BROWNING
TO HIS AMERICAN
FRIENDS

Letters between
the Brownings,
the Storys
and
James Russell Lowell
1841–1890

BROWNING
TO HIS
AMERICAN
FRIENDS

*Letters between
the Brownings,
the Storys
and
James Russell Lowell*
1841–1890

EDITED
WITH INTRODUCTION AND
NOTES BY
GERTRUDE REESE
HUDSON

BOWES AND BOWES
LONDON

NOTE – The majority of the letters in this book are copyright, and may not be reproduced in any form without permission

Letters of Robert and Elizabeth Barrett Browning
previously unpublished
© Sir John Murray 1965
Introduction and notes
© Gertrude Reese Hudson 1965
First published 1965
for the Keats-Shelley Memorial Association by
Bowes and Bowes Publishers Ltd
42 Great Russell Street, London WCI
Printed and bound in England
by W & J Mackay & Co Ltd, Chatham
Set in Monotype Baskerville

CONTENTS

REGISTER OF LETTERS, vii

ABBREVIATIONS, xii

PREFACE, xiv

INTRODUCTION, I

LETTERS from the Brownings to the Storys   21

LETTER from William Wetmore Story to Robert W. Barrett Browning (Pen)   197

LETTERS exchanged by James Russell Lowell and the Storys   201

LETTERS exchanged by Elizabeth Barrett and James Russell Lowell   351

LETTERS exchanged by Robert Browning and James Russell Lowell   357

APPENDIX I. Names of the Eldredge-Wetmore-Story families, the Lowell-White families, and the Browning-Barrett families referred to in these letters   363

APPENDIX II. Poem 'To James Russell Lowell' by William Wetmore Story, 1891   366

BIBLIOGRAPHY 368

INDEX 371

[v]

ILLUSTRATIONS

Between pages 136 *and* 137

1 Robert Browning and Pen, May 1870. *Armstrong Browning Library, Baylor University*

2 William Wetmore Story, taken in the 70's in Rome. *Peter de Brant*

3 James Russell Lowell. *Fogg Art Museum, Cambridge, Mass.*

4 Browning by Story, at Naworth Castle, September 1869. *Pierpont-Morgan Library, New York*

5 Pen's wedding, October 4th, 1887. *Miss D. Ivatt*

6 Story and his workmen outside his studio in Rome. *Peter de Brant*

REGISTER OF LETTERS

For explanation of abbreviations, see pages xii-xiii

LETTERS FROM THE BROWNINGS TO THE STORYS

Letter	Date	MS	Published	Page
RB–WWS	[Oct. 7, 1853]	TxU	HJ, I, 279–80	21
EBB–ES	[Oct. 31, 1853]		HJ, II, 56	22
EBB–ES	[ca. mid March 1854]	TxU		23
RB–WWS	March 18 [1854]	BU		24
RB–WWS	[March 21, 1854]	BU		25
EBB–ES	[March 27, 1854]	TxU		25
RB–WWS	[March 27, 1854]		HJ, I, 285	27
EBB–WWS	[March or April 1854]	TxU		28
EBB–WWS	[April 16, 1854]	TxU	HJ, I, 282–3	30
RB–WWS	June 11, 1854	TxU	HJ, I, 287–9	32
RB–SS	Dec. 27, 1854	KS		35
RB–WWS	[July 21, 1856]	TxU		37
EBB–ES	[Christmas 1858]	TxU	HJ, I, 369–70	39
RB–ES	May 29, 1859	TxU		40
EBB–Edith S	[ca. 1859]		HJ, I, 370–1	41
EBB–Edith S	[ca. 1859]		HJ, I, 370	41
RB–WWS	July 22, 1859	TxU	HJ, II, 6–7	41
RB–WWS	[July 26, 1859]	TxU	HJ, II, 10–12	44
RB–WWS	July 28, 1859	TxU	HJ, II, 8–10	46
RB, EBB–ES	[Oct. 29, 1859]	KS	HJ, II, 12–13	48
RB, EBB–SS	[Oct. 29–Nov. 23, 1859]	KS	HJ, II, 56	52
RB–ES	Nov. 23, 1859	TxU		54
RB–ES	Nov. 25 [1859]	TxU		56
RB–ES	[Dec. 3, 1859–April 22, 1860]	TxU		57
RB–SS	June 8, 1860	TxU	HJ, II, 50–52	58
RB–SS	June 15, 1860	TxU		59
RB–SS	June 19, 1860	KS		61
RB–WWS	June 29, 1860	TxU	HJ, II, 52–53	63
RB–ES	[ca. 1860]	TxU		64
RB–SS	[Nov. 9 or 16, 1860]	TxU		65
RB–SS	Nov. 17, 1860	TxU		66
RB, EBB–SS	June 13, 1861		Hood, pp. 57–58	68
RB–SS	[June 21, 1861]	KS	HJ, II, 58–60	70
RB–SS	[June 23, 1861]	TxU	HJ, II, 57–58	72
RB–SS	[June 26, 1861]	TxU		73
RB–SS	Aug. 20, 1861	Purdy	HJ, II, 90–93	75

Letter	Date	MS	Published	Page
RB–SS	Aug. 30, 1861	TxU	HJ, II, 96–98	78
RB–SS	Sept. 26, 1861	TxU		81
RB–SS	Nov. 10, 1861	KS	HJ, II, 98–102	82
RB–SS	Dec. 17, 1861	KS	HJ, II, 104–8	88
RB–WWS	Dec. 31, 1861	TxU	HJ, II, 108–9	91
RB–SS	Jan. 21, 1862	KS	HJ, II, 110–14	93
RB–WWS	Feb. 13, 1862	TxU		98
RB–SS	March 19, 1862	KS	HJ, II, 114–19	99
RB–SS	April 10, 1862	KS		105
RB–ES	July 3, 1862	TxU		108
RB–SS	Sept. 13 [1862]		Hood, pp. 69–70	109
RB–WWS	Oct. 1, 1862		Hood, pp. 70–71	111
RB–SS	Jan. 18, 1863	Yale	Hood, pp. 71–73	112
RB–SS	March 5, 1863	KS		115
RB–SS	March 27, 1863	NY		120
RB–SS	May 2, 1863	TxU	HJ, II, 135–8	122
RB–SS	July 17, 1863	KS	HJ, II, 140–2	124
RB–SS	Sept. 5, 1863	TxU	HJ, II, 138–40	128
RB–SS	Nov. 20, 1863	TxU	HJ, II, 143–4	130
RB–ES	Nov. 26, 1863	KS		132
RB–[ES]	[Nov. 26, 1863–Jan. 8, 1864]	TxU		137
RB–SS	Jan. 8, 1864	Yale	HJ, II, 145–7	139
RB–SS	May 3, 1864	KS	HJ, II, 151–3	141
RB–ES	[Aug. 22, 1864]	TxU	HJ, II, 153–6	145
RBB, RB–Edith S	Jan. 14, 1865		Hood, pp. 82–84	148
RB–SS	April 11, 1865	KS		150
RB–Edith S	July 8, 1865		Hood, p. 85	153
RB–Edith S	July 20, 1865		Hood, p. 86	154
RB–Edith S	July 26, 1865	Yale	Hood, p. 86–87	154
RB–Edith S	July 28, 1865	Yale	Hood, p. 87	155
RB–SS	Oct. 13, 1865	BU		156
RB–WWS	[Oct. 15, 1865]		Hood, pp. 87–88	156
RB–SS	[Oct. 18, 1865]	BU		157
RB–ES	Oct. 21, 1865	BU		158
RB–SS	Sept. 28, 1869		Hood, pp. 131–2	159
RB–Edith S	[Sept. 28, 1869]		Hood, pp. 132–3	160
RB–SS	Nov. 16, 1869	TxU		161
RB–Edith S	July 28, 1870		Hood, pp. 139–40	163
RB–Edith S	Oct. 20, 1871		Hood, p. 150	164
RB–Edith S	Nov. 6, 1871	PM		165
RB–Edith S	Dec. 20, 1871		Hood, pp. 151–2	166
RB–Edith S	Jan. 1, 1872		Hood, pp. 152–4	167
RB–Edith S	April 4, 1872	Yale	Hood, pp. 154–6	169
RB–WWS	Aug. 24, 1873		Hood, pp. 160–1	172
RB–WWS	June 9, 1874		Hood, pp. 162–4	174
RB–WWS	Jan. 27, 1880	TxU		176

Letter	Date	MS	Published	Page
RB–Waldo S	Dec. 23, 1881	TxU		179
RBB– Waldo S	Dec. 26, 1881	TxU		180
RB–Edith S	Aug. 7, 1884		Hood, pp. 229–30; HJ, II, 279–81	181
RB–SS	Dec. 25, 1884		Hood, pp. 232–3	183
RB–WWS	Dec. 28, 1884	Yale	Hood, pp. 233–4	184
RB–WWS	June 19, 1886		Hood, pp. 249–51	186
RB–SS	April 4, 1887		Hood, pp. 263–4	190
RB–SS	[ca. May 1887]	TxU		191
RBB–WWS	July 19, 1888		HJ, II., 227	192
RB–WWS	Sept. 30 [1889]	TxU		193

LETTER FROM WILLIAM WETMORE STORY TO ROBERT
W. BARRETT BROWNING (PEN)

			Unlocated,	
WWS–RBB	Dec. 13, 1889		from typescript	197

LETTERS EXCHANGED BY JAMES RUSSELL LOWELL
AND THE STORYS

EE(S)–JRL	[ca. 1841]	Harvard		201
JRL–WWS	[Summer 1841]	TxU		201
JRL–EE(S)	[ca. 1842]	TxU		202
JRL–EE(S)	[ca. 1842]	TxU		203
JRL–EE(S)	April 12, 1842	KS	HJ, I, 47–50	203
EE(S)–JRL	Aug. 4 [1842]	Harvard		206
JRL–EE(S)	Aug. 7, 1842	KS		208
EE(S)–JRL	Oct. 25 [1842]	Harvard		210
JRL–EE(S)	[1842]	TxU		211
EE(S)–JRL	Jan. 2, 1843	Harvard		211
WWS–JRL	Jan. 13, 1843	TxU		214
JRL–EE(S)	Jan. 31, 1843	TxU		215
WWS–JRL	Feb. 23, 1843	TxU		216
WWS–JRL	June 5, 1843	TxU		218
JRL–ES	[Late 1843]	TxU		219
JRL–WWS	Jan. 1844	TxU		220
WWS–JRL	July 29, 1844	TxU		221
JRL–WWS	July 31, 1844	TxU		221
JRL–WWS	Aug. 30, 1844	KS		222
WWS–JRL	Sept. 2, 1844	TxU	HJ, I, 72–74	223
JRL–WWS	Oct. 11, 1844	KS		225
JRL–ES	Sept. 10, 1847	Harvard	Howe, pp. 23–26	226
JRL–WWS	March 10, 1848	KS	HJ, I, 103–7	229
WWS–JRL	April 28, 1848	TxU	HJ, I, 99–102	237
WWS–JRL	March 21, 1849	TxU	HJ, I, 169–72	240

Letter	Date	MS	Published	Page
JRL–WWS	Sept. 23, 1849	KS	HJ, I, 175–83; Norton-Elmwood, I, 222–4	244
WWS–JRL	Jan. 30, 1850		HJ, I, 208–18	249
WWS–JRL	March 1, 1850	TxU		256
WWS–JRL	July 8, 1852	TxU	HJ, I, 242–5	258
WWS–JRL	Sept. 20, 1852	TxU	HJ, I, 249–53	263
WWS–JRL	Feb. 11, 1853	TxU	HJ, I, 253–7	269
WWS–JRL	Aug. 10, 1853	TxU	HJ, I 265–70	275
WWS–JRL	Jan. 9, 1855	TxU		285
JRL–WWS	July 7, 1855	Harvard		290
WWS–JRL	July 9, 1855	TxU		291
JRL–WWS	July 18, 1855	KS		293
WWS–JRL	July 20, 1855	TxU		294
JRL–WWS	July [23], 1855		HJ, I, 291–2	296
JRL–WWS	Nov. 10, 1855	Harvard	Howe, pp. 72–74	297
WWS–JRL	Dec. 30, 1855	TxU	HJ, I, 297–303	300
JRL–WWS	Jan. 28, 1856	KS	HJ, I, 313–16	308
WWS–JRL	Feb. 18, 1856	TxU	HJ, I, 309–11	310
JRL–WWS	May 7, 1856	KS	HJ, I, 322–4; Norton-Elmwood, I, 340–1	312
JRL–WWS	June 7, 1856	TxU	HJ, I, 325–6	315
JRL–ES	July 16, 1856	TxU	HJ, I, 326–8; Norton-Elmwood, I, 347–8	316
JRL–WWS	Sept. 12, 1864	Harvard		318
WWS–JRL	Dec. 10, 1864	KS	HJ, II, 147–51	319
JRL–WWS	[July 27, 1865]	TxU		322
WWS–JRL	[ca. Sept. 1865]	Harvard		322
JRL–WWS	[ca. Sept. 1865]	TxU		323
WWS–JRL	Aug. 6, 1868	TxU		323
JRL–WWS	July 28, 1872	TxU		324
WWS–JRL	Aug. 1, 1872	Harvard		325
JRL–ES	Aug. 15, 1872	KS		326
JRL–WWS	[July 31, 1877]	TxU		327
JRL–WWS	Nov. 18, 1879	TxU		328
WWS–JRL	July 25, 1882	Harvard		328
WWS–JRL	Nov. 1, 1884	Harvard		333
ES–JRL	Feb. 22, 1885	Harvard		334
WWS–JRL	Feb. 23, 1885	Harvard		335
JRL–WWS	March 5, 1885		HJ, II, 289–90	336
JRL–ES	March 31, 1885		Scudder, II, 320–1	337
JRL–WWS	June 2, 1887	KS	HJ, II, 290	338
WWS–JRL	June 6, 1887	Harvard		339
JRL–WWS	June 13, 1887	TxU		340
JRL–WWS	May 14, 1888	Harvard		340

Letter	Date	MS	Published	Page
WWS–JRL	May 19, 1888	Harvard		341
WWS–JRL	Sept. 9, 1890	Harvard		342
JRL–WWS	Oct. 2, 1890	TxU	HJ, II, 294–6; Norton-Elmwood, III, 295–7	345

LETTERS EXCHANGED BY ELIZABETH BARRETT AND JAMES RUSSELL LOWELL

Letter	Date	MS	Published	Page
JRL–EB(B)	Dec. 13, 1842	PM		351
EB(B)–JRL	Jan. 4, 1843	Harvard		352
EB(B)–JRL	July [1844]	Harvard		353

LETTERS EXCHANGED BY ROBERT BROWNING AND JAMES RUSSELL LOWELL

Letter	Date	MS	Published	Page
RB–JRL	March 9, 1873	Harvard		357
RB–JRL	Sept. 6, 1880	Harvard		358
RB–JRL	Nov. 15, 1880	BU		360
JRL–RB	Nov. 5, 1882		Howe, p. 269	360
JRL–RB	Nov. 21, 1884		Stedman, II, opp. p. 306	361
JRL–RB	May 21, 1885	BU		361
RB–JRL	May 22, 1885	Harvard		361

ABBREVIATIONS

🙆

People

EB(B)	Elizabeth Barrett (later Elizabeth Barrett Browning)
EBB	Elizabeth Barrett Browning
RB	Robert Browning
RBB	Robert W. Barrett Browning (Pen)
JRL	James Russell Lowell
EE(S)	Emelyn Eldredge (later Emelyn Story)
ES	Emelyn Story (Mrs. W. W. Story)
Edith S	Edith Story
WWS	William Wetmore Story
Waldo S	Waldo Story
Ss	The Story family

Location of Manuscripts

Berg	The Berg Collection, New York Public Library
BU	Baylor University, Waco, Texas
Harvard	Harvard University
KS	Keats-Shelley Memorial Association, Rome
Houghton	Houghton Library, Harvard University
NY	New York Public Library
PM	Pierpont Morgan Library
Purdy	Professor R. L. Purdy
Story Col.	Story Collection, TxU
TxU	University of Texas Story Collection
Yale	Yale University

Publications

DAB	*Dictionary of American Biography.*
DNB	*Dictionary of National Biography.*
DeVane and Knickerbocker	*New Letters of Robert Browning*, ed. W. C. DeVane and K. L. Knickerbocker, New Haven, Conn., 1950.

[xii]

Elmwood	*The Complete Writings of James Russell Lowell,* Elmwood Edition, 16 vols., Boston, 1904.
Hewlett	D. Hewlett, *Elizabeth Barrett Browning,* London, 1953.
HJ	Henry James, *William Wetmore Story and His Friends,* 2 vols., Boston, 1903.
Hood	*Letters of Robert Browning . . .,* ed. T. L. Hood, New Haven, Connecticut, 1933.
Howe	*New Letters of James Russell Lowell,* ed. M. A. De Wolfe Howe, New York, 1932.
Huxley	*Elizabeth Barrett Browning: Letters to her Sister, 1846–1859,* ed. L. Huxley, London, 1929.
Kenyon	*The Letters of Elizabeth Barrett Browning,* ed. F. G. Kenyon, 2 vols., London, 1897.
Landis and Freeman	*Letters of the Brownings to George Barrett,* ed. P. Landis and R. E. Freeman, Urbana, Illinois, 1958.
McAleer	*Dearest Isa,* ed. E. C. McAleer, Austin, Texas, 1951.
Norton-Elmwood	*Letters of James Russell Lowell,* ed. C. E. Norton, vols. XIV–XVI of *The Complete Writings of James Russell Lowell,* Elmwood Edition, Boston, 1904.
Phillips	M. E. Phillips, *Reminiscences of William Wetmore Story,* Chicago, 1897.
PMLA	*Publications of the Modern Language Association of America.*
Scudder	H. E. Scudder, *James Russell Lowell,* 2 vols., Boston, 1901.
Sotheby	*The Browning Collections. Catalogue of . . . The Property of R. W. Barrett Browning . . . .* (Catalogue of auction held by Sotheby . . . May, 1913).
Stedman	Edmund Clarence Stedman, *Poets of America,* 2 vols., Cambridge, Massachusetts, 1885.

IN THE KEATS-SHELLEY Memorial House in Rome there are twelve letters exchanged by James Russell Lowell and William Wetmore Story and his wife and fifteen letters from Robert Browning to William Wetmore Story. Twenty-four of these were given and three were sold to the Memorial House by Mrs. Waldo Story, the daughter-in-law of William Wetmore Story. Dorothy Hewlett asked me to edit them for the Keats-Shelley Memorial Association of London. After completing work on them, I located another group of letters belonging to the correspondence; these were bought by the University of Texas from the late Mrs. Gwendolyn Stewart, the daughter of Waldo Story.

Through the kindness of others I have been able to add to the collection, which has finally reached a total of 172. I am grateful for the use of letters in the New York Public Library, Harvard University Library, Yale University Library, the Pierpont Morgan Library, and the Armstrong Browning Library in Baylor University. For permission to use these letters and for help rendered in other ways, I am indebted to the following professors and librarians: Robert W. Hill of the manuscript division of the New York Public Library, William A. Jackson of the Houghton Library of Harvard University, Frederick B. Adams, Jr., of the Pierpont Morgan Library, Mrs. A. J. Armstrong and Jack W. Herring of the Armstrong Browning Library of Baylor University, David R. Watkins of Yale University Library, and Warren Roberts and Anne Bowden of the University of Texas Library. I am also indebted to Professor Richard L. Purdy of Yale University for the use of a letter that he owns. The ownership of each manuscript is indicated in the register of letters.

I appreciate aid received from members of the staff in the libraries where I have worked: the New York Public Library, the Boston Public Library, the University of Texas Library, the Houghton Library of Harvard University, The Armstrong Browning Library of Baylor University, the Library of Congress, and the British Museum. I owe particular thanks to Kathleen Blow of the University of Texas Library and Veva Wood of the Armstrong Browning Library of Baylor University.

Dean William Clyde DeVane of Yale kindly assisted me in my search for letters; and Miss Felice Stampfle of the Pierpont Morgan Library directed my attention to certain Story drawings.

In editing the letters, I have had helpful information from the following persons, to whom I am grateful: Elizabeth Litsinger of Baltimore; Mary McNally and Catharine Yerxa of Watertown, Massachusetts; Sarah Flannery, Patricia Maguire, Marjorie Bonquet, Kathleen Woodsworth, and John Burk of Boston; Herbert C. Philpott of Cambridge, Massachusetts; Lilly Abbott of Salem; Catherine Bonanno of North Cohasset, Massachusetts; Mabel Eiseley of Philadelphia; Donald Engley of Trinity College Library at Hartford; Roberta Sutton of Chicago; Gilbert A. Cam of New York; Ernest G. Crowsley and H. Anderson of London; L. H. Harwood of Blickling Hall, Norfolk, England; Jean P. White of the University of Sydney; and Alberto Giraldi of the Biblioteca Nazionale. Besides those whose help I have acknowledged in footnotes, I wish to thank Ruth Jones of the University of Utah and Goldia Hester of Austin, Texas.

My special thanks go to others. Signora Vera Cacciatore, curator of the Keats-Shelley Memorial House in Rome, sent photostats and provided information about manuscripts. To Dorothy Hewlett and Norman Kilgour I am deeply indebted for continuing help and kindness in all phases of the preparation and publication of this book. Mrs. Elaine Story, the wife of William Wetmore Story's son Julian, graciously answered questions about the Story family. Mr. Peter de Brant of London, the grandson of Waldo Story, paved the way for the acquisition of manuscripts, and by letters and in conversations in London has been of great assistance.

A grant from the American Philosophical Society made it possible for me to go to England in search of letters. The de Brant–Story Collection was purchased by authorization of Harry Huntt Ransom, then President and now Chancellor of the University of Texas.

I thank Dr. John D. Gordan of the Henry W. and Albert A. Berg Collection of the New York Public Library for permission to quote from Mrs. Browning's manuscripts and Professor Norman Pearson to quote from Hawthorne's Italian journals.

My grateful acknowledgement goes to the late Mrs. Gwendolyn Stewart for permission to use the Story letters; to Dr. Francis Lowell Burnett and Mrs. Esther L. Cunningham, heirs of James Russell Lowell, for permission to use the Lowell letters; and to Sir John Murray, owner of the copyright, for generous permission to use a large number of the Browning letters.

I wish to thank Messrs. Bowes and Bowes for their care and helpfulness.

THE LETTERS assembled in this collection, one hundred and seventy-two in number, were written by the Brownings, William Wetmore Story and his wife, and James Russell Lowell over a period beginning in the early 1840s and continuing down to 1890. They present, rather fully, the story of an international, three-way friendship, with Story in a pivotal position. He corresponded with the Brownings on one side and with Lowell on the other; there are, also, several letters which were exchanged directly between the Brownings and Lowell. Browning probably did not preserve Story's letters to him; some may survive, but all efforts to locate them have failed. As the correspondents lived or travelled in various countries—England, Italy, France, Germany, Spain, Switzerland, or the United States—they continued to write to each other for approximately fifty years.

The first thirty-five letters of the collection were written during the close association of the Brownings and the Storys in Italy, which was home for the Brownings during the fifteen years of their married life and became the permanent home of the Storys after two extended visits. Robert and Elizabeth Barrett were married in England on September 12, 1846, and started a week later for Italy, travelling slowly until they reached Pisa, where they stayed six months. In April of 1847 they went to Florence, intending to be there only a while and then successively move on to other places in Italy, but the weeks and months went by, and their plans changed. After they had moved several times in Florence within a year, they settled themselves in the house associated with their names—Casa Guidi. Although they spent much time elsewhere—in England and France, in cool places in Italy during the summer, and in Rome during four winters—between visits to other places they were in the Casa Guidi in Florence, Elizabeth's 'chimney corner'.

When the Brownings came to Florence the political situation was beginning to look hopeful. After Pius IX had been made Pope in 1846, he released all who had been imprisoned for political offences and initiated reforms. His liberal actions gave courage to a downtrodden Italy, whose people desired unity and freedom from Austrian oppression. One of the states that defied Austrian rule was Tuscany. Demands were made and reforms granted. While the few steps toward liberation were being gained, the action involved frightened many English residents and they fled; but the Brownings, who were interested in the movement for Italian liberty, were more inclined to stay than leave. So alive was their interest that their choice of apartment was somewhat determined by its proximity to the ducal palace, the centre of political activities. They, especially Elizabeth, became more and more intent upon the movements that fluctuated in effort and accomplishment and ultimately ended in freedom.

It was a happy time for the poets. Unbelievably cheap living eased their financial worries. Freedom and isolation were welcome to them; with books and music, writing and talking, and walks and drives they scarcely knew how the time passed. Then there was the joy of seeing the treasures of Florence. Most of the few visitors that they had, some English and some American, were welcome. Among the American visitors were William Wetmore Story and his wife.

William Story was born in Salem, Massachusetts, in 1819. His father, Joseph Story, was Associate Justice of the United States Supreme Court, pioneer in modern law school training, Professor of Law in Harvard, and author of important books in the legal field. Only a legal profession seemed possible for William. He took his A.B. and LL.B. degrees from Harvard and began his career with considerable promise for the future. He was happily married to Emelyn Eldredge of prominent Boston parents; and his circle of friends included James Russell Lowell, Charles Sumner, and others who were to become famous. In family, education, friends, and profession William Story had everything to make a New Englander satisfied at home. Yet New England and a legal career lost to a stronger urge.

In the spare hours of his youth Story painted and modelled, wrote and published poetry and critical articles, took part in discussions of literary and aesthetic problems, and indulged his love for music. The appeal of these activities conflicted strongly with the claims of his profession, and William was disturbed even though he had every reason to look forward to a successful legal career. The pressure of his background and training might have won out against his artistic inclination had he not been asked to make a statue of his father, who had died in 1845. He accepted on the condition that he might first go to Europe 'to see what had been done in art'.[1] He went in 1847, and Italy so charmed him that he was never again happy in America. He passed through a period of indecision, alternating extended visits in Europe with shorter sojourns at home, during which he longed to be back in Italy. In 1856 his period of indecision ended; he established himself and his family in Rome, the city that was to be home for the rest of his life.

It was during their first visit to Italy that the Storys met the Brownings. After some months in Rome, they spent the last of 1848 and the beginning of 1849 in Florence. On March 21, 1849, when they were back in Rome, Story wrote to his friend James Russell Lowell: 'The Brownings and we became great friends in Florence, and of course we could not become friends without liking each other'.

The Storys left Rome in May of 1849. They travelled at a leisurely pace through Europe, spending the winter of 1849–50 in Berlin and the summer of 1850 in England and Scotland, and left for America in October 1850. In 1851 the Storys returned to Italy and spent three winters in Rome, where William worked at his sculpture, leaving the city in the summers to escape the heat. In 1853 they went to Bagni di Lucca. The Brownings, too, had chosen Bagni di Lucca for the summer, and a few days after their arrival they were surprised by a visit from the Storys. The friendship begun in Florence several years before was firmly established during these months. Elizabeth said that Mr. and Mrs. Story helped to make the mountains pleasant; on donkey

[1] Letter from WWS to Enrico Nencioni (Berg).

[3]

back they went to see each other for tea-drinking and gossip. Story reported to Lowell a like satisfaction on the other side: 'Of society there are none we care to meet but the Brownings who are living here. With them we have constant & delightful intercourse interchanging long evenings together two or three times a week & driving and walking together whenever we can meet. We like them very much. They are so simple unaffected & sympathetic'.

During this summer of 1853 the Brownings and Storys planned to see much of each other in Rome in the following winter. After leaving Bagni di Lucca each family stayed about a month in Florence before starting for Rome, the Storys preceding the Brownings. Robert and Elizabeth had been disappointed repeatedly in their earlier plans for going to Rome and at last were actually to spend some months there. They and their son had a 'most exquisite journey of eight days' from Florence to Rome and entered the city in the highest spirits, 'Robert and Penini singing actually'. (The child had given himself this nickname, which later was abbreviated to Pen.) The fires were lighted in an apartment that the Storys had taken for them and they were welcomed by these good friends. Immediately after their arrival Joseph Story, six years old, became ill and died. Grief for their friends and fear for their own child clouded the first winter that the Brownings spent in Rome.

The two families were not to be together for several years. The Brownings left in May 1854 and did not return to Rome until 1858. Early in 1854 the Storys had left Rome because of their concern for the health of their daughter, Edith, their only child now. They spent the following winter in Paris and returned to America in August 1855. Within a year they were back in Europe, first spending a summer in England and then settling themselves permanently in Rome. It was in Rome that the two families were to meet again. Elizabeth suffered from the cold of Florence in 1857–58, and the Brownings decided to try the milder climate of Rome the next winter. For the remainder of Elizabeth's life—two and a half years—the two families were to live near each other, in Rome during the winter and in Siena during the summer.

The final stage of Italy's struggle for freedom was beginning, and Elizabeth had the satisfaction of seeing the liberation of most of Italy. By secret treaty Napoleon III had promised to aid Sardinia, the only Italian state with independence and strength, in case of an attack by Austria. In 1859, not long after the treaty, Austria declared war on Sardinia, and the French army under Napoleon's command came to Sardinia's assistance. Austria's losses were heavy; just when her downfall in Italy seemed inevitable, Napoleon became hesitant and suddenly issued a proposal for an armistice, which was followed by the Agreement of Villafranca. At first the unexpected move at Villafranca paralysed Italy, but after the shock wore off it provided the impetus needed to make the states forget their individual goals and unite in an effort to obtain freedom. To effect unity the Italian people wished to be annexed to Sardinia, whose strength and native ruler, Victor Emmanuel II, gave it the natural leadership in a movement for independence.

Early in 1861 the Kingdom of Italy was proclaimed under the King of Sardinia. The parts not included were Venetia, which was still in Austria's hands; Nice and Savoy, which were ceded to France; and Rome, which was under the power of the Pope. The situation had changed considerably since Pius IX had begun his reforms following his accession in 1846. His actions encouraged the Liberals, whose demands increased far beyond his expectations. Events went counter to his interests, and he tried to regain the power he had lost. The Papal states turned to Sardinia, and the Pope's attempts by threats and by force to retrieve or hold his possessions met with little success. These desperate attempts of Pius IX, who was incapable of accepting the finality of his losses, and the confidence of the revolutionaries, at one time weak and hesitant but now fearless and self-reliant, lay beneath the simmering agitation in Rome.

Elizabeth followed the events with a burning intensity that she was unable to restrain. Her interest in Italy had become a passion that blinded her to the real Louis Napoleon, whom she

[5]

confused with an ideal liberator. She, who could calmly accept harsh criticism of herself and her works, suffered greatly when Napoleon was criticized for his behaviour, never seeing the weakness or self-interest that guided his movements. As time passed she saw fewer people, but she wrote letters full of praise for Napoleon, hope for Italy, and somewhat unjustified reproofs of England's behaviour. Browning protected her from all that he could, but the vital spirit took heavy toll of her declining strength.

During the last of Elizabeth's life, to all appearances Browning was going through a period of poetic inactivity. In Rome when he was not with his family he spent his time in modelling or in social activities. Often he was with William Story in his studio or in his commodious apartment in the Palazzo Barberini, where the Storys welcomed noted people of various professions and interests and provided a hospitality that gave them a place of distinction in European social circles. In the summers in Siena the two families lived near each other, and the association was close, though Elizabeth was not always able to join the others in the frequent visits that took place.

In the early summer of 1861 Elizabeth's weakened condition made the Brownings give up their plans to meet Robert's family and Arabel Barrett in France. While they were making their customary stay in Casa Guidi between the winter and summer seasons they thought of various alternatives; one was to join their friends again in Siena, as they had done in 1859 and 1860. They were also facing the necessity of other changes. They talked of giving up Casa Guidi for a larger and quieter place in Florence and of making permanent arrangements for their winters in Rome because Elizabeth could no longer endure the cold of the north. They hoped to complete negotiations, already begun in Rome, for a small apartment in the Palazzo Barberini, where the Storys were living.

But they made no changes, nor did they go to Siena. Elizabeth caught a cold; at first her illness did not cause unusual anxiety; though her lungs were unsound, she had rallied from serious attacks before. After several days Browning grew alarmed, but on the 28th she seemed to be better and heard with pleasure encouraging political news. Early the next morning, June 29, 1861, she died in Casa Guidi.

After Elizabeth's death Browning left Florence and never returned. Story wrote to a friend:

> You cannot imagine how I shall miss him. For three years now we have been always together; never a day has passed (with the exception of two months' separation in the spring and autumn when he went to Florence) that we have not met; all the long summer evenings of these last summers at Siena he was with us, and we sat on our terrace night after night till midnight talking together, or we played and sang above stairs. All the last winters he worked with me daily for three hours in my studio, and we met either at my house or at his or at that of some friend nearly every evening. There is no one to supply his place. Returning to Rome, I have no one single intimate; acquaintances by hundreds, but no friends, no one with whom I can sympathise on all points as with him, no one with whom I can walk any of the higher ranges of art and philosophy.[1]

The friendship was natural and profitable for Browning and Story. Browning was familiar with the world of art in his early years, and the Italian environment enriched his interest and knowledge. Art, including sculpture, must have been the subject of many discussions, leaving suggestions that Browning could later turn into account. Did Browning and Story talk of Saul? Story made a statue of Saul and during his Italian years Browning completed his poem on Saul. When he was modelling under Story in his studio, Browning copied the bust of the young Augustus, the subject of a poem of his published in 1889. As for Story's own poetry, that written after his association with Browning shows Browning's influence.[2]

It is no wonder that talk never lagged for these two who were together night after night. Both liked drama and each one had

[1] HJ, II, 67–68.
[2] See HJ, II, 231–5, 239; also H. Buxton Forman's review of *Graffiti d'Italia* (*Fortnightly Review*, NS V [January 1869], 117–20).

written plays with the vain hope of a successful production. They both liked society and they possessed extraordinary social qualities. They loved Italy and they re-created her past and her contemporary life for their English and American public. Music, politics, legal subjects—these too were common interests in their sympathetic association during the last years of Browning's Italian period.

In the sixties both Story and Browning reached a turning point in their lives. Browning returned to England with his twelve-year-old son. He passed through a transitional period beset with spiritual difficulties and lacking in the spontaneity of his Italian days. Whatever concerned Elizabeth or Pen he felt deeply. Most disturbing to him were the people who he thought had taken advantage of Elizabeth through her interest in spiritualism and those who wanted to write about her life. Pen's education caused him much anxiety. He was meticulously concerned over the boy's preparation for university life, and the planning and weighing and hoping imposed a considerable strain upon him. When Pen failed his entrance examinations, it was the father and not the son who suffered frustration. Even the belated recognition of poetical merit that came in the 'sixties brought bitterness as well as pleasure.

After his return to England Browning supervised publication of Elizabeth's works, published new poems of his own and re-published old ones, and acted as Story's representative. He began the habit of setting his mornings aside for regular hours of work, no longer writing only when the spirit moved him. These literary activities occupied his days, but work was not sufficient for Browning. He needed to mix with men and women, and it was inevitable that he break through the isolation imposed by grief. He courageously resumed social contacts, and before the end of the first decade after his return to England he was a familiar figure in London society. Without restraint Browning wrote to Story of his disturbances, his work, and his efforts to resume social life. To only one other person—Isa Blagden—did Browning reveal himself as intimately in the first half of the sixties.

When Browning left Italy Story had reached a crucial point, for unless recognition came soon he would have to give up his artistic life. He had learned much and was an indefatigable worker. Comparing him with other sculptors in Italy, his contemporaries had reason to think that he deserved recognition, but he had been unable to attract the attention of the critics and the public. In his period of discouragement he must have often remembered that his mother had pronounced him mad to give up his promising legal career at home to follow the profession of art in another country.[1] His chance came when, through a provision of the Papal Government, expenses were paid for sending two of his statues to the London Exhibition of 1862——'Cleopatra', which had already become known to novel readers through Hawthorne's description of it in *The Marble Faun*, and the 'Libyan Sibyl'. Both were so well received that in European estimation they gave Story a foremost place among American sculptors.

From that time his success in the contemporary art world was assured. The high opinion of his sculpture is indicated in criticisms of his day, and many of his works were bought for public and private art collections. Among the statues that appealed to his contemporaries beside the two that established his reputation—the 'Sibyl' and 'Cleopatra'—were the 'Medea', 'Saul', 'Salome', 'Jerusalem in Her Desolation', and 'Alcestis'. The high regard that Story's contemporaries had for his works was not shared by later critics, who found in them dignity but not vigour and intensity. According to their opinion, his best portrait figures are the one of George Peabody behind the Royal Exchange in London (a replica is in Baltimore, Maryland) and the one of John Marshall in Washington.

Story's reputation did not come entirely from his sculpture; he also became well known as an author dealing with a considerable range of subjects and expressing himself in poetry and in prose. His early treatises on legal topics (1844, 1847), which long held a substantial place; a life of his father (1851); *The American Question* (1862), on the American Civil War; *Roba di*

[1] Letter from W W S to Enrico Nencioni (Berg).

Roma (1863), an informative and interesting book on Rome; *Proportions of the Human Figure* (1866); *Graffiti d'Italia* (1868), Browningesque poems; *Nero* (1875), a closet drama; *Fiammetta, a Summer Idyl* (1886), prose fiction; *Conversations in a Studio* (1890); *Excursions in Art and Letters* (1891), a collection of papers on various subjects, some contradicting an accepted viewpoint—these works (some first appeared in periodicals and later were published independently) represent the variety of his writing.

Hawthorne, that shrewd observer of the undersurface, left his own opinion of Story's versatility:

> Mr. Story is the most variously accomplished and brilliant person—the fullest of social life and fire—whom I have ever met. . . . Still . . . he left the impression on me that he is not a happy man; there must surely be a morbid sensibility; a pain and care, bred, it may be, out of the very richness of his gifts and abundance of his outward prosperity. Rich, in the prime of life, with a wife whom he loves, and children budding and blossoming as fairly as his heart could wish; with sparkling talents, so many that if he choose to neglect or fling away one, or two, or three, he would still have enough left to shine with;—who should be happy, if not he? It may be that he feels his strength, in any one direction, not quite adequate to his perception, his purpose, and his longing desire; he would rather have one great diamond, than a larger bulk and weight divided among many brilliants. The great difficulty with him, I think, is a too facile power.[1]

Another American who knew the real Story even better than Hawthorne was the sculptor's lifelong friend James Russell Lowell, to whom Story revealed the struggle accompanying his adoption of another country. After his first impression of Italy Story wrote to Lowell: 'How I shall ever endure the restraint and bondage of Boston I know not'. When faced with the decision of whether to move to Rome for good Story wrote again: 'But I am no judge of Italy & Italians, the very names fire me. I love Italy. My taste is spoilt for everything else—foolishly

[1] *The French and Italian Notebooks*, ed. Pearson, pp. 558–9.

enough. Shall I ever again be as happy as I was there? . . .
Ardently as I desire to return, I fear'. As Story and his wife
wrote of the glories of Rome, Lowell countered by recalling the
virtues of New England, and once he wrote to Mrs. Story: 'Is
W[illiam] as savage as ever against that wretched town of
Boston? Since George third nobody ever treated it so'.

Lowell never brooked criticism of America; and he took to
task any American who gave another country precedence over
his own. His love for America did not preclude the development
of affection for other countries, nor did it diminish as this affection grew. Italy he became fond of on his first visit to Europe;
Florence charmed him at once, Rome more slowly. He admitted
to more than one person that although he did not readily fall
under the fascination of Rome, the place grew upon him from
hour to hour. To one friend he wrote: 'I see that Rome has
already begun to infect you. People always begin by wondering
what other people find in the old Rookery, and end by saying
that there are so many Thises and Thats, but there is only one
Rome'.[1] England he learned to love during his residence there.
An earlier antipathy toward her, arising from his strong Americanism, disappeared; and at the end of his life England became
his second home.

Lowell was born in 1819 in Cambridge, Massachusetts, in a
house called Elmwood, rich in historical associations and
beautiful in setting. He and Story grew up in the environment
Lowell described in 'Cambridge Thirty Years Ago' (addressed
to Story and first published in 1854 and republished in a book
dedicated to Story in 1864, *Fireside Travels*) and were classmates
in grammar school before they went to Harvard. A younger
student recalled in later years having walked up and down the
street behind Story and Lowell during their grammar school
days, listening to their talk, which was often about literature. 'I
remember . . . their talking over the plot of Spenser's "Faerie
Queene" years before I had read it, and making it so interesting
that we younger urchins soon named a nook with shady apple
trees near our bathing place on Charles River the "Bower of

[1] Norton-Elmwood, I, 333.

[11]

Blisse".'[1] In college both Lowell and Story were active in social and literary affairs. Their learning did not always come through prescribed channels, sometimes to the dismay of the faculty. Exploring literary fields on their own and writing for the college paper were more attractive than going to class and to prayers and preparing assignments. Finally, on the ground of 'continued neglect of his college duties', Lowell was rusticated in his senior year.

After Lowell took his A.B. and LL.B. degrees from Harvard and tried unsuccessfully to settle himself in the legal world, he turned to writing, an interest that he and Story shared. From the beginning Lowell seemed to be in the lead in literary achievement. He soon became known in limited circles as a poet and journalist, and in 1848 he received wide recognition as poet, satirist, critic, and humourist from the publication of his *Poems, Second Series; A Fable for Critics*; the first series of *The Biglow Papers*; and *The Vision of Sir Launfal*—all in verse. Parts of some of these works had appeared in magazines before they came out in book form. Lowell contributed to various magazines and was editor of several, including the *North American Review* (with C. E. Norton) and the *Atlantic Monthly*. The creative quality of the first part of Lowell's career, in which poetry predominated, diminished as prose became a more fitting vehicle for his thought in his active and successful life of editor, professor, critic, and diplomat.

Lowell was first in Europe from July 1851 until October 1852. Part of this time he and his first wife, Maria White Lowell, spent in Rome, where they and the Storys—all friends during their youth—were together. Lowell was again in Europe in 1855–6, much of the time in Dresden, for a year's study of language and literature before he began his duties as Smith Professor of the French and Spanish Languages and Literatures and Professor of Belles Lettres in Harvard, a position he held actively from 1856 until 1877, with the exception of two years when he returned with his second wife (his first wife had died in 1853) for

[1] Thomas Wentworth Higginson, *Old Cambridge* (New York, 1900), pp. 154–5.

the third time to Europe. In 1877 he became minister to Spain and in 1880 minister to England.

His diplomatic experience in Spain, his travels, his achievements as man of letters—all prepared him for his most important position in public life, that of American minister to the Court of St. James. Lowell desired a better understanding between the people of England and of America. He believed in American democracy; he acknowledged the frequent betrayal of its ideal but had faith in its possibilities. If any man could demonstrate the best of Americanism, it was Lowell. Cultured, conservative, and literary, he was receptive to his surroundings. Temperamentally he was suited to social life, which in nineteenth-century England was an important channel for the movement of opinions. The ability as writer and speaker that had often helped him reach an immediate audience served him well as minister.

The English people lamented the loss of Lowell in 1885, when his ministerial duties ended, a few months after the death of his second wife, and many hoped that he would decide to live in England. He was too much of a New Englander to make another country his permanent home, but he returned to England every summer until he was no longer physically able to do so. He was happy in London. The crowd stimulated him and gave his solitude a protection when he wished it; he loved the birds and the parks; and he found satisfaction in the company of his English friends.

During these last years Lowell sometimes saw Robert Browning, whom he had known for over thirty years and whose poetry he had known even longer. As early as the 1840s Lowell was acquainted with the works of both Elizabeth Barrett and Robert Browning. He wrote to Miss Barrett in 1842 for a contribution to the *Pioneer*, the short-lived magazine that he helped to project, and she generously complied. In his letter he paid her the tribute of being the 'woman who has shown more true poetic genius than any poet of her sex'. He made complimentary references to both Elizabeth Barrett and Robert Browning in his *Conversations on Some of the Old Poets*, published in 1845. In 1848 he published a favourable forty-four page review of Browning's works in the *North American Review*. The possibility of Browning's influence on Lowell's poetry during this early period has been suggested by the author of one of the more recent books on Lowell.[1] At any rate, Lowell appreciated Browning's works before they received general recognition and he continued to praise them. When his daughter was in England in 1869 he referred to Browning several times in the letters he sent to her from America. At one time he wrote, 'I am rejoiced to see that the claim I made for him twenty-two years ago is now so generally admitted';[2] and at another time, '. . . he has contrived to say some of the finest things that have said in this generation'.[3] From time to time throughout his life Lowell referred to Browning's poetry in both his letters and his published works.

Shortly before Lowell's review of Browning was published in 1848, Lowell asked Story, who was in Italy, for Browning's address. A year later Story wrote Lowell that he had interpreted one of *The Biglow Papers* for the Brownings. When Lowell and his wife reached Europe in 1851, they went directly to Florence. They did not see the Brownings, who had left in May 1851 for a year and a half sojourn in England and France. For the two months that the Lowells stayed in Florence they rented Casa Guidi, the Brownings' home. In 1852 Browning and Lowell met in London; they met again there twenty years later and thereafter they continued to see each other, once in Venice but mostly in London. During Lowell's ministership they met socially at the same houses; or Browning heard Lowell lecture; or Lowell, whose entertaining was curtailed on account of his wife's poor health, invited Browning to dinner. Nor did their meetings stop when Lowell's period of diplomatic service in London ended in 1885 with the change of administration in the United States. On Lowell's return visits they saw each other in London and in Oxford. In their letters are echoes of their talk of William Story, whose intimate association with each of them was one of the bonds of the friendship between Lowell and Browning.

[1] Howard, *Victorian Knight-Errant*, pp. 242–3.
[2] Norton-Elmwood, II, 211.
[3] Norton-Elmwood, II, 213.

Story continued to see both Lowell and Browning throughout the years. He was with Lowell in Italy, in America, and in England. In the sixties he began his almost yearly visits to England, where he and Browning saw each other. In 1878 Browning, after an absence of seventeen years from Italy, began making autumn trips to Venice, so that the two men once again could visit in the country where they had first become acquainted.

Story outlived both of his friends. In the autumn of 1889 Browning and his sister went to Italy. On the way to Venice to see Pen they stopped in Asolo, where Mrs. Bronson, an American friend, had her summer home. Browning found great delight in this visit to the little town dear to him since he had visited it in 1838 and carried away the impressions used in *Pippa Passes*. Mrs. Bronson did much to contribute to his comfort and pleasure, and a visit from the Storys added to his enjoyment. When the time for parting came, the last words were spoken by Browning to Story: 'We have been friends for forty years, forty years without a break!' Browning went from Asolo to Venice, where six weeks later, on December 12, 1889, he died in his son's home, the Palazzo Rezzonico.

Just as Story learned that Browning was dying in Venice, news came that Lowell was not well. His condition grew worse in the spring, and though he improved, he had only a short time to live. After hearing of his improvement, Story wrote Lowell in September 1890, asking him to come to Rome for a visit. Lowell answered in October: 'Though I cannot come now, I am not without hope of seeing you in Italy again before I vanish. A longing has been growing in me for several years now, chiefly, I confess, for Venice, but with subsidiary hankerings after Rome and Florence'. Lowell never again saw Italy. He died in 1891 in Elmwood, the house in which he had been born. Story survived his two friends by several years, still making his home in the Palazzo Barberini in Rome. In 1895, a year and a half after the death of his wife, he died while visiting his daughter in her summer villa at Vallombrosa.

Each of the three men found a complement to his national

culture in another country; and each was honoured by other countries, the artistic works of two of them being recognized outside their own countries first—Browning's in America and Story's in England. Spiritually as well as physically, the men traversed national boundaries; yet none lost the stamp of his own country, nor his love for it.

The letters brought together here amplify our knowledge of the lives of the writers and point up the friendship existing between them. Story was one of the few people that Browning wrote to frankly and fully, and his span of association with Story was longer than that with any other regular correspondent. Lowell and Story maintained with each other their longest and most intimate recorded friendship. Besides providing additional material for the biographies of the Brownings, Story, and Lowell, the letters present information about people who were prominent in artistic, literary, and diplomatic circles, such as William Page, James T. Fields, and George Perkins Marsh. When not read as biographical sources, many letters are enjoyable in themselves and some are true specimens of the art of familiar correspondence. Except in times of personal sorrow, Lowell and Story are lighthearted and humorous, both being fond of wordplay. Browning exhibits a variety of moods, ranging from tenderness to extreme irritation.

In transcribing the letters I have kept as close to the originals as possible except for the following slight departures that seemed advisable. I have omitted words that were unintentionally duplicated. Words that were scratched through I have not transcribed since the author was obviously deleting them. I have made a few silent corrections of errors caused by haste or carelessness, such as misspelling, metathesis, and run-together words. Spellings that seem to be habitually incorrect or that do not conform to present-day usage have not been altered. Misspelt proper names are unchanged. When annotated, they are corrected in the notes; when not annotated, the misspelling is indicated in the text. I have expanded abbreviations in brackets where a footnote was not needed to explain the reference. In the body of the letter I have silently expanded Story's 'yr' to 'your'. The ampersands I have retained. When not sure of a word, I have placed it in brackets, and when my reading is particularly doubtful I have inserted a question mark after it.

Browning's punctuation exhibits certain peculiarities or lapses. He sometimes placed the comma under the dash instead of before it; sometimes made a question mark like an eye with a brow; and occasionally did not complete his parentheses and quotation marks. All of these peculiarities I have converted to ordinary typographical practice. I have transcribed his equals sign as a colon. The two dots in Elizabeth's letters do not indicate omissions; she used them in place of other marks of punctuation. In the letters of all the writers the short dash has been transcribed as a full stop when it seems to end a sentence. Lowell's only peculiarity is his capitalization of *e*, *s*, and *c* as the initial letters of words occurring within the sentence; these have been changed to the lower case. Occasionally Story used capitalization and lower case inconsistently and indiscriminately; changes have been made to facilitate the reading.

Postscripts written in the margins and inside the flaps of envelopes have been placed at the end of the letters. All addresses and dates have been given as originally written, without expanding abbreviations or altering the order to conform to a standard form; addresses and dates placed at the end of a letter have been transposed to the head; added information has been supplied in square brackets.

When I use printed letters lacking originals, footnotes indicate changes made from the printed form. Changes of dates in the heading are indicated in footnotes and the reason for making the change is given. In a few cases I knew that proper names were inaccurately transcribed by Hood; I have corrected them and have indicated the change in a note. When I have had the originals of printed letters, I have followed the original manuscript. My transcription sometimes varies from the printed transcription. Henry James, who approached his task as an artist, did not hesitate to alter the letters which he quoted. The variations between his versions and my transcriptions are too numerous to note.

I have followed the principle of identifying each person when he is mentioned the first time and supplying added information in later references only when the text requires it. Hence identifications are to be located through the index. In a few instances it has not been advisable to identify the person when he is first referred to; in such cases I used a cross reference to the identifying note. Where the text gave sufficient information, I went no further. Persons about whom I could find nothing have been noted as 'unidentified', so that the reader will know at least that a search was made. My sources of information have been cited in the notes, except when I was drawing upon such well-known reference books as *The Dictionary of American Biography*, *The Dictionary of National Biography*, and *Burke's Peerage*.

LETTERS FROM
THE BROWNINGS TO THE STORYS

B di Lucca, Friday.
[October 7, 1853][1]

My dear Story,

How good of you to write so punctually, and pleasantly besides! We shall follow your track[2] as exactly & as soon as we can—but it will not be tomorrow, after all; on Monday we *do* go, however—so it is fixed—& what a joy to see you all again after such a weary while! If you don't believe in Monday,— after so much promise breaking,—here is our method of driving disbelief out of you very effectually: will you please (prompts Ba) tell that identical old Porter he is to see that we find (English) Bread, Butter, Milk and Eggs laid in by Monday After-noon, from the accustomed purveyors of the same—"matters which do not *keep* . . tho' our love to you *will,*" —as Genese Cap^n Morris[3] probably says somewhere.

This poor dear place has given up the ghost now, & we really want to get away. So you have good apartments![4]—that is very well. I hear more about the fever at Rome than I care to infect this paper with. It rained yesterday, & to-day,—or did, a few minutes ago. I have taken to write, in default of anything better to do,—wanting to make a sketch or two (in emulation of your pencil, so happy at bridge-sides & bits of rock & water) that may bring back this last happy time when the darker days arrive—as they will, I suppose.

Meanwhile, Ba's true love to you & Mrs Story goes with that as yours ever truly,—

Robert Browning

Penini is duly sensible of the "garden" & will tell Joe & Edith his feelings there.

---

[1] Dated by EBB's letter of October 7, 1853, to her brother George. (Landis and Freeman, p. 199.)

[2] The Brownings and the Storys had been in Bagni di Lucca during the summer. They spent much time together. In entries in his diary Story told of long evenings spent in talking and telling stories; of walks and picnics, once to Prato Fiorito when the dinner, 'brought on donkey back', was spread under a great chestnut tree, another

time when they built bonfires for the children and roamed about for mushrooms and flowers, 'filling the woods with laughter'. On October 5 the Storys left Bagni di Lucca for Florence, where they stayed until November 8, when they left for Rome. (Story Col.)

³ Unidentified.

⁴ In the Villa Lustrini.

[Florence, October 31, 1853]¹

Dearest Emelyn:

I wrote to Miss Blagden² to-day about the Pantaleoni apartment.³ Thank you twenty times. Wish for me, *will* for me, mesmerise for me, that I may indeed go to bed early to-night. For Mr W.⁴ is here talking down art in Italy!

[Elizabeth Barrett Browning]

¹ Dated by EBB's letter of October 31 to Isa Blagden. (McAleer, 'New Letters from Mrs. Browning to Isa Blagden', pp. 599–600.) The Brownings, who left Bagni di Lucca on October 10, were to be in Florence until November 15.

² Isabella Blagden (d. 1873), a writer of little note but a woman of inestimable goodness, settled in Florence in 1849. By the summer of 1850 she knew the Brownings and became one of their closest friends. She ministered to Browning's needs during his last days in Florence, following Elizabeth's death. After going with him and Pen to France, where she left them with Browning's father and sister, she went to England. Later, when RB and Pen went to London, she stayed near them for a while before returning to Italy. After Elizabeth's death Isa and RB, by agreement, wrote to each other once a month. Most of Browning's letters to her are published in McAleer's *Dearest Isa*.

³ The Brownings were going to spend the winter in Rome and EBB was writing to Isa Blagden, who was there, about an apartment. 'We hear of rooms in a house occupied by Dr. Pantaleone [*sic*] at the corner of Via Babuino, Piazza di Spagna, which would probably suit us. We wish particularly to know if this is the case. Will you find out for us? Robert must have a dressing room which he could sit and write in as well—dear Isa, see to *that*'. (McAleer, 'New Letters from Mrs. Browning to Isa Blagden', pp. 599–600.) The Brownings spent

the winter at 43 Via Bocca di Leone, in an apartment the Storys found for them. (For Pantaleoni see RB–WWS, March 18, 1854, and n. 2.)

4 Unidentified.

[Rome, CA. middle of March 1854][1]

I am grieved for you dearest Emelyn, that you should be forced into doing anything contrary to your feelings on this subject, but you cannot be surprised at the fever returning as it was obvious the persistance [*sic*] of it was the price to be paid for remaining in Rome.[2] It is clearly too heavy a price—you have a treasure left to you, and to *keep it* must be after all the first object & desire with you both. For my part I do think & have long thought that it required more real courage & energy to have to stand by and count the days & know by the striking of the clock the certain approach of this terrible suffering to the poor passive darling, than to undertake actively the most painful & uncongenial of journeys. When you are gone you will begin to rejoice at going, & you will take heart again in the reblooming of the dear pale cheeks. Our duties & our happiness are identical things oftener than we can discern perhaps. I speak in deep sympathy—I have felt & feel for you, as God knows.

As for the carriage, thank you, but I am not inclined to go out today; neither Robert nor I being very well, as his note will have told you. Indeed he has a terrible headache & has been going through a mere form of breakfast.

It's disinterested virtue on our part to approve of your going away. You dont say if Edith's attack was severe or not. . & I am half *afraid* . . by what you seem to imply. Robert will try to get to you as soon as he can, so as to hear the particulars.

Your affectionate
EBB

1 This letter was probably written shortly before the Storys left Rome for Naples, so that their daughter, Edith, might recover her health. (See following note.) EBB wrote to her sister Arabel on

April 3: 'Edith's fever had taken an obstinate & threatening character. They were going a fortnight since to Naples'—but at Villetri she
became much worse. (Berg.) They were in Villetri by March 18.

[2] When Joe Story died of gastric fever on November 23, 1853,
after a day's illness, his sister also became ill.

Rome, Sat^y March 18. [1854][1]

My dear Story,

I have just succeeded in seeing P.[2] but so late in the day as to
leave no time for anything but transcribing his letter[3]—for I
think it wiser to send a duplicate to Albano[4]—fearing the neglect of the Postmasters. What can one say to you? You know
how entirely we feel for you! P. lays great emphasis on his
assurance that the quinine never produces the ague, but keeps it
off as well as the fever—and says that had the remedies been
duly taken Edie might have staid at Rome—removal being only
advisable because she did *not* take them. You have done all for
the best, I am sure. I have no time for more—you understand.
P. was out when I called first, and I was forced to see him before
writing.

Ba's most affectionate love with mine to you both,—dear
friend,

Ever affectionately yours
RB.

Pray write—we shall be so anxious.

[1] The letter is postmarked Rome, March 18, 1854, and directed
to Villetri.

[2] Diomede Pantaleoni (1810–85), Italian physician and patriot,
who was attending Edith. His name appears in the next few letters,
written about Edith during her illness in Villetri, when the Storys,
in their anxiety, sought yet questioned Dr. Pantaleoni's advice and
the Brownings defended the Roman physician.

[3] A letter from Pantaleoni was enclosed. It is in the Browning
Library at Baylor University (Waco, Texas), along with this letter.

[4] Story planned to go to Albano from Villetri, even though
Pantaleoni advised him not to.

[Rome, March 21, 1854][1]
Tuesday, 4 oclock

Dear Story,

I rec^d yours yesterday by some *procaccio*[2]—not the regular post,—too late for immediate answer—it matters the less, however, as I was unable to see Dr P[antaleoni] before 7 oclock. He wrote what you have just read.[3] On getting your distressing note this morning I have gone to him again: & he bids me tell you that the doses of quinine are too weak, and should have been given *during* the fever, not after a fit of it merely; the fits recur too speedily to allow the medicine to digest and operate, and precious time is lost: give doses of four grains every hour, and abate them when the fit is arrested—(when the *next fit*, (that is) has been prevented). Nothing else will arrest the Perniciosa[4]—and *that* is fatal here. *Don't turn back*, but whenever Edie has been two days without fever, post on as hard as you can,—*giving quinine all the time*. Nothing will be gained by going to Albano. These are his exact and very emphatic words. Of what use to add one of mine or Ba's? You know our deepest sympathy is yours in this crisis. Pray keep writing. Ba's truest love & pity go with mine to you & dear Mrs Story.

Ever yours aff^y
RB.

[1] Only Ro 21 M of the postmark is legible. Tuesday in 1854 fell on March 21. The contents indicate that the letter followed closely the preceding one, that of the 18th.

[2] 'Letter carrier'.

[3] Browning subjoined his letter to one Pantaleoni had written to the Storys. Pantaleoni's letter is in the Browning Library at Baylor University (Waco, Texas), along with this letter.

[4] 'A kind of fever'.

43 Bocca di Leone [Rome]
Monday, [March 27, 1854][1]

Robert is out and I express for him & me the joy we had in your first account, dearest Emelyn, & for myself the satisfaction which comes with this. Of course he was glad to be of any use to you, and I was glad too to play my negative part in losing him under such circumstances. May God keep you from the terror which seems past—it must have been strong indeed. Our hearts bled for you.

Oh let us be glad & grateful without recrimination or back-thoughts. We think you not just, to be candid, to poor Pantaleoni who has shown no want of feeling in the course of this crisis at least . . of that we may assure you. For my own part I think that no medical man is fairly *responsible*, if the least *iota* of his advice remains unacted upon. I should not hesitate to place my own child in his hands in the case of illness—it is all I can say.

But who is right or who is wrong need not be thought of—only dear little Edie must. Do give her a kiss from me & Penini . . a double kiss. . on her forehead, & say how glad we both are to have this welcome news. I hope the change of air will begin to do its work with other efficient remedies. If the fever keeps off, her strength will soon gain ground—a child's vitality springs like a fountain.

Robert comes in & will write a few words to Mr Story. Then, he says, I must go out with him—the first time I have been out since you went. It is very mild today. We have had a letter from the Cranches,[2] very eager about news from you, & not written, I think, in very good spirits. The Americans, they say, in Paris dont care for art—which I am afraid means that he is neglected there.

This is a scramble of a note—but the heart of what I could say at any rate, would only be that we send you our affectionate wishes & thoughts. May God bless you.

Ever yours
EBB

[1] On the 22nd, 23rd, or 24th of March the Storys sent for RB to come to Villetri because they thought their daughter was dying. She took a turn for the better and RB was back in Rome by the 25th, when he went on a picnic with Lockhart. On the 27th (the Monday of this letter) the Brownings were answering on news from the

Storys of Edith's continued improvement. (EBB to Arabel, April 3, 1854, in Berg; DeVane and Knickerbocker, pp. 73–74.)

² Christopher Pearse Cranch (1813–92), American painter and poet, and his wife, during their first stay in Europe, spent the winter of 1848–9 in Florence, where they became acquainted with the Brownings and were 'intimate' with the Storys. In 1853 the Cranches began their second European sojourn; from Paris, where they established residence for ten years, Cranch wrote his sister that even at their 'most prosperous times' they never saw ahead 'more than a few months'. In Paris they received a letter from WWS about Joe's death and Edith's illness. (Scott, *Cranch*, pp. 152, 161, 208–9, 230; see also Miller, *Christopher Pearse Cranch*, p. 17.)

[Rome, March 27, 1854][1]

I suppose your next will be from Albano. I wish it had been Frascati, I think; so beautiful did it seem last Saturday, when I went there with Lockhart,[2] whose temper got a pain in it before the day was over. I'll tell you at Albano, where I shall go on a much lighter summons than the last. There are plenty of small news we will talk and laugh over, Baths of Lucca fashion, when we meet, if all proceeds as I trust. Chorley has brought out *another* play,[3] with but dubious success I fear. Grace Greenwood[4] has printed us flamingly in her book, it seems.

[Robert Browning]

[1] These may well be the 'few words' that accompanied the preceding letter. RB refers to his recent 'summons' to Villetri and to the picnic at Frascati with Lockhart—both, from all indications, belonging to the week of March 19–25.

[2] John Gibson Lockhart (1794–1854), writer, whose great work was the biography of Sir Walter Scott, his father-in-law. Saddened by family trouble and prematurely old, he retired in 1853 and spent the winter of 1853–4 in Rome. His comment that Browning was not like 'a damned literary man' (DeVane and Knickerbocker, p. 74) pleased both Robert and Elizabeth, and Browning students today like to quote it.

[3] Henry Fothergill Chorley (1808–72), critic for the *Athenaeum* and author of various types of literature. Of the plays he wrote, three were acted, two unsuccessfully. One of the unsuccessful ones was

Duchess Eleanour: a Tragedy. It was performed on March 13, 1854, and reviewed on March 18 in the *Athenaeum*. The review consisted mainly of quotations from other reviews, in which the favourable comments were for the acting of Miss Cushman rather than for the play itself. Miss Cushman's acting, however, could not bring the needed patronage and the play was withdrawn at once. (See Henry Fothergill Chorley, *Autobiography, Memoir, and Letters* [London, 1873], II, 129–42.)

⁴ Pseudonym for Sara Jane (Clarke) Lippincott (1823–1904), author of popular works, including *Haps and Mishaps of a Tour in Europe*. The Brownings, whom she visited on three evenings in April 1854 (EBB to Arabel, Berg), are discussed on pp. 357–8 and pp. 363–4. A short passage (typical of the whole) from these pages explains the popularity of Grace Greenwood's works as well as Browning's comment: 'And now, how can I fittingly speak of the two noble poet-souls, whose union is a poem, profounder and diviner than words can compass, and of their home, doubly sanctified by genius and love? Admitted for a few happy hours into this heaven of high thought and pure affections, I am sorely tempted to leave the door ajar, and so let out upon others some of the light and music'. The pages (221–2) on Story are written in a similar style, but there are not so many of them and the adjectives apply to his statues.

Wednesday morning
[March or April 1854][1]
43 Bocca di Leone, [Rome]

My dear Mr Story

Pray dont look on me as a backer of Pantaleoni's. I have no pretension to back anybody on such a subject, & it was more for you than for him that I said what I did—it's better not to vex oneself while eating the bread, about the best way of growing the corn—that's all I meant to say. For the rest, the difference between you is simply that *he* considered & considers the liver-affection to be the result of the persistance [*sic*] of the fever. The fever after long persistance affects one or another of the organs of the body, sometimes the liver sometimes the brain .. the 'perniciosa' being Roman fever with dangerous symptoms. So he says! Also, he could not have meant to send away your child to die, because *two months ago*, as Emelyn told me the same morning, & as was patent among all your friends, he wished her to go. In his view of the case, not taking the quinine was not taking the only efficient remedy . . & it was not for you but for him, supposing him to be *responsible*, to judge of the quantity necessary to the end. Of course he might be perfectly wrong, as many wiser men have been—that is nothing at all to the question. If loyalty means a general subjection to opinion I am apt to be as disloyal as you call yourself, dear Mr Story,—but I do hold that loyalty to superior knowledge is one of the conditions of wisdom—& so do *you* . . or you wouldn't trust Sciamani.[2] The misfortune was (both to you & Pantaleone [*sic*]) that you employed him with a dyspathy between you, & an acknowledged want of confidence on your part from the beginning. You were not loyal to him because you did not recognize in him the qualities which command loyalty from you as from others.

As to the want of feeling &c, you had that impression from the first. He has a peculiar manner, which may not mean carelessness or indifference. Now, he has attended Mrs Sartoris's[3] delicate baby all the winter & she is entirely satisfied with him . .she who is a most anxious & tender mother. He snatches up political pamphlets from her table as from yours, but she reads *him* altogether differently & considers him as considerate & feeling as if he gesticulated according to the received professional hieroglyphic.

Why say anything more about Robert's journey? Never think that either he or I grudged the little trouble he took in the attempt to relieve you from a single pang of the great apprehended anguish. In my part I had more joy in seeing him come back with his good news than I had pain in seeing him go—so I was paid, you observe! I shall be glad indeed when you can remove to pleasanter rooms at Albano, & still gladder when you can get still farther away . . for *all* this atmosphere must be bad for dear Edith. *My* quarrel with Pantaleone (if you want to hear my quarrel) was all along that he did not send you off *three* months ago. See!

Tell Edie that Penini will send her a drawing. I cant bear to let him send one till we are surer of the grounds . . till she can sit up a little, dear child. It is very cheering to have such a continuance of favorable news—every day gained is worth more than itself, because the constitution at her age, if it has time for self assertion, has extraordinary spring & power of wrestling with disease. Then the weather grows finer. I hope you dont exhaust yourselves with nursing all day & night. Why not have a regular nurse which would spare you both so much? It would be good in every way. I would not have troubled you with this scribble if I had known Robert was writing. . . you have pulled us both down on you, it seems, dear Mʳ Story. May God bless you all. With love to dear Edie & Emelyn & thanks to the latter for her note.

Most truly yours ever
EBB

¹ This letter seems to follow EBB's letter of March 27, in which she had defended Pantaleoni and had referred to the 'first account' of Edith after RB's journey to Villetri.

² Unidentified.

³ Adelaide Kemble Sartoris (1814–79), vocalist and author, was of the famous acting family of Kembles. She retired from the stage in December 1842 and soon after married Edward John Sartoris. During the winter of 1853–4, when the Brownings and Storys were in Rome, the Sartorises had established residence there, and the Brownings enjoyed Mrs. Sartoris's musical evenings. Both families were in Paris during the winter of 1855–6, and when RB settled in England after Elizabeth's death, the Sartorises were living there. The pleasant relationship that had existed between Browning and Mrs. Sartoris was ruffled in the early 'seventies. (See RB–Edith S, January 1 and April 4, 1872).

43 Via Bocca di Leone, [Rome]
Sunday, [April 16, 1854]¹

My dear Mʳ Story

When Robert & I parted this morning on our different ways of attaining the Pope's benediction, he bade me, if I returned first, to begin a note to you—which I begin thus. We are both anxious to express to you, dear Mʳ Story, our gladness & true sympathy in the happy change in dear little Edith's health.

Very pleasant it is to feel this joy with you, as truly as we felt much pain with you before. Now, I do hope.. that as 'there's a tide in the affairs of men,' the turn has come to *you*, & the salt water & bitter sea weed will dash back from you from henceforth. May you never be wounded again through the objects of your love—the only wounds which *tell* in this life. The rest are scratches. As for Edith, I begin to feel almost sure of her now, & that you will see her bloom back into her old vivacity & vigour of childhood. A change into a better air will abolish the lingering effects of this pestilent climate—oh, you will let me say so now. You know it *is* full of physical & moral miasma, and when I have seen the Vatican twelve times, I shall go on to say so twelve times twelve.

Meanwhile, of course I "dont boast of having seen Rome" .. no indeed. I am properly humiliated for all my disadvantages & defects, & confess meekly in writing to England that I am the most ignorant of travellers & have seen just nothing. After this Easter hubbub however, we are going to visit galleries, villas, ruins, & crowd as much sightseeing as possible into a little space. We heard the wrong *Miserere* I believe, on Friday—but it was very fine, wrong or right, & very overcoming in its ejaculating pathos. I sate that day in the Sistine Chapel for the first time.

Then we have made various campagna excursions with Mrs Sartoris & Mrs Kemble,[2] dined in bosky vallies, & pine-wood forests, & done the proper honour to your glorious opal mountains in the distance. Castel Fusano pleases me the best. Nothing could be finer in its way.

Tell dear Edie that Penini sends her his love & a kiss, & a very bad drawing, of the artistic demerits of which he is properly conscious. It is pleasant to hear of her on a donkey, taking a comparatively strong hold of life again. If you stay at Genoa she will like the boating & the driving in that beautiful bay & country. I shall not forget our descent into Genoa from the mountains in the supernatural moonlight which touched my brain with all sorts of fantastic suppositions. I remember Robert wondering whether I was mad or not. That was in coming from Turin more than a year ago.[3]

He has come in now—and now he has written a note of his own to you. With the affectionate wishes of us both

Most truly yours
Elizabeth Barrett Browning.

We have not written to the Cranches. We are horrible correspondents as you may have perceived.

[1] The particular Sunday is identified by reference to 'this Easter hubbub' and the allusion to the *Miserere* sung in Holy Week that they had planned to hear on the preceding Friday but did not. The year is established by reference to the convalescence of Edith.

[2] Frances Anne, better known as Fanny, Kemble (1809-93), actress and author, and Adelaide Sartoris were sisters. On an acting tour in America Fanny Kemble met and married Pierce Butler, a plantation owner, but later divorced him. When the Brownings were in Rome in the winter of 1853-4, she was staying with Mrs. Sartoris. Elizabeth enjoyed telling her brother George of eccentricities of Fanny Kemble. (Landis and Freeman, pp. 210-11.)

[3] In the autumn of 1852 on their return to Italy from the visit of 1851-2 to England and France.

Florence, June 11, '54.

My dear Story,

We very sincerely sympathise with your good news—they reached us here about a week ago—as we left Rome on the 26 Ult.[1] Having got Edie well, you must keep her so. Our own child became affected by the climate a week or two before we left, and frightened us considerably—he got better the moment he left the place, just as Edie has done. The weather was delightful—but the cause is deeper than in the weather. Here, it is cool and too rainy by far. I wish I could say something about our plans—they are more than ever uncertain: if we go to London we shall pass thro' Paris without stopping, I believe. And where we pass the winter, it is impossible to decide at present. We may even return to Florence, which suits us, on the whole, better than other places. If we do pass your way, however, be sure I will bring you the cigars you desire. We found the Shaws[2] here, to lose them too soon again. We left Page[3] fighting off his fever,—a little more effectually perhaps, but far from well. I shall surprise you by telling you,—now that I *may* tell,—that he painted a magnificent portrait of me[4]— the finest of even *his* works,—just the head, which he wished to concentrate his art upon, in a manner which would have been impossible had the canvass been larger—the result is marvelous. I hate keeping secrets—but this was Page's, not mine—he even wished my wife to be kept in ignorance of it—which, of course, was impossible. And the end is, that he has presented the picture to her. Both of us would have fain escaped being the subjects of such a princely piece of generosity—but there was no withstanding his admirable delicacy & noble mindedness,—which made the sacrifice of such time and labour seem easy. I wished him to keep the picture for a year at least—but he sent it to me on the morning of our departure. So it is here, the wonder of everybody—no such work has been achieved in our time, to my knowledge, at least. I am not qualified to speak of the likeness, understand—only of the life and effect, which, I wish, with all my heart, had been given to my wife's head, or any I like better to look at than my own.

Lytton[5] goes to England in a few days—we have some pleasant evenings together. Miss Vaughan[6] is here,—Miss Hosmer[7] will follow,—the Kinneys[8] are in good case. I am trying to make up for wasted time in Rome and setting my poetical house in order. Mrs Kemble left Rome on the same day with ourselves—not in our company unfortunately, but circumstances were too strong for our wishes. She left Florence as soon as we arrived. Mrs Sartoris will be here,—or at Lucca, presently. Goodbye, my dear Story,—my wife's kind regards go with mine to Mrs Story and yourself—Penini's love to Edie.

Ever yours affectionately,
RBrowning.

Our kind remembrances to Cranch & his wife. Pray write & tell us of your next move, or continued stay.

¹ This might be read as May 20. The Brownings were to remain in Florence until June of the following year, 1855, when they left for a visit to England. The Storys were in Paris.

² Francis George Shaw (1809–82), American philanthropist, married Sarah Blake Sturgis. They, with their children, went to Europe at the beginning of the fifties and stayed for five or six years. They spent considerable time in Florence and were friends of the Brownings.

³ William Page (1811–85), American portrait painter, lived in Europe from 1850 to 1860. (Taylor, *William Page*, p. 106.) According to his contemporaries Page was a master of portraiture, but his pictures were damaged by his inclination to experiment. Portraits that were praised in wonder and gave him the name of the 'American Titian' became scarcely recognizable. EBB explained why: 'It is a theory of this artist that time does not *tone*, and that Titian's pictures were painted as we see them. The consequence of which is that his (Page's) pictures are undertoned in the first instance, and if they change at all will turn black'. (Kenyon, II, 128, 148.) Although Page was in Florence when the Brownings were there earlier, he probably first knew them in the winter of 1853–4. (See Taylor, *William Page*, p. 124.) When the Brownings came to Rome for the winter they took the apartment above that of the Pages and at once became friends with them. The strongest tie between Browning and Page was art and between EBB and Page spiritualism.

⁴ This portrait was the wonder of the moment. Plans were made to exhibit it at the Royal Academy in London. Even before it left Italy, however, it began to darken and Browning wrote to Rossetti, who was to enter it at the Academy: 'You must put it in the sun, for I seem to fear it will come but blackly out of its three months' case-hardening. So it fares with Page's pictures for the most part; but they are like Flatman the Poet's famous "Kings" in a great line he wrote— "Kings do not die—they only disappear!" ' (Hood, p. 41.) The portrait was not hung at the exhibition. Its lines obscured, the portrait, now in the Browning Library at Baylor University (Waco, Texas), holds our interest for what it once was—a 'magnificent portrait' of Browning.

⁵ Robert Bulwer Lytton (1831–91), poet and diplomat, created an Earl in 1880, was the son of Edward Bulwer Lytton. When Robert Lytton went to Florence in 1852 as an unpaid attaché to the British Legation, he became a good friend of the Brownings. His association with these and other friends who were interested in poetry encouraged his literary talent, and in 1855 he produced, under the name Owen Meredith, a volume of poetry that showed the influence of Browning, an influence that became slighter in his later poetry. (Harlan, *Owen Meredith*.)

⁶ Unidentified.

⁷ Harriet (Hatty) Goodhue Hosmer (1830–1908), American sculptress, was a good friend of the Brownings and the Storys. She lived in Rome for many years; soon after she went there she met the Brownings and made the cast of the 'Clasped Hands' of Robert and Elizabeth. (*Harriet Hosmer*, ed. Carr, p. 92.) Frequent references in the Brownings' letters testify to their friendship with the American artist during their Italian years. Later Browning became estranged from Hatty. (See R B–Edith Story, April 4, 1872, and n. 1.)

⁸ William Burnet Kinney (1799–1880), diplomatist and journalist and his wife, Elizabeth (whose child by her first marriage was the writer Edmund Clarence Stedman), moved to Florence in 1853, after he had represented the United States Government in the Court of Sardinia at Turin for three years. Just before the Brownings left Florence for the Baths of Lucca in July 1853 the Kinneys called on them; and in a letter written soon afterwards to her brother George, Elizabeth gave her impression of them, which includes the following: 'Mr. Kinney pleased us much—He has a certain nobleness of mind & opinion,—of general atmosphere—as well as considerable intelligence. . . . Mrs. Kinney dabbles in literature, wrote a review once upon Robert. . . . She is a vivacious, demonstrative, rather pretty woman . . . not especially refined for an ambassador's wife, but natural & apparently warmhearted to the point of taking you by storm'. (Landis and Freeman, pp. 188–9.)

Florence, Dec 27. '54.

My dear Story & Mrs Story,

I am very happy to hear this good news¹ & congratulate you heartily—so does my wife. Surely this will give poor Paris one pleasant association in your thoughts, will it not? I should try Germany, were I you, since Rome seems out of the question,— for I don't know that Florence has developed any new feature that would correct the first impression² she was unlucky enough to give you. We have spent a very tolerable summer there, how- ever, and are all better than when you left us—our greatest misfortune being in this sad business of the Pages,³—as we devine it, rather than understand it, for many accounts reach us, each disagreeing with the other. I fear Page is left deeply in- volved in debts of her contracting—she has not necessarily, therefore, taken anything of Cirella.⁴ Dear noble Page will be

[35]

merciful & just,—I am sure,—beyond the power or conception of the world. It is heavy on him but he will "grieve it down," as Wallenstein says.[5] I have not heard from him, nor anybody else, directly. She was kind & good & affectionate to us & to our child and we keep it in mind. Page & Cirella—a man & a wisp of straw!

I am glad indeed to find that you work despite the ungenial influences and that "Beethoven" is perfected: it seemed so fine before! I shall rejoice to have the cast you promise me— (*plaster*, you remember the stipulation. . I need not say that.) I can give you no artistic news. Powers[6] has changed his notion and drapes the pensive statue[7] you may have seen—or was it finished last year? I forget. Your own great work[8] got safely to America and begins to repay you, I trust.

Give our love to Edie—we both wish her all happiness in this best of new years gifts—and you every continuance of the same —my wife joining with

Ever yours affectionately,
Robert Browning.

[1] The Story's second son, Thomas Waldo, was born in Paris on December 9, 1854.

[2] The Storys were unsettled at this time. They preferred Rome above all other places, but the association of it with the death of their six-year-old son in 1853 put it out of consideration for a time. Paris they disliked. Florentine society had left a bad impression on them, but Story wrote to Lowell that they were thinking of establishing themselves in Florence. (WWS–JRL, January 9, 1855.)

[3] William Page's wife, Sarah, ran away from him. Details of the misfortune are given in the letter from Story to Lowell dated January 9, 1855.

[4] Don Alfonso Cirella, whom Page's wife ran away with.

[5] Coleridge's literal translation for Schiller's line '*Verschmerzen werd' ich diesen Schlag*' was 'I shall grieve down this blow'. (*The Death of Wallenstein*, Act V, scene i.)

[6] Hiram Powers (1805–73), American sculptor, who settled in Florence in 1837, was the most famous artist in his own country and in Europe during his lifetime. Soon after the Brownings went to

Florence they met and liked Powers, and EBB wrote a sonnet on his 'Greek Slave', a phenomenally popular statue. (Gardner, *Yankee Stonecutters*, pp. 27–32, 70; Kenyon, I, 334, 347.)

⁷ Inspired by 'Il Penseroso'. A month before Browning wrote this letter he described the changes to another friend; 'frankly', he commented, 'I don't understand it at all, for Milton's "Melancholy" (if this is meant for her) is said to be "like a nun" and I should have styled this a chatelaine in ecstasy, or contemplation'. (*Harriet Hosmer*, ed. Carr, p. 46; see the flattering description in Tuckermann, *Book of the Artists*, p. 289.) The statue has disappeared from the scene with some mystery. In *Lenox Library: a Guide to the Paintings and Sculptures* . . . (1877), p. 21, the following is listed: '*La Penserosa*—Hiram Powers/Modelled and executed to order,/ Florence, 1857.' The New York Public Library, of which the Lenox Library is now a part, has in the card catalogue of the Art Division notes on the statue written at various times, indicating at one time unknown whereabouts, later 'broken', then 'unlocated'.

⁸ The statue of his father.

39 Devonshire Place. Portland Place.
Monday morning.
[July 21, 1856]¹

My dear Story,

I have just read your poems² with real delight,—&, if I added,—surprise, it would mean nothing very wrong,—only that one could not have expected you to do so much in a different way from that of your earlier book.³ It is full of music & pictures, & instances of that very "objectiveness" which I remember you told me in Rome you doubted your possession of: don't doubt any more, but go to work, or rather (I congratulate you) go on working. When I say I have read the book, I intend the simple reading that takes account of the extent of what is there: I shall go into it again & inform myself more particularly: meantime I am quite sure of a great deal being very good indeed—ought I to specify—(in justice to the others)—"In Sᵗ Peter's," "The Beggar," "Castello" (admirable) "The English Language," "Couplets"? Certain of the minor poems will touch every stranger, much more myself who remember those old days. To bring up, & end with blame, as a critic should,—you might,

[37]

I think, by one or two touches have made,—& still may make,—
"The Three Singers," into quite a beautiful thing, as indeed the
conception of it *is* already: a touch to insist a little more on what,
I know, you indicate,—that the young singer was expected to
celebrate youth,—whereas all his envy went on to age—&
another to show the old singer in like manner expected to glorify
the advantages of age, which contrariwise he recurs regretfully
to those of youth,—and so the startling praise of the present
from the cripple would come out with its highest advantage.
This is all there already, I repeat,—but I fancy you might make
freer way for the light from the heart of the poem, & show it for
a little jewel, by a deepened cut or two into those side-facettes.
Only, don't spoil it.

I write this, turning from the book, with the first impression
warm. My wife is out, and I won't do her the injustice of speaking for her: but she had gone before me and told me what I
should find,—& will tell you the same with *the same* pleasure, I
am sure. How do you like Windsor?[4] With love to all, dear
Story,

ever faithfully yours,
RBrowning.

[Note added by EBB]
I have just come in, my dear Mr Story, to sympathize with
Robert in the praise of a friend, (how pleasant!) & to give you,
together with his, my true & affectionate thanks.

EBB

[1] Dated by the postmark. The address is that of the London house
belonging to John Kenyon, EBB's cousin; the Brownings were
occupying it at this date. They had spent July–October 1855 in
London, the winter of 1855-6 in Paris, and then returned to London
for the summer of 1856, after which they returned to Florence.

[2] This collection of poems (Boston, 1856) was dedicated to Lowell.
(See J R L – W W S, February 18, 1856, and n. 5.)

[3] Story had published a volume of poems in 1847.

[4] After spending the winter of 1854-5 in Paris, the Storys went to
London for the summer of 1855 before going to America. They stayed

in America until the summer of 1856, were back in England for the summer, and then returned to Italy to establish themselves at Rome. This letter is addressed to the White Hart Hotel, Windsor.

[Rome,
Christmas 1858][1]

When Penini fresh from your kindnesses & his happy day yesterday, brought me my dear Mrs Story, this too beautiful gift from you, I felt for a moment embarrassed,—but it is better I think to tell you at once that a brooch *identically the same* has been already given to me & accepted. What am I to do? I cant wear two brooches exactly alike—can I? Perhaps you will set us down as ungracious about gifts—& it is true that the sincere 'clasp of hands' (which you spoke of in an unanswered note) is better to *us* than best gifts. But my reason for begging you to appropriate otherwise this lovely trinket is too reasonable to run the least risk of being untenderly interpreted, or, what would be worse of vexing you. So I take heart to entreat you to fasten it into dear Edith's collar & to let her feel that it is not spoilt by having just passed through my hands. The sentiment of the Christian symbol, so significant & touching to us all, remains with me— while the innocent unconscious Dove floating whitely in its atmosphere of rose, suits indeed her years rather than mine. I thank you much—& I shall thank you more if you understand kindly, which you will I think.

We count on you tonight, & would fain be exacting for tomorrow night also if we thought that M^r & Mrs Marshall[2] might draw you.

Believe that among the warmest wishes of your truest friends at this season of wishes, there is none who wishes more true good & joy to you & yours, including dear Mr Story, dear Edith & the dear pretty boys, in all affectionate truth than

Elizabeth B Browning

[1] This letter can be dated by the reference to the Marshalls' visit, which took place at Christmas 1858. The visit is recorded in three other letters written by EBB—one to Arabel at Christmas (Berg) that

[39]

can be dated 1858 in part by reference to RB's meeting the new diplomat Odo Russell, who came to Italy at the last of 1858; one to Isa Blagden (Kenyon, II, 304); one to Fanny Haworth (*ibid.*, 151 [in Kenyon the letter is assigned to December 27, 1853; but references to familiarity with the David Eckleys, to the approaching visit of Miss Ellen Heaton and Miss Haworth, and to certain events in William Page's life—all point to 1858, not 1853]).

² Mary Alicia Pery Spring-Rice (1841–75), daughter of Thomas Spring-Rice, first Baron Monteagle of Brandon, married James Garth Marshall.

Siena, May 29. '59.¹

My dear Mrs Story,

Here we are, after a very prosperous journey—the weather was perfect but the vettura comes in for a due share of the praise: we went so rapidly that the day's stages were quite short & easy: I can recommend Morcatelli, the driver, as capital in all respects, & tho' his charges are high the comfort of making short days out of long ones seems well worth paying for—we were never more than seven or eight hours on the road. The Inns are good at Viterbo & Radicofani & apparently abominable at the intermediate places. I write with the man in the room waiting for my making an end.

Ever yours most truly
Robert Browning.

Ba's kindest regards—in *such* haste!

¹ The date on this letter points to an error in Huxley. A letter which Huxley dated May 27, 1859, must have been written on May 23. In the letter EBB said, 'We are on the point, that is within three days, of leaving Rome—this is monday [*sic*] and we go on Thursday . . .'. (Huxley, p. 313.) EBB said she was writing on Monday, but May 27—the date given on the letter—fell on Friday in 1859. The preceding Monday fell on the 23rd, which must have been the Monday on which EBB was writing; in that case the Brownings would have been in Siena on the 29th, the date of this letter from Browning to Story. Elizabeth's own words clarify the situation: 'This is monday' (23rd); 'we go on Thursday' (26th); 'We travel by Siena to Florence. . . . we shall do it in four days.' (Huxley, pp. 314–15.)

[CA. 1859]¹

Dearest Edith, I am very sorry, but papas are more particular than mamas, and this papa of Pen's wants him for his music, he says, and does not like the whole day to be idled. There are lessons, besides, for to-morrow. Dearest Edith, forgive us. Another day, with less obstacles, you see. And thank you for your goodness.

[Elizabeth Barrett Browning]

¹ This note was written at some time during the last two and a half years of Elizabeth's life, when the Storys and the Brownings were spending their winters in Rome and their summers in Siena.

[CA. 1859]¹

[EBB to Edith Story]
. . . by Pen's desire. He is not well, and prays you to send him for solace a certain "Family Robinson," says he, "by Mayne Reid,"² and to be sure not to remember against him his having "blotted a book of yours last year." I doubt the connection between Mayne Reid and Robinson, but speak as I am bidden. Poor child, he wants a book of some kind.

¹ This, like the preceding note, was written during the last two and a half years of Elizabeth's life. HJ said it was written 'apparently in 1860'. (I, 370.)

² *Swiss Family Robinson* was completed and published by Johann Rudolf Wyss (1781–1830); his father (Johann David Wyss) had written it.

[Florence]
Friday, July 22. '59

My dear Story,
You are quite right in supposing that in the regular course of things you would have heard from me at once: I hoped & expected to be able to beg you would take the Villa for us the next

day: but my wife became suddenly ill & very ill—she had been much affected by all these untoward events,[1] and I believe caught cold—the result was, as I say, a very painful & rather alarming attack of tightness of the chest, inability to breathe & violent cough: I called in the doctor—and, to say the best thing at once, she is much better this morning—quite well, indeed, by comparison, tho' weak with the uninterrupted sort of strangled cough that prevented her sleeping the two last nights,—her worst state, at four this morning was ended by a sudden sleep & she wokc *well*,—though very weak. Now, therefore, our business is to keep what we have gained—and I don't know so likely a way as by getting our share in your pleasant Sienna [*sic*] cool and quiet. Will you have the goodness to engage for us the Bargagli Villa[2] from August 1—to September 30. We must pay 35 f [rancescon]i a month if they won't take 30—you will do for us what you can, and we cheerfully abide by your bargain. We bring our own plate & linen. And all thanks beforehand for the trouble you choose to expose yourself to on our account.

I am vexed at what you tell me of poor Mr Landor:[3] I write to him, under cover to you, and will, if I can, prevent him doing anything so foolish as going to Viarreggio [*sic*]. I had no notion of his meaning to go to Siena till he told me he had written to you:[4] he would hear of no other plan. Now, thro' the happiest of chances, he finds exactly all & far more than he wanted, and he begins scheming in this fruitless way. His family take no notice of his letters—and, till I hear from England, which I hope to do every day, I cannot be sure that his agent or relatives will advance him a farthing: he must at all events stay till his means are assured: and were they ever so abundant, he is manifestly unfit to be trusted alone: nor can I engage to go about with him and be responsible for what happens—as to a certain degree I might in Siena. If Mr Landor is in earnest in preferring any "two-rooms," with simple board, to living with his family,—that arrangement may be made: but Viarreggio &c are "not in the programme." I will make this as plain to him as is consistent with the delicacy of communication that he requires, and, no doubt, he will acquiesce. What a load you have imposed on yourself, in your generosity—but you shall not long remain unrelieved of it, be assured. He will show you the letter I write.

I have much to do this morning before the post goes out,—but your case is urgent,—and you will understand that had I a few minutes more to spend, I would try and say some little of what I feel about your goodness the other day,—yours & dear Mrs Story's. But word of mouth will soon succeed to scratch of pen, and we shall talk together soon to heart's content. Kindest love to all from us all.

Ever yours faithfully,
Robert Browning.

[1] The shock of the treaty at Villafranca caused Elizabeth to have the worst chest attack she had had in Italy.

[2] R B did not take the Villa Bargagli; the proprietor 'raised his demands' and Browning wished to be free to make a choice after he arrived in Siena. His choice was determined finally by the advice of Elizabeth's doctor, who thought that Villa Alberti was more advantageous to her health. (DeVane and Knickerbocker, pp. 120–1; see also *The French and Italian Notebooks by Hawthorne*, ed. Pearson, pp. 557–8.)

[3] Earlier in July, Walter Savage Landor, as the result of difficulty with his family at Fiesole, had thrown himself upon Browning's mercy. When he learned that the Brownings were getting ready to go to Siena and the Storys were already there, Landor decided that he too wanted to go. Story invited Landor to stay with him. Browning took him to Siena about the middle of July and left him with the Storys while plans were made for his future. Then in his characteristically impulsive way Landor decided to leave Siena for Viareggio, but was persuaded not to go. After the Brownings went to Siena Landor moved to a small house near the villa the Brownings had taken for the summer. (For an account of Landor's last years when Browning and, to a lesser extent, the Storys were associated with him, see the following: John Forster, *Walter Savage Landor* [London, 1869], II, 561–70; the Marchesa Peruzzi di Medici, 'Walter Savage Landor', *Cornhill Magazine*, N.S., XXXVIII [April 1915], 489–98; Minchin, *Walter Savage Landor*. For a recent account see Super, *Walter Savage Landor*, pp. 468–85, 489–91.) Landor had praised Browning's early works. (See Minchin, *Landor*, pp. 15–23.) His best known comment on the poet was a sonnet printed in the *Morning*

Chronicle on November 22, 1845. Browning, in turn, dedicated the last number of his *Bells and Pomegranates* (1846) to Landor. In 1859 Elizabeth wrote, 'Robert always said that he owed more as a writer to Landor than to any contemporary'. (Kenyon, II, 354.)

4 Story met Landor in 1850 in Bath. After calls were exchanged, there was 'tea with Landor—long evening of most pleasant talk'. (Diary, Story Col.)

[Florence
July 26, 1859][1]

My dear Story,

My wife has been so ill, and the calls on my time so incessant that I was unable to tell you—what would have pleased you to know two days earlier—that I have had a very satisfactory letter from Forster[2]—kind and conclusive—he will make every effort to help poor Landor and entertains no doubt of being able to do so effectually—he energetically bids me hold himself responsible for all expense, insists on Landors finding every comfort, an attendant, and other assistance I will tell you about when we meet—but adds that he is sure there will be no need of any such effort on the part of any friend, as the brothers of Landor, with whom he will put himself in immediate communication, are "most noble, honorable gentlemen, and wealthy to-boot—& will never bear indignity to their family's head."[3] They have all been under the delusion that the Fiesole people used the greatest kindness to our poor friend, spared no effort to make him at his ease &c &c. The greatest inconvenience is, that Mr Walter Landor of Rugely [*sic*], the cousin-agent is seriously ill, dying in fact—and this may a little retard matters—but that eventually a satisfactory arrangement will be made, we need not doubt—& meantime he, & other friends just as zealous, will gladly take all the engagements that may be necessary.

I have communicated so much of this as seemed needful to Landor, beseeching him to "possess his soul in peace & quietness"—as your goodness to him, indeed, makes a very easy matter.

And now, dear Story—the moment my wife can be moved to

Siena we shall take the journey: but, as there is a stop in our negotiation about the "Bargagli," let me profit by it to beg dear Mrs Story will let us know, before we decide on taking it, what I overlooked in my usual stupid way for the grounds and groves and other external beauties—my wife is tenacious of a ground floor—no stairs to ascend: now, which of the *three* at our discretion is the *stairless* villa? I am able to satisfy her about the coolness and picturesqueness of situation—but I forget all the rest. Can you help us again without finding the bore too exorbitant? We thank you most heartily for all your goodness but if we arrive uncertain as to the villa we take we will proceed at once to the inn which we have good experience of. I will write again on receipt of the letter I venture to expect: I will buy the ink & attend to the other desires.

Yours affectionately
RB

My wifes truest thanks & love, and prayers to be excused for this heap of trouble.

[1] HJ correctly dated this letter 1859, but he stated erroneously that it followed the one dated July 28, 1859, by Browning. (HJ, II, 10–12.) The proper sequence for the July letters is the following: July 22 (RB waits for directions from England concerning arrangements for Landor); July 26 (RB has just heard, through Forster, about arrangements to be made in England for Landor); July 28 (RB refers to the letter written the 'day before yesterday' with directions concerning Landor). Browning himself dated the letters of the 22nd and the 28th.

[2] John Forster (1812–76), historian, biographer, and critic—was Landor's literary executor. Forster furthered Browning's reputation from the time he wrote a favourable criticism of *Paracelsus* through his collaboration with Procter in editing the *Selections*. Unfortunately with his kind heart Forster had an overbearing and possessive manner, which made Browning's association with him difficult, and the friendship grew cold in the sixties.

[3] As the result of Forster's communications, Landor's brothers provided money, and for the rest of Landor's life Browning became in effect his guardian, managing his affairs and soothing his troubled spirit.

My dear Story,

I wrote to you hurriedly the day before yesterday—since then two most kind communications have reached us from your Villa. I told you that Forster had written energetically begging me to take every care of Landor till he could make new arrangements with the Brothers & Agent—the serious illness of the latter being all that prevented the matter from being very speedily terminated. I wrote on the same day to Mrs Landor demanding in a mildly-gruff way clothes, books, plate, pictures, residue of cash—in short all that poor Landor, by a note just received, desires me to obtain thro' the good offices of the Commissary of Police![1] However, diplomacy being more efficacious than frank fighting, I simply *wrote*, as I say,—and yesterday was favoured by a visit from Mrs Landor all butter & honey (save an occasional wasp's sting overlooked in the latter when she occasionally designated her husband as "the old Brute"!). The end is, she gives up all we require—the clothes, this very day, to Mr Kirkup,[2] the rest as soon as possible. I will bring them with me—and the note I enclose may set our poor friend's mind at rest on that point—but it will also serve another purpose, I trust —induce him to take that lodging you were so fortunate as to place at his disposal. Of your own goodness & generous hospitality you will not let me speak, nor is it necessary—but it *is* necessary, not on your account at all so much as on his own, that Landor should now fairly try the experiment which he was bent on making, and show whether he can indeed live independently of the immediate superintendence of his family: the question is not, which of his friends will be ready and happy to entertain him as a guest, but whether he can ever be anything else— which his wife very emphatically denies. I should certainly like to see how he sets about it—and I strongly press on him in the note the necessity of taking those lodgings for a single month and finding how he likes the way of life he was determined to adopt. In a month, we shall know exactly what his means are, and can contrive how they may be turned to the best account. He must try *now*, because a failure can be easily redeemed. Had

I supposed he would stay with you more than a day, I should have made quite other arrangements. Your goodness, however, has tranquilized and strengthened him and may contribute greatly to the success of the experiment. I have only room to thank you, or try and thank you and dear Mrs Story & Edith for their extreme kindness to us: we mean to go to Siena the first day that my wife is able to make the effort. She is decidedly better but still very weak: we mean to be as happy as possible for these coming two months and therefore, to avoid any precipitation and mistake, we will go to Siena, attack the triangle of villas in succession, armed with those capital plans, and establish my wife to her mind—as I know will be soon done. We thank you for all your far too generous offers and would accept them, be assured, were it at all necessary to do so. Let us once arrive & the rest will be an easy matter.

My wife's love to you both—Peni's especial love & thanks to Edith, whose commissions he will be proud to execute.

Ever yours faithfully
Robert Browning.

---

[1] On July 27 Landor wrote to Browning: 'A shower, a very slight one, yesterday, reminded me that I had only a thin coat on, and not another to change. In vain I applied to my family for my cloathes [sic]. Before you leave Florence, will you apply to the authorities for an order that my son deliver them up, and also my plate, together with whatever may remain out of the £110 left with him, after paying what he proposed I should pay for my board and other expenses, of which his mother told me he kept an account to a *quadrino*!' (Minchin, *Walter Savage Landor*, pp. 28–29.)

[2] Seymour Stocker Kirkup (1788–1880), artist, antiquarian, and ardent believer in spiritualism, was born in London and settled in Florence. Because of his strange, almost weird, personality a number of his contemporaries left a record of him and his manner of living. In an account by Nathaniel Hawthorne he is described as 'rather low of stature, with a pale, shrivelled face, and hair and beard perfectly white, and the former of a particularly soft and silken texture. He has a high, thin nose, of the English aristocratic type; his eyes have a queer, rather wild look, and the eyebrows are arched above them, so that he seems all the time to be seeing something that strikes him with surprise'. (*French and Italian Notebooks*, ed. Pearson, p. 485.) RB had

an affection for this childlike and kind old man and bore his absurdities on spiritualism with an easy tolerance. Kirkup had been a friend of Landor's since the 1820s. As an old and trusted friend he did much for Landor in the time following his final break with his family.

[Casa Guidi, Florence
October 29, 1859][1]
Saturday Morning—shame on us!

My dear Mrs Story,

I wanted to begin the answer to your note (most kind note) of two days ago—& so have stupidly prevented Ba from thanking you at once. She will do *that* for herself presently—but I am anxious to say that our surprise and my—something like consternation at finding you had gone away after all, and without getting what I supposed was necessary, and on a Festa-day when banks are shut,—you must know it was considerable,—I don't like to think of it even now, though your note gives such pleasant assurance of matters having somehow gone right. I believed it impossible that you could leave that afternoon, having sounded Story on the subject & felt the bottom of his mind on the subject at three o'clock or nearly. We went out on a sudden instigation of mine—just to the Cascine, & were back within an hour & a half.

You need not be told how entirely we owe you the delightful summer we have spent at Siena: its one fault was its briefness. Ba is hardly so well as when she was let thrive in peace & quiet in that dear old Villa & the pleasant country it hardly shut out. She is forced to see more people, & talk oftener than suits her. I am very anxious to get away and see no obstacle to our doing so by the end of the first week in November when Mr Landor will be finally established in his winter quarters.[2] We are papering & carpeting and doing things superiorly. He is quite well,—as gentle & affectionate as ever—and I shall regret his loss more than there is any use in dwelling upon, now that it must be. Ba enters the room at this moment saying "I wish we were in Rome!" Tell us,—for we count on your goodness,—the day you

[48]

expect to be there—and, when you get there, any news about houses,—sunny ones & prices of the same: in short, as usual trouble yourself infinitely for the sake of us poor do-nothings in return, who can't even keep at home one afternoon when we might be of some slight use. Goodbye now—for a very little time, I trust: love to Story to Edie—truest felicitations to you on the rosy cheeks of the Boys—kindest regards to Wild[3]—indeed, more grateful & affectionate remembrances rise up as I write than one can well put in a letter—or, indeed, in a speech.

Ever yours most sincerely
Robert Browning.

[Continued by EBB]

who has written so much & left so little room between me & post-time that I can only say amen to his affectionate thoughts—yes—I am very anxious to get to Rome. Nothing keeps us but the Landor necessity. The air here (since it has turned to damp) and too much talking make me feel more *unsound* than I have done lately—& the prophecied-of massacre at Rome (toward the imagination of which Dall' Ongaro[4] contributed poetically, two evenings ago) does not alarm me so much as thoughts of the tramontana. The Venetian poet threatened us also on other points. But I am stedfast in the faith that things are going excellently. Even dear Mr Story must approve of the locking up of the newspapers against the bishops' charges. Let us pray that the Pope[5] & his Antonelli[6] wont give up an inch. The danger is that they give up. Will nobody help the Pope away? My kingdom for a horse..or rather a mule—or rather a boat from Porta [*sic*] Anzio. Then the emperor's last promise to the Tuscan delegates that there sh^d be no intervention[7] . . neppure Napoletano[8] . . is worth something.

So sorry we were to miss you—and who would have thought it after what Mr Story said to us? Till your note came we even held a little to the probability of your returning for a week or fortnight. But the boys checks confuted such an idea most reasonably, of course. Thank you a hundred times for your kindness in caring to have Penini. But he was well the next day. And then, parting with him would be hard. I did so once to my own sister for a week—and he cried every evening of the time,—& I almost did the same. He was six years old then, & he made a vow "never in his life more to go away from papa & mama." It wont be kept—the more's the pity. Still up to this time, he will not go, he says. But you are none the less kind. Tell dear Edie with my true love, that I had my jacket arranged with the pretty patriotic buttons on purpose to receive her that unlucky morning. Love to all of you.

Affectionately always
Elizabeth Barrett B.

[Written by RB inside flap of envelope]

Since writing, arrives a letter from Cartwright[9]—he is urgent on us to take the apartment above that occupied by Mr Jones[10] in the Corso last year. He represents it as precisely what we require—(number of rooms, sun in abundance, third floor no more difficult of access than a second—) ending with "I honestly believe that in all Rome you will not find a more suitable apartment." He further says if he can agree as to price, he will himself take the Jones' apartment—& presses for an immediate answer. Now, what do you say? Is not the Corso very noisy? Is it healthy there? Can we do better, do you think? They ask 60[sc[udi]] a month for *five* months—with a prospect of diminution if we take it for longer. We both of us want your opinion before thinking of a decision—forgive all the trouble, if you can! On returning to the letter, I find the bedrooms look to the back, over a convent-garden.

[1] HJ dated the letter 1859 (II, 12). RB headed it Saturday, and October 29, 1859, the postmark on the letter, fell on Saturday.

[2] Browning made an arrangement for Landor to live in a lodging house kept by EBB's former maid Wilson, now Madame Romagnoli.

[50]

[3] Hamilton G. Wilde, or Wild (1827–84), American portrait, genre, and landscape painter, studied in Europe. (George C. Groce and David H. Wallace, *The New-York Historical Society's Dictionary of Artists in America* [New Haven, Connecticut, 1957]; see also Tuckerman, *Book of the Artists*, p. 486.)

[4] Francesco Dall' Ongaro (1808–73), Italian writer. He was educated for the priesthood, which he gave up in order to encourage and educate the people for Italian unity. Elizabeth liked Dall' Ongaro and respected his work. (Kenyon, II, 375, 130–1; Hewlett, p. 334.)

[5] EBB wrote to a friend on November 2 of this year: 'What I'm most afraid of after all is lest the "Holiness of our Lord" should agree to reform at the last moment. It's too late; it must be too late—it ought to be too late. . . '. (Kenyon, II, 349.)

[6] Giacomo Antonelli (1806–76), Italian Cardinal, unscrupulous in his defence of the Holy See and of his own interests during the struggle between the Papacy and the Italian *Risorgimento*.

[7] After Villafranca Napoleon promised that there would be no foreign intervention. However, his promise of non-intervention was sometimes inconsistent with his threats. (See King, *A History of Italian Unity*, II, 96, 103.)

[8] 'Not even of Naples'.

[9] William Cornwallis Cartwright (1825 or 1826–1915), A Liberal, was a Member of Parliament from Oxfordshire, 1868–85. He married Clementine Gaul, lady-in-waiting to a Pomeranian princess, knew languages well, and lived abroad many years, chiefly in Rome. Walburga Lady Paget knew him in Florence and included him in her gallery of portraits. 'There was Mr. Cartwright, a man of versatile talents and many languages, Liberal by conviction, and with a liberal conscience, a pleasant man to all except to his own family. He had an ungainly Polish wife, who had run away with him dressed as a page, but who could speak no language at all but her own'. (*Embassies of Other Days*, I, 252.) After inheriting property in England, Cartwright settled in his native country. 'He quickly attained a position of some authority with regard to foreign politics, from his intimate knowledge not only of languages but of peoples and leading men'. (*The Times*, November 9, 1915, p. 7.) Cartwright and his wife knew the Brownings in Italy, and the friendship with RB continued after Elizabeth's death.

[10] Browning had in his address book the name of Mr. George Jones, 63 Corso.

[51]

Florence, Monday.
[October 29—November 23, 1859]¹

Dear Friends,

We fear you must be fixed at Leghorn for a day or two longer, so black are the signs of this morning—& so take advantage of your stay to thank you, though but in a word, for all your kindness. We are quite of your mind about the objections to the proposed Rooms in the Corso, and are in no sort of hurry. We will gladly & gratefully wait for your report. Cartwright tells me to-day that he has taken the 2^d floor (the Jones') till June, and is anxious that we should profit by what he considers a good chance—but even his friendliness can't bring the sun to that back bedroom, unluckily. Those streets leading to the Pincio are clearly preferable. Understand, therefore, that we shall relieve you of none of the trouble you are bent on burdening yourselves with, and shall decide on nothing till you arrive in Rome.

After all, if you linger by the sea some few days the good gained there will be so much the more confirmed. Such a day as is now inflicting itself on us! Re-enter Rome with fine weather if you can.

I have seen Jarves² and been seen by him here one evening—and can assure you all is comfortably settled in the matter of the picture criticism: I also explained the thing to Kirkup.

I hope we may find an apartment the moment we go to Rome,—your offers are not the less gratefully received by us, you very well know—but I have only time to add that my wife's best love & thanks go to you both with those of yours ever affectionately,

Robert Browning.

[Continued by EBB]

I, for one, dear friends, have no 'feeling' *for* the Corso—rather against it—though in case of disturbances I shall rather like than otherwise being "there to see"—yes, indeed. A sunshiney bedroom is just as necessary as a sunshiney salon. For the Gregori-

[52]

ana, there is this objection—one cant get at carriages easily, I believe, & we are dependent on such conveniences. But your kindness and science together are to be trusted wholly. Nothing sunnier & pleasanter than the Bocca[3] can be found—only the sitting room is small, and the height great.

I congratulate you on your Urquhart[4] fanatic. There are fanatics of all colours, now-a-days. News from Naples are threatening in this Monitore[5] just opened. Whoever goes mad among the enemies of Italy, she gets the advantage by it. May they go mad therefore.

As soon as the rain ceases & I can get out, I will go & see your charming little Duchess.[6] I like her & honor her house— here in Florence, I mean.

Robert hasn't told you that whatever Can Giallo[7] may be doing poetically, his master is active. Robert *might* tell you that a poem on the goddess Diana[8] was produced the other day for instance, which had the peculiarity of being so exceedingly indecent (for Diana or any other goddess, or woman) that it might be objected to by less prudish critics than Moncton Milnes.[9] Robert might tell you of it, & MIGHTN'T send it to you. Dear Edie—may God bless her.

Affectionately yours
EBB.

[1] This letter was assigned by HJ to 'some moment' of the 'couple of years' previous to the winter of 1860–1. (II, 56.) The year 1859 is written in brackets on the letter in someone's handwriting besides Browning's. The letter was written in that year between the letters of October 29 and November 23, as is obvious from the contents of the three letters.

[2] James Jackson Jarves (1818–88), pioneer art collector and writer of books on art, is best known today for his collection of 119 paintings, acquired by Yale when it was the only collection of early Italian pictures in America. He and the Brownings knew each other in Florence, where Jarves lived from 1852 to 1884. (Francis Steegmuller, *The Two Lives of James Jackson Jarves* [New Haven, 1851].) From references to Jarves in both the letters of EBB and RB it is clear that Elizabeth was more attracted to him than Browning was, an attraction that can be explained by Jarves's interest in spiritualism.

³ In the winters of 1853–4 and 1858–9 the Brownings were at 43 Via Bocca di Leone. In the winter of 1859–60 they were at 28 Via del Tritone.

⁴ Unidentified.

⁵ The Brownings depended on the news from the anti-papal *Monitore* and later circumvented the police in order to receive it in Rome, where it was banned. (Kenyon, II, 371–2; McAleer, pp. 51, 67.)

⁶ Elizabeth wrote to her sister Arabel in June 1859: 'Then the Duke & Duchess of Cassigliano have called on us—(an acquaintance begun in Rome though they live in Florence.) She was a princess Barbarini, & he is the eldest son of that Marquis Laiatico who had so much to do with the change of government here & has gone officially to Piedmont'. (Berg.)

⁷ Landor's dog, a Pomeranian, given to him by WWS.

⁸ 'A Dialogue in Verse between Diana and her Nymphs' is one of the Landor manuscripts listed by Sotheby in the *Browning Collections*. (P. 53, item 240.)

⁹ Richard Monckton Milnes, first Baron Houghton (1809–85), politician, poet, and biographer of Keats. His success as a host and his great number of friends gave him a conspicuous place in Victorian society, where his path often crossed Browning's. Milnes's extensive and fine library contained a well-known collection of erotica. (James Pope-Hennessy, *Monckton Milnes: The Flight of Youth* [London, 1951], pp. 113–22.)

Florence, Nov. 23. '59.

Dear Mrs Story,

When your note (full of kindness as it could hold) came to us more than a fortnight ago,—I was expecting that any day after the 8th Nov—when Mr Landor was to be definitively disposed of I should be able to write that we were certainly to be at Rome by the week's end: that very day, or perhaps the next, the cold weather surprised us, and ever since we have been expecting & hoping for just such a decided change in it as will allow us to believe in three or four warm days for our journey by Siena: such changes always arrive, so far as we remember, and yesterday seemed the prophet of all we want,—but this morning is clear, sunny and cold again. Be sure that if we can risk the journey we will—our preparations are made, we could set out three days hence or earlier. It was so unfortunate a necessity,— that of domiciling dear old Landor, beside arranging other matters concerning his interests—and one could hardly foresee this extension of the first cold days—for where is the St Martin, or your Indian summer? One good thing is that if we can but arrive in Rome, from your kind account, we shall meet with but little difficulty in housing ourselves, i.e. sunning ourselves, fully to heart's content in the deserted English & American quarters. Hatty[1] wrote to us two days ago and mentioned something about a capital house in Via Felice[2]—"which Story had probably written about"—has he done so? Nothing reached us, at all events. Both of us feel more grateful than we shall try to enlarge upon for that offer of your house on our first arrival— and we know your sincerity & generosity enough to believe that you would really be indifferent to the inconvenience for the sake of serving us so effectually—but indeed we shall not need your goodness in this respect—(I think we use it freely enough in the other matters!) We will sleep one night at the Hotel,—pass in review in the course of the next morning the apartments that you recommend, and get settled by nightfall at latest. I will write to you the moment our course is decided: I shall trouble you to remember the *lascia passare*[3] for the frontier as well as the City-gate—but all particularities the *last thing*! I write with a visitor talking with my wife (she has been suffering, rather, from over-visitation). I don't know that she will be able to add a word to mine: I can safely send her love to you all, if nothing more. She is not particularly weak or unwell, and could face the troubles of a journey quite as well as last year,—had we but last year's mild weather!

Mr Landor told me last night that he had written to you & Edie two weeks ago. He seemed very desirous of hearing something in return. He is well and comfortably lodged for the winter—but is irritable, too often, at little misconceptions, for-getfulnesses of his own, which no solicitude can provide against.

I will leave off with more love to you all, & more hopes of seeing you all very soon again from

Yours affectionately ever
Robert Browning.

¹ Harriet Hosmer.

² During the winter of 1860–1 the Brownings lived at 126 Via Felice in Rome—now Via Sistina. (See Hewlett, p. 334.)

³ 'Persons travelling in their own carriage should write before-hand to their correspondent, or banker at Rome, or to the British Consul, requesting that a lascia-passare may be forwarded to the frontier, and another left at the gates of Rome, in order to avoid the formalities of the custom-house. The lascia-passare is never granted to persons travelling in public carriages'. (Murray's *Central Italy* [London, 1850], p. 3.)

[Florence]
Nov. 25. (Friday) [1859]¹

Dear Mrs Story,

You will have got my letter,—sent the day before yesterday, when I received your kind note. The weather has broken up at last—we hope & will, at least, endeavour, to leave on Sunday or Monday² at latest. I have only time to renew truest thanks & to beg that you will send the lascia-passare to the Frontier (somewhere by Radicofani) as well as to the Gate. We shall try to bring Pen's pony³ with us—if that be difficult, we shall send him slowly—but can any "order" do anything for us should we bring him?

You know how much we thank you, how much we desire to see & be with you. We go to the Hotel d'Angleterre—unless some such clear good fortune in the way of a House as it would be worth your while to mention in a note, left for us at the Gate, should render it needless.

Ever yours, in utmost haste lest a minute of
the morning be lost, with Ba's love to all,
Faithfully ever
Robert Browning.

[1] 'Friday' was placed in parentheses by RB. The year is established from comments in this letter that relate it to the preceding letter.

[2] They did leave on Sunday (27) or Monday (28). EBB said they arrived in Rome on December 3 (Saturday) after a six-day journey. (Kenyon, II, 357.)

[3] Browning bought the pony in Siena; Elizabeth reported that it 'travelled like a glorified Houyhnhnm' to Rome. (Kenyon, II, 354.)

[Rome]
Tuesday E[y].
[December 3, 1859–April 22, 1860][1]

Dear Mrs Story,

We were expecting to be able to enjoy your company this evening in case you were good enough to give it us: my wife, however, continues so unwell that I feel you would prefer any other evening to this,—will you understand & forgive us? (for I too remain worried by my vile cold, & have kept the house again all day).

I read the "Westminster"- which you can, if you please, transmit to Mr Parker[2] when you have done with it.

Ever yours most truly,
R Browning.

[1] The Brownings were in Rome from December 3, 1859, until June 4, 1860; Theodore Parker was in Rome from October 19, 1859, until April 22, 1860. This letter was written between the Brownings' arrival and Parker's departure.

[2] Theodore Parker (1810–60), New England preacher, writer, and reformer, went to Italy in an effort to regain his health, first to Rome and then to Florence, where he died. When he arrived in Rome he found Americans that he had known in Massachusetts, among them William Story. Parker and the Brownings met and admired each other. (See Weiss, *Life of Theodore Parker*, II, 382, 390, 406, 409–10; and Kenyon, II, 355, 388.) EBB wrote to Arabel of him: 'He has eyes like light itself, and his forehead is as a mount of vision, an extraordinary man in many ways'. (Berg, December 7, 1859.)

Dear Friends,

I said I would tell you how we found things & fared on the Orvieto road: we arrived at 4 yesterday afternoon and preferred resting here for four & twenty hours to going forward at once. We travelled 48 or 50 miles delightfully the first day & reached Viterbo early: next morning we began the new part of the journey—continued 30 miles at a stretch and got to Orvieto, thro' a pleasant, placid country—(*such* work of Luca Signorelli at the Cathedral!). On Wednesday we advanced to Ficulle,— but for Ba's fatigue, it would have been better to push on to Città della Pieve where a fresco of Perugino's is worth the trouble of a longer journey,—& the comfort of the Inn would have been much greater: but it was our own choice to divide the way *so*. We reached Chiusi early—having travelled all day thro' exquisite scenery. We felt the heat—not intolerably however, nor before this third day: there was never any dust to mention. We left Chiusi at nine, or later, yesterday (I got up early every morning and saw sights for an hour or two) and reached Sinalunga by 1 oclock—had there been an endurable inn, Ba might have rested sufficiently to proceed to Florence— but she was forced to choose between the kitchen & the carriage & preferred the latter—so here we stopped, as I began by saying. We were perfectly served throughout—the Vetturino caring for all things, and his charge for the three days & a half amounts to 19 scudi—2 pauls—I paid the service myself: surely this was not much. The end is, we have had a delightful journey, which Ba has born very well on the whole—tho' the whole business is far more fatiguing than by the short stages on the Perugia Road.

I have seen Aliberti[1] & *all but* arranged with him for the Villa—I have also seen Nencini—who is to receive your box to-day and take care of it: he had heard nothing from you on the subject, & perhaps you wished it to be conveyed to the Villa thro' other hands—but he told me that the "magazzinaggio"[2] would be considerable if there were any delay in removing it— though it seemed best to consign it to him.

[58]

We are going in a few minutes—what shall I say that you dont know? How grateful we are for all that is past & how hopeful of more pleasures in your company. If we can do anything at Florence, you know how you will oblige us by letting us know. Kind love to you all—Wild and all—from all of us

Ever yours faithfully & aff [y]
Robert Browning

[1] The Brownings were on their way from Rome to Florence, where they were to stay about a month. As in 1859 the Brownings and the Storys spent the summer in Siena—the Brownings at the Villa Alberti and the Storys at the Villa Belvedere. The Storys made arrangements for their villa through Nencini.

[2] 'Warehouse charge'.

Florence, June 15. '60.

Dear Friends,

Truest thanks for your kindness,—the letter & the package brought by Mr Field.[1] You had not received the letter which reached you, I hope, the day of his departure: I gave it to "Pippetta," the last thing, to put into the post, as we left Siena: if it have miscarried,—I may say briefly that we travelled prosperously thro' a beautiful country and that I, leaving Ba to rest herself, saw wonderful things at Orvieto & Chiusi. She was too fatigued to proceed at once to Florence from Sinalunga—we stayed twenty four hours at Siena, & reached Florence happily this day last week. Since then, she has not left the house, nor do I press it on her,—considering that repose is best for her just now. I have ended our negotiation with Alberti,—for three months on the old terms with some advantages,—and we are to be there by the 7th of June[2] *at latest*: joy to our reunion!

You have been perfectly good in executing all our commissions so exactly. Can I make you any sort of return in kind—do nothing for you here? Shall we really see nothing of you in Florence? The weather is very cool, & it would be pleasant to

[59]

go about with you. We liked Mr Field much—all but in the shortness of his stay: by this time you have lost dear Wild, too. I would have gone down for one goodbye day,—pleasant-painful as it might be—but there is *so* much for me to do here,—after an absence & before an absence, you understand! I have been writing for so many half hours this morning that the pen quite refuses to do better than in the scrawling you see! So I will just say that I found Landor quite well,—very affectionate to us & to you. I will take care of the (interesting) papers & letters, & bring them with me—but most thanks for the two photographs —so admirable, we all think.

Ba has not yet delivered your letter to the Duchessa di Casigliano—but will do so the first day she can go out. Her best love to you all—with mine & Pen's. He was proud indeed of dear Edie's letter. I hope Mrs Eldridge & your Brother[3] have borne the journey well. It will be only like your kindness to write a word to tell us how & where you are.

Ever yours affectionately
RB.

[1] John W. Field (1815–87) of Philadelphia, who spent much time in Europe. He was a friend of both Lowell and Story. In a letter dated May 7, 1855, a friend introduced him to A. H. Clough: 'He is a man of forty years old, who having made fortune enough for his own and his wife's . . . moderate wants, is now leading a life of complete leisure. He is one of the frankest, most honest, open-hearted men I ever knew. . . . He has "a talent for friendship",—with a cordial, sympathetic manner which is the real expression of his feeling. He has more love for literature and art than cultivation,—and he appreciates everything much more through his affection than through his intellect'. (*Letters of C. E. Norton*, ed. Sara Norton, I, 127–8.) In the autumn of 1881, over twenty years after Browning and Field met, they saw each other in Venice (DeVane and Knickerbocker, pp. 269–70); Lowell was also there (Houghton, bMS Am 1239.1). Later Field, Lowell, and Story were in Rome, 'telling over old stories and reviving old associations'. (Norton-Elmwood, III, 94.)

[2] Browning meant July.

[3] One of Emelyn (Eldredge) Story's brothers listed in Appendix I.

Dear Friends,

We received Edie's note—& only put off thanking her & you for it, & for so much beside, in order to be able to tell you that Ba had executed your commission & carried your notes to the Duchess of Casigliano: it seems strange to say that she has only just done this,—having left the house for the *first* time this morning—not that she felt unwell after the journey—but simply *tired*—so I let her rest. She is now quite well & strong again. We were both of us delighted with those earnest, engaging & perfectly good young great people: Ba intends to write to you directly—& will tell you more about them & other persons & things—but I am determined to send a word without further delay—because a word back again will oblige us so much: for we want to know how you are, how you like your house,—what you please to tell us, in short. I suppose—you got my letters at last—not only the one I sent from Siena but the other from Florence,—& that you know all is arranged with Alberti about the three months' occupation "to begin July 7, at latest." It is very cool here just now, but the heats will begin presently & we shall go on the first warning. I fear Landor will be best let alone[1]—tho I have not made up my mind: he is very comfortable & cool where he is—very cheerful & satisfactory in most respects—he took tea with us last night & sent me a copy of verses, the first thing this morning, "made before his breakfast" —"Lead from Casa Guidi Windows,"[2] he calls them. We find very few friends here—the Forbes[3] remain, & the Westons[4] are just arrived: shall I transfer to them that most interesting letter of Mrs Apthorpe's[5]—who, I observe, desires that they may read it?

Do you indeed, as dear Edie pleases to assure us, miss our neighbourliness (what word must I use?) Be assured I want your presence quite as much & more. We all look forward to three happy, productive months at Marciano.[6] I found Frederick Chapman[7] here, nephew of our Publisher—& he has rather quickened our laziness—he talks about new editions & other encouragement. Aurora Leigh: *Fifth* is getting ready & the second of "Before Congress"[8] is imminent. We had to get ready some dozen of packets for him, & so turn his presence & departure to account—this must explain our silence since we arrived. I have got my cast from the face of "Keats"[9]—such a beautiful & characteristic thing. I wish you could see it, & am not prevented bringing it to Siena by any other considerasion [*sic*] than that of the fear of a smash—*that* would be dreadful indeed. One could photograph it well, could one not?

I look up to ask Ba what I shall say on her behalf, till she can dispense with my help & lo she is asleep! No. Pen has waked her up with a question about his riding—so she sends her best love with mine, and repeats that she is very tired. So goodbye—till you write again,—kindest regards to Mrs Eldgridge [*sic*] & Mr Eldridge,—I hope they are enjoying themselves. Do give me something to do for you, if you don't go to Florence yourselves.

> *Ever yours, most affectionately*
> *Robert Browning*

(see this paper, which
it is too late to change!

---

[1] Landor did go to Siena again, just as he had gone in the preceding summer.

[2] Sotheby lists the following item: 'Landor (W. S.) Lead for Casa Guidi Windows, Auto. Poem, 26 lines (*one couplet written twice over*), 1 p. 4to, signed in full and dated *June* 29, "in the morning before breakfast".' The catalogue explanation of the poem is this: 'The "Lead for Casa Guidi Windows" is about Syracuse and Garibaldi, and was no doubt written shortly after the latter's conquest of Sicily in 1860.' (P. 53, item 243.) This poem must be 'Syracuse', published in *Heroic Idyls*, 1863. (*The Complete Works of Walter Savage Landor*, ed. Stephen Wheeler [London, 1935], XV, 123.)

[3] The Misses Forbes, Casa Grazzini, are listed in Browning's address book.

[4] The Weston family was from Weymouth, Massachusetts. In the Weston papers in the Rare Book Room of the Boston Public Library there are references to European visits of various members of the Weston family. Twice in the 60s Browning wrote Story of having seen one of the Misses Westons in London. (March 19, 1862, and

May 3, 1864.) Maria Weston Chapman (1806–85), one of the family, was largely responsible for the best known of the anti-slavery gift books—the *Liberty Bell*. It was in this publication that EBB's 'A Curse for a Nation' was first published in 1856—the poem that many, when it was later included in *Poems Before Congress*, erroneously thought a pronouncement on England. In Sotheby there is listed a presentation copy of the issue of the *Liberty Bell* in which 'A Curse for a Nation' was first published, inscribed 'To Elizabeth Barrett Browning from her affectionate friend Maria Weston Chapman, Weymouth, Massachusetts, U.S. January 29th, 1856'. (P. 111, item 861.)

⁵ Eliza Apthorp and her husband, Robert Apthorp, were in Europe with their son, William Foster (1848–1913), who was partly educated there and who eventually became an outstanding music critic.

⁶ The Villa Alberti is in Marciano, two miles from Siena. It is now called Villa Marciano. (Hewlett, pp. 318–19.)

⁷ Frederic Chapman (1823–95) succeeded Edward Chapman as head of the publishing firm of Chapman and Hall.

⁸ *Poems Before Congress*, published in March 1860. This was the last volume of Elizabeth's poems published during her life. It was coloured strongly by her political feelings and, consequently, was severely attacked by the critics, who did not always understand the poems. (See Hewlett, pp. 324–5.) Because of the disapproval of the poems Elizabeth, as well as RB, must have been gratified by the possibility of a second edition. (See Kenyon, II, 394, for comment made by EBB.)

⁹ Sotheby lists the following: 'A Plaster Death Mask of Keats, on circular base'. (P. 160, item 1394.)

Florence, June 29. '60.
Dear Story,

True thanks for your kind & welcome letter: I was going to answer it leisurely, when there is a sudden occasion of writing to Nencini,—for Landor determines at last to accompany us, and I want the old quarters for him, where you helped to make him so comfortable last year. So I just write a word—without prejudice to the other few words I mean to write before we set out, to say that, for ourselves, the best news I can communicate

[63]

is that we start for Marciano & you all, to-morrow week—as I have just apprised Alberti. Won't you like to see another month or two of dear old Landor & Can Giallo? (He has just come to me for picture-money,—such pictures!)[1]

I will procure the French books, if they are to be found here: think of any other commission, I may be lucky enough to be entrusted with. I shall hardly save the post & must leave off with kind love from Ba & Pen to your whole circle: what a pleasure to think we shall so soon meet again!

> *Ever yours affectionately*
> *Robert Browning.*

Would you have the goodness, whenever you engage your piano, to secure for me the same that I had last year—at the same terms? And beg that it may be transferred to the Villa on *the* 7th so that we may find it on arriving?—and will you forgive this troubling you?

[1] Landor gave free reign to his enthusiasm for painting. A derogatory impression of his artistic taste and practices in purchasing pictures, as the result of comments made by some of his contemporaries, has led two recent biographers to write in his defence. (See Super, *Walter Savage Landor*, pp. 179–80; and Malcolm Elwin, *Landor* [London, 1958], pp. 217–18.) Browning sometimes referred lightly to Landor's whims and fancies, as he did in this letter, but he was fully aware and appreciative of his endowments. With his own interest in art Browning doubtless was sympathetic with the motives that lay behind Landor's choice of pictures.

[Siena or Florence, CA. 1860][1]

Dear Mrs Story,

All thanks for your kindness, on the part of us all. Will you let us go to you to-morrow instead of to-day?—as some arrangements have been made about a drive of our own, & Mr Landor's coming in the evening, which it might be difficult to alter. You know very well how I miss my evenings but what can I do? I have just received a letter from Lady W.[2] which I send. Love to Story, Edie—& indeed everybody. Pen will be with you as you so kindly ask. Ba says all this thro' me & is as affectionately yours

as, yours ever,

Robert Browning

Whenever your servant goes the way of our *envelopes—waiting to be gummed*—will he be so kind as to get them? I have forgotten all about the shop.

¹ This letter was written before Elizabeth's death (1861) and in all probability after Browning started his guardianship of Landor (summer of 1859). It was written in Siena or Florence. The Brownings, the Storys, and Landor were all in Siena in the summers of 1859 and 1860; and during these last years of Elizabeth's life the Storys, on their way to and from Siena, sometimes went to Florence, where Landor had his permanent residence and where the Brownings stopped for a while in Casa Guidi between winter in Rome and summer in Siena.

² Lady William Russell (1793–1874), distinguished intellectually and socially, was the wife of Lord William Russell (1790–1846), high in diplomatic service. While she was in Rome in the early 1860's she was injured in an accident. Although she never entirely recovered and seldom left her house, she did not give up her social life after her return to England. Among the eminent people who went to her home were many foreign as well as English friends; 'it was a privilege to be one of its recognized habitués' (*A Great Lady's Friendships*, ed. Lady Burghclere [London, 1933], p. 19). Browning, who had met her son Odo in 1858, was acquainted with her by February 1859, when he was visiting in Rome (Huxley, p. 307); and Story probably met her during the same visit. As later references in these letters indicate, Browning, after his return to London in 1861, often went to see Lady William, who received her friends every evening. (An undated, unidentified newspaper clipping giving the facts of her life and an account of her written by Mrs. Story are in the Story Col.)

[Florence]

Friday Mᵍ.

[November 9 or 16, 1860]¹

Dear Friends,

I write in all haste to save the post—but have only to tell you that the enclosed Bill was brought to me this morning by the Proprietor of the Villa de Lyon,—he begs you to pay the amount to Brown, Casa Fausti, near the Corso—his agent: I would have paid it, of course, but thought the more prudent way would be to send it to yourself.

How I wish we had been "off" a fortnight ago! The cold is greatly inconveniencing Ba already—we shall take the first mild day & run for our lives, depend upon it. You know how you are missed by us all. Love to you from Ba, Pen &

Yours affectionately ever
Robert Browning.

Page is writing on Art in the "Indep"[2]—I will bring the numbers. I send the *third* "Galignani"[3] with this, & directed a letter to you on Tuesday. I have got Landor photographed in very deed—& am presently to receive a proof: he vowed he would commit no such folly, up to the last moment.

[1] The date is indicated by the appearance of William Page's articles in the *Independent* in October and November 1860 and substantiated by the reference to the photographing of Landor (see Minchin, *Walter Savage Landor*, p. 111) while the Brownings were in Florence, between October 8 (see Sotheby, p. 78, item 441) and November 18, when they left for Rome (see RB–SS, November 17, 1860). From Browning's statement that they would leave as soon as the weather permitted, it can be inferred that the letter must have been written on the Friday of the 9th or of the 16th, not long before their departure from Florence.

[2] Under the general title of 'The Italian Schools of Painting' the following articles by William Page appeared in 1860 in the *Independent* (New York): 'Raphael and the Pre-Raphaelites', October 11; 'Raphael and His School', October 18; 'The Venetian School and Titian', October 25; 'Titian', November 1.

[3] *Galignani's Messenger* (1814–1904), founded by Giovanni Antonio Galignani in Paris and widely read by Englishmen on the Continent.

Florence, Nov 17. '60.

Dear Friends,

We start to-morrow, Sunday—I just write this, in utmost haste, to tell you why we precipitate our departure. We have just received the worst news of poor Mrs Cook[1]—and if the next

[66]

post brings the calamitous intelligence I cannot but expect—
we should not be able to leave at all—& what the effect would
be on Ba, of mental & physical suffering together, you may
imagine—so I am determined to get her off to-morrow—we
shall therefore arrive on Friday, I suppose. I dare say you will
kindly take our letters at the post so that we may be no longer
in suspense than is necessary. Also—you will understand to say
"no letters!" should you meet us—so as to allow me to get the
first reading & break any bad result as much as I can.

How kind, your letter from Terni,—and the messages which
Mrs Bruen[2] delivered! But *that* all goes of course now,—tho'
we are none the less grateful. We shall soon see you & thank you,
I hope. The weather is just what we require. We have the
Vetturino who enabled us to travel so comfortably last year—
but I have had no time to plan for a better arrangement as to
Inns &c being, as I said, in the utmost haste. I have a letter for
you from New York—& sent one to you, or saw it directed at
the post, a few days ago. I paid Goodban's[3] bill.

Poor Ba is in no condition to say anything—but would if she
could. Please tell Mr Russell[4] that I venture again to bid people
address my 'Nazione'[5] & 'Athenaeum' to *him* so shall I hope to
get them unmutilated.

Ever yours affectionately
Robert Browning.

[1] EBB's sister Henrietta, who married Captain William Surtees
Cook in 1850, died November 23, 1860. (See McAleer, p. 66; and
Landis and Freeman, pp. 251-2, for RB's account of the effect of
Henrietta's sickness and death on EBB.)

[2] See RB–WWS, November 10, 1861, n. 10.

[3] Edward Goodban of Florence is listed under 'Printsellers' and
'Booksellers' in Murray's *Central Italy* (1867), p. 86.

[4] Odo William Leopold Russell (1829–84), first Baron Ampthill,
diplomat. Odo, his brother Arthur John, and his mother Lady
William Russell, as friends of both Browning and Story, are often
referred to in these letters. Browning met Odo Russell in Rome in
late 1858 (EBB to Arabel, Berg), when he was beginning a term of
service that lasted until 1870.

[5] 'The leading journal at present [in Florence] is the "Nazione". It is consitutional in politics, and, on the whole, ably conducted.' (Charles Richard Weld, *Florence: The New Capital of Italy* [London, 1867], p. 201.) Issues of *La Nazione* for June 30, July 1 and 2 following EBB's death were still in her desk when it was put up for sale by auction in 1913. (Sotheby, p. 153, item 1317.)

Florence, June 13, '61

Dear Friends,—are you really at Leghorn? I had such a fancy that you would be detained longer than you hoped, as to feel it useless writing; but I hear you must be really arrived now,—and how glad we are—Our own journey[1] was prosperous enough, with favorable weather. We rested a day at Siena and got in tolerable plight to Florence on the Wednesday evening—before the saddest of all mornings![2] My wife was thoroughly tired, of course,—has not attempted to leave the house since,—but is regaining strength now. Our journey to France would be absurd and is given up[3]—I have no notion where we shall choose to spend the warm months. I saw Alberti at Florence and Nencini[4] also—as surmised, both the Villas[5] are perfectly at our disposal and are likely to continue so—I can hear of nobody intending to molest us—what do you say? Florence is empty of stranger-folk, we are absolutely quiet from morning to night.

Did I overwhelm you with commissions that day of our departure? Whatever you found intolerable, I do trust you threw over, in pure kindness to us.

And the apartment?[6] Have you heard anything more from agent or principal? No word has reached me, you may be sure; we are both of us anxious to know.

We found Mr. Landor very well and rationally disposed,—looking, as you may imagine, without a lock of hair or tuft of beard! He wished to look "younger," say some—"cleaner" suggest others. He was glad to hear what news I could give him about you all. And now,—what news do you give us? How is Mrs. Story,—relieved from those vile headaches which seemed as if they would never go, those last days of our stay in Rome? And how are you, dear Story, who were wanting change, we

[68]

fancied, after all the great doings of the year? And Edie and the Boys,—tell us they are well as soon as you can. Only to be at Leghorn! But for how long,—and what is to be done next? Can we help you in any poor way here in Florence? Ba will put in a word for herself—and I shall then begin calculating post arrivals and looking—so eagerly—for more than a word from you. All love to you all from

Yours affectionately ever,
Robert Browning.

[Continued by EBB]

Ba can only write a word—she has not the heart—in the face of this great calamity—what a return to Florence!—I have felt beaten and bruised ever since—though the banners are all out this morning for the as-good-as-official "recognition of Italy"— but there's a crepe on the flag, and the joy is as flowers on graves—May God save Italy without his angels.

I sent about the corset, dear Emelyn,[7] but the business takes time and is not finished—

When shall we see you?—Peni talks much of writing to Edie—

Your affectionate EBB

[1] From Rome, where they had spent the winter.

[2] The death of Camillo Benso Cavour (b. 1810), Italian statesman, on June 6, 1861. Through his work the unity of the greater part of Italy had been effected.

[3] For a family visit. Without having recovered from the shock of the death of her sister Henrietta in the preceding November, Elizabeth suffered from the 'great calamity'—to use her words—of the death of Cavour, the man who was so much a part of her hopes for Italy.

[4] Printed 'Mencini' in Hood.

[5] Villa Belvedere and Villa Alberti.

[6] The Brownings were trying to lease an apartment in the Palazzo

Barberini, the palace in which the Storys had an apartment. (Sotheby, p. 78, item 441; see RB–WWS, June 21, 1861, and Introduction.)

⁷ Printed 'Evelyn' in Hood.

Florence, Friday.
[June 21, 1861]¹

Dear Friends,

Don't let me miss another post-hour and leave your letters, so kind & pleasant to us both, unanswered. You tell us nothing of yourselves however. Mrs Story was far from well three weeks ago.

First, there's no doubt you can have Villa Orr² how & when you please. Nencini said the owners wanted money, would never have refused an offer,—in short I took it for granted that any conditions so reasonable would be accepted unless I gave too early notice of the possibility of your return. "There was nobody and would be nobody"—he said. Alberti will be at least as accomodating. Should you incline to the Baths of Lucca,—I hear of the propitious emptiness of that place also, how any terms will be caught at. What do you think of Viareggio which seems rather attractive to folks this season,—and is praised for its sea and six miles of sand?

How kindness 'self you have been in all that troublesome negotiation for the apartment! It will all come to nothing, we begin to fear, as the days go by & bring no tidings. As the chair could be appended without disfigurement to the house, one sees no other reason against us than that fears & scruples shake the Prince and we shall probably drop off in the shake—a great pity, though!

Yes,—very good news,³ good symptoms on every side for Italy: the main of it is effected, let us hope,—"tutto è salvo,"⁴ and the less of delay in these plaguy *"dettagli"*⁵ (vide today's *Nazione*)—the better. As you put to me that poser, "Is the Queen insane or Catholic?"—I can only resort to my old sheepish answer—"don't believe!" I have no sort of private information, but see a spread of English newspapers daily and can only couple their absolute silence with Antonelli's knowledge and commentary, and make the too customary conclusion. The Court Circular[6] yesterday mentioned that the Queen had driven, in plenty of company, to Richmond and returned thence, on Saturday last,—and, on Sunday morning, had attended service in Buckingham House Chapel—as long as she can so perform in public it will not matter much if she be secretly mad and confidentially a papist, I suppose: but I remember, so long ago, when she was lame and unable to stand upright,—then bent upon marrying nobody but Lord Elphinstone,[7]—then a Tory to the backbone,—then mad as a March hare—but that was twenty five years ago,—and such a "then" with this "now" soon turn to, not improbably.

How hot, how unpleasant to be so far away from you, how pleasant to hope soon to see the good summertime again as of old in your company! We all want the same things exactly— can it not be? Ba is stronger & better, but has not yet left the house. Few friends are here. Landor has cut off his beard— treasure your photographs! As you have ours,[8] by the bye, dear Mrs Story, please to help yourself to heart's content—and keep the residue till you see us. Who knows but I may really run over some morning if I can be spared? Do not *you* intend, on the other hand, to see something of Florence before the final settlement? How it would delight us all,—but you know that. We hear less of American news than when we were at Rome, and abundantly despise our own mean newspaper-articles. All love to you all from us here—do be good and write to us, as soon as there is anything to say,—and sooner.

Affectionately yours ever
Robert Browning.

[1] Someone besides Browning wrote the year '1861' in brackets on the same line with 'Florence, Friday'. The letter can reasonably be placed on June 21, 1861, the Friday that fell between June 17, the date of the Court Circular that RB had seen (see n. 6 below), and June 23, the date of Browning's next letter to Story, written on the Sunday that Browning was to make the visit he proposed in this

letter. R B would not have written of going 'over some morning' to see the Story's after the night of June 22–23, for from that time till her death on the 29th Elizabeth was too ill for him to be away.

² Villa Orr, another name for Villa Belvedere, where the Storys stayed in Siena.

³ Cavour's loss was a great one, but Bettino Ricasoli, the Premier who succeeded him, continued the work for a unified kingdom—to the gratification of those interested in Italian unity. The evening before her death, one week after this letter was written, Elizabeth was talking of 'Ricasoli's identity of policy with that of Cavour'. (DeVane and Knickerbocker, p. 138.)

⁴ 'Everything is saved'.

⁵ 'Details'.

⁶ See *The Times*, June 17, 1861, p. 9.

⁷ John Elphinstone, thirteenth Lord Elphinstone (1807–60), Governor of Madras and Bombay. He was in the Royal Horse Guards from 1826 until 1837, when he was appointed Governor of Madras, an appointment, it was said at the time, made to put an end to the rumour that he and the Princess were in love. Browning is saying that the Queen's behavior 'now' is not improbable in the light of her behavior 'then', twenty-five years ago.

⁸ The last photographs of EBB were taken on May 27, 1861. (Sotheby, p. 78, item 441. See also DeVane and Knickerbocker, p. 141.)

[Florence]
Sunday, 6 1/2.
[June 23, 1861]¹

Dear Friends,

I meant to go down to you to-day and thank you, better than by words, for your photographs & the note,—but Ba, who caught cold in some strange way two days ago, suddenly became much worse—& last night was alarmingly attacked by the old obstruction at the chest. I had to fetch a Doctor in the middle of the night who stayed with us till morning,—it really seemed as if she would be strangled on the spot,—and that for six hours together! At five oclock she began to get thro' it, and since then has been much better. I shall be forced to leave this burning place as soon as she is able—*where* do you go? I will write to-morrow and tell you how she is. In your letter you incline to Viareggio,—do you? Or the old Siena? Or the Baths? Or any place up in the mountains, such as Corvigliajo, 30 miles hence on the Bologna mountains, said to be as cold as Switzerland, with one inn & no resources beyond its romantic scenery. Let us be together if we can. I will send your letter this evening (to the D[uchessa] di C[asigliano].) Such a fright this attack has been—suppose we had been pleasantly travelling! This is scribbled to save the post. All love to you all, Ba bids me say

Yours aff^y ever
R Browning.

---

[1] Henry James stated that this letter of 'Browning's, in Rome, must have been of May, or thereabouts, 1861, and have preceded but by a few days their last return to Florence'. (HJ, II, 57.) Both the conjectured place and month are wrong. In the letter RB described a bad attack that EBB had had the night before, an attack that we know from two other letters (Hood, p. 60, and McAleer, pp. 79–80) she had on the night of June 22–23 in Florence.

[Florence]
Wednesday, 2 oclock
[June 26, 1861][1]

Dear Friends,

Your notes of last night & today are come safely. Ba has been very ill indeed but is better I hope & think, to-day. She had a restless night, which I thought would not have happened, as the day was better: she is inclined to sleep today & the cough is less troublesome—with *none* of the first alarming symptons,—but her weakness is extreme tho' we do all we can to strengthen her. The moment she recovers we shall go to the easiest & coolest place, probably Siena—her recovery will be slow,—one lung is entirely congested & useless. There was some cold caught—then this more formidable accident became known. Pen is quite well. I could write of many things but really want spirit & time.

All thanks for all your kindness—coming here would distress us to no purpose. Ba can see no one, of course. We need no assurance of your entire goodness & sympathy. I have letters &c but of these another time. Lytton[2] is here & very assiduous in calling for news. Treat me better than I deserve & write news, now & at all times, of yourselves. I grieve to hear dear Edie is again unwell,—that ought not to be, so persistently. Love to you all from us all.

Ever yours aff^y

RB

I have sent your packet to the D[uchessa] di C[asigliano]. What exquisite photographs,—what a delight to have! Mr [Boott][3] sent the packet of Ba's *cartes.* I suppose, the Pony-thing had not arrived when you left. To give a touch of interest to my note (full of our poor selves) I copy a bit of a letter just come. ("our queen is not insane, nor in the least approaching it. She held an immense drawing room yesterday—not easy to do, had such been the case. She felt deeply her mother's death for two reasons—one that P. Albert would not allow her to be sent for till so late, when the D. of Kent was beyond the power of recognising her—& the *on dit* is, that it was very long before she forgave her husband for this act: & beside this, it is believed perfectly by everyone that her mother died a R. Catholic, which was a great grief to her—this is received by all as a fact!" Cartwright has also written, & is set out for [Garstarin],[4] Dicey[5] from Turin &c &c

---

[1] This letter was written between the 'first alarming symptoms' of the night of June 22–23, after which the doctor reported that 'one lung was condensed' (Hood, p. 60), and the 29th, when Elizabeth died. The Wednesday between those dates fell on the 26th.

[2] Robert Lytton, now Second Secretary of Embassy in Vienna, was visiting Florence during EBB's last illness.

[3] Could this be Francis Boott?

[4] Did Browning intend to write 'Garstein'? This word, like a number of other words in the letter to his friends, shows Browning's disturbed state of mind; many letters in the words went awry. I made

silent changes in words that were not written as Browning usually wrote them: I corrected a few misspellings, pulled together disjoined words and disjoined words run together, and corrected one error in tense.

⁵ Edward James Stephen Dicey (1832–1911), author and journalist, published *Rome in 1860* (dedicated to the Brownings) and *Cavour —a Memoir* in 1861. In September 1861 he published an article on EBB in *Macmillan's Magazine*. (See McAleer, p. 89, for RB's reference to the article.) After visiting the United States in 1862, he published *Six Months in the Federal States* (1863).

"Chez M. Chauvin, St Enogat près Dinard,
Ile et Vilaine. France."
(or, 151. Rue de Grenelle, Fg St Germn.
Aug 20. '61.

My dear Friends—for so let me write to you all, as I was used to talk in those days which already seem so good & old—the first thing I fear is that you never received a letter I sent you,—that is, sent Edie in reply to one addressed to Peni—and failing which, you may have thought me more inattentive than I really was: indeed, I feel I should appear to all but such affectionate eyes as yours, wanting in gratitude for many very touching proofs of your goodness—but you will understand, after all. I wrote, copying precisely the address which Edie gave, tho' I can't remember *what* I wrote. No matter, as I can tell you all you so kindly require to know, and far more precisely than was possible then. I *did* leave Florence at last—on the 1st of this month—accompanied by Miss Blagden, who has devoted herself to me & Peni, disregarding health, convenience & all other considerations. We took the straight road,—too well known to me,—& reached Paris at last—for, being encumbered with Peni's pony we could not travel by express. I had meant to cross over to London for a day or two's talking with Arabel Barrett,¹ but the process of going over the old ground, stopping at the old Inns &c was too much—and I found it impossible to go farther: Paris also is unbearable to me, and I only breathe freelier since we arrived at this wild, primitive & lonely place—by

[75]

St Malo—with a solitary sea, bays, sands & rocks, & green, pleasant country. Miss Blagden left Paris on the 10th—, in a very indifferent state of health,—for London. I shall stay here till the autumn sets in,—perhaps a month longer,—and then, after just a day or two spent in Paris, shall finally settle in London for the winter & spring. I mean to get a very good English Tutor, capable of preparing Pen for the University without, if possible, necessitating the passage thro' a Public School: and if I delay this, as my original notion was, I may lose the critical time when the English stamp (in all that it is good for) is taken or missed. I have written to various friends about my projects, and shall be glad to profit by their experience: such a school as dear Edie described would have been desirable had Peni been brought up in England from the first—but I distrust all hybrid & ambiguous natures & nationalities and want to make something decided of the poor little fellow. I find, by myself, that one leans out the more widely over one's neighbour's field for being effectually rooted in one's own garden. Meantime we shall get thro' the next three or four weeks with various success—for Pen is quite well, strong, red as a brick, and amusing himself all day with his grandfather,[2] who, at the age of seventy-nine is absolutely unchanged. I see no difference whatever except in the greyer hair, and a touch or two of rheumatism which does not prevent three long walks a day. Pen rides, bathes and does well generally. My sister is better, and finds the loneliness & roughness of the place to her taste.

So much about myself, as you enjoined: now I may say how glad I feel that you appear to be enjoying yourselves, that the brave boys must be as you desire, that dear Mrs Story & Edie cannot have gone far wrong: you did not tell me explicitly & ought to have done so. Go to Rome & only mind me, as remembering how unremitting have always been your endeavours,—& how successful,—to make me & mine happy there. I shall never forget: there will be all the good of it. But I shall see you whenever I am able,—won't you come to England next summer, or spring? It was in your plans, surely. London may suit me better than a brighter place for some time to come—but I shall have no ties, no housekeeping, nothing to prevent me from wandering about, if circumstances permit. I want my new life to resemble the last fifteen years as little as possible—it is idle, talking just yet, however.

I deeply feel with you about the disaster at Bull's Run[3] so far as I know anything about it from having glanced at a single newspaper: I only know that the good cause has suffered, & that we all suffer with it. As to scurrilous articles in the "Times," I have had the satisfaction of never seeing the outside of that paper—but quite sure am I that its habit of deliberate maligning will have found exercise in this and every other matter interesting humanity. How can you mind such writing? I look to the end, the success, with every confidence—but, as I said, I have missed all the details of this misadventure. You must & will do better & best another time—& meanwhile, the fewer big words on all sides, in any sense, the better!

'Tanhäuser' is written by Lytton & Julian Fane[4]—the latter's are the songs, which are poor. Julian Fane wrote a volume years ago which the "Times" reviewed much in the way you now describe: I conclude that his father's being Ambassador to Austria then, & his brother Earl of Westmoreland now, has some little to do with the "Times'" admiration. Lytton, to whom the best part of the book belongs, has no such influence. He gave me the book, told me Fane was publishing the secret everywhere, and spoke modestly enough about his own estimation of the thing. I have just heard from him,[5] by the way,—he must be at Vienna by this time.

And now—it is hard to say "good bye," which of late years has always gone along with "we shall so soon meet again & so merrily!" Go you, dear Story, on in your admirable way—nor altogether without me who shall continue as interested in your work as when I could see it in progress from the little door of the room by the garden.

True love to you all—from yours ever

affectionately & gratefully
Robert Browning.

Peni sends his love also, his best love, to Edie & you all.

¹ Arabel Barrett, unmarried, gave her time to religious and social work.

² Robert Browning, Sr., had moved to Paris in 1852, where he lived with his daughter, Sarianna, until his death.

³ One of the early battles of the American Civil War was that of Bull Run (July 21, 1861), in which the North was defeated.

⁴ Julian Henry Charles Fane (1827–70), diplomatist and poet, fifth son of John Fane, eleventh Earl of Westmorland. In 1852 Julian Fane published a volume of poems, 'which soon reached a second edition' (DNB) and in 1854 a translation of poems by Heinrich Heine. Robert Lytton and Fane met in 1856 and became good friends a few years later, while Lytton was in Vienna. *Tannhäuser*, a narrative poem, was published under the names of Neville Temple (Fane) and Edward Trevor (Lytton). For Lytton's comment on the success of the poem see *Letters from Owen Meredith*, ed. Harlan and Harlan, pp. 190–1.

⁵ For this letter see *Letters from Owen Meredith*, ed. Harlan and Harlan, pp. 173–6.

Chez M. Chauvin, Sᵗ Enogat près Vilaine,
Ile et Vilaine, France.
Aug: 30. '61.

*Dear Mrs Story—dear Friends all—*your letter, & news of your health & well-being was a comfort to receive: I shall tell you so at once,—and that you caused me a delay of two days by addressing to Paris: this place is just by Sᵗ Malo, in Bretagne, and well known to the Post-Office if not on the maps. I wanted to tell you that your note to Russell somehow missed him—he called on me in Florence, perhaps a week after your departure,¹ & had heard nothing of it,—but promised to effect the matter: I grew frightened however, & wrote myself to Hooker²—with complete success: Hooker overcame the reluctance of Alessandri,³ and sent the "negative," carefully packed, to Paris—where it still is,—I cannot be *sure* it is unbroken, but may hope so, I suppose—you can therefore send the copy to Mrs Shaw⁴—to whom I will write when I find myself "up" to it. I had a very exact picture made of the room in Casa Guidi⁵—after vainly trying to get it photographed—& of this picture I have photographs—giving a sufficient idea of it—which I will send you: both the negatives (of two photographs, differing in size) which I had secured, were broken—but they were ill packed, & may be replaced easily. I think I shall not examine the state of the invaluable one till I get to London. Then I will procure copies & send to various friends who have desired them, Mrs Bruen, Mrs Crawford[6] &c. You must know that I feel your affection, as I remember all your past goodness—but I can't write about anything. I could perhaps speak—if we were together. But to write freezes me altogether. Tell me about yourselves—whatever interests you will deeply interest me. I read no newspapers, know absolutely nothing of what has been going on the last two months. I feel impatient at doing nothing, & long to begin with Pen. It is useless doing any more now—he may as well get in as great a stock of health & strength as is possible—it will all come into use presently in our grim London. (It is ungrateful of me to say this, with so many kind friends proposing to put light into the coming gloomy winter, but I feel so, & may say so to you.) I should be glad to know exactly where the following friends, who have written to me some time ago, *now are*, or may certainly be found in time,—Mrs Bruen & Perkins[7]—Mrs Tappan's Sister,[8]—you know,—who was at Rome last year with her daughter. Mrs Mary Shaw,—I remember now. People move about, in Switzerland, and I cannot be certain of reaching them.

Miss Blagden will not return to Italy—at all events, not before she has made an endeavour to live in England. She goes to Clifton, in all probability, where Miss Cobbe[9] is to see her comfortably settled. I cannot believe she will bear the change. She has given up her Villa, where she was counting upon a joyous summer with Hatty. I blame her for all this, but unquestionably like it in her.

Dear Edie's letter to Peni was hard to bear in one respect—I *did* remember so vividly the two last "24th August"[10] days! all that took place on morning & evening. Dear Edie will know I am keeping for her a little thing her affectionateness will take & preserve for those old days' sake.

[79]

Is there a likelihood, as she gives one to understand, of your going to England,—or at least of William's going next year? It would be a delight to look forward to *that*.

Don't tell anybody about *those rooms*[11]—I should hate to hear that the first comer who could climb the staircase had entered in & taken possession. This is very silly, I know. But I only think & write sillinesses just now.

I only *heard*—know nothing but by hearsay—of the dreadful death of Mrs Longfellow.[12]

The staying at Casa Guidi was not the worst of it: I kept in my place there like a worm-eaten piece of old furniture looking solid enough, but when I was *moved*, I began to go to pieces: I am getting "mended up" here, & shall no doubt last my proper time, for all the past.

Where is Miss Dempster?[13] at Skibo Castle as before? I have a letter (to my wife) which I want to answer.

Forgive all stupidities—the trusting *them* to you implies real love, to be sure, & I am always lovingly & gratefully

Yours ever

R Browning.

Landor remains under my care. Lytton is very kind,—has written to me three times[14] this fortnight: he is at Vienna.

[1] The Storys had gone to Florence when they heard of Elizabeth's death.

[2] Packenham and Hooker, who engaged in transactions with American banks, forwarded parcels, works of art, etc. (Murray's *Rome and its Environs* [London, 1853], p. viii.)

[3] Allessandri was a Roman photographer. R B wrote to his sister on July 5, 1861: 'I have a perfect Photograph of Ba taken a week before we left Rome, and hope to be able to secure the plate'. (De-Vane and Knickerbocker, p. 133.) Ten years later Browning, in giving a photograph of E B B to someone, explained that it was the last taken of her and that the name on the back was of the Parisian photographer who reproduced it from Allesandri's negative. (McAleer, p. 357.)

[4] This may be Mrs. Sarah Shaw.

⁵ Reproduction of the painting is in Sotheby, p. 7, item 14.

⁶ The wife of Thomas Crawford. (See WWS–JRL, March 21, 1849, n. 1.)

⁷ The wife of Charles Callahan Perkins. (See RB–WWS, November 10, 1861, n. 10.)

⁸ Mary (Sturgis) Shaw and Caroline (Sturgis) Tappan were sisters. Mrs. Shaw's daughter was Mary Louisa Shaw. (R. F. Sturgis, *Edward Sturgis*, p. 43.)

⁹ Frances Power Cobbe (1822–1904), philanthropist and religious writer. In 1860, when she was in Italy, Elizabeth was impressed by her as being 'very acute, and so perfectly without Continental prejudices, that she didn't pretend to much interest even in our Italian movement, having her heart in England and with the poor'. (Kenyon, II, 398.)

¹⁰ Browning must have had in mind Edith Story's birthday, which actually fell on August 23, not 24, according to WWS (Story Col.) and Phillips (p. 74).

¹¹ Lytton wrote to RB on the 24th of this month: 'Cottrell told me at Florence, before I left, that he had let your house for a short time. It is fortunate, but I cannot bear to think of it'. (*Letters from Owen Meredith*, ed. Harlan and Harlan, p. 179.)

¹² She burned to death when her dress caught fire.

¹³ Charlotte Louisa Hawkins Dempster (1835–1913), novelist and essayist, was born in Scotland and died in Cannes.

¹⁴ Published in *Letters from Owen Meredith*, ed. Harlan and Harlan, pp. 173–9.

Paris, Sepʳ 26. '61.

Dear Friends,

You will in all probability have heard from me before you receive this—which is just meant to accompany the photographs I have an opportunity of sending. I received your combined letters at Sᵗ Enogat, and will answer them the moment I am settled in London—whither I go in a day or two: but I cannot say too often how grateful I am for your goodness.

Let William take care of his health, on which so much

depends—and fight like the man he is against all these adverse influences.[1] What a comfort if I can see you again in the summer!

Ever yours affectionately
Robert Browning.

[1] Browning explained to Robert Lytton what the adverse influences were: 'Story has been unwell and out of spirits: the lucklessness of the Northern States involved his own prospects, the Trustees of a fund for a statue to Quincy, of which the commission has been given to him (and which statue is three-parts finished in marble) announce "no effects" (what became of them?); another patron renounces a "Beethoven", done absolutely; and his bust of Theodore Parker, he much fears, is lost at sea! These are sad announcements, and made just when there is an inevitable clipping of incomes, uncertainty of receipts, and the rest of it. However, he has springiness of mind, and will not break for a little'. (*Letters from Owen Meredith*, ed. Harlan and Harlan, p. 187.)

1. Chichester Road, Upper Westbourne Terrace.
Nov. 10. '61.

My dear Friends,

The last day I spent at St Enogat, I remember I was bent on writing an answer of some sort to the letters, brimful of kindness, which I had received just before: I had to go to St Malo's however, & could not get a clear quarter of an hour—I meant therefore to write on arriving at Paris: the end is, that all this while I have said nothing—& as a consequence heard nothing. But you do know my feeling to you all, & whether it is likely to [grow] less now. I have one of my old headaches this morning,— cannot attend to Pen, nor go out for a walk (in the rain)—a duty of religion enforced on me at leisure minutes—so I will chat a little with you, if you please, as if I came in, the dear old way—taking my seat by the corner of the "mobile," whatever it should be called, where my elbow goes so well—& there you are in the customary places! Well, I stayed at Paris only a day or two, being impatient to get to London on many accounts. I saw Mr Burridge[1] (nobody else)—he was far too kind & good with Pen as usual: I gave him some photographs & notes with them for various friends,—& something, a note, I think—for you: I cannot hear whether he has arrived at Rome or no. I had an adventure in going to Boulogne—was strangely misinformed as to the proper train—that which transports horses—and the people refused to take me: I proved the fault was theirs (having their printed paper to show) & also their officials', and explaining the loss of time & money they would put me to unless I was suffered to take Pen's pony by the express-train (my own, that was to have been, went without me)—declared (in all good humour, for they were polite enough) that I would prosecute them: I was upwards of two hours in this weary work of battling with them—"it *could not* be"!—but at the last moment, literally, it *was*—they pushed me into the train, put the horse-box on, which there was no time even to pay for, & so I got off, reached Boulogne in time to get the pony thro' the custom house, & consequently not miss the boat direct to London which sailed two hours after midnight: missing moreover the accident which happened to the "proper train for me," which I certainly should have taken had they beaten me, & which was run into by another train at Amiens having "22 wounded & 10 or 12 killed," said the "Times" two days after. Another strange thing happened while I was in the train. I had been thinking much of the meeting I had with Tennyson ten years ago[2] when he was the first person I chanced upon in Paris,—I must have told you, for it always impressed me—well, I, in like manner, not having seen an English friend since I left Florence, put my head out of [the] window at the Amiens Station—out came Tennyson & entered a carriage: he was changed, had a great beard, but I could not be deceived: at Boulogne I met him in the doorway & was re-assured—but I kept out of sight. When the luggage was disposed of, Pen proposed to go & see the quay: the Folkestone-boat was on the point of starting. I said "I'll show you Tennyson"—& presently he came forward with his wife & two beautiful children—they seated themselves a few yards from me: I pulled my hat over my face,—not that they would have recognized me—& so saw them off. Odd, is it not, to leave

Florence twice, and twice meet, for the first English face—Tennyson's! I wonder whether he, also, had missed the afternoon train & its smash. I arrived at Arabel Barrett's, stayed with her a fortnight, then came to this lodging, a few doors off: her kindness has been perfect & it is a great relief to have her at hand for Pen—her knowledge helping my ignorance. She has suffered much since my coming from the sudden death of Octavius Barrett's wife—which happened a week after the poor thing's confinement: & yesterday came the news of an uncle's[3] still more sudden death. I have seen nobody but her, whom I could possibly avoid seeing—always excepting people whose information might be of use for Pen: I am still unprovided with a Tutor for him—wanting the best possible: I cannot decide yet whether to send him to Eton before Oxford—there is much against, & nearly as much in favor of *that* scheme. If the question is found to lie between giving up all other advantages now acquired or acquiring, & only securing Greek, Latin & gentility at Eton, I shall give up these last: if the rules of Eton will allow me to keep Pen with me so long that enough Greek & Latin may be added to what he is now learning, I will risk the neglect of these for two or three years at Eton—but not otherwise. Everybody is very kind & it is promised that Pen will have particular favor & advantage: but he is so good & goes on so well that I cannot bear the thought of suspending Music, French, German, Italian & Drawing—to gain Latin & Greek *now* instead of two years later, merely because boys are not admitted to Eton after fourteen—& he is twelve & a half: it is amusing to hear my informants talk—(people entirely qualified to speak on the subject, of course)—they say (actually, & not in joke)—"If your boy has a private Tutor till he goes to the University, he will be so much more advanced than those of his own standing he will find there, that the effect may be disastrous—he will look down on his fellows, & they, naturally, take a prejudice against him: the advantage at Eton is *not* of getting scholarship, but of-of-of"—why, getting aristocratic connexions & friendships, which in England is the chief end of man! In a week or two, I shall decide: meantime, all the teaching falls on me, even the music, as of old: for everybody is away, & I want to make no provisional arrangements, but get settled once & for a long time: one German master happened to be at hand, & I secured him, as wanted more urgently than anybody else—but, I assure you, this will all be over in another week,—& I shall have to turn my mind to other matters. Pen is in a very satisfactory state: his health perfect, apparently—his good temper, docility & application really praiseworthy. He is much grown, much changed—you certainly would find it hard to recognize in him the old Peni with the curls & pretty dresses.[4] He rides out daily alone—looks quite old enough for that. He remembers you all every day, & probably every hour. I shall make his eyes sparkle when I tell him I have written to you. My own time (to end with all this about myself)—every minute is taken up—I have much to do with the printers, & shall have for some weeks more. I see nobody—have only called on people about business— the main business being about Pen: there being what is called "nobody in Town," there was no need to enquire who made the exception.— I shall presently go about, I suppose, for people have been very kind indeed. Miss Blagden is opposite in a house no farther from this than your ball-room from the green drawing room. She came last week & will stay three months at least,— pleasantly for me.

Now, tell me in turn how you are & what you do and mean to do, so far as you can: the last letter was saddened with disastrous strokes which had glanced on you from the general struggle in America: have your fears been justified? I want earnestly to be assured, as I have been hoping, that better expectations have displaced them. I cannot understand, for instance, that business of the evaporation of the money subscribed for the Statue—if it ever was there, where can it be gone to? And has the Bust of Parker[5] actually been lost? Story talked of the "work in his studio being suspended"—that cannot be altogether the case surely? At any rate, the two great works[6] are to come to London, are they not? And *my* bust,[7]—I recollect that you mentioned its having been begun,- is the progress of *that* suspended also? I have put myself out of the way of hearing

[85]

all this, which interests me so much, by stupidly delaying to give even my address,—that, I dare say, would have drawn a few lines from your benevolence. *Something* Story must be doing —& discouraging as neglect (comparative) & perverseness (positive) may be in common cases, he must live them down & through & be sure of the end. You will also tell me, I hope, all your household doings which used to interest me so much in the happy old days—what is Edie doing now? The poor Abbé[8] is no longer employed, I suppose. Tell Edie I forget none of my promises to her,—for instance the autographs—but I only once opened the desk where they lie, & let it fall again: when I make up my mind to examine, I shall do it effectually. Are you coming to London, yes or no? Can I do anything for you now or then? You have taken the measure pretty accurately, I dare say, of what I am worth in the way of returning the countless kind-nesses laid by in my heart—but you *do* know that if I can try at some poor return I will—so enough of that.

It is not because I do not feel the deepest interest in the American news that I rather turn from writing about it—parti-cularly to you who understand so much more,—foresee, & perhaps apprehend more than can the uninstructed here. The grin of the "Times" may be hard to bear, but indeed the feeling of the few people I see is altogether free from its malicious self-satisfaction: I never hear a word for "the South,"[9] even from those who think the North underestimated its strength, & despair of a better issue than separation: *we* say, fight it out to the last—but for English lookers-on, who abjure heroics, to say that—would be saying "Do yourselves as much harm as you can." The Italian hope deferred again is also a weariness—but not worse, I think. Dear Friends, we feel together, hope together, —did so & will do so! Here is a "length," as the actors used to say. Remember me to any friend that still cares to know. I heard from Cartwright yesterday. Diceys go to you immedi-ately. Can you tell me where the Bruens & Perkins[10] are? The Eckleys[11] are coming here presently. I can't stay longer with you in the cheerful room, so goodbye, Story, goodbye, Mrs Story, goodbye, Edie, & God bless you all. *RB.*

¹ 'Dr. Burridge, an American dentist, very highly spoken of, and much employed by the Roman nobility and foreign residents'. (Murray's *Rome and its Environs* [London, 1867], p. xx.)

² See Kenyon, II, 15.

³ Unidentified.

⁴ In July RB had written to his sister: 'Pen, the golden curls and fantastic dress, is gone just as Ba is gone: he has short hair, worn boy-wise, long trousers, is a common boy all at once: otherwise I could not have lived without a maid'. (DeVane and Knickerbocker, p. 133.)

⁵ When Theodore Parker was in Rome in 1859–60, Story modelled a bust of him. It was not lost; three years after this letter was written it was reproduced in Vol. II of Weiss, *Life and Correspondence of Theodore Parker*, and it is now in the Boston Public Library. The monument set up in 1891 in place of the original one on Parker's grave in Florence was designed by WWS.

⁶ 'Cleopatra' and the 'Libyan Sibyl'. (See Introduction.)

⁷ Companion busts of RB and EBB, which are in the Keats–Shelley Memorial House in Rome, were made by Story. The first, as Story explained, was made of RB in Italy: 'The last thing I did before leaving Rome was to make a bust of him which his wife was good enough to call "perfect". It was made for her as a present, but, alas! you see the end of that'. (HJ, II, 69–70.) Story made the bust of EBB after her death; Browning's concern over it shows up in later letters to Story.

⁸ In a report on Pen in December 1859 EBB had written to her sister Arabel that Pen was to have instruction under a Roman priest three times a week—two hours at a time—with Edith Story. 'He likes the idea of this except that a priest should be the instructor! Pen has the horror of "priests" which people catch in the sacred precincts of Exeter Hall. I really have to scold him & lecture him'. (Berg.) See also Whiting, *The Brownings* (Boston, 1913), p. 188.

⁹ The pro-Southern feeling was strong in England at this time. Browning, in his first difficult months in London, obviously had a limited view of English opinion of the American Civil War.

¹⁰ Browning usually referred to the Perkins and Bruens together. Charles Callahan Perkins (1823–86), a wealthy American art critic who engaged in and supported musical, artistic, and educational activities, married Frances Bruen, daughter of Rev. Matthias Bruen of New York. WWS referred to Mrs. Bruen and Mary Bruen. (WWS—ES, November 9, 1867; September 1, 1877, Story Col.)

¹¹ Mr. and Mrs. David Eckley, wealthy Americans, knew the Brownings in Italy. Mrs. Eckley (Sophie) and EBB were intimate friends in 1858 and 1859; then something happened (seemingly in part connected with spiritualism), and Sophie 'found herself discovered'. Whatever she did, Elizabeth's feeling toward her went to the other extreme. Browning wrote in later years that he had one charge against Mrs. Eckley: '. . . she cheated Ba from the beginning—and I say, in the bitterness of the truth, that Ba deserved it for shutting her eyes and stopping her ears as she determinedly did'. (McAleer, p. 314.) Browning wrote with agitation about Sophie to Story and Isa Blagden. The visit he referred to in this letter was probably the one discussed in a letter to Miss Blagden in 1868. (McAleer, p. 295.)

1. Chichester Road, Upper Westbourne Terrace.
Dec: 17. '61.

Dearest Friends, & dearer than ever just now!— The parcel¹ & letter have this moment arrived & I lose not a minute in telling you so,—as also that I will go this morning & see with Dicey what is to be done—I *much* fear little or nothing, beyond some cost of publishing—which you may expect, I should say: perhaps immediate circulation, even in a cheap & popular paper, which would put your thoughts into thousands of heads at once, would be better than any delay in trying for the more dignified journals, & certainly than the pamphlet-form: this miserable affair of the "Trent"² has so changed the object of interest for the moment. I have not even glanced at your writing, so anxious am I to assure you at once on the above-mentioned points, but I know that we agree in feeling *here*, as in other matters—& probably do not differ even in appretiation [*sic*] of facts, as in old subjects of dispute when our feelings went equally together. I think English judgment of the Northern procedures has been wrong from the beginning,—just as of the French procedures (will you let me say) in Italy: our people expected in both cases that the pure & simple *right* in the case would be declared & rigorously carried out without one let or stop or diplomatical fetching of circuits—"Italy shall be free, & Slavery abolished, absolutely, at once & forever." At the first hesitation in face of difficulties, we cried out, "Italy will *not* be freed, nor slavery

extinguished, after all"—& our sympathy stopped & irritation
began—as if the *spirit* of all we would have sympathized in were
not actively alive all the time, & taking the crooked road to
what, in this poor world, is only reached by a straight one "as
the crow flies,"—far above our heads, and rather near the
heaven. The *spirit* of all Mr Lincoln's acts is altogether against
slavery in the end: but in apprehension of the result of losing the
uncertain states, he declared his intention to be quite otherwise:
you understand this, & the English did *not*, & so all the work of
the "Times" was "cut out for it"—and, just as in the Italian case,
every measure now taken by the North in the direction, plainer
& plainer, of complete emancipation, will be considered as
"forced upon them." It seems besides as if no mistake on one
part can be met without two or more mistakes on the other, to
make up for their coming late into observation: so the malice
of the "Times" provoked abuse enough on your side, &
threatenings quite beside the purpose—because our neutrality,
poor, hard cold thing indeed, was the worst you had to expect,
and in no moment of the fear of a terrible result for the cotton-
operatives here, did anyone dream of taking part with the
South. This sad affair of the "Trent" puts all this away, however—our people hold to the *bone* they have got in their jaws
this time—that *a naval lieutenant is not an admiralty-judge*: if you
put things as they were, so far as possible,—let the prisoners be
restored with an acknowledgement that the seizure was wrong,
I think the "Trent" ought in fairness to be considered as taken
into one of your ports & subject to adjudicature: if our lawyers
are right, you will have to restore her & pay for the detention,—
if your authorities,—the ship is yours, envoys & all. There is
remedy for our wrong in the legal way, & no other: but you are
too likely to say—"the ship *would* be confiscated, the damages
infinitely greater,—this twitching the sum in dispute out of the
waistcoat-pocket is kinder than issuing writs & imprisoning the
debtor 'while *he* demurs'—if the debt be disproved after all, the
writ & expenses will all fall on *you*—whereas carry off my money
& I lose *that* decidedly, right or wrong—moreover you treated
me thus at Charing-Cross!" So it seems we may fairly say, &

you fairly do—but who can be sure he sees clearly, once the bad blood setting towards the head? Come what will, *I*—insignificant unit here—make no 'war' in my soul with my truest brothers & friends: noone ever had cause to love a country better than I, who have so long been only not an American because people can hardly experience such generosity except as strangers. Nor do I mean ever to go into the matter again with you, dearest of all American friends, which our respective lawyers will wrangle out for some time yet—I *hope!* Here is a first bitter fruits of the business, that this letter which I have been meaning every day to write in reply to your *two* precious budgets of home news that gave me pleasure like pain & pain like pleasure, so recently—this letter proves, as you see, something altogether foreign to what it should be if true to my heart & responsive to yours: it is all written moreover while Pen is practising at my elbow on a grand piano in a very little London room: but my minutes (I dont know whether I began by saying) are numbered & disposed of from morning till night,—I never had so much to do, or so little pleasure in doing it, or anything. I will tell you when I write next (which must be as soon as I know anything decidedly about your pamphlet)—how I am provided with Teachers for Pen & what I mean to do with him for the present. But having scribbled what I really doubt whether you or anybody else can read or understand, in determination to say *something* at once—I will leave off for a day or two. Truest love & thanks to dear Mrs Story & Edie for their letters: Pen is quite well. All regards & remembrances from us both to the Abbé when you see him. Other friends I mean to write to very soon.

> *Ever yours affectionately & beyond*
> *fear of change,*
> Robert Browning.

---

[1] It contained Story's exposition of the case for the North during the Civil War, which first appeared as three letters in the *Daily News* (December 25, 26, and 27), later reprinted as *The American Question* (London, 1862). HJ (II, 103) erroneously gave the dates of the letters as December 26, 27, and 28.

[2] At the beginning of difficulties in the United States the Unionists' strong protest against lack of sympathy in Great Britain resulted in an exchange of violent diatribe. Nerves were tense when, in November 1861, Captain Charles Wilkes of the United States Navy seized two Confederate commissioners off the British mail steamer *Trent* and imprisoned them in Boston. Englishmen were outraged at the report; they felt that war was being forced upon them. At the demand of the British Government the prisoners were released in January 1862, and since the English did not really want war and decided that the Union wanted no war with them the agitation subsided. As the air cleared England took measure of the American situation, a reaction set in, and the final result of the Trent affair was better English feeling toward the North. (See Donaldson Jordan and Edwin J. Pratt, *Europe and the American Civil War* [Boston, 1931], pp. 21–47.)

1. Chichester Road,
Upper Westbourne Terrace.
Dec. 31. '61.

My dear Story,

There is just a chance that I may get a few words off by post-time, late as the hour is: I will try hard. You must have received the three numbers of the Daily News (Dec. 25.26.27) containing your paper. Dicey sent them—all your thanks are due to him.[1] I put the M.S. in his hands at once, & he succeeded in his endeavours as you see: but unluckily there was *no time* to refer to Mr Adams[2]—the Editor said this "slack week's" occasion must be seized—and so good an occasion was not let slip: for indeed every day puts the past question deeper in the background beside the terrible interest of the new question[3] altogether distinct from it. The inaccuracies therefore must be corrected in the pamphlet, should you please to reprint it so. Mr Adams has been communicated with, & no doubt will explain, if needful. Your position, so far from London, makes excusable the slip to which you refer: those cases have been turned & tried till they are dry dust now, and it is said that Americans & English *here* are of one mind about them. Oh the pity of it all! Captain Wilkes with his instincts, & law studies *extempore*, & notion of "embodied dispatches"! To quarrel about such a man's "notions"! And no words, nor love indeed, on this

[91]

side, can help at all! Indeed you are wrong as to men's "fury" here. I have not heard one man, woman or child express anything but dismay at the prospect of being obliged to go to war on any grounds with America—but every one felt there might be an obligation as stringent as a slap on the face in public from one's bosom friend. But I've done.

I wrote (I ought to say) the moment your packet arrived: you had my letter, I hope! This new, dear letter comes warmly into the grey cold corner where I am keeping alive this last day of my last good year. Next year, next hundred years will change nothing in my gratitude, and love: nor in your goodness to me, I know. Bear with this hurry this once. I will try now & tell you many a little thing next time: I mean to go out & see friends as I used. I shall be able to gossip with you. Meantime, I run in & shake hands, & sit by the fire as of old—see you always & love you always—do believe.

So God bless you all, dear three friends! I am groping for the paper in the dark & cannot see it as I do your faces. Pen sends his truest love to you, & to the brave "Boys"—with mine.

Yours aff^u ever
R Browning.

Certainly, the Exposition[4]—& unchanged in every respect—were it but as a realization of P. Albert's desire.

---

[1] At the end of the 60s Edward Dicey became editor of the *Daily News* and may well have been contributing to it when this letter was written. His sympathies, as well as those of the *Daily News*, were with the North.

[2] Charles Francis Adams (1807–86), American minister to the Court of St. James (1861–68). On January 21, 1862, he wrote to WWS: 'Mr Dicey, before yours reached me, had been to me about publishing your letters. . . . On reading them, they appeared to me so very deserving as to elicit a decided opinion even before your direction to cause them to be put in a collected form had reached London. Since then Mr Dicey has been kind enough to put the proof sheets under my eye. . . '. In reference to corrections of 'points in American History', Adams wrote: 'That you should have been able to do so well in this respect has surprised me, as I could scarce

imagine you better provided [with books on American history] at Rome than I am here'. (Story Col.)

³ The Prince Consort died on December 14, 1861. The reference may be to the behavior of the grief-stricken Queen. She communicated with her ministers through intermediaries until they reminded her towards the end of the first month of bereavement of her duty of direct communication. (Sidney Lee, *Queen Victoria* [London, 1904], pp. 324–5.)

⁴ In an article in *The Times* on the International Exhibition, the following statements were made: 'For some days after the lamented decease of the late Prince Consort, an idea was almost universally entertained that the approaching Great Exhibition of this year would be deferred to another and more auspicious time. . . . But a moment's reflection will show that such a course could never have been contemplated without a positive disregard for the memory and wishes of the late Prince himself . . .'. (January 16, 1862, p. 7.)

1. Chichester Road, Upper Westbourne Terrace.
Jan. 21. '62.

Dearest Friends,

I wrote two hurried letters to you, weeks ago, about the American letter—& meant to say something more leisurely at the first opportunity—which is *now*, & not earlier, you shall hear why. A fortnight ago Pen was attacked with what they supposed would be small-pox: after a day or two of anxiety enough the ailment proved nothing but *chicken* pox—kept him a week in bed, another week in the house, & finally has dismissed him as it found him: "had there been any encouragement in the system it would certainly have gone on to small pox" says the doctor, & I take my comfort out of that: really believing we have got off very fortunately. Peni took up lessons again yesterday—is out in the snow just now—& I at last write the word or two which your kindness will take as if they were worthier. First, I am very glad that, on the whole, the matter of the "Letter" may be pronounced successful thro' Dicey's energy and opportunities: it would have been better could the supervision have been given to Mr Adams as you wished, but the great point was to

[93]

secure such an advantage as the columns of the "Daily News"—
a first-class paper—and you understand that, no doubt. I don't
remember whether I told you my own poor opinion of the
extreme cleverness of the exposition of the question: the Trent
affair was necessarily less complete in its handling than we
should have found it had you been nearer the law-books. Of my
heartfelt delight in the issue of *that* thing, why try & speak?
Don't mind the mean, vindictive "Times"—everyone here
understands the difficulties that have had to be overcome, and
thinks the reparation complete & handsome too: the purpose of
the North is also understood at last—and if the event of the
struggle seems less certain here, than to your politicians, there is
no longer the notion that "slavery had nothing to do with it:"
the "Commissaries" will be received with the contempt they
deserve, and the antecedents of both gentlemen are kept profi-
tably in mind here. On the other hand, this blocking up
Charleston seems inconsistent with any hope of eventual success
on your side—for what will you do if Charleston becomes loyal
again? There may be better reasons for such a step than we can
see—let us hope so. Dicey will be a good interpreter, at least, of
Northern intentions & accomplishments: he is gone, you know,
—for some months: I gave him a few letters[1]—you, however,
will do whatever he wants in that way, & as hardly anybody else
can. I am heartily glad he goes.

Of myself—so little to say,—my life is as grey (or yellow) as
this sky, one snow-bank above head at this minute. I make up
my mind from week to week, *next* Monday I will begin & call on
my friends—but this fortnight of anxiety was a real excuse,—
next week, I still say. I see hardly anybody, but mean, I assure
you, to alter all that for abundance of reasons. I have got,
besides, a Tutor[2] to my mind—rather than to Pen's perhaps—but
he is sound to the core in grammatical niceties and will put the
essentials of scholarship into the said Pen's head, I think: a grave
taciturn indefatigable man, who returns to the charge with his
gerunds & supines till the miracle is accomplished: not such
pleasant teaching as the dear Abbé's, but Pen is growing fast in
every way and wants to understand serious work: his behaviour

is very satisfactory,—he gets good habits of attention & diligence daily—& continues as childlike and docile as before,—rather grows more so. I have a very good German music master,—who will be of great use,—learns German, Drawing, Dancing & other matters, as much as he can properly bear. I cannot but think that such an education pursued for three or four years will send him to the University in better plight than if he threw up all study but that of Latin & Greek for the same time, *plus* Eton manners good & bad. I shall go on thus, at all events, for another year. I am convinced that our method was, in this case, the right one—of generally enlarging the knowledge first of all, by the introduction of various studies, however imperfectly apprehended—and then going back to re-learn, and more exactly, what was superficially gained at first. And so I make myself somewhat more quiet upon what gave me a deal of trouble and anxiety at the beginning. And for me,—my end of life, & particular reward for myself will be—one day—years hence—to just go back to Italy—to Rome—& die as I lived, when I used really to live. If you knew—but you *do* know & can conceive how precious every mud-splash on the house walls of Rome is: how every minute of those last six months in Rome would *melt up* into gold enough for a year's use now, if I had it! But I have *not*, & must think of something else,—as, that you at least are there, where you were, as you were. But come here, all the same, for you can go back, you know. Surely you will all come,[3]—will you not, for the Exposition—which (I told you truly in my last note) is to go on just as it was intended: let me know what you *do* intend—& how far advanced is the Sibyl. And, dear Mrs Story, do *you* please write me more of those letters that I was so delighted to have, and that stop of a sudden: why? I will try and make some sort of return in my lame way, by repeating to *you* all the news that occurs when I go my rounds and see people you know—whose very letters are in a pile here, unanswered, but not always to remain so (observed for the hundredth time). You may know—what I have left out in my account of the daily work that I have been painfully engaged with the Printers, and am not yet absolutely out of their hands: the book, advertised long ago[4] by the publisher, will not appear for a month at least. I shall send it to you the first thing. (Since writing this paragraph, arrives an invitation from Miss Wynn[5] to dine and meet Mr Maurice[6] only,—& I have accepted it—as I said I would.) There is a note from Pen to go with this—if Edie knew how happy her letters make him—& I should be ungrateful indeed not to add—& me also—she should give us more & more: how does the music proceed,—including the singing,—*that* is not abandoned, I hope. I have just written to Cartwright—for the first time since I was here—very black it looks when actually put on paper. Dear Story, tell me what you can about the studio— let me smell the wet clay once more, and hear the birds & the goat thro' that dear little door to the left: I would send my kind remembrances to M. Boncinelli[7]—if he cared to have them, & he may, in his good nature. Have you to do still with that clever Lombard artist? Probably not—but as for your being idle, I don't believe it. By the bye—Mrs Cholmeley[8] wrote the other day and mentioned the death of poor Gajassi:[9] if there is a sale of his effects, and the cast of Byron's head by Thorwaldsen,[10] (with his "points" on it) is to be sold for what you consider a moderate price, I should be glad to have it—supposing that there is no trouble to you, & that Boncinelli attends such sales as of old—keep it in your studio "till I come."

I want you to tell the many & true friends I have in Rome— & elsewhere when you write to them, how they are all like portraits in the one habitable room of a house. I go in among them many a time in the course of the day & night. The Bruens & Perkins—whose kind & dear letters to me are still unacknow- ledged, but not forgotten, any more than the photographs which are theirs by every right: I have only just succeeded in getting impressions in Paris from the plate—which is found to be in perfect condition—I shall supply all friends therefore.

And now—goodbye: if you knew how the minutest news of your daily life interest me, you would register every chip that is picked up on the carpet. How is Wilde? I have his picture of Peni facing me[11]—give him my true love. But you need no tell- ing how I think of old friends. How is the weather with you?

[96]

Here, singularly mild & fine days till a few touches of frost & snow surprized us—the thaw is even now beginning. It is clear that Pen needs fear nothing—he never was better, or freer from cough. How are Edie's headaches? And Story's general health continues as well as when you last wrote? Don't forget to remember me most kindly & particularly to Mrs Dicey[12]—to Lady William—(how is she—the accident had just happened, & I have heard nothing, of course, since your letter.) There is no protracting this final shaking of hands—in decency I must leave off—Pen's truest love to you all—with that of

Yours affectionately ever
Robert Browning.

[1] To America. DeVane and Knickerbocker has one of the letters. (P. 143.)

[2] G. K. Gillespie. See Browning's letters to Gillespie when Pen failed his examinations for matriculation at Oxford (Reese, 'Robert Browning and His Son', p. 793), and indications of kind remembrance of him during these and later years (Hood, pp. 129–30; 159).

[3] The Storys did go to England. Near the end of the visit Story wrote to a friend: 'My visit to England has been delightful; everywhere and from everybody I have received the warmest kindness and hospitality—such as I never can forget.' (HJ, II, 74.)

[4] EBB's *Last Poems*, published in March by Chapman and Hall.

[5] Charlotte Williams-Wynn (1807–69), daughter of Charles Watkin Williams-Wynn (who held important political offices in England), was interested in literature and public affairs. She kept in touch with prominent people in Europe and had close friendships with F. D. Maurice, Carlyle, and Baron Bunsen. (*Memorials of Charlotte Williams-Wynn*, ed. Harriot Hester Lindesay [London, 1878].)

[6] Frederick Denison Maurice (1805–72), divine.

[7] In the Story papers there are several references to Boncinelli: he was working on the marble of one of Story's statues; he was giving his opinion of one of Story's sketches; he was keeping Story's household keys during the absence of the Story family. (Story Col.)

[8] Under 'Bankers' in Murray's there is the following entry:

'Messrs. Plowden, Cholmeley, and Co., 234, Corso, chiefly employed by the Roman Catholic residents and visitors'. (*Rome and
its Environs* [London, 1867,] p. xviii.) Lowell refers to him as an
English banker. (Houghton, bMS Am 1239.2.)

⁹ Vincenzo Gajassi is listed in R B's address book.

¹⁰ Albert Bertel Thorwaldsen (1770–1844), Danish sculptor. The
account of his interview with Byron when he made a bust of him in
1817 is worth reprinting. '. . . that was in Rome, when I was about
to make Byron's statue; he placed himself just opposite to me, and
began immediately to assume quite another countenance to what
was customary to him. "Will you not sit still?" said I; "but you
must not make these faces".—"It is my expression", said Byron.
"Indeed?" said I, and then I made him as I wished, and everybody
said, when it was finished, that I had hit the likeness. When Byron,
however, saw it, he said, "It does not resemble me at all; I look more
unhappy." ' (Hans Christian Andersen, *The Story of My Life* [Boston,
1871], p. 183.)

¹¹ This picture of Pen on his pony faces p. 181 of T. J. Wise,
Bibliography of the Writings . . . of Elizabeth Barrett Browning. Hamilton Wilde painted it while he was staying with the Storys in Siena
in 1859 and gave it to Mrs. Browning. (Kenyon, I I, 344.)

¹² This is not the wife of Edward Dicey, for he married the daughter of Maria Weston Chapman in 1867. Mrs. Gaskell referred to a
Mrs. Dicey who had spent several winters in Rome and was there
during this winter. (*Letters of Mrs. Gaskell and Charles Eliot Norton*, ed.
Jane Whitehill [London, 1932], p. 95.)

1. Chichester Road,
Upper Westbourne Terrace.
Feb. 13. '62

My dear Story,

I wrote you a long letter, to follow two short ones—not very
long ago—but your generous ways,—Mrs Story and Edie com-
bining with you,—make me apprehensive about never so little a
shutting up of the hand usually too liberal, and there come
fancies of the post's playing one false, which I want relieved by a
word from you, so direct under cover to Cartwright. If you are
only busy,—let me know through Mrs Story: what I most want
to be assured of is that your intention of going to London holds

good. I am often asked to verify the praises of the Sybal [*sic*] which are rife in the papers and always boast of having seen the erection & completion of her: you will certainly find yourself well known and eagerly expected—*come*, therefore!

Cartwright has told me of Lady William's severe illness—& (this morning) of her improvement in some degree. I hope the best—but fear the very best will be little satisfactory.

My own days go on as usual—& so I best like it, wanting as little further change as possible. The book[1] is done—[it] cannot be published for another month. I will send it to you the moment I have it. I go out a little,—have called on friends, old & recent, —mean to accept all invitations henceforth: am just made a member of the "Athenaeum,"[2] by the committee, and in short am like one of those well-appointed cockney sportsmen who are accoutred from head to heel in sporting-gear, with the primest of guns & perfectest of pointers, & who only want nerve to pull the trigger—till, you see, I aim full at *you*—"bang"—here's my shot of a letter, and I bring you down in the shape of "la dovuta sua risposta"[3] to

all of yours affectionately ener
RB.

[1] EBB's *Last Poems*.

[2] Milnes and Edward Twisleton were instrumental in the election of Browning to the Athenaeum Club. (T. Wemyss Reid, *The Life, Letters, and Friendships of Richard Monckton Milnes* [New York, 1891], II, 79; and Houghton, bMS Am 1408.) RB wrote to Twisleton: 'You must make me aware of the decencies of the position to which your kindness has exalted me'. (Houghton, bMS Am 1408.)

[3] 'Your due reply'.

1. Chichester Road, Upper Westbourne Terrace. March 19. '62.

Dearest Friends—

Three letters, from one or another of you! & the pleasure they gave me, I can't,—honestly can't tell you: will it be told you in any degree by the fact that I sit down at once to obey the desire in the last (that carried by Miss Gaskell)[1] "that I should write just a word *at once*"—here is the word, never minding the injustice it does the many things calling for many words: but my time is almost wholly taken up—first by work of a morning then by going out of evenings—did you not bid me do that too? I ought to be able to return your news by mine, & state particularly *who* was where, as you do so pleasantly: but it really goes out of my head the next morning: moreover, what a difference between your Roman names and such as I might remember? I *will* remember some things however,—as first, that I saw Miss Weston lately: that Miss Dempster wrote & appointed a day to be seen at Reeves'[2]—speaking delightedly of a letter from you: I met her sister too. The Brother is travelling in Spain: she looked better &nd in spirits. I dined two days ago at Mrs Marshall's fathers, Ld Monteagle,[3]—she was well,—would perhaps come to town later: Aubrey de Vere[4] is in Athens or thereabout. I daresay Rome will have, as usual "all roads lead to it:"—tonight I dine with Emerson Tennent[5]—but I can't go on with the week's work: enough is said to show you that I try and see old friends— when my true *treat* would be an evening over the [pile] of unread books,—or a morning with the old coat & wet clay. Oh, the [Storys]! Well,—Rossetti has had a miserable loss of his wife, a month ago—she took an overdose of laudanum one evening— they had dined out, returned early, & he had left her for his class at the working-mens 'Institution'—coming back he found her in a stertorous unnatural sleep, & presently found an empty bottle —got assistance, but in vain. He is in trouble indeed, poor, kind fellow. I met Dickens at dinner the other day—looking very well & young. Thackeray has just resigned the Editorship of the Cornhill. Why should I not trust to you, what I know you will keep to yourselves—but what will certainly amuse you, as nothing else I could write is like to do? What good in our loving each other unless I do such a thing? So, O Story, O Emelyn (dare I say, for the solemnity's sake) and O Edie—the Editorship has, under the circumstances &c &c been offered to—*me*! I really take it as a compliment because I am, by your indulgence, a bit of a poet, if you like—but a man of the world and able editor, hardly! They count on my attracting writers,—I who could never muster *English* readers enough to pay for salt & bread! My first answer was prompt enough—that my life was done for & settled, that I could not change it & would not—but the conveyer of the message bade me consider, in a flattering way & I took the [week] to do so accordingly: I can't be sure how I shall answer,—that's the end: for I have rather an impulse —first to get the salary, which Pen might find something to do with,—next to figure as a man actually capable of choosing better articles from the quantity always on hand than have illustrated the Cornhill,—and last, to try what the business is like. It requires *merely editing*—no line of my own writing—(*that* would be another matter.) On the other hand, the little to do ought to be honestly done, might take more of my time than I choose to part with,—and what do I want with more money? I shall diplomatize accordingly—write for a full statement of what I am expected to do, if I accept, and what, and for how long, I am to receive in that case—one farthing less than Thackeray got, apart from the price of his substantive articles I shall not take, of course: and if I don't like the terms, the publishers have my bow, I have my little piece of satisfied conceit, and *you* have what is amusing you dear three, I engage!

Seriously, now that I care not one whit about what I never cared for too much, people are getting goodnatured to my poems. There's printing a book of "Selections from R B"[6]— (SCULPTOR & poet) which is to popularize my old things: & so & so means to review it, and somebody or [other] always was looking out for such an occasion, and what's his name always said he admired me, only he didn't say it, though he said something else every week of his life in some Journal. The breath of man! Now, that reminds me—I was invited to dine last night with General Lodwick[7] to meet a "great genius just from Rome, of whom Gibson[8] thought wondrously,"—in short, Aesi[9] and her mother! I was previously engaged but shall call this afternoon, if I can, & hear how the performance prospered.

I went to Paris three weeks ago (accompanied by Pen) saw my father to heart's content (in his eightieth year, perfectly well in body & mind & strong as thirty years ago)—saw no one else but Mad[ame] Du Quaire,[10] & came back on the eighth day. I wish the absence from London could be to-morrow: the little book[11] is to be published—& if books were to be distinguished as formerly by a great red edging, this ought to have something of the kind round it without help from the printer. Reviewers will have my heart in their rough hands for the next month or two: but I am not very formidable—witness Mr Thornton Hunt, who has *not* printed the letter of his fathers which I meant to give him —but, in place of it, without a word to me, (as he confesses in his preface) has printed *our* letter to his father![12] He knew I should have refused leave to print such a thing in the most energetic terms possible—so he takes leave. It is hardly worth noticing further, that he prints my writing, which he can't read, so as to make it pure nonsense in parts—as he also confesses in his preface. He has printed William's letter to him as well as the letter of his father—but there was reason for *that*,[13] in the nature of the communication. I ought to be angry, but can't—I shall simply, when quite sure of myself, write & say what I think of his proceeding, & then propose to give his father's letter in exchange for the one actually printed,—which he shall cancel. There's nothing in my letter I care about except the indecent nature of the exposure—it's just as if, being at my toilette, some clownish person chose to throw the bed-room door wide: (there's enough of it.) Now, you, dearest friends, if you don't keep your word, what shall I say or do? Come and let me see you. I rejoice in hearing that the Statues are sent off:[14] I speak about them before they arrive: not to have my report lose *all* value in their presence. All happiness to them & to you. Of friends,—I rejoice heartily in the recovery of Lady W[illiam] & will write a word to her, since you encourage me,—I had indeed thought of doing so. Lady Charlotte Locker[15] & her kind husband called at Paris on my Sister,—give them my truest regard: tell her, I have something for her when I can see her—also, for Lady Augusta,[16] but who can reach her now? All remembrances, & all they imply, to the Perkins & the Bruens—I wish dear Mrs Bruen had helped me earlier with her discoveries of character,[17]—but never mind. Mrs

Procter[18] was [told] by a believing friend—"that Mr Home[19] particularly felt the annoyance of being perpetually confounded with the Mr. Hume Mr B. insulted & Mr Trollope[20] abused—it was quite another man!"—Eh, my friends? Thank the dear Abbé for his loving word to Pen: Pen will answer it presently, & I will write to you again: but give me another drink of the Roman air when you care to send me rejoicing thro' the grey drear lengths of days here! For I *am* grateful whatever poor creature I be in all else—& ever your affectionate *R B*

Pen's dearest love to Edie & the Boys & you both. He is quite well. I don't refer to news of a certain sort,—gladly rec^d however. I had r^d what you sent, but it was better to see the very things.

[1] Elizabeth Cleghorn Gaskell (1810–65), novelist, with her two oldest daughters, had enjoyed the company of the Storys during a stay in Italy in 1857, when she met the Brownings.

[2] This may be Henry Reeve (1813–95), man of letters, who was editor of the *Edinburgh Review* (1855–95). Browning had his name in his address book.

[3] Thomas Spring-Rice, first Baron Monteagle of Brandon (1790–1866), Member of Parliament, was instrumental in Irish reform.

[4] Aubrey de Vere (1814–1902), poet and prose writer, whose mother was sister to Lord Monteagle.

[5] Sir James Emerson Tennent (1804–69), English politician and author.

[6] 'Selections / from the / Poetical Works / of / Robert Browning. / London: / Chapman and Hall, / 193, Piccadilly. / 1863'. *SCULP-TOR & poet* does not appear on the title page. John Forster and Bryan Waller Procter edited this selection of Browning's poetry. Both men had long supported Browning and hoped this volume would extend his reputation; it did contribute considerably to the circumstances in the 60s that established the poet's reputation.

[7] On October 18, 1873, *The Times* reported the 'death, on the 28th of August, 1873, of General Peter Lodwick, of the Bombay Infantry'. In his address book Browning listed him as Lieutenant General Lodwick, 63 Westbourne Terrace, Hyde Park.

[8] John Gibson (1790–1866), English sculptor, who was a pioneer in encouraging a revival of coloured sculpture, went to Rome in 1817 and lived there until his death, returning to England only for visits.

⁹ My conjecture is that Aesi is Adelaide Ironside (1831–67), a native of Australia who painted and wrote poetry and lived in Rome from 1856 until her death. Browning again referred to Aesi in a letter to Miss Blagden on June 19, 1867: 'Now all I want *for myself* is to be forgotten in some out of the way place in Italy or Greece, with books, a model and a lump of clay & sticks—am ready to take up poor <Aesi's> broken thread of life'. (McAleer, p. 269. The occurrence of 'Aesi' in the letter to Story confirms Mr. McAleer's reading of an unusual and difficult proper name.) Adelaide Ironside went with her mother to London in 1855, and during the next year they went to Rome, where they made their home for the rest of Adelaide's life. In Rome she became a friend of Gibson's. (Obituary notice in *Athenaeum*, May 11, 1867, pp. 624–5; *Dictionary of Australian Biography* [Sydney, 1949]; William Moore, *The Story of Australian Art* [Sydney, 1934], pp. 1–4.)

¹⁰ Frances Mary Blackett before her marriage. 'Of old Northumberland race, married to a Frenchman, then widowed, childless, and loving the world, of which she took an amused view, Mme. Du Quaire seemed in those days, with a home on each side of the Channel, to have had neither in Paris nor in London a sacrifice to make. She had kept each intimacy without giving up the other— which was really to know how to live'. (HJ, II, 121.)

¹¹ EBB's *Last Poems*.

¹² The letter from RB and EBB was published in *The Correspondence of Leigh Hunt*, II, 264–8 (later republished by Hood, pp. 47–50). The correspondence was edited by his son Thornton Leigh Hunt (London, 1862). Earlier in March Browning had told Miss Isa Blagden what he thought of Thornton Hunt's behavior (McAleer, pp. 101–2); and in 1877, in answering a question of H. Buxton Forman concerning the publication of the letter, he again expressed his disapproval (Hood, p. 177).

¹³ In the Leigh Hunt *Correspondence*, W. W. Story's letter to Thornton Hunt precedes and explains the letter from Leigh Hunt to Story. Through WWS, S. Adams Lee, an American, asked if he could give a present of $500 to Hunt. The gift was declined and Lee thought it was not wanted because he was a slave holder. Actually it was declined because Hunt had been hurt by Dickens's easily recognized portrayal of him in the character of Harold Skimpole in *Bleak House*. Dickens presented in an unflattering way Hunt's belief that one should receive as well as give, and Hunt confessed to Story the shock that Dickens had given him. (II, 271–5.)

¹⁴ The Roman Government paid expenses for shipping Story's 'Cleopatra' and the 'Libyan Sibyl' to the London Exhibition, to be

placed in the Roman Court. (Berg, Letter to Enrico Nencioni.) They were so well received that Story's reputation was established.

15 First wife (d. 1872) of Frederick Locker (later Locker-Lampson and daughter of Thomas Bruce, seventh Earl of Elgin, who brought the famous Elgin marbles to England.

16 Lady Augusta Bruce (1822–76), sister to Lady Charlotte Locker, married Arthur Stanley, Dean of Westminster, in 1863.

17 Probably refers to the David Eckleys.

18 Anne Procter (1799–1888), stepdaughter of Basil Montagu and wife of Bryan Waller Procter (1787–1874), better known as 'Barry Cornwall'. Mrs. Procter, intellectually and socially gifted, knew and was known by many famous people. Browning regularly went to her Sunday afternoon levée. (George W. Smalley, *London Letters and Some Others* [New York, 1891], I, 303–5.) When Barry Cornwall was a well-known poet and Browning was not widely recognized, he strongly supported the younger poet and predicted his fame. (James T. Fields, *Barry Cornwall and Some of His Friends* [Boston, 1876], pp. 31–32.)

19 Daniel Dunglas Home, or Hume (1833–86), American medium born in Scotland, had a large following in Europe, including people of high standing. He was in England when the Brownings were there in 1855. EBB, who was much interested in spiritualism, and Browning went to a séance which Home held in Ealing. Later in spite of Browning's strong disapproval of the medium and his tactics, Home was foolish enough to go to the poet's house; but after the violent scene that took place he avoided ever meeting him again. Browning openly and strongly expressed his dislike of Home, poetically (in 'Mr. Sludge, the Medium') and otherwise.

20 Thomas Adolphus Trollope (1810–92) also went to Ealing to a séance, which he described in *What I Remember* (New York, 1888), pp. 260–2. After a later prolonged observation of the medium his impression was a 'disagreeable one of doubt and perplexity'. (P. 265.)

1. Chichester Road,
Upper Westbourne Terrace.
Apr. 10. '62

Dearest Friends,

I got the second of the letters this morning, & will answer it at once, if but by a word. I will try earnestly & do anything that may be possible: I seem powerless however in this great place.

Last night I was dining with a friend in Parliament (Grant Duff)[1] with two strangers, who were similarly dignified, & one of them asked my opinion (for he was on a committee obliged to make up its mind on that point) as to who was the best *English* Sculptor—whereupon, turning Irish for the good occasion, I told him & the rest what I thought of the Cleopatra & the Sibyl —ending by formally asking the whole table "How can I get to help the proper placing these statues?" Whereupon said one & all,—"There's no way: a contributor may advocate his own claims, if he's present—but nobody else." Don't think my zeal is quenched—especially by the receipt of [that?] second letter— but I want you to hope very little except from the merits of the statue. Write to *me* a letter, referring to Mr Adams' & his presumed power,[2]—I'll send it with enforcement of my own, which will be only a repetition of what I told him a fortnight ago when I sate by him at Emerson Tennents. Don't let me forget a curious thing last night,—a Lady something—or other turned to me & said "I know you are a great friend of the Storys"—(then came the proper tribute to you)—"I knew them when they lived at the Porta Pinciana—& saw the *sketch* for the Cleopatra—& am happy indeed to hear that it is so realized." In my stupid way, though I talked to her on that hint, I never asked who she was— (rather large, with an aquiline nose,—I'll find out.) All my interest in the Exhibition will go to the works you send, & a few more. There is an order to go & see the Interior lying unused on the table since a fortnight. I pass the building without lifting my head to see—though its prodigious ugliness has not quite escaped me: I go out every night to dine in a cold-blooded way, and have had the occasion often to say what I thought about these works—did so the night before last at John Murray's,—at breakfast last Sunday with Milnes,—always indeed, because the matter goes to my "genio," & I enjoy doing it. To-night I dine at the Milmans[3] & meet people (the Ashburtons[4] I believe)—& shall be ready to plant a word. *But burn this letter, I entreat, for it's too sub-editorial in character.* And there! you surely never thought for a moment that I meant to accept Thackeray's glories whether discarded by him or subtracted by the Firm? I was simply amused at the notion of their coming to me—and a little flattered: I at once, however, told the messenger that there was no chance of my accepting—but he bade me think it over for a week: I coasted the week out, & then wrote that I had no sort of inclination to do anything of the kind, but that it was due to the politeness of the Publishers to give every attention to their proposal, & if, therefore, they would put it into black & white, stating explicitly what they wanted of me & what they would give me in return, my answer should soon follow. Since then,— silence!—as I expected: tho', from something I heard, they seem to have wanted the thing more than one would have fancied possible. All's as well with me now as it ever can be, and, as you say, what has Editorship to do with me?

I never told of that *quartiere*[5] to anybody—(of *where* it was)— and am sure the indication to it never came from Miss Blagden. They wanted to let it, I suppose, at bottom of their hearts, & took the next offer: I should have liked to go there one day—, whenever Pen's education is over—but never mind. I will send the book[6]—I hesitated at first, as I thought yourselves might be coming—but you are *not*—that is clear! Take my love, all three of you—I will write again very soon: tell Lady William how happy her recovery makes me,—and the hope of seeing her here. Pen is wonderfully well. *Yours affectionately ever, Robert Browning*

The Lodwicks, with whom I dined last week enquired most warmly about you, & charged me, if you came over, not to let you forget them. I dined with Bulwer[7] tête-à-tête last Monday & found him very pleasant & friendly—& so strangely like Lytton in many respects,—only younger, really! Burn all this rubbish, I *pray* you—that I may be encouraged to write more.

[1] Sir Mountstuart Elphinstone Grant Duff (1829–1906), statesman and author.

[2] As early as September 6, 1861, Charles Francis Adams, in reply to a letter from WWS, had sent information concerning the representation of the United States at the Exhibition and the 'placing of articles'. (Story Col.)

³ Henry Hart Milman (1791–1868), poet and historian, became Dean of St. Paul's in 1849. He is remembered chiefly as a historian.

⁴ William Bingham Baring, second Baron Ashburton (1799–1864), married Lady Harriet Mary Montagu in 1823. She died in 1857 and the next year he married Louisa Caroline, daughter of the Right. Hon. James Stewart Mackenzie (1827–1903). In the early 'seventies Browning proposed to Lady Louisa in a tactless fashion, and the strained feelings that resulted made complications for them and for their friends. The effect of the outcome of the proposal upon Browning was reflected in his poetry. (See DeVane, *A Browning Handbook*, pp. 368–9, 406–7, 504; W. C. DeVane, *Browning's Parleyings* [New Haven, Connecticut, 1927], pp. 89–91; W. O. Raymond, *The Infinite Moment* [Toronto, 1950], pp. 116–28.)

⁵ The apartment in the Palazzo Barberini that the Brownings were negotiating for when Elizabeth died.

⁶ EBB's *Last Poems*.

⁷ Edward Bulwer Lytton (1803–73), novelist and politician, raised to the peerage in 1866, the father of Robert Bulwer Lytton.

19. Warwick Crescent, Harrow R^d
July 3. '62.

Dear Mrs Story,

I received a note from Rossetti this morning telling me that his sister was so unwell as to be unable to go out on Saturday—& that the meeting of us all was put off accordingly: you will have heard as much by this time, no doubt. I forgot all about it & stupidly engaged myself for Saturday—not to L^y Goldsmid's,[1] however,—as you seem to expect. I see nothing of you—but it can't be helped. Has William got my letter appointing an interview with Chapman[2] for Friday at 1. oclock? I only saw the managing-man, but liked *his* alacrity & evident good will in the matter: if Friday won't suit, he must write himself & fix another time.

Ever yours aff^v
R. Browning.

I observe some mistake in your address as given in this note—*15*—& you told me *17*—& to *17* I directed the letter yesterday.

[1] Louisa Sophia Goldsmid (d. 1908) married Sir Francis Henry Goldsmid (1808–78). Julian Goldsmid was their nephew.

[2] Edward Chapman, head of the publishing firm of Chapman and Hall or his successor, Frederic Chapman. While he was in London, Story was arranging for the publication of his *Roba di Roma*.

Chez M. le Maire de Ste. Marie
près Pornic, Loire Inférieure
Sept. 13 [1862][1]

Dearest Friends:

I have no more than a word to say, but you will take that of me with your old goodness. The letter of Aug. 28th arrived safely—you must let me hear once more of you before we leave this place, which will be very soon now, unless the fine weather should be prolonged extraordinarily. Our arrangements are for going on the 24th. Pen seems to enjoy himself so much and the daily swimming must be so good for him, that I should decide for another week, but we must stop a few days in Paris. At any rate we hope (*I* hope, at least) to be in London a few days after the beginning of October, and shall we not find you there? Indeed it cannot well be otherwise, and what a comfort to look forward to—never mind the pain after it all! I never much expected you would be able to do as you wished (I know) and pass a few days with us here. It was too hard, indeed impossible. Our early time was made sad enough by the sudden illness and death of our hostess, the Mayor's wife—a young woman leaving four little children and the husband who feels her loss. But things go on as usual now—three weeks since then. I did not mean to give you the notion that this place at all resembled Dieppe; the country is solitary and bare enough, but the sea is everywhere and the land harmonises entirely with it. I like the rocky walks by the sea and complete loneliness. At Pornic, gaiety enough, but it does not reach us. Mrs. Bracken[2] strolls with us of an evening—the boys fish and divert themselves. I brought some old books with me, and read odd things in Latin and antique French. Let me remember that I made a note for William of a passage about the Evil Eye[3] in Cap: IV. Lib. IX Auli Gelii Noctium Atticarum in which quoting from Plinius secundus, he says that those in Africa who have such an eye possess a double pupil to it—a ghastly circumstance! In another crazy old Latin joke book, I came upon the "Piper of Hamelin" done into verse, by one Lucas Lossius[4] who has simply left out the whole story of the rats and only mentions the spiriting away of the children as a singular instance of the devil's power. He makes him a bag-piper moreover.

Now, *how about the purchaser of the statues*?[5] Do tell me. I am very glad the book[6] is in hand. If you write at once, I shall get your letter, and a great delight here, but if you cannot manage it, direct to 151 Rue de Grenelle, Faubourg St. Germain. I am really anxious to know and hear. Pen's true love with mine to you all. My Father and Sister's kind regards and my complete stupidity all go together.

from your ever affectionately,
R. B.

---

[1] The date, assigned by Hood, is verified by RB's reference to the death of the Mayor's wife. (See McAleer, p. 125.)

[2] RB often wrote of Mrs. Mary Egerton Bracken and her son, Willy Bracken, as well as of other members of the family, to Isa Blagden. He described Mrs. Bracken as a 'woman of a mild mournful voice over minute grievances, chiefly culinary, but really devoted to Willy' (McAleer, p. 219); and followed Willy, Pen's friend, through childhood, vacation days, university life, and marriage, at times comparing him with Pen. (McAleer, *passim*.)

[3] 'The Evil Eye and Other Superstitions' was first published as an installment of *Roba di Roma* in the *Atlantic Monthly*, June 1860 (V, 693–704). When *Roba di Roma* was published as a book, the chapter 'The Evil Eye' was an enlargement of the earlier work, one of the additions being the passage Browning called Story's attention to in this letter. The chapter was omitted when *Roba di Roma* was reduced to one volume and was later published in *Castle St Angelo and the Evil Eye* (London, 1877).

[4] Lucas Lossius (1508–82), German musician.

[5] On June 19, 1862, RB wrote Isa Blagden that he knew Story had refused £1,500 for the 'Sibyl' and there was talk of his getting

£2,000 for the 'Cleopatra'. He later heard that Story had received £2,400 for them. (McAleer, pp. 107, 138.) Story himself said he was offered £3,000 for them. (Berg, letter to Enrico Nencioni.)

[6] Story's *Roba di Roma*. Eight of the chapters of this book first appeared serially under the same title in the *Atlantic Monthly*, running from April 1859 until June 1860. Story enlarged and revised these and added thirteen chapters to make up the two volumes that Chapman and Hall published in 1863. The book went through at least eight editions.

Ste. Marie, near Pornic
Oct. 1, '62
Address (Paris) 151 Rue de Grenelle
Faubourg St. Germain

Dearest Friend,

We leave this place tomorrow, hope to be in Paris by Friday night, and in London, say, a week after that. If we could meet once or twice more before you go away, it would be pleasant indeed. I rather fancy we may, supposing that friends will continue to snatch at you, and that Chapman and his printers will not be more miraculously expeditious than usual. Anyhow, I rejoice heartily in the sale of the statues—a good comfortable fact, freeing you from any *back-thoughts*[1] and bother. William has a clear way before him and may do what he pleases. I see from here the complacent curl in my friend the Tuscan's fat cheek and mouth, he of the studio, and that nice sympathetic helper (I forget both their names for the moment)—it will delight him also. All of which I shall not see, but it will do William good, and I expect the fruits in many a fine and true thing to come.

These last news from the North[2] are admirable and consolatory, and I think, by such poor glimmer of light as comes to me, that the Italian news[3] is far from discouraging. I go away with a sort of beginning of joy chimes in my ears. At all events, I go away with Pen in prodigious force—he has taken his fifty-first good swim in the sea, is brick-coloured and broad-shouldered— he wants to see you all, as you may suppose—you and Edie.

If I get a word before I leave Paris—on your receiving this—I shall know what I am to expect on arriving in London. I might lose some days by waiting to enquire about you till I arrive, and, according to the promise of your letter, I may extend or curtail my stay in Paris, by a day or two. Remember that the "season," for publishing is terribly early in October. Forster writes to me that he will not let the little collection of my things,[4] which has been printed and ready more than two months ago, appear before "the middle of November at very earliest." Of course you can't wait till then,[5] and I understand little about the ways of such successes.

We are glad indeed to hear that the Boys are so flourishing. Pen's love to them and to you goes with mine, you know, and the best regards of my father and sister.

Ever yours affectionately,
Robert Browning.

[1] Before Story's works became known through the London Exhibition of 1862 he had not been able to sell them and he thought he would have to abandon art and return to America and the profession of law.

[2] Browning probably referred to the Battle of Antietam (September 17, 1862), in which the North was victorious. Since *The Times* announced the news on September 30, he could hardly have heard it in Brittany. He had not had time to hear of the Emancipation Proclamation of September 22.

[3] Garibaldi's recent defeat in the mountains around Aspromonte had been a humiliation for Italy, and the 'glimmer of light' was very faint.

[4] The *Selections*. The Preface was dated November 1862. The book came out on December 22, 1862 (Landis and Freeman, p. 283), and carried the date 1863 on the title page.

[5] To publish *Roba di Roma*.

19. Warwick Crescent, Harrow Road.
Jan: 18. '63

Dearest Friends,

Long as the time is, since I have written, the fault cannot have been mine, *that* I know. When you left, the run of ill-luck in letters, appointments & so on, was extraordinary. Mrs Sturgis'[1] invitation, which I had made up my mind to accept, came too late—a quarter of an hour before the last starting of the train, which it would have taken an hour to reach: your own letter apprising us of the going away next morning came also too late: but I hardly regret this last, as such partings are no good. Well, I could tell *you* nothing, you know, and you would not tell us whether you were alive or dead, for ever so long, till one day a dear letter from Edie was sent from Walton,[2] nearly a month after date: this was followed by a second better (because longer) than the first, and it reached us as swiftly as surely: but, lo—the courier on whom I counted for the carriage of the little book[3] she was good enough to want, set off in a hurry for some reason, at a few hours notice, and I had nothing to do but wait for the next. Here is the book for her, with more love than should go with so little a thing, and true thanks for what I was allowed to see in her letter when Pen had done with it—which was not at once. Now let me go to another matter: a month ago, at least, I received one evening the proofs, five or six, of the "Evil Eye" with a note from the Printer to Chapman, saying that there were duplicate passages, and other difficulties and that they could not proceed —& another from Chapman to myself, adding that he had just got a telegram from you urging the immediate publication of the book, and asking me to help: I supposed that for some reason, probably connected with republishing in America, you were in some sort of author's fix—so did the business at a sitting,—that is, I corrected English, Latin & Greek, suppressed two repetitions of passages, and otherwise did the needful, and carried the proofs to Chapman first thing next morning: but had I known that *after all* there would be the delay of another month or more, I should have taken my time, and made sure that no error escaped me—which at present I can only hope: another thing— of the Greek quotations, some few were partially accented, the rest *not*—and, under the pressure of time (or the lack of it) I thought it safest to remove all accents, as the regulation of them is a ticklish business: as to the references, I could not of course attempt to verify them, though I changed one or two,—(the wrong Idyll of Theocritus &c.) Chapman tells me, you have been good enough to destine a copy to me,—thank you heartily for it,—but as it is not yet here, I cannot see what is done or undone,—but the sum of it all is, that I fancied you were in an emergency, and that the thing must be got out of hand *at once*: with a single day's leisure I should have done better work, though not with a better will.

I go every now & then to Lady W[illiam]'s,[4] and hear—if there is anything to hear: she seems to me tolerably well, though she complains greatly of pain, and makes no effort to walk—there can hardly be any great improvement expected: but her good spirits and great cleverness are remarkable as ever. I met at her house a Mr Grey[5] who had seen you, & spent a pleasant evening with you.

But I can't chronicle all these people that come & go before me, and whose very names I forget next day: why do I like so much to hear gossip from you and fancy that London news can no more interest you than it does me? You throw bits of porphyry & marble pavement from Rome, and I have only London mud, that's the fact. Give my true love to all Roman friends—the Perkins, Bruens: the Lockers,[6] Hatty,[7] Miss Cushman.[8] I cannot say I am dull here—I work, or, at least, am employed all day long. Pen is growing a great fellow, and a dear good boy besides: I am much satisfied with him. He rows every day almost, and capitally,—rides too, though the pony is getting little indeed. I believe I have done the best for him. Now I shall leave off: do you, Mrs Story, you, William, & you Edie, remember me whenever half an hour is disposable, and set it down with charities and almsgiving. Story is of course getting on with his Saul[9]—if it isn't the grand thing we expect, shan't he catch it! Tell all about the Boys, & yourselves & your neighbours and be sure of the affectionate gratitude of yours ever *R Browning*.

[1] Julia Overing Boit Sturgis (d. 1888) was the third wife of Russell Sturgis (1805–87), London banker, who had been a lawyer in Boston before he became a business man. In 1849 he stopped in London on his way from the United States to China, where he had already prospered in business. In London he accepted an invitation to join the firm of Baring Brothers and Company, the Mercantile Banking

House, and in 1873 became senior partner. He had many literary and artistic friends. (Hidy, *The House of Baring*, pp. 83, 579; Sturgis, *From Books and Papers of Russell Sturgis*, pp. 253–61.) It seems that Browning met the Sturgises through the Storys.

2 The Sturgis home, Mount Felix, was at Walton-on-Thames 'in a superb house, in the Italian villa style, terraced down to the Thames, built for Lord Tankerville, too expensive for him, and bought by the American banker'. (Adams, *Richard Henry Dana*, II, 110.)

3 RB's *Selections* of 1863.

4 'Lady W's' is transcribed 'Lady A's' in Hood. The reference is to Lady William Russell.

5 Unidentified. Hood wrote 'Mrs. Grey'.

6 The Lockers were in Rome in the winters of 1861–2, 1862–3, and 1866–7. During the last winter they lived in an apartment that the Brownings had lived in. (Locker-Lampson, *My Confidences*, p. 158.)

7 Hatty Hosmer.

8 Charlotte Saunders Cushman (1816–76), American actress, who started her career as an opera singer and shifted to drama. Her fame was established in her first season of acting in London in 1845. She spent several periods of her life in Italy. In the letters and journals of WWS and the letters of the Brownings there are references to her association with both families.

9 The *Quarterly Review* praised this statue: '. . . among the most remarkable novelties of the Roman studios last winter was Mr. Story's model of "Saul tempted by the Evil Spirit"—a figure of extraordinary power, and, as we believe, thoroughly original. . . '. (CXIV [July 1863], 250. For a description of the statue see Phillips [pp. 148–9].) Story made several copies of 'Saul'. He sold one to Theo Shillaber for £1,600 and another to Count Palffy for the same amount. (Notebook of 1888, Story Col.)

19. Warwick Crescent,
Upper Westbourne Terrace.
March 5. '63.

Dearest Friends,

Of the few words I shall be able to write,—what use in giving any to excuses and beggings for pardon? I do seem to know

[115]

that you understand my first satisfying people outside—& then sitting down quietly with the inmates of my soul's little house. The long letter from Mrs Story was wholly a comfort & delight: how shall I get another if I say nothing in reply? Yet you see how foolish I am. But I have been unwell, bilious, full of cold & cough, with work of various kinds to occupy me for hours and hours, and a continued press of engagements—going out as I do every evening—& you remember what *that* means. However I wanted this to be, have got it, & like it. I don't reckon among engagements the time I am able to spend with L.^y William[1]— the pleasure is complete there, & unattended by the slightest drawback: I dine with her, sit with her, & go away (as I did last night) only the more anxious to return (as I hope to do this evening.) She is certainly much better,—takes a little exercise in a sort of go-cart, can sit up to dinner,—for the rest, is the perfectly delightful person you know,—or rather, more so, by virtue of the six months more of her that I have been allowed to enjoy—so now, no more of company, but all of *you*. First, true congratulations about Story's book: Chapman showed me his stock the other day,—but a hundred or less copies unsold,— said he should produce a new edition, having one vol: still in type—but of this you must have heard—as of the various reviews[2] which have been unanimous in their chorus of praise. He engaged to send you these thro' the Foreign Office and I hope has done so. I told you about my endeavoring to correct the text of the Evil Eye, in the space of four hours—all, as I was given to understand, between us & the public: had I guessed that weeks would intervene—(why, I don't know)—I would have tried to verify the notes which are "shaky." It is very pleasant to observe, as I do continually that you are in mind though no longer in sight—everybody speaks most cordially and expresses interest in the forthcoming works. I hope & trust the "Saul" may be all I have a right to believe. A letter from Odo Russell to his mother spoke of it in the highest terms—a letter that arrived yesterday. I want not to forget to tell you that in a profoundly stupid lecture which (to my amazement and discomfiture) I heard Cardinal Wiseman deliver some time ago,[3]—

[116]

he made one good point, by praising the ethnological science which came in aid of art in the case of the "Sibyl"—"*O si sic omnia!*" for he was deplorably long, wonderfully wrong, and anything you like but strong—all of which you will see when you see the printed Discourse. I had faith in his tact, you know.

Pen is quite well—except for a rather obstinate cold & cough (I caught mine of him.)—and continues to give me great satisfaction. I have just succeeded in entering him for residence at Balliol, Oxford, in 1867, if we live & do well. It is the best college in Oxford, by all testimony, being *Jowett's*—a reading college exclusively—and conferring great honor on those of its inmates who distinguish themselves. His name was most kindly put down simultaneously by Jowett & Dr Scott,[4] the Master, each signifying to me his intention of being useful & kind to Pen when he should need it. I believe I have done the best in the course I decided on: he learns more than at school, seems to enjoy himself quite enough, and proves really so good, conscientious & respectable, that I am content with things as they are. He is much grown since you saw him. Last Sunday, he & I, stepping into a carriage on the underground railway found—Macpherson![5]— who could hardly believe Pen to be the boy of two years back. I daresay your boys are as much advanced: do you still hold to your project of sending them to Eton? It will bring you to England, for one good thing. How do they get on? Any news of the poor Abbé? And Edie, "out" now—is she enjoying herself? Now, be constant to the old tradition, and continue to do me all the good & kindness, while I simply accept & gratefully do nothing: tell me all about everybody & everything: as for Macpherson, he seemed to have much of Rome in his beard & hair—I felt unwonted love for him—& so it is with the many people I meet,—whom I knew there and fancied I never could care three straws about. In a week, we go to Paris i.e. on the 14. till the end of the month: then we stay four months & then,—*not* to Italy, alas! How kind Mrs Sturgis has been you can hardly imagine. She asked us to spend the Christmas week there,—it was only too pleasant to be possible: I had engagements of old standing. I write to you now through her goodness in apprising me of her departure.[6] I wish her all the delight she deserves—and you will do your utmost to help in *that*. I send with this a little book,[7] not to be published for a fortnight yet. You got, no doubt, the little thing[8] I sent, thro' the Foreign Office, for Edie. My old books are getting printed, and so slowly that I shall not be able to bring out the new book[9] till Autumn: wanting to draw a distinct line between past & present.

Everybody is crazy—literally—about the entry next Saturday of the Princess:[10] the crowd will be enormous. I heartily wish I were out of it all—but must place Pen, and, being caught in the current, may as well see with a good grace: Pen goes with L^y de Grey,[11]—I go to Devonshire House,—which comes of not caring for a thing. The weather has been magnificent for the last day or two, but can hardly *last*, I fear.

And now I've done—little enough, but, as I began by saying, the more will be your charity to answer. Give my love to all friends, acquaintance, indifferents and enemies, if I have any. Pen is away, but I know what I ought to say for him. Landor is quite well though he had a significant attack two months ago or more: he wrote to me on the occasion of his completing his eighty-eighth year,—just one of his old letters!

Goodbye, dearest friends,—all three, or all five of you, be assured I always think of you and never without comfort and perhaps hope—hope for the years at *the end*.

Affectionately yours meanwhile, then
and ever,
Robert Browning.

Thanks most heartily for the Robi di Roma: which I received since writing last.

I scribble what you will read, hard as the pen can drive, & never return to it—take it & forgive it *so*.

---

[1] From Frederick Locker-Lampson's account it is easy to see why Browning enjoyed himself with Lady William: She 'continued her studies [after her accident in Rome], leading a life of apparently satisfied aspiration, and surrounding herself with and governing (she had a genius for command) a varied society of distinguished and

pleasant people; for, though of advanced age, she retained a keen interest in many things, more especially in such as appertained to her *monde*—her politics, her books, her china, her pearls, her *causerie*, her religion, and her cats: not forgetting the babble of the great world about and beyond her'. (*My Confidences*, pp. 372–3.)

2 Of *Roba di Roma*, containing the chapter 'The Evil Eye'. Some favourable reviews that appeared in 1863 were in the following periodicals: *Athenaeum* (January 24, pp. 115–7); *Saturday Review* (February 21, pp. 243–4); *National Review* (April, pp. 426–42); *Examiner* (April 18, pp. 245–6).

3 The lecture was delivered at the Royal Institution on January 30, 1863, and was published later in the same year under the title *Points of Contact Between Science and Art* (London).

4 Benjamin Jowett (1817–93) followed Robert Scott (1811–87) as Master of Balliol in 1870. Jowett's fine influence upon young men who came to Balliol was well known, and Browning wanted Pen to be under such leadership. Even with Jowett's help Browning did not succeed in overcoming Pen's indifference to academic life.

5 Robert Macpherson, a Scotsman (grandnephew of the translator of Ossian), who settled in Rome to study art. As an artist he accomplished little; as an art connoisseur and as one of the first photographers in Rome he was more successful. Several of his contemporaries left records of his striking appearance, especially of his auburn beard. (Freeman, *Gatherings from an Artist's Portfolio*, II, 201–33; WWS–JRL, August 10, 1853; Huxley, p. 63.)

6 For Rome. (HJ, II, 122.)

7 Essays by EBB that had appeared in the *Athenaeum* in 1842 were prepared for publication in book form by RB and published in 1863 by Chapman and Hall under the title *The Greek Christian Poets and the English Poets*.

8 His *Selections*.

9 *The Poetical Works of Robert Browning*, three volumes, and *Dramatis Personae*.

10 The Crown Prince married Princess Alexandra, daughter of the King of Denmark, on March 10, 1863.

11 Henrietta Anne Theodosia (1833–1907), wife of George Frederick Samuel Robinson (1827–1909), third Earl de Grey (1859), second Earl of Ripon (1859), and first Marquess of Ripon (1871).

Dearest Friends,

While I was away, Arthur Russell[1] called this morning bringing your letter & leaving word that he will start tonight for
Rome: I must send a scrap,—together with such thoughts!—
along with him. I & Pen have spent nearly a fortnight here—
only with my Father & sister—and in two days,—on the 29th we
return for our four-months' work. You should not talk so, &
tempt so—it cannot be, you know—for Pen must really work
hard for Balliol which is the reading College, and its examination (even for entering) "no shame in any sense" as Jowett writes
to a friend of mine: I believe we shall manage it very well, but
not unless we try—that's certain—& we mean to try,—where-
fore no Rome, no *you*—except in remembrance & hope. I was
vexed not to see a minute of Mrs Sturgis in London: tell her how
I sympathise with what must be her delight just now: even here,
the weather is magnificent.

Now about this new "manifestation" of our friend's:[2] I
weigh my words when I say it does not astonish me one whit nor
in the least degree add to my acquaintance with that very peculiar mind which I had reasons of my own for thoroughly studying long ago: I dare affirm that I know that character in enough
of its ins and outs, turns & twists,—and you, of course, remember that I *did* know it of old,—those who did *not*, have all this
novelty to learn, & admire. Of the story you tell me,—that is,
of her charges against the poor fellow,—I do not believe one
syllable, nor that the "paper" is other than either a forgery or,
just as likely, an acknowledgement extorted on false pretences
from his miserable folly—which thus meets its punishment—
some punishment being proper enough. I am in no doubt that by
those cheating "manifestations" of which I have heard him
speak, she could have prevailed on him to sign seal & attest
anything: by such means she was in the habit of pushing &
shoving him wherever it suited her purpose: and such was his
infatuation that I really think he did *not* believe in her at the
bottom of his heart, though in his prodigious passion for her, he
was determined to believe: he would really have given up soul

& body for her. I am sure he has never been "false" to her—except in suppressing the grain of common sense which, as I say, at bottom of his heart, led him to disbelieve in her,—never "false" in the most microscopic degree. It is, on her part, wickedness enjoying & turning to account, something like insanity but not quite: she might be insane, and probably will be, but *was not*, at least when I knew her. Surely the husband's friends will counsel him to let her go to the devil: I don't expect he *will*, however. I did not know they were still in England—fancied you spoke of them as in Rome: you must have meant the others of the name. Mr R:[3] will never be imposed on by the story, if he considers a little. But don't ask *me* to write or enquire or testify, I who am no sicker of her in my soul than I was four years ago.

Now I have done: we go in August, if all be well, to some quiet seaside place, just as before—Pen's health & growth seeming to call for a couple of months of that life,—probably we shall return to Pornic. I have much work to do,—bring out my new Edition presently, the new things[4] in the autumn. I rejoice in William's various successes: his "Roba" has done capitally & is like to do—you see the new Edition. As for "Saul" I expect great things and enjoy them beforehand. Won't you write? It is only too pleasant: and Edie—*she* will write for old love's sake, tell her: Pen is out but I shall gratify him by sending his best love to you all—with mine, who am

Ever yours affectionately
Robert Browning.

All regard to friends,—Hatty, the Bruens & Perkins, my friends at the Studio.

[1] Arthur John Edward Russell (1825–92), son of Lady William Russell and Lord George William Russell; private secretary to Lord John Russell, 1849–54; Member of Parliament for Tavistock, 1857–85. His residence was the meeting place of political and literary society. (Frederick Boase, *Modern English Biography* [Truro, 1892].)

[2] This and the following letter (May 2) indicate that Mrs. Sophia Eckley was making an accusation of unfaithfulness against her husband. They were later separated. Neither here nor in other

references to the Eckleys does Browning express the animosity for the husband that he did for the wife.

³ Unidentified. Hardly Mr. Odo Russell.

⁴ *The Poetical Works of Robert Browning*, three volumes, and *Dramatis Personae*.

19. Warwick Crescent,
Upper Westbourne Terrace, W.
May 2. '63.

Dearest Friends,

What a time since I have heard from you! I got a letter from Story nearly a month ago—a full chord, & then, instead of striking up myself, I began to count I can't say how many bars' rest—thirty days of it about—always meaning to lead off with a fresh subject presently! If I had written *two* days after, and told you any little thing—for instance, how I went, the day after, to Chapman's, and found that he had already printed off the first volume and was working double tides to despatch the second,¹—you would have,—some one of you three,—replied to me, as you will now. To go on,—I easily reconciled myself to the (perhaps) fortunate impossibility of chopping & changing—a vile business: your book has succeeded remarkably. Chapman told me, two days ago, that he was getting rapidly through the new edition,—the praises have been universal and hearty,—why not let "well" alone? And we *must*, this time,—but so you will *next* time, if you take my advice.

Next, "Saul"—I wish you & us all joy of it: I know it will be all I hope,—Arthur Russell speaks in the highest terms of it,—and other opinions in the same sense have reached me,—that is right. And now,—the new Statue, what will that be?² Give me another to expect.

I told Mrs Story what I thought about the pleasant charge against that hardened reprobate, Don Juan redivivus, & so on, poor dear good simple David.³ His sister's defection don't surprise me one bit more than his wife's,—though on quite different grounds. I never knew but a very little of Miss E[ckley]:

who was, had one cared to look into the matter, a far more curious study than her sister-in-law—for you had a person neither stupid, nor vain, nor pretentious, nor scheming, nor false in any discernible way, who yet, for some inexplicable reason, chose not to see, or by some miracle could not see, what must have been perked in her face daily and hourly. You know that those inventions about spirits &c were not at all more prodigious than the daily-sprouting toadstools of that dunghill of a soul,—lies about this, that & the other: I am convinced that even her Husband caught a sight of these,—indeed, more than once, came full upon some outrageous specimen,—& then resolutely shut his eyes and said black should be white to the end of the chapter: but then, *he* was in love. I remember once inadvertently telling him something she had said, about an invitation "she had reluctantly accepted to please *him*"—whereas, as he cried in amazement, "she had forced *him* to go, purely to please *her*." I saw his face change, and was afraid he would go home and explode: not he! It was gulped down, and ignored thenceforth & forever. But for his sister to gulp and ignore,— I can't explain, but it must have been so—and I shall continue to believe that *here* has been a swallow of a camel, where no gnats nor black beetles have been "strained at". My own fancy is, that the intercourse with Lady A.[4] It has fired Sophy with a noble emulation—the interest and mystery of the "injured wife" —the glory of becoming a Lady B *in 24. mo*! and from the *wanting this* to the oldest of the old ways of *getting this* was, as Hamlet says, "as easy as lying"; and the more that I discover the perfect *ease* of it, the more do I feel humbled before minds so made that to them the immense difficulty of lying appears an impossibility, and who accept Sophy with her wallet of wares for an angel laden with roses. *I* accept her now as a familiar blotch on a picture of the past—and I solaced myself the other day by placing two portraits of her, one on each side of a delicious drawing of a "model" in the costume of Truth, just given to me by Leighton.[5] I should like above most things to have a good talk with her: no hurting *me*, alas!

I'll leave off, or wait to go on—when an answer comes.

Robert is quite well: Lady W[illiam] more & more dear & delightful—she suffers much, but recovers now,—I am hopeful as to the result, and that she will yet walk as she can talk. I dine with her to-day: she always asks (did ask two days since) "when I heard last from you." Let me tell her something soon! Now, all love to you all, all memory and some hope from

Yours affectionately ever

Robt Browning.

¹ Second edition of Story's *Roba di Roma.*

² 'Sappho'.

³ David Eckley.

⁴ Unidentified. The sentence stands as Browning wrote it.

⁵ Frederic Leighton (1830–96), Baron Leighton of Stretton (1896) and President of the Royal Academy of Art (1878). While he was in Rome in 1853 working on his painting 'Cimabue's Madonna', he met the Brownings. The friendship with the poet that followed developed into a staunch and lasting one. (Martha Hale Shackford, *The Brownings and Leighton* [Wellesley, Massachusetts, 1942], *passim;* Mrs. Russell Barrington, *The Life, Letters and Work of Frederic Leighton* [London, 1906], I, 145–6, 146n, 149, 169; II, 29n, 51–52, 65, 225, 304–5; MS. letters from Leighton to Browning at Baylor University.)

London, 19. Warwick Crescent, Upper Westbourne Terrace. July 17, '63

Dearest Friends, It is the old story—you have sent a beggar a heap of money, and you don't surely expect him to send *you* money again: you gave me two wonderful letters—for Edie's seemed as one to me also—and I know I felt as grateful as your hearts could desire. All the same, I would, or Pen would, have written at once, had not Edie's account of your doings puzzled us— "You were to leave for Leghorn at the end of the week" (no use in writing to Rome, then!) "and perhaps go to Switzerland"— (nor use in trying to catch you at Leghorn, consequently.) Pen began to write a long while ago & I enclose his [conversation?].

[124]

I at last bethought me of Mrs Sturgis & wrote to her for your address—& it comes this morning after a week's delay because she had hurt her arm: this scrap shall go to beloved Siena there-fore—where I am better contended to fancy you than elsewhere: I cannot remember which the *Belvidere* [*sic*] villa is—tell me exactly—but I will not prompt you—sure, that when you *do* gratify us again it will be in the old way—the best of all talking and writing, to my taste. We stay here till the end of July—then go to Paris, & I think to the same place as last year[1]—the ex-treme quiet and rusticity are so good in their kind. I am very tired with work and play, as it is counted, and want some weeks for myself. Probably Mrs Bracken and her boy (of Pen's age) will go with us again. I attribute much or at least something of Pen's good health and continued growth to the sea-change. He is quite well, long past the poor pony which, to avoid an acci-dent, I gave away lately. He certainly satisfies me on the whole —without more *love* for lessons than (at bottom of my heart) I should like, he learns respectably, and, I expect, as well as a school boy with half the difficulty. Best of all, he is as simple and truthful as boy ever was—really all I wish in that respect. His rowing does him infinite good: & he cuts no bad figure in his white dress, managing a boat like a feather to perfection. Well, this has been a busy season. I have gone out constantly, but not too much of my experiences stays in my head—except a general feeling of thankfulness and wonder at people's kindness. Lady W[illiam] will be your first object of interest—very dear, & exceedingly clever, as well as admirably patient under her pro-longed imprisonment: I much fear the summer is slipping away, and will hardly find her prepared to make the effort of leaving home—indeed she has not yet even left the house: it is no doubt discouraging to go through real pain on the chance of finding oneself the better—but unless the effort be made, how is any strength to come? The general health seems sadly affected by this vile indoor life. Still, one sees little of this *late* of an evening, when visitors and their contribution of news bring out the old colour and quality,—and you know how pleasant *that* is. Another invalid here is no less than A. Tennyson—who is kept in bed by an ambiguous sort of *rash*, eruption—suppressed hay fever or irregularly-acting vaccination,—the learned don't know: I saw him and found him his fine self, two days ago—affectionate and simple as ever. He has poems which will be printed soon—of one, "Enoch" (the Fisherman or Sailor) friends speak highly. Ruskin is back from Switzerland, & well: I see him now & then, with Dickens, Ristori[2] (I sate with her twice at dinner lately)—and a few others you would care to know,—and plenty you may guess.

I sent all your photographs to the proper people, except Ly Ashburtons—she has not been in town and I keep it till the last thing, at all events. Thank you most heartily for mine—beautifully true, and charming in themselves, they are,—Edie's excepted,—the solitary one,—which is very different from Edie in the groups—still we are grateful for it & everything. At Paris we shall probably get Pen done again—you shall of course have it, though I don't pretend to compete with you in generosity: the boys look capitally, and are evidently doing as well as possible. I never expected you would come to England this year—and for reasons, wholly independent of me, I could not go to Italy this summer: but next year I *must* go, if I live. I confess, I never think of seeing you again satisfactorily till the end of things here—till a few years more go by—and they *do* go like a dream—that it should be already two years, all but a few days, since I left Italy! I hope to end my life in the land I love best—and what with work and troubles of great & little degree, five or six years will pass, if I don't pass them—so one day a very aged person will come knocking &c as in the story books! Meantime, William will have become very famous. I quite believe in what you tell me, and others tell me—and that the Saul will be a noble work and great success. The other works,[3] did you not say they were to come to England?

If you are your old selves you, one, all or each of you will first of all write to me *here*—up to July 31: thenceforward, to Paris (R.B/ 151. Rue de Grenelle, Faubourg St Germain,)—all letters will be forwarded to me,—from Paris, that is. And I will so enjoy them, and the thoughts of you all, as I sit in the room óverlooking a few cottages, and the church, and so to the sea! Edie's letter, with its account of Litzt[4] was delightful. She must write more. Who lives at the old villa,—ours? And at Landor's —& Orr's,[5] if you are really out there. And the people—who is there dead, or just the same? Tell me, won't you? Last Sunday who came here but Annunziata:[6] she called in Paris on my sister for my address: I was out—she left word she would call on Tuesday or Sunday—so it will be on Sunday. She is with L^y Duff Gordon.[7]

Remember—but I must have said this before—you cannot tell me the number of flies that buzz in your window without interesting me. I believe if you made mere crosses on the paper, I could read the sheet full. Landor wrote yesterday,—was very well: he has been ill, dangerously so—but seems likely to bear up against his eighty nine years. All love to you all, now & ever from yours affectionately

Robert Browning.

[1] Sainte Marie, near Pornic, in Brittany,

[2] Adelaide Ristori (1822–1906), Italian actress. Browning and Story both had a special interest in the actress from the country they felt close to, but they did not fall in one or the other of the extreme camps of criticism, as was often the case with commentators on Ristori's acting. Browning thought she had sensibility but not imagination. (Huxley, p. 245.) Story considered her 'more simple, natural, and impulsive' in 1849 and 1850, when she played chiefly in comedy in Italy; and 'more stately, elaborate, and calculated in her art' after she changed to tragedy. (*Roba di Roma* [London, 1891], II, 228.)

[3] 'Sappho' and perhaps 'Medea'.

[4] Browning had trouble in spelling *Liszt*. In 1886 he spelled it *Litz* and *Listz*. (DeVane and Knickerbocker, pp. 324, 325.) Story was a friend of Liszt. ('Romance of Beautiful American Marchesa Peruzzi de [*sic*] Medici', *New York Sun*, April 27, 1913, Section 4, p. 4. See also Rudolf Lehmann, *An Artist's Reminiscences* [London, 1894], p. 270.)

[5] Another name for Villa Belvedere.

[6] When Wilson, the maid Elizabeth brought from England, left

the Brownings in 1857, she was replaced by Annunziata, who worked for them until Elizabeth's death. Annunziata's visit gave Browning both pain and pleasure. (McAleer, pp. 166–7.)

7 Lucie Austin (1821–69), author, married Sir Cornewall Duff-Gordon in 1840. She lived the last part of her life in Egypt, where she died of consumption. She was in England from June to October of 1863, when Annunziata may have been her maid.

Ste Marie près Pornic, Loire Inférieure
Sept. 5. 63

Dear Friends,

Both your letters arrived here—William's three weeks ago, and Edie's the day before yesterday: the delight they give me you can hardly guess—yet by some fatality—not perversity—I delay answering and prevent myself from getting more of your goodness. As it is, Pen happens to bring me his letter, ready to explode, and it needs must leave this place in a quarter of an hour if it would catch the post at Pornic: I shall only scribble a word or two, & leave myself in your hands & hearts. Here are we in the old place, just as we left it last year—and I rather like it better on acquaintance—the barrenness of the country is not a bad thing—the silence, and surrounding sea, all one could wish. The weather however, is broken up & autumnal. They say here, that never was so hot and unvaried a summer: we came in for the end of it—not that I object to the blusterous wind & bursts of rain—but the bathing gets colder. I bathe daily, & fancy it is particularly good for me, body & spirit. Pen has been somewhat unlucky, he caught cold somehow, bathed prematurely, and suffered in consequence—he is now nearly well again, and keeps his red cheeks & broad shoulders. The Brackens, mother & son, are in a house close by, and the two boys, just of an age, enjoy each others company. I know nothing about friends in London—no letters follow me here (except from Paris) and I can only hope that everybody thrives more or less. L^y W[illiam] was to go to Walmer[1] if possible. Rossetti, I saw just before I quitted London—he lives after an easy fashion in a large old house at Chelsea, amid carvings and queernesses of every picturesque kind. I will certainly give him your message & remembrance on my return. Let me notice that one of your parcels of photographs directed to Miss—(I forget the name) (Howard?)[2] was returned to me as I came away—your address having been to an apartment she occupied last year—the people of which had no notion of her present *habitat*: if you can direct me how to find her out, I will do so. L͟y A[shburton] will, I hope, return to England soon—& shall receive her packet. Now I have done with England and all in it—let me breathe Siena to the end of my five minutes. It was indeed stupid to fancy you could have been unfaithful to the old Villa[3]—but the "Orr"-name used to be enough for me. There is something in this place, that brings Siena to my mind *always*—no two places were ever more unlike—but the autumn feeling, winter cares, comparative idleness and stoppage of one's life, beside the stillness—these are here, as they used to be there. Dearest Edie, I wish you many and many another happy birthday & that you may change as little as possible! I am really glad that the little friend [Barberina] is going to do well,—as is very likely: she seemed, from the mere glimpses of her I had, to be very good and graceful. The other Florence family is admirable. Oh, Napoleon! Do we really differ so thoroughly about him, after all? No understanding comes out of talk on such questions, because one presses to the support of the weaker points,—not necessarily untenable, but weak—and the end is, *these* seem the argument. But I never answer for what any man *may* do, if I try and appreciate what he *has* done: my opinion of the solid good rendered years ago is unchanged. The subsequent deference to the clerical party in France, and support of brigandage, is poor work—but it surely is doing little harm to the general good. As for the party of action, one sees the main chance tolerably clearly from this distance: Austria is enormously strong just now, and if Italy attacks her without France to help, she will rue it, that's too likely. Goodbye, since I needs must say it. Do well, & keep well, and remember me as ever as

Yours affectionately
Robert Browning.

Any news of Mrs Eckley? Somebody saw her name in Galignani's address book, the other day. I am very anxious to see the book of proportions.[4] How shall you return to Rome? By sea, I suppose. Well, two of my English years have slipped away—if I live, (and I am particularly well) I shall have plenty of Italy yet. I bring out two volumes of new things[5] (men & women—but under some other name, to please the publisher)

[1] Walmer Castle was once the home of the Duke of Wellington. In 1881 it was a residence of Lord Granville (Walburga, Lady Paget, *Embassies of Other Days*, II, 338), who was closely associated with the Russell family diplomatically. He may have occupied Walmer Castle when Lady William Russell went there in 1863.

[2] Unidentified. The name was added above the line.

[3] Belvedere.

[4] Story's *The Proportions of the Human Figure* was published by Chapman and Hall in 1866.

[5] *Dramatis Personae*.

Nov. 20, '63.

Dear Friends,

Oh me, the delay that has been in answering your last letter, Edie's dear little note! Have you thought hard things of me, or been sure, like your good selves, that there was no wrong in the silence—after all. But to business, for Odo Russell goes to-morrow. I forwarded the parcel to Lansdowne House[1] at once, and hope you know as much. I did the same by L^y Ashburton's, on her return. And now, listen! Chapman formally asked me to do what you shall hear. He said you had agreed to reduce the two vols: of R[oba] di R[oma] to one for hand-book use: that your abstractions were not sufficient, accompanied as they were by new matter: and that something more must be done to effect your purpose as well as his own: I at first refused decidedly—on the ground that you had pleased yourself, and I could not & would not cut away what you wished to leave. I bade him send

[130]

me the proofs, however, which I engaged to correct thoroughly. He said somebody else must attempt it in consequence. When the first proofs arrived, I bethought me—and made up my mind that you would be safer under my hand than any other's. I accordingly went through the whole book again and, with proper tenderness, have only touched a few corroborative passages which do not interfere with the text, and may be supposed to answer the purpose of *notes*—so can be producible at any time in another shape. There was no removing any of your own descriptions or remarks—but some of the historical notices of early times are not so immediately to the present purpose of the book and may be postponed—let us say. Thus in the paper on the Jews, while all the part relating to the medieval and modern state of things is retained, some of the more recondite & preliminary matter is removed. Also, I much fear, the final note on the Population of Old Rome must be given up: I shall see, at the very end,—but, according to the project, something must be sacrificed—the volume would otherwise be too bulky: and I preferred, as I say, detaching what might be used separately hereafter, to breaking up the pictures and discourses in the book which are in immediate request. At all events I have done my best,—and certainly better,—inasmuch as more liberally to my author,—than the regular man of all work would have done: but the task is an ungracious one, and I don't like it—though I like you to judge of it, for you will understand & forgive. To make amends, be sure that what is printed shall be flawless and perfect as care can make it. This much said, I will *go on*, the first day I can find, and write in my old way—not having time now for the many things: only adding, that Pen is quite well, and that I wish I were with you,—words cannot say how much. After all, will it not be kindest to write at once to me and tell me how you bear with my meddling? Oh, you'll say, he has done his best, whatever that may be, and I forgive him. I ventured to give Geo[rge] Barrett a letter to you—sure you would show him kindness for old times' sake. All love to you all.

Aff^y.
Robt Browning

¹ The third Marquess of Lansdowne (b. 1780) had died in January of 1863. The parcel may have been for the fourth Marquess of Lansdowne (1816–66). In the Story Collection there are two undated letters sent to WWS from 'Lansdowne', who wanted to buy one of the statues of Cleopatra.

19. Warwick Crescent, Upper Westbourne Terrace.
Nov. 26. '63.

My dear Mrs Story,

I was certainly going to write to you this day: how pleasantly your letter pushes me into my writing-room where I begin what you see, I can't tell you, but suppose you guess. Probably a scrawl of mine, got through at the Club¹ amid comers & goers, in utmost hurry & worry,—will have reached you by the Russells: I had not time to do more than *scrawl*, I repeat: well, I have to re-assure William about a fear expressed in it, and say that the appendix on the Population of Old Rome *can* be got in, to my great satisfaction: I could only act, you know, on Chapman's assertion that the book must, in your interest as well as his, be somehow reduced—and if so, I preferred lightening drapery and pedestal and letting the real Story-statue alone: as it is, there is really no harm done,—only a few *corroborative* passages postponed (as I like to call it) and the book runs along more sprightly than ever: as for corrections,—if what I made, be but attended to,—the text will be faultless pretty nearly. So much for that—be sure that I really like doing it for its own sake, beside yours: and if the treatise on Proportions wants me, —mind,—I shall much more want, & expect, *it*. Next, Hume!² Look for no explosion from me, any more than from a spent squib: why? "That's tellings," as schoolboys say. Of course, William could do nothing but attend to Mr Mitchell's³ recommendation—equally of course he will keep Hume within the studio's bounds, and introduce him to the *modelli* if he wants improving company—tho' after all this is unfair to such of them as I have known. I saw the fellow's face for one minute, last year, at a party—Lady Salisbury's⁴—and can't help flattering myself that the sonorous announcement of my name had some-

[132]

thing to do with his prompt disappearance. By the bye, Mrs Bruen wrote to me most kindly—I never got her letter & invitation to go to Boulogne till long after she must have left: thank her cordially for me, if you please. She mentioned Sophy's[5] story, and promised to convince *you* of its truth whenever she should see you,—tell her, with my love and with proper frankness, that anyone who has ever believed in Sophy, as she undoubtedly did, should lay that enormous mistake to heart. I decline entertaining, much more, believing, the evidence, unless absolutely *ocular*, of any such person: why, they have once taken chalk for cheese, or rather prussic acid for primrose-essence, and should ever after go into a corner when chemicals are to be tested. That Eckley has found her out, chosen to open his poor infatuated eyes and see what was staring him in the face, and,— horrified thereat,—changed one devil for another,—that is in itself possible enough: but Miss Eckley's opinion of Sophy's declaration, even backed by Mrs Bruen's acceptance of the same, is as good as the shopboy's assurance that his master, this time, has made no blunder without the bottles. If I be judged to give myself airs of superiority, the simplest answer would be, I *am* demonstrably superior in this, seeing that I cried "poison" at first sniff—and suffered more, from maintaining it, than from any incident in my whole life: is one to get *no* good out of *that*.

Most capital is your description of L^y A.[6] whom I exactly fancy! He *would* have it so, & has got it: I always liked him much, & liked his wife much.

Thank you deeply for your goodness to George[7]—I expected something like it, however. He is what you say of him: over-refined, I suppose, for bustling barristery, which he threw up three years' ago,—also for country life, which he seems sick of: he wrote to me from Rome, before seeing you— full of delight in it, which was a good sign. Oh, you in Rome! The very words are music to my heart: if I live, in Italy I will finish living and die to my content. I keep it steadily in view, and rather liked to hear a not overwise Italian reply to me, the other day, "What are five or six years, to wait?"—Not that I regret one step I have taken since: so far my object in coming here really seems to have been attained as nearly as under human conditions is possible: Pen is in a very satisfactory state: his health, growth, words and ways, I am bound to be more than contended with, ambitious and nervously anxious as I am. He has now been two years at work—my desire having been that he should advance *generally*, not at the expense of any faculty mental, moral or physical—and he *is* advanced enough: his temper and character I accept thankfully: he is increasingly attentive & observant, with a reserve, self respect, and even (let me say) dignity of bearing which strikes others more than myself. Dr Mussy,[8] the clever French doctor in vogue just now, happened to meet him at dinner and told me afterward he had been greatly struck by his *attentiveness* "I should expect" he said "that he never loses a minute of his time,—is always *observing*, no matter what—and I consider that the most valuable characteristic in a youth of his age." The private tuition certainly succeeds so far—I believe that he will be a good Latin & Greek Scholar: indeed I was surprised yesterday to be shown by his grave teacher,[9] (the earnestest of pedagogues) what a considerable series of sentences he had just translated viva voce into Greek without a fault: our system would be impossible at a school—it is *oral*: Pen translates *orally*,—using grammar and dictionary on the spot,—Latin & Greek into English or vice versa—two hours of this, three times a week, are worth the whole week spent in "stewing" over books, after schoolboy fashion,—it is condensed work: of course he prepares other exercises with me: and I find the general character of his studies come into use now: for instance, he has great aptitude at scanning and verse-making from his musical sense: will scan twenty lines of Virgil without a mistake. Three years more of this, surely will send him to Oxford ripe for action. Then his drawing is very good, his music sufficiently so, considering the poor hour a day he can give it—while French, German & Italian are in good forwardness. I have clever masters, & Pen really loves them all. (Tell Edie I bought a first rate piano the other day and would give my ears to hear her sing with its accompaniment. I can listen from this distance to her voice.) I tell you all this, knowing you will like to have it—

[134]

also, the realisation of it is the one pleasure I have. I hope & trust you will tell me all about your fine boys as freely: I want one thing, you may want another, and there are various ways to even the same end,—but I shall be anxious to watch any way to any end,—and always open to criticism on *mine*.

The Russells will soon be with you: I saw little of Odo, but found him most kind & cordial: Arthur is a dear and admirable person, unjust to himself in not coming into fuller prominence. Lady W[illiam] is all you say of her. I wish I could be with her every day of my life—but at nights, the day's resolve goes, too often, because of sheer weariness,—soul and body halting under social requirements. I wish I could register the dinners—because I like to draw out *your* notice of such—but sufficient for the day is the dinner. I get through & get done with it, pleasant as it often is. I did read that "Macbeth"—article[10]—capital, & with a compliment to *me* in it, moreover, after William's inveterate habit!—the funnier because of a criticism on "Mr B."[11] that followed,—noticeable for its mixed nature,—over-laudatory, perhaps, and candid in the main point of giving to me the exact canon of composition whereby I live, move & have my being. He says, I seek a central effect, and only wish the details to be subordinate and seen by a reflected light from the whole: exactly! simply, it is wrong, he holds—and "right," I maintain. Then he overlooks whole poems & plays written to exemplify the very things he says I never even try to do: people used to ignore *all* I had done,—now they recognize a bit and ignore the rest—"pazienza"! And the "bit" is absurdly accounted for—"my long acquaintance with Priests & the Confessional"—I who never spoke to any other priest than our little Abbé for two minutes in my life!

What is this "*new* Cleopatra"[12]—a new conception? good luck to it & us! That is a shameful calumny against Hatty:[13] I have seen her working at it, in various stages—not that I want *that* assurance of Hatty's honesty,—knowing her as I knew Sophie.[14] O Rome, O Story, my master!—I have just finished the fitting up my little studio, lying waste since you saw it—there is clay in, and modelling-tools, and I shall set to work at once—letting the memories curl round me while I preposterously meddle and make! I seem as if it would solace me beyond gin & water—some people try *that*. Our clay is white, not the rich Roman *brown*.

Now, is this a letter or no? Write to me soon, for charity. Take my true love, all three of you! Pen has got his old friend Willie Bracken in the next room. Mother & son settle close by, that the boy may go to the London University: there is therefore a good, gentle, intelligent companion for Pen—a *desideratum* obtained. I bring out a book in the spring[15]—it is delayed a little to take advantage of the sort of success (for me) that the edition[16] is getting: there are reviews reported in progress which will better come out first. I'll send the new things, to be sure—and did *not* send the Edition because a prettier one is in prospect. Goodbye—once more all love to you all from yours ever affectionately

R Browning.

Pen's deep gratitude for the slippers which are not yet received but shall be acknowledged,—he bids me say.

[1] The Athenaeum.

[2] This reference is made clear by a passage in a letter to Miss Blagden, dated December 19, 1863: 'Hume went to Rome with a letter from Mr Mitchel to Story, asking to become his pupil: Story refused, but got him a studio, conceiving himself bound to do so much by the letter: Mrs S. wrote me this: of course Hume immediately wrote to England . . . that S *had* taken him as a pupil—it is Story's own business,—he chooses to take this dung-ball into his hand for a minute, and he will get more & more smeared'. (McAleer, pp. 182–3.)

[3] Unidentified.

[4] Mary Catherine (d. 1900), second wife of James Brownlow William, second Marquess of Salisbury.

[5] Mrs. Eckley.

[6] The mystery lady of the Eckley complications.

[7] George Barrett.

Robert Browning and Pen, May 1870. The inscription is in Browning's own handwriting.

James Russell Lowell.

William Wetmore Story, taken in the 70's in Rome.

Browning by Story, at Naworth Castle, September 1869.
Despite the clear signature these drawings were previously
attributed to the Earl of Carlisle.

Pen's wedding, October 4th, 1887. This previously unpublished photo was taken outside the church at Pembury, near
Tunbridge Wells.

Story and his workmen outside his studio in Rome. The entrance is on the left.

[8] Henri Guéneau de Mussy (1814–92).

[9] G. K. Gillespie.

[10] 'Distortions of the English Stage: "Macbeth",' in the *National Review*, vol. XVII [October, 1863], pp. 292–322.

[11] The criticism is on pp. 417–46 in a review of *The Poetical Works of Robert Browning*.

[12] In her list of statues modelled by Story, Miss Phillips placed 'Cleopatra Remodeled' under the year 1864. (Phillips, Appendix.)

[13] Harriet Hosmer had been accused of plagiarism. When the accusation was made in the *London Art Journal* and *The Queen* that her statue 'Zenobia' was the work of someone else, Hatty sued for libel, but the suit was withdrawn and a retraction published by the editors. (R. B. Thurston, 'Harriet G. Hosmer', *Eminent Women of the Age* [Hartford, Connecticut, 1869], pp. 582–3.) WWS defended her in a letter in the *Athenaeum* of December 19, 1863 (p. 840). RB wrote to Isa Blagden: 'I don't think I should have troubled my head about such a charge in such a quarter, had I been she'. (McAleer, p. 182.)

[14] Sophia Eckley. RB defended Hatty here, but after his unfortunate proposal to Lady Ashburton Hatty turned against him and took Lady Ashburton's part. In his letter to Edith Story of April 4, 1872, Browning expressed bitterness toward Hatty.

[15] *Dramatis Personae.*

[16] *The Poetical Works.*

[November 26, 1863–January 8, 1864][1]

[First part of letter cut away]

. . . most tragical issues, I promise you.

It was stupid in me to give my letter to the Russells—who did not go immediately, and perhaps are only at Turin by this time. But you must have been sure of my understanding entirely your proposal—the pure. . . .

[Portion of letter cut away]

And now,—about the "Bust":[2] I shall tell you my mind, because you deserve it,—and so does Story, who knows my belief in his genius, and power to do whatever can be done: *can* this be done? In that face, which I shall not apply any epithet to, the inner light of the soul was used to fill up all deficiency, and—for me—transfigure all actually there: this light gone, what can replace it? A painter's skill, perhaps, who can give a few leading points and leave the rest to fancy: but a sculptor must *make all out*—and his facts will be the dead facts—do you wish for these? I should turn away anxiously from such. I have been endeavouring to do this very thing, spite of my conviction of its impossibility,—with every help from photographs, pictures, and my memory—and Leighton's skill,[3] memory and affectionate zeal—but it could not be, and I think never can. If you think otherwise, of course I will send the photograph you mention—but I want you, in our common interest, to consider well before you begin what—I much fear—will only end disastrously. Story will do his utmost—as no one will—but! and then we shall all be sorry. Now decide—and understand that if I am wrong, it is a happy chance indeed. Give those dear friends my old love: I am going to write in a day or two, when Pen's letter of gratitude can accompany mine—Edith will know for *what*. You may also safely give something very like my love to every stock or stone, much more man or woman, in Rome. Pen's warmest remembrances, he bids me say. Arabel is very well. Mrs Robinson[4] but poorly.

Ever yours affectionately
R Browning.

[1] This letter follows the one of November 26, 1863, with a reference to the letter carried by the Russells and precedes the one of January 8, 1864, which continues the topic of Edith's present and of the bust of Elizabeth.

[2] Of EBB. Story made a bust of her after her death to go with the one he had made of RB in 1861.

[3] Frederic Leighton designed the monument for Elizabeth's grave in the Protestant Cemetery in Florence.

[4] Mrs. W. C. Robinson, 30 Russell Square, is listed in Browning's address book.

London, 19. Warwick Crescent, Upper Westbourne Terr:
Jan. 8. '64.

Dearest Friends all,—At last—but not too late for your goodness,
I know,—comes my letter: I could not write earlier. I have
wronged Pen somewhat, however, seeing that he has really
written and then, in despair at waiting for me, tore up his per-
formances—you feel, even at your distance, how his cheeks
glowed at getting those choice slippers and charming words
from Edie: they (the slippers) are made up—but not worn yet,
—too precious for that! Now, for myself: I finished, *last year*,
correcting the book[1]—the delay in getting it out was none of
mine, depend on it: but there is a good deal of new matter,
beside corrections, and the Printers would do it no quicklier.
You may have got a copy by this, for aught I know. If the
printers attended to my corrections, all is right now: I am sure
you will forgive me if anything may seem *over*corrected, in some
trifling matters—but I wanted the book to be right,—not merely
blameless so far as my strict share in it goes: thus, I try at uni-
formity in the titles *Saint* &c—since we say, St Augustine, I say
St Bernardino, not San.—S^t not Sta Anne—&c. &c. Also, when
an English expression or word is referred to as original, if *that*
is Latin, I give it rather than Italian,—equally a derivative,—
when this last would look like a blunder—e.g. "beaks of ships
(rostri)" I change to the real "rostra," & so on: the book reads
well throughout, and nothing is lost, you will see, except the
early history of the Jews,—all the statistics are in,—so good luck
to it! Always,—if you are satisfied with my doings,—let me have
the correcting your labours of this kind. Next, I have to thank
you for all your kindness to George,[2] who expresses himself
warmly on the subject: poor fellow, his illness is very annoying
at this sight-seeing time, in a strange place. He writes to me
about that impossible Bust: it can only be from his little
acquaintance with the procedures of Art, especially your Art:
for a painter might give a few traits in full and leave the rest to
one's fancy—but a sculptor must make a whole somehow,—and
for me, at least, the result would be, "the better—the worse."

[139]

To strangers an idealization might do very well. In the Tomb now constructing[3]—the central circle will contain no attempt at a portrait, much as I should desire it, but a simple "Poetry" with no pretence at anything but a symbol. George thinks there would be help in the magnified reproduction of the photograph made at Hâvre: he does not remember that it is an ambrotype, —beneath, or at the back of, glass,—incapable of being reproduced, as a picture would be with a glass over it: even the original is not in a state to be sent to Italy, having been cracked across the face in its last passage thither—the least motion would divide it. I can quite believe that George, seeing what you can do,—Saul and Sappho,—may hope even this might be within your compass: but, I know it will never be[4]—and I hate that you should even try vainly to do anything,—and *that*, of all other things. Understand me—dear Story! I shall write to George—the first disappointment will be easier to bear than a later one. If you made a beautiful head which we could not bear to look on!

Poor Thackeray![5] I was to have met him on Wednesday 23^{d} at dinner—we talked about his empty chair: he was to dine next day, 24, at another friends where I was certainly to see him —and where heard, on arriving, what had happened in the morning. He was no worse than I ever knew him,—in higher spirits than of old,—I often met him. He never got rid of the silly way of doing himself injustice by affecting—but never mind now—one has forgotten all about it.

Pen is out skating—we have bitter frost: he is very well, save for the remains of a cough he caught by going to a hot place & out again, without a great coat: I have much to do to-day— how gladly I could begin to dream upon paper about you, Rome, and years to come—but I can't keep this long. All love to you all,—best new year's wishes: shall I see you, I wonder? It is just in the dice that I may. Remember me to all friends— Perkins, the Bruens, Hatty and the rest. How is Wild? Here is his beautiful little picture opposite me. All regard to him. Do write soon,—*Ever yours affectionately, R Browning.*
How about Mrs Eckley?—and the poor fellow? Lady W[illiam]

is very well, on the whole. Love to Mad⁰ Duquaire, particularly. She writes great things of Sappho.

1 *Roba di Roma,* condensed to one volume.

2 *George Barrett.*

3 Monument for EBB's grave.

4 George Barrett wrote Story on July 19, 1864. 'By all means perfect your work, as it will be perfected by its translation from clay into marble. . . . R. Browning's opinion & feelings upon such a matter should of course be regarded most tenderly but I think that he looks upon your attempt with fear, not dislike, & that he will be as much gratified with the result as I shall be'. (Story Col.)

5 He died during the night of 23–24 of December.

19 Warwick Crescent, Upper Westbourne Terr:
May 3. '64.

My dear Friends,

True thanks for the good, long, but never long enough letter, which crossed my scrap through Miss Blagden's enclosure: I was wishing even more than usual to hear something about you: don't keep me so long waiting another time, pray. I want to get the present sent to-day, so shall only be able to say a very little. Of the Bust¹—I have told you: I could not but fear & be repugnant for reasons as utterly removed from any suspicion of Story's power to do anything short of miraculous, as one thing well can be from another: Miss Blagden & you both think a miracle *has* been done, and I believe in miracles though I don't count upon them. I may easily be morbid, & the Bust is not meant for me: that a beautiful work would come from the genius I always recognized, is a very natural matter. One day I shall see,—waiting hopefully meantime.

I am happy to hear—as I do on all sides—of the applauses, and proved appreciations by purchase, of the statues: what come to London, I shall go and enjoy.

[141]

Next, about the floating reports[2]—oh, my beloved ones, con-tinue to do me the justice of not accounting me a fool, you who have called me great things in my day! The two names you give come with a difference of funniness: I don't object so much to Miss G: because I know well enough how *that* bubble was blown, Lady Westmorland[3] having told me the other day: it was simply a cackle of our dear Lady W's at the egregious joke of an *"angelic* attraction"—helped by a piece of impertinence of Milnes! who was at a dinner where she would not sit near him, as she told me, but at the other end of the table by me—of course, seeing that I was bidden take her downstairs—so he went grinning monkey-fashion about my "attentions"—in the com-pany of some twenty other guests! The other lady—now, let's remember! I met her last year at a party at L⁷ Belper's,[4] spoke to her a minute, got an invitation next day to go to some Aunt of hers who was to have some music, didn't dream of going, and a week or two after, on meeting the lady at another large party was, not so much "cut" as fiercely abused by the lady as "want-ing in the attributes of a poet—*gentleman*, she would not say"—I patched up the quarrel as well as I could, and saw her once again, for a minute and a word, at Mrs Bates',[5] whither, like me, she had gone to bid Miss Weston good-bye—eight months ago, about: since then,—. These are promising signs, I hope. Briefly & practically, when I feel my will going by those symptoms, I'll tell *you*, first people of all, so, till then, you know what to say.

I think I told you that Robert was sent to get fresh air & a holiday in the country: he returns to-night, quite well—for I doubt if there was anything to "recover" from: he hunted with the stag-hounds, & was in the saddle eight hours one day, riding 25 miles & more: he is a great, strong boy, and as good as gold—having written to me, of his own accord, every day since he left. He can fence, row, box, ride & swim with any Eton Boy, I sus-pect—and as for everything else, Latin & Greek, the advocates of Public Schools always begin by crying out "Oh, of course you'll beat us *there*." "The dodge" seems to be—after school is done with, at seventeen, say,—why, take a tutor and begin to learn really!" I am in no fear therefore that your fine boys will be the worse for their living in Rome/ May 4. I was beaten in my effort to get this off yesterday. Pen is returned, great, brown and radiant with what he has seen and done. They have been very kind to him everywhere. Well, I ought to regale you with accounts of my own goings-on, the dinners and the at-homes,— and I know that such a part of my letter would not be the least amusing one—only, it is so flat an affair to me,—at all events, the retailing or even remembering it, that I should not answer your benevolent purpose, which is to do me good, not you—are not you happy enough out there? So let the glories of the Academy Dinner,[6] & L^y de Greys, on Saturday,—Forster's, and the D^{ss} of Cleveland's,[7] on Sunday, (Monday-relâche, because of the expected Pen) last e^g Lady Colvile's,[8] to-morrow L^y Harry Vane's,[9] & so on, & so on—let me bury these under the hopes of occupying any *ultimo piano* in Rome one day: what do you mean by talking about the ending of the lease in the P: Barberini— that you would ever, in any conceivable circumstances, leave Rome? I am not sure, however, that I might not incline to try the South, Naples or Sicily, when the railways overload Rome, as they seem likely to do. But don't let us think of that now. I do not call the week or whatever it may be which I suppose I shall have to spend in Florence a return to Italy, any more than Father Matthew[10] called taking the sacrament wine-drinking. I don't think more about it than that, if it must be, it will be in the first week of September, or thereabouts. I cannot spend the rest of the time there, because I owe it to my Father & Sister—whom I have not visited this Easter as I ought to have done. I shall send you my Poems[11] when they appear—on the 21st. They have been delayed thus long to suit the requirements of Mr Fields,[12] who made such an offer as induced me to conquer my repugnance and let him print some of the things in his Magazine before publication here: when he got them safe, he informed me that the money (stipulated to be in English pounds) should be forthcoming—in better times! Suppose I had reversed the process, required the money *first*, and then announced that when my invention was better, I would remit the owing verses with five per cent interest,—meanwhile praising extremely the quality of his cheque! But enough of him. Good-bye, all dear five of you, big & little! Pen's kindest love, he sends, with mine. I should like to hear Edie sing—but what should I not like to do? Give all remembrances to everybody. I am sure I forget nobody. Lady W: is suffering from neuralgia. I hope to see her to-night. Goodbye, and be happy as long as you can.

Affectionately yours
Robert Browning.

¹ Of EBB.

² That Browning was going to marry. Miss G. was possibly Mary Ann Virginia Gabriel (1825–77), musical composer of considerable note, who married (1874) George E. March, author of most of the librettos for her operas. The other lady was seemingly Miss Bonham Carter (d. September 6, 1865), sculptress. (*Robert Browning and Julia Wedgwood*, ed. Curle, pp. 65, 69.) There were other floating comments on him and Julia Wedgwood (*ibid.*, pp. xvi–xviii, 117–18) and the rumour that he was going to marry Jean Ingelow (1820–97), the poetess (Isabella Fyvie Mayo, *Recollections of Fifty Years* [London, 1910], pp. 197–8).

³ Priscilla Anne Fane, Countess of Westmorland (1793–1879), linguist and artist, daughter of third Earl of Mornington. She was the wife of the eleventh Earl of Westmorland and mother of Julian Fane, both referred to in these letters.

⁴ Amelia Harriet (d. 1890), daughter of William Otter, Bishop of Chichester, and wife of Edward Strutt, first Baron Belper (1801–80), authority on free trade, law reform, and education.

⁵ Lucretia Augustus Sturgis, cousin to Russell Sturgis and wife of Joshua Bates (1788–1864), one of the three managing partners of Baring Brothers. Joshua Bates left his home in Massachusetts in 1816 or 1817 with $5.00 and by 1857 had to his credit $4,000,000 and much prominence in England. (Hidy, *The House of Baring*, pp. 82–85; Sturgis. *From Books and Papers of Russell Sturgis*, p. 105.)

⁶ The banquet for the opening of the annual exhibition of the Royal Academy was given on April 30. In the toast given to literature by John Forster was the following: 'I see poetry in some pleasant forms known to you all, and especially in that of Mr. Browning, one of the most original thinkers as well as one of the first poets of his time.' (*The Times*, May 2, 1864, p. 8.)

⁷ Grace Caroline (d. 1883), daughter of William Lowther, Earl of Lonsdale, and wife of William John Frederick, Duke of Cleveland (1792–1864).

⁸ Frances Elinor, daughter of Sir John Peter Grant, married Sir James William Colvile (1810–80), a judge prominent in Indian affairs.

⁹ Catherine Lucy Wilhelmina (1819–1901), daughter of Philip Henry, fourth Earl Stanhope, married Harry George Vane, who succeeded to the Dukedom of Cleveland in 1864 on the death of his brother.

¹⁰ Theobald Mathew (1790–1856), Irish priest, called the 'Apostle of Temperance'.

¹¹ *Dramatis Personae*, which was published on the 28th, not the 21st.

¹² James T. Fields (1817–81), American publisher, edited the *Atlantic Monthly* from 1861 to 1871, in which were published 'Gold Hair' in May and 'Prospice' and section VI of 'James Lee' in June of 1864.

Cambo, près Bayonne, Basses Pyrénées.
[August 22, 1864]¹

Dear Mrs. Story,

This writing has indeed been good of you—I was just meaning to tell you about our doings, which are not come to an end yet. We had a fancy to try a new place, Arcachon by Bordeaux, and reached it in two days' easy journeying—only to find, what was a few years ago a beautiful pine-forest, turned into a toy-town with boulevards traced through the sand-hills, *tirs-au-pistolet*,² a Casino and other French institutions, and the whole full to the edge of strangers—there was nothing to be had, though I spent a couple of days in trying my luck: we looked at an adjoining old town of a different sort, La Teste,—nothing to let there,—so we determined to go on to Bayonne, and did so, hoping for rest to the foot sole at St Jean-de Luz: this is really an exquisite little place, with a delicious sea, and great mountains in the back-ground—every house taken, *everyone* of not a few: I regretted it the more, that Pen had one good swim and enjoyed every thing, sands and water: last we braved the awful

Biarritz—but liked the noise and crowd of it still less than Archachon,—the prices, moreover, were calculated for Diplomatists, ambitious senators, and so on: there seemed no course open to us—pushed up at the very end of France as we were—but to "lie by" in some quiet place till the bathers should begin to leave St Jean,—they never stay long, in France, but come & go in a crowd: and here we are at the Cambo, a village in the Pyrénées fifteen or sixteen miles from Bayonne, in repute for its mineral waters, but out of the season now, we thankfully find: the country is exceedingly beautiful, the mountains just like the Tuscan ranges, with plenty of oak & chestnut woods, and everywhere the greenest of meadows—the great characteristic of the place—the little fresh river that winds in and out the hills & vales, the *Nive*, comes from Spain, which is three hours' walk off: this is the Basque country, moreover, the people talk French with difficulty, and charming girl-faces abound,—there is no lack of necessaries or even something over, and we have some fifty visitors—but after a few yards striding one is alone to all intents and purposes: I went two days ago to see a famous mountain-pass, *le pas de Roland*,[3] so called because that Paladin kicked a hole in a rock, which blocks the way, to allow Charlemagne's army to pass: very striking and picturesque it was, while the meadows by the river-side were delightful. But it is strangely hot, in spite of the greenness, though this morning there is Scirocco and approaching rain: the wind being so many puffs from a blast-furnace. Well, our plan is to stay here three weeks longer—till the 13th and then spend the rest of our holiday at St Jean—say three weeks,—bathing assiduously to make up for lost time: there will be room and to spare, and we may recover our position—for the last two years in that dear rough old St Marie,—stark-naked as she was of all comfort, to the British mind,—put this smug little village in unpleasant relief: I don't see the sea all day long. On the other hand, my sister, who never was so far south, is delighted with everything—for we have *cicale*, and other unusualities. Moreover, there is a certain temptation which we *may* be unable to withstand,—and if so, farewell to St Jean! We are within an easy day's journey of

[146]

Madrid, and Pen's ears prick up like unto one of these Spanish mule's at his mates on a hill-top: after all, one would sacrifice something for a sight of the Titians and Velasquez: still, I hold for the original scheme, till forced to strike my flag. Be where we may, we return to Paris in the first week of October, and if you are really to be found there,—how good it will be, you know well enough. I shall content myself with saying that nobody used to the quantities of you, which I can boast to have been, could bear the miserable London allowance with such superhuman equanimity as I think you appreciate in myself, spite of a mock reproach or two. Now in earnest, I am grieved to hear that Story has been ill,—I supposed that the quiet days and perfect friendliness at Walton would set all wrong right. You see, you need to keep trimming the family boat, which don't make way unless every member of the crew is in his exact place, well and merry. Why should Story work and worry and spoil everything? This is a great shame, of which you tell me—surely whoever knows, and has an opportunity of telling the story properly will be glad to do so. What can Newton mean by holding his tongue?[4] And why not do at once, what will have to be done at some time?

See what a letter I have scribbled before breakfast time, to save the post which starts early! I know nothing whatever of London news, never letting my letters find me out here—they lie in a heap till my return: of course, I take care that any news from Landor[5] shall come straight, as it has just done. I get one or two weekly newspapers, that's all. If you *do* incline to write again, before the 13th Sept., it will wipe out many sins, I moderately say. Of course I talk no nonsense about your coming *here,* thirty miles perhaps from the sea! If you have a passion for adventure, and want to peep into Spain,—why,—of course, there's our St Jean-de Luz, and of course other delights: but I'm past illusions. Let us catch a week of you at Paris,—*that* may be done.

Pen—here in the room—"sends his very kindest love to all *and* to Edith": I subscribe my name. Give my truest regard & affectionate remembrance to Mr & Mrs Sturgis. All kindest congratulations to Ly W[illiam] on her amended health: I don't

forget her injunction, and shall write soon. My own party is quite well, my father perceptibly younger than last year—he walks, draws and reads all day.   *Ever yours affectionately*
Robert Browning.

¹ Dated by the letter to Julia Wedgwood written on August 20, in which RB said he had gone to the Pass of Roland that morning. (*Robert Browning and Julia Wedgwood*, ed. Curle, p. 43.)

² 'Shooting galleries for pistols'.

³ It is fairly well accepted that Browning decided upon his plan for *The Ring and the Book* when he went to see this 'famous mountain pass'. (See DeVane, *Handbook*, pp. 321–3.)

⁴ Sir Charles Thomas Newton (1816–94), archaeologist. In 1861 he was made keeper of Greek and Roman antiquities at the British Museum. 'Newton's keepership at the Museum was marked by an amazing wealth of important acquisitions, which were largely attributable to his personal influence or initiation'. (DNB) Browning's reference is to Story's help in the acquisition of statues for the British Museum, for which Newton had not yet given him public recognition. It was given later.

⁵ The last of many references in these letters to Landor. He died in September of this year. Until the end Browning continued to manage Landor's affairs.

Saty. Jan. 14. 1865.
My dearest Edie,
Many thanks for your kindness, or rather your naughtiness in wasting so much of your time in making such a beautiful pair of slippers for a stupid fellow like myself. Why they are more fitted for a prince than for me! However there is one thing which is that you may be assured that I shall wear them out (although they ought rather to be put under a glass case) and that in doing so they will cause me to remember you still oftener, (although I don't think that there is much danger of my forgetting you). I must ask for your forgiveness for my not hav-written to you before but really this is the first moment that I have had since Xmas to write in.

[148]

. . . The weather here is anything but wintery—today it is almost temperate outside and as yet we have had no skating. You must answer this stupid epistle—for I want to hear about you all. How are Mr. and Mrs. Story, and the two young prize-fighters, whom I had the honour of meeting in Paris?[1] I wonder if there is any chance of our seeing each other soon. I hope you will come over here next summer, and that if you do come, I shall see a little more of you than last time. Give my love to Mr. and Mrs. Story, and to the above-mentioned members of the "P.R." and of the Society for the encouragement of the "Noble Art of Self-Defence." As I have nothing else to write that could possibly be interesting to you, I think that I had better shut up.

Do write to your aff[te]

old Bob[2]

[Continued by R B]

My dear Edie—or rather, dear friends all three—I have kept this letter of Pen's far too long, meaning to do myself something like justice in another of my own—but as the week gets on, I see the best way will be to be content with a word or two. I am literally engaged all day long. I heard, after some time on my arrival in London, that your Papa had been seriously ill,—was that true?— and, after a rather shorter interval, that he was quite recovered. I hope whatever was wrong is right again: take care that he spends his energy with regard to the many years wherein it is intended to last—not all at once,—he knows that, well as I,— but you must make him mind his knowledge. I hear very little from, that is, about you—a word from Ly. W[illiam] now and then: it is all my own fault, I ought to take care and satisfy myself. But why does [not] a good, great budgetful of news arrive now and then to me the unworthy from Mrs. Story, who engaged to find me in food of the kind? How I should enjoy it now! Well, the days and weeks and even years go by, and, by my reckoning a couple of years more and Pen will be full-fledged: in two months he will be sixteen. I can't think of what I may do in my own idleness then—for thinking of all the care that will begin again, about him. It's for the best, of course. How are the boys, big fellows now—have they a master, or what do

[149]

they do, and what is meant to be done with them? And you, how do you like Rome, all of you, after the London gaieties? What is brooding in the Studio? I don't care much to know who is at Rome, Lord This and Mrs the Other. So, you see, though somewhat tardy, acknowledgement has been made copiously enough for the good office about the statues:[3] I have not seen them,—to my shame,—can't find the clear morning to bestow, however worthily,—they can wait, moreover.

I shan't give you gossip now—nor make this into anything but a long-drawn sigh to have wings and flee to the blue country. Florence will not be itself much longer, by all accounts, —Poggio[4] to be built over, and all up, far as Fiesole, they say. I don't care, it's all gone anyhow. Good bye, dear Edie—and goodbye, the dear others! If you have already any plans for the Summer, you may as well tell me: can it be possible you will come here? No! Yes! No—Yes.

Ever yours aff^y,
R Browning.

[1] R B and his son, returning from their summer holiday by way of Paris, and the Storys, just arriving in Paris from London, saw each other briefly. (McAleer, p. 194.)

[2] Pen Browning.

[3] Credit was given at the end of an article entitled 'New Sculptures at the British Museum', published in the *Athenaeum* of November 26, 1864 (pp. 709–10).

[4] Extensive changes were made when the capital was moved from Turin to Florence in 1865.

19. Warwick Crescent,
Upper Westbourne Terrace, W
April 11. '65.

Dear Friends, I was happy indeed to get your letters—Edie's first, & now this satisfactory one. I had no notion when we met & parted in Paris so hurriedly that anything was wrong with you (in my writing you must each of you pick out his or her own *whos* and *yous:*) I only supposed that London Life had done its usual work: and having already exceeded my stay abroad I was anxious to get home again: for I used to idle enough in Italy—but here I stick to my business honestly. At all events, you seem quite recovered now, and must take care & keep so. "Medea"[1] will be a sight to see,—and I rejoice that so good a fellow as Goldsmid[2] has the "Saul." I shall be able to see it, moreover, with the rest of the world. As for the Bust[3]—you could never mistake my feeling of fear of the alterations that seemed unavoidable: I know very well that if such a miracle of reproduction could be expected from any human being, it may from *you*. Many people, quite competent to pronounce judgment, have declared that such a miracle *is* accomplished in the present case: all the more will be my prize, of course. But I was put to so much pain by a well-meaning artist here, two years ago, who was bent on reconstructing something out of photographs and pictures, and did fail so entirely,—that the approach to anything like the pain impressed me, certainly, at the time. I know your immense superiority not only in art but in the knowledge which the art is to use: and whatever be the result there can be no annoyance to me: there *was* before.

Well, we are in the Easter lull, before recommencing with double spirit in a fortnight: I & Pen mean to go to Paris next week for a few days to see our people. Pen is a great fellow now, with incipient moustaches, and made his appearance the other night at a party in the actual coat & white tie—inevitable but bitter! His whole great soul was wrapped up in the Boatraces last Saturday, when Oxford again beat Cambridge, the cool long & strong stroke against the spurt and spasmodic dip: the English do best by sticking to the English way. And don't you be fancying there's any panic in us about Canada[4]—those fortifications are considered useless by the people who expect to have to fight—and if we *have not*, so much the better, but as we get promises of it from right & left, it's not easy to disbelieve them altogether.

I am very sorry that you should have your painful experience of Chapman's slowness[5] in rendering an account: that is his old vice—I bade you be prepared for it: he is in like arrears with me. It admits of no excuse at all, and you have a right to give it what ugly name you please—which name if *he* dislikes, the remedy is in his own hands. I will speak to him about it in a day or so. The Booksellers generally give accounts only once a year—but he engages to do otherwise, and don't keep his word: I have not myself the genius of making such men mind me, and they know it.

As for the work you so kindly care to know about, it is all in one way, about the Trial-Book[6]—my poem will be long enough, for one thing.

Spring is upon us of a sudden, and pairing-time is evident: Octavius Barrett re-marries next week: I even hear this morning that Milsand[7] (you know him?) is on the point of marrying. All the better!

I must try and see more of Lady William than I have done of late: I am overcome by engagements. I continue to hope for better things in your part of the world than that the imbecility there will last forever. Is Mrs Trollope[8] dead?—very ill, I know —but nothing so sad is known here as yet.

Goodbye—this is a poor scribble, but it may go—your generosity in answering it will be the greater. Pen's love with mine to you all.

Ever affectionately yours RB.

I am very anxious to hear from Cartwright who is in sad trouble I fear, with illness of his children & of himself, poor fellow.

[1] 'The figure [of Medea] is one of Mr. Story's earlier works and is undoubtedly one of his best'. (Taft, *The History of American Sculpture*, p. 157.)

[2] Julian Goldsmid (1838–96), third and last Baronet, inherited large financial holdings, and, as was characteristic of his family, was prominent in public life. He had a remarkable art collection.

[3] Of EBB.

[4] During the early part of the Civil War, when feelings between the North and England were tense there was some fear in England of

Northern aggression in Canada, but it subsided. The fear was revived when the North was victorious. The English were afraid of the new feeling of power in the North and of its grievances against England; and they were afraid that with the habit of war the armies would prefer marching against Canada to being demobilized.

⁵ Browning often complained to Edward Chapman for his tardiness in rendering accounts. For this and other reasons he changed publisher soon after the middle of the 'sixties. (See letters to Chapman and Appendix C in DeVane and Knickerbocker for an account of R B's relationship with him.)

⁶ *The Ring and the Book* was the work alluded to and the main source for it was the Trial-Book (the Old Yellow Book), which Browning found on a bookstall in Florence in June 1860 and read at once. Not until several years later did he begin to compose his poem, which reached a length of 21,116 lines. *The Ring and the Book* was first published in four parts (November, December 1868 and January, February 1869).

⁷ One of Browning's most gratifying friendships was with Joseph Antoine Milsand (1817–86), French critic, with whom he became acquainted in Paris in 1852. (Th. Bentzon, 'A French Friend of Browning—Joseph Milsand', *Scribner's Magazine*, XX [July 1896], 108–20.) For an account of his engagement see McAleer, p. 213.

⁸ Theodosia (Garrow) Trollope (1825–65), author, died on April 13. She was the first wife of Thomas Adolphus Trollope.

19 Warwick Crescent,
Upper Westbourne Terrace, W.
July 8. '65.

Dearest Edie,

What will you have thought of this week's silence, after sending me and Pen that kind note and request? I thought I should be able to go to-day, and waited to become sure before sending word,—but, after all, you know very well how we both of us long to see as much of you as we can. I want to get to Mount Felix¹ as early in the morning or afternoon as may conveniently be, and walk about the beautiful grounds. Shall it be next Saturday?—unless there should be visitors, for we want to have you to ourselves, for the little time there is left us.

I want you, too, to tell Mr. and Mrs. Sturgis how glad I shall be to see them again: I have no time,—can never call, much less leave town for a day, but I neither am forgetful nor ungrateful, I hope: It is now the end of the season, (and *my* working season, besides—for I have written *8400* lines of my new poem[2] since the autumn,—there's for you!)—and there is a little breathing-space before going away. Pen's love is especially sent to you with that of

> *Yours affectionately ever,*
> *RB.*

[1] The home of the Russell Sturgises at Walton-on-Thames, where Edith was staying while Mr. and Mrs. Story were in the United States.

[2] *The Ring and the Book.*

July 20, '65

Dearest Edie:

If we go to Mount Felix on Saturday shall we find you alone, and will Mrs. Sturgis bear with all this stupid fuss that I seem to make, and let us come early, and give us some luncheon, and let us go—not late?

If visitors are expected, we will take another Saturday: that Goose—Pen would not go without me, finding that I really meant to go some time or other!

Kindest regards to Mr. and Mrs. Sturgis,

> *from yours affectionately ever,*
> *Robert Browning*

May I have a word in answer?

19 Warwick Crescent,
Upper Westbourne Terrace, W.
July 26. '65.

Dearest Edie,

If I was "perverse," I am now paid for my perversity—since I find that I shall have to leave London without seeing you, after all the pleasant things that were to have been. Letters from

Paris induce me to hasten our departure, and next Saturday,—the day I meant to ask leave to pass at Mount Felix,—will break on us in London & set on us in Paris—(poetically expressed.) Pen's vexation is what it should be: he went to the Academy last Saturday hoping to meet you there—but to no purpose. Perhaps you will still be at Mount Felix in October, when we return—in the very beginning of it,—if so—but where is the use of proposing pleasant things,—they never come to good now—with me, at least.

Thank Mrs Sturgis exceedingly for me: "perverse," indeed, because, being only able to excuse myself from other people's invitations by saying—"I never accept such,"—and finding life bearable in consequence,—I don't give way to the temptation the first time that it would be delightful so to do!—Then, Regattas—what has a grey owl like me to do with Regattas & the lovers of the same? No, no! the dark for me!

I want to tell you that the Bust arrived yesterday: I have hardly looked steadily enough at it yet: there are some things admirably reproduced there—more, by far than I thought possible—nobody else could have saved them, or made so beautiful a thing. Tell your Papa so, when you write.

Ever affectionately yours
Robert Browning.

We go to Ste Marie, near Pornic, as we did two years ago & the year before—to the Mayor's house, just as before. Willie Bracken & his mother go also,—though we don't travel together.

July 28. '65.

Dearest Edie,

Indeed it was impossible for either of us, Pen or myself, to get to you to-day: the kindness of your invitation remains with us both. We go off early to-morrow—and whether we meet or no, shall always keep you in mind and be, as

now, affectionately yours,
Pen & RB.

Kind regards and thanks once again to Mrs Sturgis. Love to your Papa & Mama when you write.

> 19 Warwick Crescent,
> Upper Westbourne Terrace, W.
> Oct. 13. '65.

Dear Friends,

I am just come back[1]—are you here still? If so, you must not go away till I have seen you somehow. As I know nothing about anybody since I left London, I am ignorant in your case—but I want much to know—& so does Pen.

> *Ever yours affectionately*
> *R Browning.*

[1]Browning left London on July 29 to go to Paris, then to Sainte Marie, near Pornic. There he remained until October 1, when he started his return to London via Paris.

> 19 Warwick Crescent,
> Upper Westbourne Terr; W.
> Sunday Mᵍ [October 15, 1865.][1]

Dear Story, You will have found my letter, if you had not seen it when you wrote—not that it is needful to tell you that I should greatly enjoy one more word with you all. The letter reached me at eight o'clock last evening—Had I imagined you were at Chapman's yesterday,—why, I passed the shop!

To-day I have engagements I can't put off. All I can say is— if you find it possible to say "We shall be at such a place, at such a time," —any day—I will certainly be there.

Whatever happens, and whether we are to see each other sooner or later—I am always yours as ever. I begin to see a pin-point of light out at the end of this London life,—Italy at the end of a few years more, you know!

I wrote to Edie as soon as the Bust came—as I had been frank in confessing my fears, you may depend on the honesty of

my wonder and delight. Would you like me to take it for a portrait, when I publish a "Selection"[2] that is projected?

Ever affectionately yours
R Browning

[1] Hood's conjectured date for this letter is July 30, 1865. The
month date, July 30, is not right. Browning was not in London
(RB–WWS, July 28, 1865), and Story could not have been at
Chapman's (the publishers) the day preceding the 30th, for he was
still in the United States (HJ, II, 184). The letters of October 13, 15
(my date), 18, and 21 form a group concerned with attempts of
Story and Browning to get together since both had been away from
London and Story would soon return to Rome. From the sequence
of attempts, made clear in the letters, the Sunday morning of this
letter can be identified as October 15.

[2] *A Selection from the Poetry of Elizabeth Barrett Browning*, published
by Chapman and Hall in 1866.

19, Warwick Crescent, W.
Wednesday night.
[October 18, 1865][1]

Dear Friends,

I did myself no good by the return thro' the cold & rain on
Monday:[2] my cough, and a headache, kept me at home yesterday: and to-day, having left the house with the intention of bid-
ding you goodbye, the effect of the air makes itself so unpleasant,
that I write this at a friend's house, and mean to go back at once.
If, by any chance, you do not go tomorrow, send me a word and
I will try and see you at 5. Pen is to return on Friday.

Ever affectionately yours,
R Browni[ng][3]

[1] Someone besides Browning dated this letter October 13, 1865,
on the envelope. The figure '18' on the postmark was read as '13'.
The dating of October 18 (Wednesday) fits this letter into its proper
place in the sequence of the letters written in October.

[2] He had made an effort to see Story.

[3] Torn away.

19. Warwick Crescent,
Upper Westbourne Terrace, W.
Oct. 21, '65.

Dear Mrs Story,

I am more vexed than you can be at all this missing & playing at cross-purposes, but how can it be otherwise? I first heard from William on Saturday night, hours after you left Town:—on getting Edie's note on Monday, I posted off to Cataldis',[1]—then came your note appointing Wednesday at 5 till dinner-time (I did not understand that you wished me to meet you at the Museum)—and on Wednesday came the Telegram: the fact is, you are here, very properly, to be busy,—& I can only hope to catch you by chance. Fancy—if I wrote to-day to say I would go to Walton[2] on Monday,—I should probably go, find you called to Town,—and returning, get the letter to tell me so! No—it won't do, my dear friend, and we must wait better years. Moreover, the reason I do not leave Town, when once fairly settled in it, is, as I have always truly declared, because I *cannot:* I take the longest possible holiday, and, that over, shut my eyes to any diversion from my business in this place: where should I go, if my purpose were to enjoy myself merely, rather than to those entirely kind friends who treated me as they did when I last visited them? I should think that is unnecessary to say! I go nowhere, and am obliged to make no exception, if I would not offend other people. I just went to Oxford in the summer—but that was a business-matter.

The end is,—tell me any evening, or morning, when you will be at Cataldis', and there you will find me. I should indeed like to see Wild again.

I wrote about a portrait to William—but have thought of another for the present book:[3] I can use *his* hereafter with advantage, if he allow it.

Love to you all,—kind regards to Mr & Mrs Sturgis.

Yours affectionately ever
R Browning

[1] Cataldis Hotel.

² The Storys were probably at the home of Russell Sturgis.

³ *A Selection from the Poetry of Elizabeth Barrett Browning.* Browning had considered using Story's bust of EBB for portrait (see RB–WWS, October 15, 1865), but he used as frontispiece a head of EBB with the caption 'in early youth'.

19. Warwick Crescent,
Upper Westbourne Terrace, W.
Sept. 28, '69

Dear Friends,—it is a real comfort to fancy one can do anything for you, however minute,—anything akin to the handing a rug or carrying a hat-box: it is too horrible to be quite cut off, as I am now, after two months absolute indivisibility![1] Tilton's[2] speedy removal is more than ever necessary to me,—keep it in mind when you are able to give him a push! But about the poor little commission: I enclose you the Ticket,—all is safe and waiting your arrival.

This morning I called, in company of my sister, on Mr. and Mrs. Eldridge,[3]—they arrived last evening only; they leave London, on the 3ᵈ—or perhaps the 4ᵗʰ—for Liverpool, whence they depart on the 5ᵗʰ. Mr. Shaw[4] is expected to arrive tonight or tomorrow: he sails with them: not so Miss Williams[5] who remains in Paris, at the Hôtel d'Orient, Rue Neuve des Augustins, intending to pass the winter at Cannes or Pau or Arles. She is not quite so well as before, though far from an invalid. We did not see your Brother, who was busy somewhere somehow. There,—I wish I had something more to tell, as an excuse for continuing this effort at intercourse!

I found all well at home, but was weary, myself,—today, however, I feel well enough. The day is exceedingly warm and fine,—unseasonable, I suppose. You really should be in no hurry to return—that is, when once you have reached London, —it is still Summer-time with us,—what then at Rome?

Good bye, dear Friends,—I get a little of the light of your faces, as I bid you remember

Yours affectionately ever
R.B.

¹ In August the Brownings and the Storys had been among Lady Ashburton's guests at Loch Luichart in Scotland. In September they were at Naworth Castle, one of Lord Carlisle's homes.

² In editing this letter, Hood identified Tilton as Theodore Tilton, 'editor of *The Independent*, in which in former years some of Mrs. Browning's poems had appeared'. (P. 355.) At this time Theodore Tilton (1835–1907) was very active in the United States in his promising career of journalist and lecturer and could hardly have been given a push by Story toward a speedy removal. Did RB wish to obtain quarters in the Barberini occupied by John Rollin Tilton (1828–88), American landscape painter, who went to Rome in 1852 and retained residence there until his death? (See DAB and HJ, II, 305.) Browning often talked of returning to Rome to live.

³ Mrs. Story's brothers who were living at this time were James Thomas Eldredge and Charles Warren Eldredge.

⁴ Unidentified.

⁵ Unidentified. Not Charlotte Williams-Wynn, who died in April of 1869.

19 Warwick Crescent,
Upper Westbourne Terrace, W.
[September 28, 1869]¹

Dearest Edie, it is good indeed of you to care about a special word for yourself, when I have told Mr. and Mrs. Story all the little there is to tell. Since you exact it, know then that I was tired and out of sorts on my arrival at 10 o'clock; and, having somehow got out of my good old habit of soundly and expeditiously sleeping, I continued to weary myself in bed,—but in the end the sleep came, and I woke aware of the accustomed curtains and furniture, and none the worse for a little tossing and tumbling. I sincerely hope your ailments,—far more important than mine, —have been disposed of as easily. You seemed nervous and fatigued,—take care of yourself, will you?

I found some letters of no particular interest. One from Leighton's sister² mentions that she has no idea where he can be, —such licences can some people permit themselves! You will hear from the other letter how I went to see your Aunt³ and found her.

How stupid one feels at this vile writing after two months' live real talk! I shall get more used to it, I dare say, after a little practice; but at first,—why, I begin as you see—and end as you expect—for what news will there be in my telling you that

> *I am ever affectionately yours?*
> *RB.*

I saw Trevilian (so they pronounce, but probably don't spell it) just now,—he is going to be married to-morrow, and struck me as not exuberantly joyful.

If you get news of any interest, you will be kind in writing, you know; also "whether or no," as the Negro said.

---

¹ Hood dates this *ca.* September 1869. It can be definitely dated as September 28, 1869, by the reference to Trevelyan's marriage on the following day. Sir George Otto Trevelyan (1838–1928), historian and author, married Caroline Philips on September 29, 1869.

² Alexandra Leighton (1828–1903), sister of Frederic Leighton, married (1857) Colonel Sutherland Orr, who died in 1858. She met Browning in the winter of 1855–6 in Paris, and after she settled in London in 1869 they became close friends. At the request of some of the members of the Browning Society, of which she was a devoted member, she wrote the *Handbook to the Works of Robert Browning* 'with the encouragement and help of the poet'. (DNB). After Browning's death, his son and sister asked her to write the life of Browning, and she turned to the Storys for details of Browning's life during the years of their close association with him. (Story Col.) When Mrs. Orr's *Life and Letters of Robert Browning* was published (1891), Story gave his opinion of it to his son: 'I have as yet only glanced at it—& it seemed rather colourless to me—but Mama thinks better of it & is busy reading it. B's letters are not vigorous or characteristic or light—& as for incidents & descriptions of persons & life it is very meagre'. (Story Col.)

³ Mrs. Eldredge.

Blickling Hall, Aylsham, Norfolk.
Nov: 16. '69

Dear Friends,

I ought to have written long before, I very well know: but there were many difficulties in the way. I got your notes in

London, and could perhaps have seen you—but those dismal good-byes are best avoided, and I shall rather busy myself with the hope of saying "how do you do?" all the more cheerfully next year. The fact is, the holidays are over, with (for me) an end of boys'-play, which,—it is said,—men ought to know when to leave off: and "left off" it all is, I very sincerely assure you. I am seeing all my sober friends, and still have visits to pay before I settle down to my work at London,—whatever that work is to be: I go from this beautiful place[1] (worth fifty Ashridges)[2] at the end of the week,—then to Wrest,[3]—then to Highclere,[4] then, —home, I hope. Pen is at work, I believe,—preparing for "Smalls": he has an ugly cold which he can't shake off. If I were in London, I would send by Odo Russell,—who leaves next Saturday, some photographs &c—another occasion will offer itself, I dare say. Well, you are in Rome, happily settled by this time: I incline less & less to be there with the crowd, and should grow bilious at the nine hundred & odd bishops:[5] however, they will "clear out" in due time, and leave the place much as they found it. I hope you are all well, and that the weather is not as unhealthy as the sickly heat here,—for *hot*, it is: we have a cold day or two which promise to "brace" us,—and then back comes the Indian summer: you at Rome may be broiling possibly.

I wish I had news of any kind, to give my letter a touch of importance,—but little reaches me, and my ears get deaf to even that little: I shall best "shut up," as Pen would say. Good bye, dear Friends, let us meet and, if it may be, have fun again next year. With all love to you all, believe me

ever affectionately yours,
Robert Browning.

[1] Blickling Hall, a famous mansion built in the early seventeenth century. In 1869 it was the home of the eighth Marquess of Lothian (1832–70). An earlier house on the estate was the home of the Boleyns, and Anne spent much of her childhood there. Blickling Hall, together with about 4,500 acres, is now owned by the National Trust.

[2] Ashridge Park, near Berkhamstead, Hertfordshire, one of the places belonging to the third Earl Brownlow (1844–1921), son of Lady Marion Alford.

³ Wrest Park, near Ampthill, Bedfordshire, was one of the residences of Earl Cowper of Wingham (1834–1905). Browning dedicated *Balaustion's Adventures* to the Countess Cowper.

⁴ Highclere Castle, near Newbury, Berkshire, was one of the residences of Henry Herbert, fourth Earl of Carnarvon (1831–90).

⁵ The Vatican Council, the twentieth oecumenical council of the bishops of the Roman Catholic Church, opened December 8, 1869. Its main business was the proclamation of the Pope's Infallibility, giving the Church authority over civil and political rights. The actual result was the downfall of the Pope's temporal power. The Catholic States were unsympathetic with Papal Infallibility, which was out of keeping with the times, and the Papacy was left without defenders. In September 1870 the Italian Government seized Rome, which was proclaimed the capital of Italy.

19 Warwick Crescent,
Upper Westb: Ter:
July 28, '70

Dear Edie, I write at Pen's desire—the poor fellow being unable himself to do so. I had to leave London last Wednesday, and on returning two days after, I found him very ill from exposure to the sun on the day he crossed the Park to call on you: there seemed nothing, however, to hinder my keeping another engagement on Saturday—but on Monday I found him in an outrageous eruption of the measles: the violence of the attack may have helped to end the ugly thing all the sooner,—for to-day he is plainly convalescent, beyond any expectation of the doctor, who saw him four times yesterday: this is the second time he has been visited by this pleasant intruder (the measles, not the Doctor!). He is anxious that you should not dream of enquiring about him,—a formality altogether unnecessary, for— red and hardly recognizable as he was on Monday, he is at this moment studying the newspaper and digesting a good breakfast—in bed, of course. (Since writing the last word, the doctor confirms me in all I conjectured, and promises that the cure shall be complete in a week or so.)

[163]

I suppose I ought also to notice that passage of your letter in which you speak of "the strange misunderstanding between us all—in the existence of which you cannot even believe, though one lives to learn many things." I am quite ready and glad to accept Mrs. Story's kind assurance that I *did* misunderstand the omission of the customary notice,—to which I have got used for the last eight or nine years,—that you had arrived in London. Pray let there be an end of all thinking or talking about it, and let our next meeting, whenever it happen, make amends for the mistakes of this year. Give my kindest regards to your Father and Mother, and remember me as

ever affectionately your
RB.

19, Warwick Crescent, W.
Oct. 20, '71

Dear Edie,

Thank you exceedingly for your letter alongside Pen's writing; fortunate he is to be enjoying himself with you[1] while I endure the steaming unhealthy heat surrounded by everything that is ugly. Pray don't talk about "Rome," unless you wish to throw this place into even stronger shade than naturally belongs to it! No chance of Rome for me this year, if any year!

It was no word nor half-word of Pen's that induced me to send the message thro' him—natural enough, I hope—that I had been prevented sending copies of my little thing to anybody except three or four people whose addresses were known to the Publisher,—since I left town the day that he professed to publish the Poem.[2] On returning, I got a few copies for my friends,—and are not you a friend of mine still? All I wanted him to do was to explain why there was such an ado about next to nothing in the shape of a book.

I shall look forward with great pleasure to the promised sight of you this next week—if you are destined to increase the comforts of London,—at some cost to yourself, I fear. I am glad Pen has seen those beautiful places, and in your company. Give him my love,—he will excuse my not writing, or writing through your tongue if it will kindly charge itself with the no-news that I and Sarianna are very well.

Ever affectionately yours
Robert Browning

¹ Browning had been staying with friends at their places in Scotland—the Benzons (see RB–Edith S, December 20, 1871, n, 1) and Lady Ashburton. When he returned to London, his son, who had been with him, remained a while longer. The Storys were in Scotland too.

² *Balaustion's Adventure*, published in August 1871.

19. Warwick Crescent, W.
Nov: 6, '71

Dearest Edie,

I was very sorry to find that by failing to see you all on Saturday I lost my last chance of doing so before your departure. I was really unable to go out,—though,—never mind the "inability,"—I certainly would have made the effort had I supposed you were so resolutely on the move. As it is, I am very happy indeed that I saw you all; and shall look forward to seeing you again with all the old affection and desire. One little thing I meant to say,—that, if you remember, I promised you the *very* original of a little poem of mine,¹—blots, scratches and so forth inclusive: here it is,—I wish it were worthier your acceptance.

Give my kindest love to your Father & Mother. If there are things likelier to happen than a journey to Rome on my part,— yet, Providence & Pen assisting, such a delight might not impossibly be in store for me. "Meantime, all my wishes flee / To the home beyond the sea"²—as dear old Procter sings.

Ever yours affectionately
R Browning.

¹ 'Hervé Riel', first published in the *Cornhill Magazine* in March 1871. The letter to Edith and the manuscript of 'Hervé Riel' that accompanied it are in the Pierpont Morgan Library.

[165]

[2] The following lines are from 'On a Lady Slanderer' by Bryan Waller Procter (Barry Cornwall):

> Meantime, all my wishes flee
> To thy nest beyond the sea!

19 Warwick Crescent, W.
Dec. 20. '71.

Dearest Edie,

You bade me, in the kind little note you sent from Paris, write to you at Rome and say that I was coming. I am always "coming" in one sense, so far as wishing and even hoping go; but this winter is to be the usual dismal affair for me in London, too certainly. Mr. Benzon[1] tried his best to get me to adventure in his company: but, after all, the difficulty will be for me rather to leave Rome, when I once get there, than to *go*: his visit will be a very short one. So, he takes you my new little book,[2] and I write to warn you that I expect you not to care three straws for what, in the nature of things, is uninteresting enough, even compared with other poems of mine which you have been only too good to. What poetry can be in a sort of political satire, made the milder because of the present fortunes of the subject?[3] So, all you are to understand by the gift of the thing is that, for want of better, it is my best at present. Give my kindest love to your Father and Mother. Neither I nor Pen have been abundantly well, of late, but I am well now and he is better.

Ever affectionately yours
Robert Browning.

[1] Ernest Leopold Benzon (1819–73), a good friend of both Story and Browning. He was a 'shrewd German-American who had amassed a fortune in business'. He and Frederic(k) Lehmann (see RB–JRL, November 15, 1880, and n.1) were partners in the firm of ironmasters, Naylor, Vickers & Co. (Moscheles, *Fragments of an Autobiography*, p. 320.)

[2] *Prince Hohenstiel-Schwangau*, which Browning had worked on while he was staying at Benzon's place in Scotland in the autumn of this year. (McAleer, p. 367.)

[166]

³ After Napoleon III's defeat at Sedan in September 1870 and the subsequent fall of the Empire, Napoleon spent the remainder of his life in England.

19. Warwick Crescent, Jan. 1. '72

Private

Dearest Edie,

First and last of all,—truest good wishes to you and everybody yours, for this year and whatever years are to follow after! Then, thank you very much for your letter, and the kind things you say about me and the little book;¹ only, I don't think, when you have read more, you will find I have "taken the man for any Hero"—I rather made him confess he was the opposite, though I put forward what excuses I thought he was likely to make for himself, if inclined to try. I never at any time thought much better of him than now; and I don't think so much worse of the character as shown us in the last few years, because I suppose there to be a physical and intellectual decline of faculty, brought about by the man's own faults, no doubt—but I think he struggles against these; and when that is the case, depend on it, in a soliloquy, a man makes the most of his good intentions and sees great excuse in them—far beyond what our optics discover! I really wrote—that is, conceived the poem, twelve years ago in the Via del Tritone²—in a little handbreadth of prose,—now yellow with age and Italian ink,—which I breathed out into this full-blown bubble in a couple of months this autumn that is gone —thinking it fair so to do. What is the poem you allude to, which "I talked about at L[och] L[uichart]."³ I have absolutely forgotten—if you tell me, and I still am of the same mind about it, I will try and keep alive what you will have helped me to recover —when this thing I am now engaged upon⁴ (half-done, now) is out of hand.

And now, with respect to the "question quite between ourselves." I only know of one person in London, not "whom I would call my enemy," but who openly professes herself such,— Mrs. Sartoris. Three years ago, I found she was complaining to people that I had quarreled with her, she didn't imagine why—

while, all I knew was that she had discontinued inviting me to her house. *I* didn't imagine why. I met her a year after at Wrest, passed some days in her company, thought all was right again. She accused me of "dropping her," I replied that she had "dropped me"—for the kindness was all of one side, in the nature of things, I had no home to invite her to, and could only accept her invitations—which ceased to come. To be sure, I might have "called"—but I never was one of the intimates she kept aware of her movements,—as to when she would be in town for a day or two, and as suddenly away again,—and, moreover, I never feel inclined to take much trouble to pick up a friendship anybody lets fall for so little reason, to dirty my hands by so doing. Last season, just before May's[5] marriage, I met the whole family at dinner,—sat by Mrs. S. and found her friendly as of old,—and I took the occasion, from something she inquired about, to write a friendly little note next day. But then happened this that I shall tell you. Two years ago, *just* before we went to Scotland, Miss Gabriel[6] gave me an account of her grievances against Mrs. S.—which account I received, never forgetting 1st that it was a one-sided account, and 2ly that if the conduct she complained of were truly described, there was nothing in it, which, *a la rigueur*, could not be excused after a fashion into a fault of judgment and temper,—nothing therefore which prevented the friendly feeling I showed, and, in turn, wished to get again at Wrest as I have mentioned—but this last year, Lady A[shburton] began upon me one day about the "utter falseness of Miss G."—"having just heard the whole story from Mrs. S." We got no further in the story than the first sentence "Miss G. wrote to Mr. Greville,[7] with whom she had little or no previous acquaintance"—because I interposed—"with whom she had an intimate acquaintance." That was a point necessary to be cleared up, because all Miss G's veracity would have disappeared, were the facts otherwise. Accordingly I called on Miss G.—picked out a couple of the shortest notes from a heap she had retained,—for a purpose,—and sent them to L^y A. that she might see for herself whether the writer was "intimate" or not with Miss G. The letters were returned to me with an expression of convenient wonder how—but I will transcribe from the letter itself—"The world is out of joint"—and "I can't imagine how two tales so entirely different can both be true." Both could not, indeed, "be true," but, with that evidence, it was pretty clear which was false. I make no doubt this was at once reported to Mrs. S. who is consequently, I have as little doubt, from many circumstances that are come to my knowledge, "an enemy of mine"—for which, be assured, I care not three straws, nor do I trouble myself to inquire what she [has] said, written, or done in return for my "making the two tales look so very different." If poor Hatty[8] heard some third tale, and at once threw up her old friend, I am sorry for her. The whole business has turned out too blessedly for me to much concern myself as to how it happened, and by means of whom.

Ever affectionately yours,
R Browning

[1] *Prince Hohenstiel-Schwangau.*

[2] Where the Brownings lived in Rome during the winter of 1859–60.

[3] Loch Luichart, Lady Ashburton's place in Scotland.

[4] *Fifine at the Fair.*

[5] Mrs. Adelaide Sartoris's daughter, May, married Evans Gordon.

[6] See RB–Ss, May 3, 1864, n. 2.

[7] Possibly Henry William Greville (1801–72), diarist.

[8] As the following letter (April 4, 1872) shows, it was not Mrs. Sartoris who said something that caused Hatty Hosmer to give up her old friend Browning.

Belton House,
Grantham.
April 4. '72.

Dearest Edie,

Thank you very much for your letter & all its kindness: I have only a short quarter of an hour at my service, but I want to answer it with no more delay than I can help—and, to get done with the one unpleasantness first,—what you tell me about Hatty & the "intimate friends" and their report of me which made her cut our old & long friendship short,[1] is the one touch wanting to confirm my impression of her behaviour in that matter: I suggested that her authority *might possibly be* Mrs Sartoris, not at all because I saw reason to suspect her of anything worse than a little disliking, with or without reason, which she had, & still may have for aught I know,—but from a remainder of respect to Hatty—who *might have* paid attention to any story reported by somebody who, at all events, was intimate with all three of the parties concerned,—myself, Hatty and Lady A[shburton]—she turns out, however, to have thought it quite just & proper to listen to people I never by any possibility can have mentioned Lady A's name to,—(for I *know* well to whom, and under what particular circumstances, I ever was induced to mention the name,)—and then, without giving me a hint of what the story was, how I might explain it or expose it,—to take on herself to write that letter: that is,—to say she took it on herself,—for I don't believe any such nonsense, or that she was anything but the cat's paw of Lady A. in the business,—who, knowing she had only succeeded, after nine or ten months' teazing with her invitations, to get me to promise to visit her for one day, and so get handsomely done with it all,—wanted to have the air of shutting the door in my face with a final bang,— fancying that she could coax me round the back-way the very next day,—as she did by sending a servant & a letter of invitation to the house in Park Lane. I have told her my mind so thoroughly about *that*, and so effectually relieved myself from any further bother of the kind, that I need not bring up the nauseating remembrance: she & I have met once since, and I felt excused from even looking at—much less, speaking to her. But I should like to know,—whatever the story may have been,—what business Hatty had with my behaviour to L^y A. in L^y A's house? I suppose that Lady A. did not suppress what she considered the capital point of her quarrel with me when she foamed out into the couple of letters she bespattered me with: yet the worst she charged me with was,—having said that my heart was buried in

[170]

Florence, and the attractiveness of a marriage with her lay in its advantage to Pen: two simple facts,—as I told her,—which I had never left her in ignorance about, for a moment,—though that I ever paraded this in a gross form to anybody is simply false: but had it been true,—does Hatty instantly practise impertinence on any friend of hers who intends to make an ambitious or mercenary marriage? As for her devotion to Lady Λ: begetting this chivalrous ardour in her,—Lady A has got plenty of friends quite as intimate, who never fancied for a moment that they were called on to fight her battles. For instance, I have been a week here with Lʸ Marian Alford,[2] whom I was especially invited to meet,—she, I fancy, has received the utmost of Lady A's confidences, and heard whatever there was to hear: and nothing can exceed the friendliness with which we converse day after day: which is only to say, that she is a rational woman of the world, valuing her own independence, and understanding that there are two ways of telling a story. So, now, I have done with Hatty, for once & always. Had I believed stories about *her*, many a long year ago, and ordered her away from people's houses on the strength of them, I should have lost a friendship I used to value highly: but I have gained some pleasant memories by being less ready than she to believe slanderous gossip,—and,—as she has elected to know me only through the reports of others, though I would have shown what they were worth in a minute, had she given me the opportunity, —so shall our relation be, and no otherwise, to the end of time. I scribble all this as fast as the pen can drive, but you will understand, and help all with your sympathy & intelligence, I know.

Well, I am glad of all you tell me,—of the Statue's[3] success, of your approaching visit to London, of the enjoyments, in various ways, you tell me about so pleasantly. I have come here for a little change & relaxation,—my six months' stay in Town having begun to get the better of me. Pen is with his kind friends in Scotland, whence he writes in good spirits to-day. I shall return soon, having to "go to press"[4]—pressure, indeed! All my love to you all—don't let this dry indignant letter hide the true feeling that is under it: this, I trust, will be the last of my returning to that detestable subject. *Ever affectionately yours, dearest Edie,—R.B.*

¹ Hatty Hosmer was not the only mutual friend who was affected by the jarred relationship between Browning and Lady Ashburton after her rejection of his unflattering proposal. Story was caught up in the whirlpool of emotions; but since, quite naturally, it is easier not to assume the quarrels of friends, Story, as time passed, seemed willing to take up the former friendship with Lady Ashburton. When he was in London in 1875, he wrote to his wife: 'I enclose you a letter from Lady Ashburton which I have just received. It is a fathom-deep burial of the hatchet & I shall go & see her. She is affectionately mine. Well! no matter—let bye-gone be byegones'. (Story Col.)

² Lady Marianne (or Marian) Alford (1817–88), daughter of the second Marquess of Northampton and wife of John Viscount Alford, was artist, art patroness, and authoress. She spent much time in Rome, where Browning and Story had known her. According to the letterhead Browning was visiting at Belton House, one of the residences of the third Earl Brownlow, Lady Marian Alford's son.

³ Probably 'Semiramis'. (See Phillips, Appendix.)

⁴ *Fifine at the Fair* was to be published about a month later.

St. Aubin-sur-mer, par Luc, Calvados
Aug. 24, '73

My dear Story,

I ought not to think any proceeding of yours "singularly kind"—but I can't help doing so in the case of this long, particularizing letter, written amid so much to distract your attention—most full of interest it is, of course, at whatever trouble to yourself it may have been produced. Pen kept me sufficiently informed about the main result of every one of these sad days—but attempted no more, and I understand for the first time the nature of poor B's attack.¹ What can I add but that I am deeply interested in the news I wait for each morning? How sorry I am, there is no need to say. It struck me as exceedingly fortunate for our friend that you were at hand—your services must have been valuable indeed. What an extinction of the light of that pleasant

[172]

party,—even if there be an escape from the worst we have to fear. This will have done no good,—to say the least of it,—to Mrs Story who was benefiting by the stay at North Berwick according to Pen. His note,—a day later than your letter,—mentions her being expected at Pitlochrie on Monday.

I am sure Mrs. Benzon understands how much I feel for her on this terrible occasion—if it could be otherwise, I would write every day. Give her my most affectionate regards. My presence at Allean would be a pure incumbrance, I very well know. Indeed, I fancy you oppressed with such a multitude of counsellors. Well,—at all events, I am not so circumstanced here as to be in unnatural contrast, thro' the gaiety of St. Aubin, with the misfortune at Allean. I and my sister walk, bathe, breathe fresh air enough, have our friend Milsand's company, and thereupon send another day to its account. I have out a little reading between whiles. The weather is not so constantly fine as last year,—seems to have broken up already. We have made just one expedition in a jolting cart-carriage; and yet three weeks of our term have been somehow got rid of. While I write, it is raining heavily. I know that you always take just this opportunity,—of country quiet,—to write, and otherwise turn your short holiday to account. You must stay the longer in England, and catch, if possible, whatever you lose just now. I write, as I cannot but feel, lumberingly—and with a weight of foreboding and dispiritedness—but my object may have been gained—for all I want is to thank you deeply, and associate myself, despite of the distance, with your anxieties and friendly feelings. My sister is not very well,—has a bad cold,—but feels as gratefully as I do your kindness in this matter—and all others, indeed.

Ever affectionately yours
Robert Browning

This is pricked on a bare deal table with an iron pen.

¹ In August, Ernest Benzon took sick at Allean House, his place near Pitlochry, Scotland, while Story and Browning's son were visiting there. (Story Col.) He died on September 14. (*The Globe and Traveller* [London], September 16, 1873, p. 7.)

Dear Friend, I write at once on the impulse of having seen Mr.
Lowell[1] last night at a party—to my great pleasure—and *then*,
having heard from him the impossible news that you were not
coming to London this year![2]—which was a most unpleasant
thing to hear. Can it be? Here is Story a regular member of the
"Athenaeum,"[3] and all for nothing! At all events, reconsider the
matter, and if there be no very good reason for such a step, pray
don't take it. I believe, you see, in what you tell me of your completely reestablished health,—otherwise, *that* would overbear all
other considerations. At all events, the most likely way to *know*
instead of conjecture merely what you intend doing will be to
write—so I write. And if you are really purposed to stay away
altogether, I think you will be disposed to answer me *nearly* at
once. However, I ought to have told you earlier that I duly
waited on the Semiramis[4] and had every impression you could
desire or expect of her grandeur and voluptuousness. I don't
know what they intend to do with it—there is a sale of pictures,
next week, but nothing else. The books seem all in their places.
I know exactly as much as I wish,—i.e. nothing at all,—about
the arrangements under poor Benzon's will.[5] The bust, which
I am anxious to see, is sure to be a great success—of course,
the mere cast would have helped nobody by itself. Story knows
how to keep faces in the gallery under his hat. Mrs. B[enzon] is
very well,—doesn't go out, but sees old friends of an afternoon.
Lily[6] is quite well, and the boy gets a big fellow; but you may
hear of all this and more from herself, perhaps. My best report is
to be of Pen. It is now four months and a half since he has been
at steady work,[7] and there must be immense good in that. His
master, Heyermans,[8] evidently *is* the master, and, from Pen's
letters, which are unremitting, I can see that he is happier than
he ever was in his life. What a load this lightens me of. Who can
judge better than you? He has never once budged from his
butcher's-shop-lodging, and it is *I*, this time, who begin to be
anxious that he should change the air and otherwise relax a

little. If no other scheme presents itself, I and my sister will join him in an excursion somewhither in the autumn. We don't go to France, at any rate. Neither I nor my sister have been very well—our abominable weather may be to blame. I caught cold three weeks ago, and got otherwise out of order, but feel better at last. Lady W[illiam] is very fluctuating in health,—sometimes apparently at death's door,—then, a step backwards, and she is almost her old self again. The V de R's[9] are here and will do much for her. I see every now and then that contemptible Lady Ashburton, and mind her no more than any other black beetle—so long as it don't crawl up my sleeve. The town is very full and busy, just now, but the season will be a short one. Do tell me, by a word or two, what you are likely to do. Your two young men are quite well, apparently, and Edith was about to visit Florence, when you wrote. Did she go? What a wonderful affair this American band of believing ones—as a product of your common-sensical country, seems to us here! I dined in company with Gen. Schenk[10] last evening, and wish I had remembered to ask him about it. Lowell (but that was at another house) looked very well. He stays here for a fortnight only. His wife was with him. B Trollope[11] is notable also for her singing. She was present, and it only seemed yesterday when Pen and the little lady cantered about on ponies side by side like two butterflies. Well, some good things remain. My true love for you all—take it!

RB.

[1] Lowell and his wife had been in Europe for two years and were to sail for America near the end of June.

[2] Story did go to London in the autumn of 1874.

[3] Arthur Russell wrote to Story on March 10, 1874, that he had been elected a member of the Athenaeum, 'one of the 9 illustrious men who are annually chosen'. (HJ, II, 317.)

[4] A statue owned by Benzon, which Story had made.

[5] Mr. Benzon bequeathed to RB a valuable collection of arms (Sotheby, pp. 150–1, items, 1,291–1,300), which suggested some lines

in Browning's poem 'A Forgiveness'. (For a comment on the bequest see *The Diary of Alfred Domett*, ed. E. A. Horsman [London, 1953], pp. 181-2.)

6 Lily was the adopted child of Mr. and Mrs. Ernest Benzon. (Hood, p. 357.)

7 Pen Browning had made it quite clear that he had no inclination for the academic side of university but much enjoyment in sports and billiard playing. In despair his father concluded that he was 'unfit for anything but idleness and pleasure', (Landis and Freeman, p. 295.) After leaving the university, Pen continued a carefree existence while the poet vainly tried to find what work his son was fit for. (Landis and Freeman, pp. 292-7.) But it was Pen, not his father, who, in the midst of idling, found by chance what attracted him— painting. His father lost no time in setting the wheels in motion for study and training in art, for which Pen showed talent as well as interest.

8 Jean-Arnould Heyermans (b. 1837) of Antwerp.

9 Unidentified.

10 Major-General Robert Cumming Schenck (1809-90) was United States Minister to Great Britain from 1871 to 1876.

11 Beatrice Trollope (1853-81), daughter of Thomas Adolphus and Theodosia (Garrow) Trollope, was a precocious child. Her fine voice had caused the 'best teachers' in Florence to beg for the 'privilege of taking her as a pupil'. (Lucy Poate Stebbins and Richard Poate Stebbins, *The Trollopes* [New York, 1945], p. 232.)

19. Warwick Crescent, W.
Jan. 27. '80.

My dear Story,

It says something for the delight I always have in getting news of you, that there was a sort of pleasure when I found your letter last night, even though I feared it might refer to this sad business. You do not seem aware that I have already heard every essential particular you mention from the parties themselves: Mr Benson[1] having written to me at length on the 1st—and (in reply to my answer) on the 9th of the present month,—and Miss Fletcher wrote also on Jan. 12th. If they had shown you what I wrote in return, I hardly think you would have expected I

[176]

could say anything more—as there is no new circumstance to remark upon. Indeed your own admirably lucid co-ordination of the facts previously stated in Mr Benson's and Miss Fletcher's letters only makes the case more unintelligible than ever. Those facts are that Ld Wentworth[2] was absolutely "in love" up to the moment when he broke off his intended marriage for whatever was the cause: what *that* can have been I have no notion—certainly it must differ altogether from the causes alleged or surmised, as far as I know them. If the reason for the divorce was simply "incompatibility of temper"—there is no imputation of very serious blame on either party to the suit,—and one hardly understands why Mr Benson should have been a sufferer from "a cabal of seven years growth against us which has formulated and repeated calumnies," abominable enough: and he attributes to the "poisonous and soiling current of Roman iniquity,"—which has found "unscrupulous agents interested in hurting us in London & defeating Lord W's purpose,"—the rupture in question. If that is so, not a word about it appears in Lord W's letter, it would seem. Miss Fletcher's mistake as to her own age is too trivial for notice—if unconnected with some other circumstance more important,—and, besides, has been satisfactorily accounted for. What then effects so extraordinary a change in the feelings of a man resolutely bent on carrying out his purpose and altogether independent of anybody? Miss Fletcher attributes it to influence exerted at his sister's[3] during two days: up till then he had "written to her each day for six weeks": on the second day, he "declared the engagement to be in abeyance"—and the rest followed. If nothing quite new had occurred, this would be inexplicable. Lady A. welcomed the news of her brother's intention most warmly the moment she was apprised of it—we heard *that* at Cortina: and, in W's letters up to the last, "she sent me kind messages, even urging that there should be no delay to the marriage." How, then, could she be induced to start any but a *new* objection—and what weight could any nonsense about "a different social grade" have with her brother—as Miss F. supposes? Once again, I comprehend nothing as the facts are stated: remember, I have not the least knowledge, or guess even, at what W. would say in justification of his conduct. I have not seen him for more than two months, and never referred in the remotest way to his engagement at any time since he acquainted me with it in Cortina. The practical result of all this miserable work should be assuredly that, in spite of the bitterness and disappointment,—which cannot well be exaggerated,—Miss F. is bound to be thankful that—even thus—her union has been prevented with Lord W. if his character should prove as she estimates.[4] For if such a love as she believes in could be paralyzed at its culmination by such a very nothing as she discovers,—what would have been her security a week after actual marriage from a far more terrible *volte-face* occasioned by the merest of trifles? The worst outrage one could fancy would be to imagine that some compensation would lie in the escape with a realized title and fortune: and I cannot pretend to wish that such an adventure should be attempted. She must go on—however hard the business of authorship may now be—with what began so well,—and, to my feeling,—could she share it,—always on the supposition that she is confident of having been utterly and causelessly wronged,— to *my* feeling, the regret for what she has lost would vanish soon enough.

> *Ever affectionately yours*
> *Robert Browning.*

I say nothing of the much I would otherwise have to say about yourselves. All New Year happiness to you all. My Sister wrote to Mrs Story to some such effect.

---

[1] The situation referred to in this letter is explained by Mabel Dodge Luhan. Mrs. Fletcher ran away from America to Italy with Eugene Benson, her son's tutor; and when her husband divorced her, she married Benson. They settled in Venice with her two children— the son and a daughter, Julia Constance Fletcher (the Miss Fletcher of this letter). Lord Wentworth (later Lord Lovelace), Byron's grandson, fell in love with her, but members of his family kept him from marrying her. She remained unmarried, cherishing her romance throughout her life. (*European Experiences* [New York, 1935], pp. 290–300.) Miss Fletcher (b. 1853), whose pseudonym was George Fleming, was the daughter of Rev. James Cooley Fletcher of

America. She was a novelist, playwright, and for a time a reviewer for *The Times*.

[2] Lord Wentworth (1839–1906), the author of *Astarte*, had married (1869) Fanny Heriot, who died in 1878; he married Mary Caroline Wortley in December 1880.

[3] Lady Anne Isabella Noel (1837–1917).

[4] Hawthorne, in recording his visit to Newstead Abbey, included unfavourable comments that he had heard on Lord Wentworth. (*The English Notebooks by Nathaniel Hawthorne*, ed. Randall Stewart [New York, 1941], p. 491.)

19, Warwick Crescent, W.
Dec. 23, '81

My dear Waldo,

I am sure you do me the justice to believe that whatever event makes you "altogether happy" finds me—I may say, finds all three of us, my Sister and Pen as well as myself,—in the truest sympathy with you. If your Father & Mother approve of the measure,[1] as I am delighted to hear they do, that circumstance is proof enough you have made a capital choice—to say nothing of my confidence in your own judgment and good taste. Since I began this letter, one for Pen, originally directed to Antwerp, —was put into my hand. The said Pen, poor fellow, is lying down with a headache—no doubt the consequence of a rough passage the day before yesterday: he managed to read it, however,—is very happy in your happiness, and will himself write as soon as he is well again—which will not keep you long waiting, I hope. You have probably heard from kind Mr Field of Pen's luck in selling his two pictures (one, the Hanover Gallery big affair) to Mrs B. Moore[2]—and of her gracious behaviour in the matter. I am not going to repeat with variations how much I congratulate you and wish you all good Christmas wishes. Give my best love to your Father & Mother and Julian, —love in which my Sister shares equally,—and believe me ever, my dear Waldo,

Affectionately yours
Robert Browning.

¹ Thomas Waldo Story married Ada Maud Broadwood in Rome in April 1883. She was the daughter of Thomas Capel Broadwood of Lyne (in Sussex), England, and Mary Davidson (Hennen) Broadwood, formerly of New Orleans, United States of America.

² Mrs. Clara Sophia Bloomfield-Moore (1824–99) of Philadelphia, authoress and philanthropist. After the death of her husband she spent much time in London, where, as in Philadelphia, 'her house was a resort for artists, musicians and authors'. (*National Cyclopaedia of American Biography*, IX, 473.) She met Browning in 1879; the friendship that followed she described in her article 'Robert Browning' in *Lippincott's Magazine* (XLV [May 1890], 683–91). She bought 'The Dinant-Market Woman' for herself and 'The Delivery to the Secular Arm', which had been exhibited in the Hanover Gallery, for the Pennsylvania Academy of Fine Arts at Philadelphia.

19. Warwick Crescent. W.
26th Dec: 1881

My dear old Waldo,

I do wish you all happiness and congratulate you most heartily!¹ Certainly, more so than these hackneyed words can convey: but we ought to understand each other without words and phrases, since our friendship began before you could speak and when I was a babe! I should have delighted in being able to grasp you by the hand, and, indeed, had been intending to go and see you all, this winter: but my plans have been upset by an opportunity presenting itself of working in Paris, in the studio of a friend, under Rodin the sculptor & I am going in for a dose of modeling which, I take it, is a surer road to knowledge of the figure than drawing in black and white. I hope our meeting will not be put off again for long and must content myself with hearing all about you and Ju-² from my Father and aunt who are full of your kindness to them. They are both well, and my Father seems especially flourishing. I hope you are all well also —mind you give my kindest love to Mr & Mrs Story and to Edie, next time a letter goes to her:—perhaps, she is with you— as well as to Ju: I want to see *the* picture.

Ever most affty yrs
Pen

[180]

Let me have some news of you soon. I am the worst hand at letter-writing *I* know!

¹ On Waldo's engagement.

² Julian Story.

19, Warwick Crescent, W.
Aug. 7, '84

My dear Edie, What else am I to say? Your kind letter arrived two days ago, and the Book¹ has followed quickly. It is not so very "little" an affair; and, in the fear that, when my sister has finished it, I may have to begin my own reading, and end it so late as to lead you to suppose that either book or letter has gone wrong, on this account I write at once to thank you most heartily. My sister says the autobiography is *fascinating*. I can well believe it, for I never knew such a work to be without interest, and this of Dupré must abound in precisely the matters that interest me most—but it happens also that your father read aloud to me, at Venice,² a considerable portion of your performance, and very greatly was I delighted by it. To be sure, I should welcome any work of yours and be disappointed indeed if it were otherwise than I have a right to expect. When I have thoroughly gone through the book, I will write again, if you permit me—as I know your old memories will be indulgent in the case. I was most happy to hear from your father's friends the Curtises³ of Venice, who are here, that his health is greatly improved; that of your mother has not suffered, I believe. There is not much likelihood of our going to Italy this autumn, the silly quarantine regulations effectually hinder our attempting that; and in no case should I—probably—trust myself in Florence again—but such an event might be, and if you are within reach, you will be certain to see the old friend—who always rejoices when he hears of your well-being, and trusts it may continue.

Pen is very well, at Dinant, just now, painting landscape in the open air. I have told him already of the book which I know he will delight in reading. I am occupied this very day in sending his statue of Dryope to Brussels, where the exhibition will give it a chance of being judged by better knowledge than is found here.[4] Your own brothers' works are capital—Julian's picture at the Grosvenor is admirable, in many respects, above the works on each side of it; and Waldo's statuette is exceedingly good also. They have, each of them, enjoyed a better education than is easily obtainable here.

My sister sends her kindest love to you. She had, some weeks ago, a serious attack of *peritonitis* which gave us alarm at one time—but she is herself again—after five weeks' confinement to bed. We are ordered to find mountain air for her, and must somehow manage it—but our Gressoney in the Val d'Aosta[5] is a barred paradise at present. Switzerland is our resource, I suppose. What do you think? We get, this moment, a word from your mother to say she—or "we"—may be seen in town this day only, as she leaves early tomorrow. I shall contrive to call this evening, and will keep my letter open to make it worth your reading by my news.

Friday, Aug. 8. I spent the evening very pleasantly with your father and mother at the York Hotel. They are, both of them, perfectly well and in excellent spirits. Their plan is to go somewhere for a week or two's refuge from the heat, and thence, returning to London, get to Rome as soon as the difficulties on the frontier are removed. For ourselves, we hope to leave in a day or two for St. Moritz, where Mrs. Moore offers us lodging in a villa she rents there.[6] My sister's state is beginning to require immediate change, and I have apparently no alternative. So, once more, goodbye and God bless you, dear Edie! Offer my best respects to your husband and believe me ever affectionately yours

Robert Browning

[1] Edith Story (now the Marchesa Peruzzi) translated Giovanni Duprè's *Thoughts on Art and Autobiographical Memoirs*. It was published in Boston in 1886, with an introduction by W. W. Story.

[2] When Browning left Italy in 1861 he was not to return until 1878

and then not to Florence. He went to Venice, where he made fairly regular autumn visits for the rest of his life.

[3] Daniel Curtis, an American who with his family settled in Venice, was a friend of both Story and Lowell. His home, the Palazzo Barbaro, was near the Palazzo Rezzonico, where Pen Browning lived. When Browning, just before his death, was with his son in Venice, he spent considerable time in the company of the Curtises; and after Browning's death Ralph Curtis, the son, who was an artist, was written 'about a cast being taken of his face and hands'. (*Diary of Miss Evelyn Barclay*, ed. A. J. Armstrong, p. [5] and *passim*; also Houghton, bMS Am 1239. 1; James Rennell Rodd, *Social and Diplomatic Memories*, Second Series, 1894–1901 [London, 1923], pp. 44–45.)

[4] The Royal Academy had rejected 'Dryope', Pen's most ambitious work, and the sting that Browning felt was still fresh. (Reese, 'Robert Browning and His Son', p. 796.)

[5] When they were staying here in the preceding summer Browning described the place as the 'most beautiful little cluster of cottages nested in a valley or rather pass through the Alps, just under Monte Rosa'. He and his sister reached their destination by a seven-mile ascent on mules. (DeVane and Knickerbocker, pp. 288–9.)

[6] Villa Berry, St. Moritz, Ober Engadine. (For an account of the visit see R B's letter in Whiting's *The Brownings*, pp. 252–3.)

19 Warwick Crescent W
Dec. 25, 1884

Dear friends,—

I make haste to say that I have just received your letter with its enclosures, and will give them to Mrs. Moore at once—she having arrived from America last week. I read them, according to your desire, and can judge what has happened, plainly enough, through an unfortunate mental peculiarity of seeing only, for the time present, the desirableness of an acquisition—and afterwards discovering that this looks otherwise in another light, and forgetting what has been said and done—and, in this case, written—under the first impulse. Nothing could cause much greater inconvenience, or subject the author of it to more serious misconception—a lighter word than you would naturally use to qualify it—but I have had considerable experience, and should hardly entertain very seriously any proposal to acquire a work of art which was not acted upon at once and past mistake —that is, a mistake in Mrs. Moore's mind as to what she had originally—beyond question—intended to do: it is a sort of "thinking aloud" instead of thinking in silence, and speaking definitely at last. I have a real sorrow that a lady, whose nature I know to be generous in the extreme, should, by a failing of this kind, cause—in other cases than the present—a doubt of the existence of generosity and something more important: but so it is.[1]

In my letter of a week ago, I forgot to say how grieved I was at the death of poor Hamilton Wild—of which I had been informed by Mr. Field—those were good days when we foregathered at the Villa in Siena![2] But this is Christmas Day, and I have many unopened letters lying beside me. I thought it best to acknowledge yours at once. So, with true Christmas good wishes for you and all with you, believe me ever

Affectionately yours,
Robert Browning.

[1] Browning was so appreciative of Mrs. Bloomfield-Moore's purchase of Pen's works that he felt inclined to make a case for her. As time passed her behavior caused him to express some criticism of her to Pen (Hood, pp. 276, 321) though the friendly relation continued until the end of his life. After seeing Mrs. Bloomfield-Moore in 1890, Story wrote to his son Waldo that she was 'full of excuses & pretences'. (Story Col.)

[2] In 1859. (See RB–SS, January 21, 1862, n. 11.)

19. Warwick Crescent. W.
Dec. 28. '84.

My dear Story,

I called yesterday afternoon at the house of Mrs Moore to deliver, as you desired, the two letters—hers and your own: but she was not visible, being confined to her bed by a bad cold, and I left the papers in an enclosure. By the evening post those which you now receive came here—with no other word in the envelope,—and I have the simply unpleasant business of returning them. I heard about the misunderstanding some three years ago,—hardly if at all, since,—and am very sorry to find matters are no better but apparently worse than before. Indeed, I gathered, from what I heard at the time, that Mrs Moore was still ready to buy any new work of yours, of which no "replica," by consequence, could already exist—the difficulty being in that respect, and not so much as to subsequent copying. If the fact of the Statue being itself a "replica" was duly explained to her, I fail to conceive what the objection could be to abiding by the terms of her agreement. I understood, besides, that if she had seen and been satisfied with the Statue, as she endeavoured to do at Paris, she would have accepted it in spite of what she considered disadvantageous circumstances,—but the owner was away, and her dissatisfaction had no chance of being removed. I can only be (once again) very sorry for what seems past remedy.

Mr Hurlbert[1] has just written to me concerning the Hawthorne calumnies.[2] I can have no objection to anybody hearing that I think them monstrous. The bringing in my wife and myself as witnesses of the spiritualistic experiments at the Villa Montauto is absurd—as might have been known by Mr Julian had he looked at his Father's "Notes"—wherein no mention of our names will be found, though he dwells on the minutest incidents: we had left Florence a month before he took the Villa, nor returned there till long after he was out of it. This piece of inexactitude,—the first bit of the book I fell upon,—warned me effectually off the premises. So much may be said "on my authority"—but I object to making any statement which may give Mr Julian the happy chance of an altercation in the newspapers: letters and letters!

Pen came here nearly a fortnight ago—very unwell: but we doctored and nursed and brought him round again. His love goes with mine and my Sister's to you and all with you.

I am, my Dear Story, ever affectionately yours

Robert Browning.

¹ William Henry Hurlbert (1827–95), American journalist and author. After 1883 he spent most of his time in Europe, but had to leave England in 1891 as the result of a suit for breach of promise, which, however, he had won. At the time of his death (in Italy) there was still a warrant against him in London. A letter by Story to the editor of the *Standard* (London) printed in the *Sun* (New York) on December 8, 1893 (p. 6) helped to refute charges against Hurlbert.

² The passage on the Brownings in Julian Hawthorne's *Nathaniel Hawthorne and His Wife* (Boston, 1884) included the following: 'In the year 1858 Nathaniel Hawthorne was living with his family in the Villa Montauto, just outside the walls of Florence. Among his near neighbours during that summer—the summer of Donati's comet—were Mr. and Mrs. Robert Browning; and they were often visitors at Montauto. Mrs. Browning was at that time deeply interested in spiritualism. . . '. (I, 30.) The publicizing of EBB's interest in spiritualism was abhorrent to Browning. Some of his letters to Elizabeth's brother George in the 'eighties show how much he feared what the public would say on this score when he was no longer alive to prevent biographizing and publication of letters. (Landis and Freeman, pp. 304–28, *passim.*)

19, Warwick Crescent, W.
June 19, '86

My dear Story,

I received last night the packet of M.S.—all thanks to your kindness. Had I mustered courage enough to look at the originals—undisturbed in their repose of fourteen years since I copied them for you—I should probably have given neither you nor myself further trouble in the matter—but my memory was hazy as to the precise charge which I intended they should meet —and fancied they were more than what they prove to be—a simple answer to the assertion (if it was really made) that I had been making endeavours to renew a relation of even ordinary acquaintance, instead of resisting cajoleries and pathetic appeals, for two years together, that I should do so. As bearing upon the writer's veracity this was evidence enough. And even with respect to the calumnies which Lady A[shburton] exploded in all the madness of her wounded vanity—I was not aware at that time of what I have had abundant knowledge of since—how thoroughly her character as a calumniator was understood by those most intimately connected with her—and how little credit would be given to assertions of this sort in my case. I retained exactly as much as I was disposed to value of the esteem and attention of every one of our common friends and acquaintance,—and in two instances—when I chose to volunteer an explanation of the causes of my feeling with regard to her,—I found that her nearest relatives had undergone precisely similar treatment. One of these,—whom I only became acquainted with a few years ago,—told me she herself had been treated as—and called to her face—"a thief."[1] There would seem therefore little use in casting about for means of defence against such a charge from such a person—*posthumous*, as her cowardice would take care that it should be. I shall nevertheless abide by your advice, and retain the original letters—giving such directions for their ultimate disposal as you very properly suggest, and indeed as I had always intended. So, enough of an odious experience—which had, however, the effect of enabling you and Mrs. Story to prove yourselves effectually and admirably my friends, as there is no need that I should gratefully acknowledge now.

Last week, my sister was on the point of going to Paris— where Milsand is unhappily far from well. My own engagements would not allow me to leave with her, but I was to fetch her back in a week. On the evening before her departure she had a severe return of the inflammatory attack which she suffered from two years ago. By prompt remedies the danger was averted—and she is convalescent, though weakened by ten days spent in bed. She is to get up for half an hour, this morning. Pen who was to have accompanied her to Boulogne, stayed till we had assurance that he might do so without apprehension. He left on Sunday for Dinant. "Our Palace"[2] will belong to us in due form, if there be any justice in the law-courts whither the case is relegated. My lawyer has no doubt of the event. He considered that I paid too much for the property and that as the Vendors' conduct "left them bound but myself free" I might preferably get a better bargain elsewhere—hence his hesitation to proceed against the Montecuccoli who, moreover, i If withdrew from the agreement, would no doubt intreat me to fulfil the same. But I decided to try conclusions with these "mascalzoni,"[3] and the proper "citazione"[4] has been issued, and my advocate selected. The delay will be tiresome, as the Montecuccoli are entitled to some forty days' grace, when a Venetian could claim a week only, or thereabouts. Moreover these people know that, whenever they please to take it, my money is waiting —meanwhile they collect the rents from the existing tenants. I leave myself no room for such news as are at hand. It is bitterly cold here—beyond example in June. I will give your message to Lowell, whom I saw two days since,—and shall see next week at Oxford, where Jowett's vice chancellorship ends in a festive bouquet of fireworks at Commemoration[5]—wherein a degree will be conferred on Dr. Holmes[6]—whom I have seen much of lately. Mrs. Bronson[7] and Edith[8] are here enjoying themselves and greatly adding to our enjoyment. They too go to Oxford. The Curtis family[9] will be here presently, I am glad to say. They were at Amsterdam when I heard last. You know the strange turmoil of politics in which we are engaged just now, and which will be intensified in a week or two. I met Gladstone at dinner the day after his defeat—and never saw him in higher spirits. I am dead against him, however. All true love to you both—from

yours affectionately ever,
RB.

[1] Since most Browning readers know Lady Ashburton only through one of Henry James's floating descriptions (HJ, II, 195–8), a more sharply focused account by a contemporary will help in the interpretation of the Browning-Ashburton association and of the references the poet made to Lady Ashburton (Walburga, Lady Paget, *Embassies of Other Days*, I, 280–1):—

'Louisa Lady Ashburton was a frequent visitor to Rome. She was most attractive and very remarkable. She always lived in Miss Hosmer's house and bought her statues. Generous, violent, rash and impulsive, ever swayed by the impression of the moment, she was necessarily under the thumb of somebody. Bevies of impecunious artists hovered about her like locusts, trades-people made fortunes out of her and adventurers found her an easy prey. Everybody thought her enormously rich, because, with princely generosity, she threw large sums away for any object that caught her fancy. Though she not infrequently offended, she always fully and graciously retracted, and her smile, with the light in her dark eyes, under the straight brows, put me in mind of lightning amongst thunderclouds. 'A woman of this type had, of course, staunch friends, as well as bitter foes, for she was all contradictions. . . . At her homes she varied between untold kindness and unmitigated tyranny. When she asked friends to her country houses she had either no room for them or she made hay of their rooms, whilst they were staying there. At her dinner parties she generally had more guests than she expected and more women than men. . . '.

² Palazzo Manzoni. This fifteenth-century Venetian palace had greatly impressed Browning, and he was delighted at the prospect of owning it, but in the end he did not acquire it. There was a delay in the negotiations, and Browning learned that the structure was at fault. His disappointment in not getting this palace, which was intended for Pen, was forgotten only when his son acquired the Palazzo Rezzonico.

³ 'Ruffians'.

⁴ 'Summons'.

⁵ The commemoration of founders and benefactors, which took place on June 30 in the Sheldonian Theatre, was reported by *The Times* (July 1, 1886, p. 7). One sentence reads thus: 'Shortly afterwards arrived the Vice-Chancellor and procession of University officials and doctors, among whom were conspicuous Mr. Robert Browning and Mr. Russell Lowell'.

⁶ 'A warm reception was given to Dr. Oliver Wendell Holmes, and the solitary good thing of to-day was hit upon by the fortunate individual who asked, "whether he had come up in the one-horse shay".' (*The Times*, July 1, 1886, p. 7.) In 1882, when Oxford conferred the honorary degree of D.C.L. upon Browning, a prankster dangled, from the gallery, a red cotton nightcap above his head.

⁷ Mrs. Katharine De Kay Bronson (d. 1901), a friend of Browning's last years. 'She was a most accomplished and scholarly woman, whose goodness of heart and charm of manner were paralleled by her range of intellectual interests and her grasp of affairs'. (Whiting, *The Brownings*, p. 288. For Browning's friendship with her see *ibid.*, pp. 242–95; Mrs. Bronson's articles 'Browning in Asolo', *Century Magazine*, LIX [April 1900], 920–31, and 'Browning in Venice', *Century Magazine*, LXIII [February 1902], 572–84.)

⁸ Edith Bronson, later the Contessa Rucellai.

⁹ The Daniel Curtis family.

19, Warwick Crescent, W.
Apr. 4. '87

Dear Friends, I got the letter of which I enclose a copy, two days ago, under the following circumstances.[1] A Mr. Shortall,[2] of Chicago,—with whom I had some correspondence last year concerning the representation there of one of my plays by an amateur company—wrote to me, last week, to say he was just arrived in London and about to depart thence, but wished first to see me for a few minutes. I replied I should be happy to see him, and on Friday he called accordingly,—a pleasant kindly person. He had—you will observe—no need of anybody's intervention on his behalf. The writer of the letter I subjoin chose to address me in the way you will see; and I think it due to you— hardly necessary as it may be—to show how far impudence can go. Pray do not even reply to this recurrence of mine to a hateful subject—but as you have so lately looked over the letters etc. of Lady Ashburton, you may as well know how the chief agent in that business professes to feel for me whom she slandered. Of course, I never have said a word about her to Lady Marian—whom indeed I have only met once, at poor Houghton's,[3] since I saw her in your rooms at London, as you remember, when Lady A. "tried on" conciliation—not quite with such effrontery however.

Although this is no letter-proper, only a brief notice I think necessary, I cannot help sweetening the page by mentioning that Pen writes in warm terms of Julian's picture for the Salon,[4] —full of cleverness, he says. I trust you are both well. Our winter has been abominable, and I found myself decidedly the worse for the want of my customary dose of the divine Italian air.

Ever affectionately yours
Robert Browning.

[190]

[1] Hatty Hosmer's note introducing Shortall, a copy of which which accompanied Browning's letter, reads as follows:

Churchside
Denmark Hill
March 31 [1887]

My dear Friend,
Here comes a very affectionate ghost from the Past. This ghost, however, has very often been with you in spirit though absent in shadow, and it was glad you had not forgotten her,—as Lady Marian assured her not long since, your enquiries proved. Now she is coming in the flesh to explain its long seclusion. In the meantime, pray smile kindly upon my friend Mr. Shortall who presents you this, and believe that I am as always

Affectionately yours
Hatty Hosmer

[2] Probably John G. Shortall (1838–1908), lawyer, of Chicago, who came to the United States from Ireland. After retiring from business in the 70s, he gave his time to public affairs and was active in literary and musical circles in Chicago. Since the Proceedings of the Board of Directors of the Chicago Public Library indicate that he, a Board member, did not attend meetings from January 8, 1887, through April 23, 1887, he may well have been in England at the time of Browning's letter. (*The National Cyclopaedia of American Biography*, VI, 458–9; letter from Mrs. Roberta B. Sutton, Chief of Reference Department, the Chicago Public Library, September 12, 1961.) I have found no record of an amateur production of a Browning play at or near this time.

[3] Who died in 1885.

[4] Julian Story's 'Épisode des Massacres de Septembre, 1792' was described and the design pronounced 'powerful and admirably studied' by the *Athenaeum* for June 25, 1887 (p. 836), in an account of the Salon exhibition in Paris.

[CA. May 1887][1]

Dear Friends, I have too long delayed saying what I can truly say that I felt as much astonishment as delight in seeing the extraordinary progress of Julian,—his picture is admirable for anybody to have painted it, and wonderful for comparatively a beginner. I was more prepared for Waldo's Bassi Rilievi,[2] but they are very charming too,—though not in as good a position as they should be for a full display of their grace & refinement.

Both painter & sculptor have "a future" within easy reach if they will only go steadily towards it. It gave me & my sister great pleasure to see them here. Pen, too, was much gratified by meeting his old friends again—a circumstance that will happen, I hope, without so long an interval as, this time, has been the case. Dear Friends, I cannot be sure we shall meet in Venice this autumn: I am turned out of house & home[3] by a Railway, and must get shelter somewhere by the winter: but if I can possibly manage to escape, you may depend on it I will. I trust you both are well. All kindest regards to you from

Yours affectionately ever
R Browning.

[1] This letter was written in or near May, after Browning saw the exhibition at the Grosvenor and before he moved to De Vere Gardens.

[2] In an account of the Grosvenor Gallery exhibition, the *Saturday Review* (LXIII [May 28, 1887], 768) reported that Waldo Story sent 'creditable work'.

[3] RB moved to 29 De Vere Gardens in June. In July he and his sister went to St. Moritz and returned to London in September.

29 De Vere Gardens, W., July 19th, 1888.

My dear Story,—I had just telegraphed to Dulwich[1] that I should be unable, to my great regret, to go there this morning, when your message comes—still more adding to my regret. I have a vile cough, and a general sense of indisposition which quite prevent my attendance on an occasion which I think will interest you—as it used to do in my case. *Ever affectionately yours,*
Robert Browning.

[1] The Dulwich Picture Gallery was near Camberwell, where Browning lived in his youth. Early in his life he became familiar with its pictures in the frequent visits with his art-loving father. In 1855 the Brownings and Lowell had been at Dulwich together. (Norton-Elmwood, I, 310–11.)

Asolo, near Treviso: Sept. 30. [1889][1]

My dear Story,

I can't help obeying the impulse I have had this long while to get some authentic news of you & Mrs Story, and to ascertain whether a note, I left for you at the Hôtel from which you wrote to me, ever reached you. I was in the country when it came, and, immediately on returning, called to see you but was told you had just left—only for a day or two; I repeated my call after that interval, and, finding you still away, bade them give you my note aforesaid—and, hearing nothing further, I left London quite uncertain how things were going with you—for you spoke of Mrs Story's health requiring the advice of Jenner[2]—and I fancy it may have been to the I. of Wight, where he was attending on Prince Leopold, that your visit was paid. So, to clear up all this uncertainty and set my mind at ease, I dispatch this scribble from the Asolo I made acquaintance with more than forty years ago, and have always had a longing to see once again.[3] My sister & I suffered from a disastrous experience last year,[4] and we determined to take our holiday after another fashion this time: so, after a few hot days in Paris, we went at once to Splügen, the village at the entry of the Pass: there we stayed in solitary satisfaction for five weeks in a house of which we were the only inhabitants,—walking ourselves weary, day after day, amid the fine scenery there,—the Via Mala on one side, the Bernardino pass on the other, the Chiavenna road before us,—with all sorts of diversions from the straight path to right & left. A week ago, the weather fairly warned us away—the mountains were covered with snow and the cold was proportionate—we crossed therefore to Chiavenna and Colico, and, by Bellagio, reached Lecco—whence we made for Verona: after a couple of days passed there, we got to Treviso, and—in pursuance of an old desire of mine, rested at this very primitive place, in the most unsophisticated of inns—where we mean to complete a week's stay, and, next Friday, proceed to Venice—there spend a fortnight, and then turn our backs to the pleasant South. I don't know whether I miscalculate entirely in supposing that you may possibly be in Rome again: if you are, I rely on your kindness to tell me something of yourself by a word or two to me at Venice, *poste restante:* if business or amusement are detaining you else-where,—at all events you will know how really anxious I am to get all the information in my power. Mrs Story wrote a tanta-lizing letter to my Sister, holding out hopes of a meeting which never came to pass. It was provoking that I happened to be away (a rare thing with me) just when you might have been sought and found. Be sure, however, that you and all your belongings are never out of my mind—though the actual sight of you is too rare now-a-days! My sister sends her kindest love to you & Mrs Story: and I am ever, my dear Story,

affectionately yours

Robert Browning.

¹ Dated by Browning's last visit to Asolo, which he made in 1889.

² Sir William Jenner, first Baronet (1815–98), physician, was appointed physician extraordinary to Queen Victoria in 1861.

³ On Browning's first trip to the Continent in 1838 he had dis-covered Asolo and loved it, and his feelings never changed. In 1878, after an absence of forty years, during which he had seen many places in Europe, he returned to find that his early love for Asolo had not idealized it. On this last visit in 1889 the reality of its charm and beauty affected him even more than ever.

⁴ The journey in 1888 was made with too much haste for Brown-ing's diminishing strength. Just after he reached Primiero he wrote Mrs. Bronson of his 'rather trying journey, what with the heat and his indisposition' (Whiting, *The Brownings*, p. 272), and just before beginning on this last journey in 1889 he wrote to his son, 'I am in an altogether different condition from this time last year—the day . . . we arrived at Primiero'. (Hood, p. 316; see also Orr, *Life and Letters of Robert Browning*, p. 387.)

LETTER FROM WILLIAM WETMORE STORY TO

ROBERT W. BARRETT BROWNING (PEN)

Rome
Palazzo Barberini
Dec. 13, 1889[1]

My dear Pen

We only received last night the very sad news of your Father's death—and I cannot tell you how deeply it has affected us—We had constantly nourished a hope that with his strong constitution he would get over this attack— and the final news came to us like a terrible blow—He was one of my oldest and dearest and most valued friends—and the world seems poor now that he has gone—Yes! for it is not only a loss to us who were his personal friends, it is a terrible loss to the world—that nothing can ever make up—The last words he said to us when we said good-bye to him at Asolo were "We have been friends for forty years—aye—more than forty years—and with never a break"—How true it was—There was never a break—never a cloud on our friendship for a moment—and the more I knew him the more I loved him—and the more I admired him—He was one of the best and noblest of men—Alas! that I should have to say, he was—I do not think that a small or mean thought ever knocked at the door of his spirit—much less even—was allowed to enter—Ever large hearted as large minded, grand in all his impulses—generous in all his feelings—vivid in his enthusiasms and the most living man I ever knew—I cannot believe it possible that he has gone from us forever—

We look back on those last days at Asolo with truest pleasure —What a delight it was to see him and hear him—and it will always be a precious remembrance—After we left him there we went down to Siena where we all used to live together in those summers long gone—and the whole place seemed full of memories of him and your mother and you—Almost—it seemed, as I stood on the terrace of the old Villa, where we sat and talked so many pleasant days that I could hear the very tones of his voice.

I wish I could offer you and Miss Browning and your wife any consolation, that I could say a word to alleviate this terrible sorrow—But what is there to say—I can only press your hand

and say—my heart is with you—and this helps not at all—or
at best so very-very little—

Where is he to find his last resting place?—Will it—can it be
in Florence as I would hope, beside your mother—I hope this
may be possible—

My warmest and most heartfelt sympathy for you *all*—in
these sad days—We all join in love—and best wishes—for you
all.

Ever your most affectionate
W. W. Story

I suppose your Father never received a letter I wrote him some
ten days or so ago—when from all we heard we supposed him to
be quite recovered from the attack of Bronchitis.

---

[1] This letter tells of the last visit of Browning and Story in
Browning's beloved Asolo. On October 31 Browning arrived in
Venice, where he took pleasure in the restorations made in the
Palazzo Rezzonico and in his walks and visits with his friends. He
had not long to live, for he took a cold and the bronchitis that fol-
lowed weakened his heart. He died on December 12, 1889. (Details
of these last days in Venice are given in the *Diary of Miss Evelyn
Barclay*, ed. A. J. Armstrong.)

LETTERS EXCHANGED BY JAMES RUSSELL LOWELL
AND THE STORYS

Friday Morning.
7 Otis Place. [Boston]
[CA. 1841]¹

Dear James,

Will you take tea with us this evening? the girls are to be here & I hope we may have a right merry time, you must come.

Will you ask William Story for me? tell him that it is a *tea-party* & the hour is 7.

> *Yours most truly.*
> *Emelyn.²*

¹ This letter would presumably bring together the four people of this portion of the Browning–Lowell–Story correspondence—Maria White (one of 'the girls') and her future husband, James Russell Lowell; Emelyn Eldredge and her future husband, William Wetmore Story. It was written before the engagement of Emelyn Eldredge and WWS, *ca.* August 1842 (Story Col.), and possibly after the engagement of Maria White and JRL, in November 1840. It was addressed to 9 Somerset Court.

² In September 1841 Lowell sent Emelyn Eldredge the following lines, part of a poem that is among the Lowell manuscript letters in the Keats–Shelley Memorial House. Doubtless it belonged to the class of poems that Lowell said he 'would gladly suppress or put into the Coventry of smaller print in an appendix'. (Prefatory Note to Elmwood, IX, v.) I quote, therefore, only the stanza referring to Emelyn Eldredge and her friend Maria White: 'So, ere I saw, I loved thee / For her dear sake alone, / But now that I have known thee / I love thee for thine now'.

[Boston]
Wednesday P.M.
[SUMMER 1841]¹

Dear Bill

This is the only sheet of paper you have, & I am afraid to look on the other side of this for fear of finding a blot 'or something,' & you have not any packthread so I have used all your wax. I did not get your note till this morning, so I could not send the book yesterday afternoon as requested. I went to Reid's & enquired for "Fairest Maiden" & he said he had it not. Whether he has or not I don't know. It is so hot I can't write straight or anyway. I am almost enough melted to seal this note myself. I hope the book will come safe. Remember me to the ladies, & so I am

Your just not melted friend
J.R.L.

P.S. I am now melted.

¹ This letter was addressed to Story in Salem but bears no stamp or postmark. It was evidently written in Story's law office. The 'Fairest Maiden' must refer to Lowell's first book, *A Year's Life*, published in January 1841. The dedicatory poem begins thus: 'The gentle Una I have loved, / The snowy maiden, pure and mild. . . '. In the second stanza Lowell offers his book to one like Una, meaning Maria White, to whom he was engaged.

No 4 Court [Street, Boston]
Mond[ay, CA. 1842]¹

My dear Emelyn

I was at Watertown yesterday & I think, from what Maria² said, that if you were to write to her & ask her to come & spend that part of the week with you during which your mother is at Greenwich, she would do it. Your letter inviting "Col Richardson & lady"³ did not reach its destination. Take my best love & give part of it to the Angel.⁴

Yr true friend
J.R.L.

¹ Lowell's address was 4 Court Street in 1842 and the first part of 1843. The upper right-hand corner of the letter is torn away.

² Maria White, whom Lowell married on December 26, 1844, lived in Watertown, several miles from Cambridge.

³ Unidentified.

⁴ The 'Angel' was possibly Emelyn's youngest sister, Mary Elizabeth.

No 4 Court Street [Boston]
Monday [CA. 1842]

My dear Emelyn,

I have just had a letter from the "blessed child"[1] in which she says that she shall be with you this afternoon (if it do not storm) prepared to stay a week.

Confess that you never [saw] any paper so thin as this & show it to the Only when she comes in, for I have bought some for her to write to Phranque[2] on.

Yrs ever

Jemes

Tell the Angel that after a good deal of philosophic investigation & laborious research I have come to the conclusion that she is a wixen. I thought it proper to let her know this as soon as possible.

[Written by a blot at the top of the page] This blot is unaccountable.

[1] Maria White.

[2] Frank Heath, whom Lowell referred to in 'Some Letters of Walter Savage Landor' and identified in a footnote: 'This friend was John Francis Heath, of Virginia, who took his degree in 1840. He was the handsomest man I have ever seen, and in every manly exercise the most accomplished. His body was as exquisitely moulded as his face was beautiful. . . . After leaving college he went to Germany and dreamed away nine years at Heidelberg. We used to call him Hamlet, he could have done so much and did so absolutely nothing. He died in the Confederate service, in 1862'. (Elmwood, VIII, 55 n.) The 'only' was Maria White.

Boston 12 April 1842
No 4 Court St.

My dear Emelyn

Last night I called at your house & saw your mother & the angel. They were both well. Maria read me a part of your letters, with which I was properly edified. I am glad Jane "Shore"[1] is so charming a person. She will be quite an addition to "the band"[2] when you bring her on hither with you. She will be introduced, I imagine, to a quite new & strange, & I trust, pleasant, state of society. I mean in our own little circle.

You are very gay, I hear, in New York, balls &c being the standard amusements provided for every evening. You remember I prophesied that Miss M. E. Line would soon get *accustomed* to such extravagancies. But the most unbounded imagination never went so far as to suppose that she would *like* them. Ah! we poor puritanical Boston people will seem quite tame & flat, I am afraid, to young ladies who have been in the everyday society of Moustaches, & who have met foreign ambassadors facetoface. One thing I beseech. Do not bring home a New York dress which by the extravagant tastes & propensities of the skirt will preclude the possibility of a friend's walking with you on one of our narrow sidewalks.

And so you have seen a "New York transcendentalist." Truly, it is hard to imagine such a personage. However, by steadily bracing the mind to thinking of angels in tournures or in French boots & moustaches, one can gradually recall the natural state of the mind & prepare it for receiving the idea of the strange species abovenamed.

But, my dear Child, I will leave nonsense, & say half a dozen serious words. I have an excuse in the fact that I yesterday returned from Salem where we had spent "Fast" week. You were all that we missed. We had a very good time indeed, doing, of course just what we pleased. We waltzed, or acted Charades, or enjoyed tete a tetes on the stairs or in the library, or joked or did *something* all the time. An ingenious friend who was patient enough to count the number of puns made in the space of twenty minutes, found them to be 75, or a little more than three in a minute. The recoil from such a state of mind is either into stupidity or a greater degree of nonsense. In my case, I experience an agreeable mixture of both.

I am glad you have been to see Page. I think he is, in many respects, the most remarkable painter we have, & I freely confess that I had rather have his portrait of Mrs Loring[3] than *the* Vandyke. If you see him again, do give him my very best remembrance & love. I wish Jane Shaw[4] were going to be painted by him. Has he finished his picture of Jephthah's daughter[5] yet? That will, I hope, establish his fame. The fault of Page has been a propensity to try experiments, a propensity ruinous to present & often to lasting success—as Lionardo [*sic*] da Vinci proves. He has hardly ever profited by what experience he had already gained, so desirous has he been of acquiring more. In short, he has seldom painted as well as he could.[6]

I should advise you also to visit Mrs Child.[7] Of all American women who have yet put their minds in print, she has shown the most of what can be truly called genius.

Visiting persons like Page & her will keep your heart balanced when it is in danger from the fashion & frivolity of which you must necessarily see so much. This is the glory of Art. It is She who has nursed the soul & kept it alive so long. It is She who keeps fresh in us some touches of our higher nature, some memories of a more divine & blessed life. I have not any fear for a heart so pure & true as yours is, my dear Emelyn, but if I were exposed to similar influences I should take the same remedies myself. I should read more poetry, the more fashion & hollowness I saw. For it is impossible for any one otherwise to save themselves from infection.

This letter is miserably written because I did [it] with a steel pen & because I irretrievably injured my handwriting in writing long articles with a similar tool. If you stay in N. Y. long enough I shall write again till when I remain as now & ever your true & loving friend

J.R.L.

P.S. Don't get engaged to anybody who will carry you to N.Y. We want you here.

[1] A play upon the name Jane Shaw. See n. 4 of this letter.

[2] Five young men who had been friends in Harvard University, including Lowell and Story, and sisters of four of them formed a group known as 'The Band', 'The Club', or 'The Brothers and Sisters'. They met for amusement and serious discussion of various topics and looked upon Lowell and Maria White as their King and

Queen. The Band had some members in addition to the inner circle, and Emelyn Eldredge was one of them. (Edward Everett Hale, *James Russell Lowell and His Friends* [Boston, 1899], pp. 70–77; Higginson, *Cheerful Yesterdays*, pp. 75–77; Phillips, p. 72.)

[3] Possibly the wife of Charles Greely Loring (1794–1867), the eminent Boston lawyer, in whose office Lowell worked in the early 'forties.

[4] This letter is addressed to Miss Emelyn Eldredge/care of Franklin Shaw Esq/ New York/ N. Y.

[5] Although great things were predicted for 'Jephthah's Daughter' and Page made many sketches for it, the painting was never completed. (Taylor, *William Page*, pp. 97–99, 248–9.)

[6] Page painted Lowell's portrait (which faces p. 116 of Vol. I of Scudder) during the winter of 1842–3, and Lowell dedicated his Poems of 1844 to Page. A few years earlier the two men had met and started a friendship that lasted a lifetime. They had an affectionate regard for each other and each had a high opinion of the other's work.

[7] Lydia Maria Francis Child (1802–80), American authoress and abolitionist, whose best writing was on slavery. Although she said that her natural inclinations attracted her more to literature and arts than to reform, she had little creative ability. Lowell paid tribute to her in *A Fable for Critics*. (Elmwood, XII, 69–73.) Howard has called attention to the part Lydia Child played in the lives of Lowell and Maria White. (*Victorian Knight-Errant*, pp. 46–47.)

[Boston]
Thursday Morning.
August 4th [1842][1]

My dear James,

I wished to write to you from New York in answer to your kind letter, but I found no time when I could do so with any degree of satisfaction to myself. Still most dear to me were those kind words, most welcome & cheering.

At first I knew you only through Maria. She was the only friend I had ever loved as entirely as it is in my nature to love. And she loved you—then you became a part of my Maria thought. And then I came to feel that you were my friend and if

I have not come to you with the story of my joy & sorrow I have felt that you were just as fully in my confidence. There is no concealment in my disposition. I can not seem what I am not—but there are feelings which deep in my soul I cherish far-far above words. I can not speak of them to any—no voice has this mighty feeling. I look in upon my own heart and I see the life which is there, has given no evidence of itself to the world—the full high aspiration of my soul—the strong & noble purpose in life—unalterably deep love in my heart—these have no sign given to any. Some thing will come, what has lain dormant then will become roused & waked. And the magician must be Love. Think not that I shall be deceived, no lighter feeling can I mistake for this which is so to renew my life. I have never thought I loved but I have longed to love some one worthy & great, a soul deep & pure. I feel that I can give as pure & holy a love as woman ever gave. I know there is strength in me. I feel that I have within me that which can not fade, which will grow to highest life. I feel that I can stay a strong mind, & in my heart sustain & cherish eternally even the strongest & wisest. Do not fear for me. I can tell when I am loved, I shall not need to look back upon past experiences, to hold up before myself examples of faith lost & love not returned. No woman ever had a larger faith & God will surely give to this a wisdom which shall make me to stand firm as a rock. You said I should be unhappy if I loved a man ardent & in passion & it must be one strong consistent & firm. I can think of no meanness or weakness in him I shall love. I must have the strong arm. But I can never suffer from neglect or coldness, this is what you meant I think. I do not fear it, I will make myself worthy the love of him I love, I shall hold it & progress it must even as my love must. If ever the time comes when I can say to all men—"this is my love here have I put my faith" you will see that you need not fear for me. You will see that I am a woman grown. Securely I shall rest, no wavering, no doubt but even perfect faith.

Dear James, you are a true friend to me. I know it & would often have told you that I felt this—but it was not then to be spoken. How little do we know what argument our lives to our neighbors creed hath proved. Little do you know the influence which has come to me through your love for Maria & through the holy purity of your every act.

Maria is the most beautiful woman I have ever known. When I am with her I realize that I am in the presence & friendship of one of the holiest among women. When I am with her I am content to live in her joy to read only the book of her life—then I lose myself & some times even I have forgotten my own existence as a living & thinking being. I do not tell Maria of my life because I put it aside as far as I may when I am with her to be more entirely with her in hers. And because too I have found no voice as yet to speak for me. It is not that I want faith & trust in her.

I have written what I should not have been able to say to you & what I have wished to write many times. I know you are a friend indeed. And you must know now that I do put my trust in you. You were ever the kindest & best of friends & all your words have given me hope & comfort. I wished to write to Maria but I have not time this morning.

Yours in truest faith & friendship—
Emelyn.

[1] The year 1841 is written in the margin in another hand besides Emelyn's, but August 4 fell on Thursday in 1842, not in 1841. Lowell's letter dated August 7, 1842, is a prompt answer to this one.

Boston, Sunday Aug 7. 1842
No 4 Court St.

My dearest Emelyn

I find your letter lying on my desk. I have just come from Providence, having gone so far with Page. I am not so fit to answer your letter as if I had not been up at 4 this morning, but I wish to answer it *now*. As it is you will not get this till tomorrow.

My beautiful friend, I have two deep reasons for feeling great interest in the man whom you shall love. First, the love I bear you which the love of a brother perhaps could scarcely parallel, for we seem but the more bound to those who are not tied to us by blood since they are our brothers & sisters by a wider law & a more beautiful dispensation. The next is a more selfish one— it is that in your husband I would fain have a *friend*. Not that I stand in need of more love than that with which Maria so encircles & luminously enfloods my soul—but the very fulness of my love to her makes other objects for love (on whom to bestow the overflowings of this heaping cup of my heart) needful to me. And this, dear child, let me say is the stamp of a true, perfected & everduring love. If you ever love a man *wholly*, if your love for him turns all your affections into one deep channel & divides you ever so little from other objects, if you say to your heart "Now thou art in thy duty, now thou lovest & cherishest but one & dreamest of him only, therefore take thine ease, thou hast much goods laid up for many years, I will pull down my old barns & build greater, wherein I may garner the overflowing harvest of thy love for him only". Oh be sure that this is the seal of a love as yet most imperfect of a love in its rudest & most elementary form. Love may be & is, in whatever form, its own reward— yet has many a true heart sorrowed & many loving eyes have been blurred with bitter tears as they looked on the unrequiting face which to them was sun & moon & sky & stars & all the glory of outward & inward nature.

I had written to the top of the page yesterday. I have finished the sentence which was then in my heart. Since then something has arisen to my mind which decided me not to finish this letter as I had intended. Truth to myself which God knows I hold dearest, & truth to you required this acknowledgement. The obstacle to my writing, dear Emelyn, is nothing which could breathe a breath to dim for an instant my crystal trust in you & in your love of me. Yet is it something which hinders me of that utter freedom without a full sense of which I cannot write a line. Neither has ANY THIRD PERSON WHATEVER influenced me in it.

No doubt, as we grow older & older—*we* shall become every day further asunder—but let us trust that nothing can ever divide our *hearts* or any hearts once as truly united as ours. We all of us have our weaknesses, these hearts must "wear earth about them"—but as you know & (better) as I know myself I have a true & humble hope to be true & noble. As surely as I put my faith in this heart, which beats so now that my firmness of hand fails me to write, I shall ever be your faithful, loving friend. If I have ever gone too far in my friendship—I mean in *your* opinion—for an instinct from God has always taught *me* that in friendship (whatever there may be of not far enough) there is no too far, you will forgive for love's sake. Whatever betide, from now through all Eternity, you may always look to me for a full & happy sympathy & put all faith in the best

of your loving
J.R.L.

I trust to you to show this to *none*. I do not fear to have all I write shown to all if need be, but I have sometimes found that implications may be coined of words, & a *false* meaning put in the lips of the truest heart, I would wish (for I do not know exactly what I have written) that you would burn this, or if you wish to keep it, keep it to yourself wholly.

[Boston]
Tuesday Oct 25ᵗʰ [1842][1]

My dear James,

If you see Frank Shaw[2] in the course of the week will you give this letter to him, if you do not will you take it to Maria yourself on Friday, it will be as interesting then as it is now & as it is not a single letter I will not send it by mail.

Come to see me when you can & I wish that were very often.

Yours most truly,
Emelyn.

[1] This letter was sent to 4 Court Street (Boston), where Lowell had his law office in 1842. October 25 fell on Tuesday in 1842.

[2] Lowell sometimes addressed Francis George Shaw as 'Frank'.

4 Court Street [Boston]
Thursday [1842][1]

My dear Emelyn

I have been busy night & day all the week or you would have
seen me. I write this to say that I shall come to see you this
evening, expecting the pleasure of escorting you to the lecture.
Give my love [to] the fairhaired & blueyed "angel."

Yrs truly &
Lovingly
J.R.L.

[1] Lowell had his law office at this address in 1842 and part of 1843.
Emelyn Eldredge was living in Boston.

[Boston]
Thursday Morning. Jan 2 '43.

My dear James,

I know you will give my letter kindly greeting, and the words
I shall send to you fresh from my heart will meet your love &
sympathy. Therefore, this sunny morning I set me down to talk
with you—and most dear friend, the joy I must find in this
commencing is after all the first & truest impulse.

I know it seems, nay it is, to you as to myself a long time
since we have met, & I do believe you would have had it otherwise & would have looked in upon me but for your hurry &
business. Not less however do I feel myself drawn to tell you of
myself, the hopes & experiences of my life—, the sweet friendship flower that has grown up in my heart, planted in the days
of our first acquaintance & nourished by the dews of Heaven to
be a strong & healthy plant, kept green in these days by the sun
of memory & a firm faith in the future. Many times when I
would have spoken of this my love for you I have been restrained
in the consciousness that these words are commonplace & are
not the fitting robe for my feeling. But in this world of ours it is
beautiful that such things are commonplace, at least in the
expression for that is somewhat.

[211]

For a time my tongue was bound, by circumstances which to my eyes became neccssity. I could not speak to you & Maria of the new life that had come to me[1]—but in your true eyes I have looked & found such assurance of peace & light in the end, that it was hard to realize that any thing new could be told you on the subject. All my life long I shall remember this silent sympathy which to my anxious, fearful heart was as the blessing of the Angels.

Now that the day has dawned & I walk forth in all the glory of my love, with every trust in God, my love & myself, in the serenest atmosphere of love which knows no fear or distrust any where, when my life is so peaceful & my soul moved by the infinite, holiest presence of God & truth—I am far worthier to be your friend, I have a new strength, I am a truer woman & all my sympathies have deepened.

No where on this wide earth beats there a heart whose nobleness & purity, whose rare integrity of principle my soul has learned to reverence & love so much as yours. Give me from this fountain that gushes so clear & fresh for all. Let me be your sister, as in a careless [moment] have you named me—take William for your brother, and you will find that he has a heart & soul noble & true. Ah! he is beautiful & good & true.

It is so hard to speak of what is so deep a feeling with us, I go about the world sighing for a word which shall speak the thing I feel. Ah! there were never any so full & deep, that they the measure of the infinite could speak.

Let me tell you now—for I am limited to this one sheet of paper for space & have a world of matter to lead me off from the fact—how much the "Pioneer,"[2] is liked by your friends & such of the world without the pale of friendship as I have had speech with. Every body likes it, & there is only one prophecy & that, success. I as being best able to speak for myself would tell you of my delight in it, you will do all I know, be all—say all. Do not stay away from us longer than you must[3] gain all the strength you can—take a new lease of life. Come back to us, let us not be out done in appreciation by the stranger, or in our consideration of the prophet. Some thing we miss, some thing that every day gave earnest of truth & depth when by the hollowness & insincerity of many persons we were oppressed— the surest refuge a true & lofty soul. I had a letter from Maria yesterday, she, dear child goes on her daily round of duty with a true & womanly dignity, now that you are so far off and yet most near.

I hooitated some time before I wrote this letter, knowing how numerous your list of correspondents must be & feeling unwilling to add to your duties. Do not answer this letter—do not write to me. I shall hear through others & I shall be content. It cannot surely, be well for you to write much & we dont incline to retard your recovery. Dr Elliott[4] may be kind & loving, but we are kinder & lovinger.

Maria is coming to make her long visit in town as soon as you return. Write no more letters—save your eyes. God bless you & keep you.

Yours in truest love. Emelyn.

Mr Page saw every body, heard every thing—he will tell you all, I have forgotten all if I have known any thing of the doings of those you are interested in & although I find it hard to leave you now still I have no new thing to tell you, unless it be true that that which can never grow old must be new.

[1] In 1842 she became engaged to William Story.

[2] *The Pioneer*, a monthly literary magazine, started by J. R. Lowell and Robert Carter. It ran through only three issues— January, February, and March 1843. A high standard had been set for the magazine, which included contributions from Poe, Hawthorne, and Elizabeth Barrett. (Introduction by Sculley Bradley to a facsimile of the *Pioneer* [New York: Scholars' Facsimiles and Reprints, 1947].)

[3] Lowell was in New York undergoing treatment for his eyes.

[4] Dr. Samuel Mackenzie Elliott (1811–73), born in Scotland, became a well-known oculist in New York. He was treating Lowell's eyes.

Dear Jem—

I think I feel well enough to send you a line this morning—in consideration of the fact that sunshine, so long denied to us, has at length been prevailed upon to appear.

You know of course I suppose that Bill W's[1] engagement is broken off—by Jane S.[2] I for one, am glad of it. I never thought she appreciated the frank & true whole-heartedness of Bill, and growing up within the walls of sectarianism, she seemed to have lost that breadth and freedom, which keep the mind & heart open to the sunshine of Truth. I don't think she was frank & confidential in her intercourse with Bill, either and fear, that she knew that she did not love him & would not marry him, before she went to Mobile. That, at least, I thought when I was there. Alls well now however—and Bill will love a nobler woman yet.

Andrews[3] has finished the Genevieve very well, & is printing it with a sort of violet-ink—which produces a more agreeable & softened effect, than the black ink. Upon the whole I think it will look very well. I was astonished to find that he never had read the poem, which I forthwith recommended him to do. He is quite an intelligent man & talks well—& has a genial feeling for art, which makes me think that he will improve in engraving. He thinks that the art of e[ngraving] is not at all understood & appreciated. But I don't know about that. All the scope that an engraver can have seems to me to be in reproducing the feeling & sentiment of the painter by a different medium, he has no chance for creation—nor play of fancy, and this excessive exactness, and irretrievable nature of the substance he works in, necessitate a certain cautiousness & timidity.

Nothing new is going on—but the election of Governor, which comes off to-day & Morton[4] will be the man.

Do you ever see Page & Dougherty?[5] do you taste the flavor of Downing[6]—now & then? or are you imprisoned, forbidden shell fish & those delights wherewith the delicate appetite loves much to dally,—and obliged to keep one of Waldo Emerson's lustrums of spare diet. How is it with you my friend in this

matter of food. Have you wet pellets over your eyes of zinc &
lead water for hours? Do you wear green specs & moustaches &
pass for a Lieutenant of adventures as on the John Dwight
night? Or what are your circumstances? A deplorable sense of
nothing at all in the middle of your body—called by Physicians
nausea & by the sufferers themselves by no cognomen, but by
their friends, home-sickness—or how? If you are not eyeless,
let me hear a word from you—& thank me for this

Yours very truly

W. W. Story.

¹ Probably William A. White. See WWS–JRL, February 23,
1843, n. 7.

² Jane Shaw?

³ Joseph Andrews (1806–73), engraver, did engravings for the
first two issues of *The Pioneer*. 'Genevieve', which illustrated Coleridge's poem 'Love', was designed by Story (under the name of
I. B. Wright) and engraved by Andrews for the February issue.

⁴ Marcus Morton (1784–1864) was defeated in this election of
1843. He was candidate for Governor for sixteen successive years, but
was successful only twice.

⁵ Addison Dougherty, the brother of Sarah Dougherty, who
became the second wife of the often discussed William Page of these
letters.

⁶ Andrew Jackson Downing (1815–52), author and first great
American landscape gardener.

New York Janʸ 31 1843

My dear Emelyn,

If you were not my sister (as I have always loved to call you)
before, I am sure your dear letter, which came like a fresh dewy
breeze upon my heart, would have made you so. Dear, fountain
hearted woman, be sure always of my truest love—& if I have
sometimes, perhaps, presumed too much upon my brotherhood,
it was all from love of you & of right.

I could not help writing you just a word. But I am forbidden to write by D^r E[lliott] on pain of retarding my cure, & I have three more letters which I *must* answer, beside writing something for the Pioneer—if I can.

God bless your kind woman's heart again & again!

> *Goodbye & be to me only*
> *as I am to you*
> *J.R.L.*

[Boston]
February 23rd 1843.

Dear Jem—

I should have written you many times ere this, but that whatever time I could give to writing, which is necessarily small, I devoted to the Pioneer,[1] which is very nearly the same thing as you. So you'll not think I was forgetful of the 'Young Raphael." Even now I stop a little gap of time before a Bankrupt examination to which I am doomed this morning, to say nothing, for that in fact is just what I have to say. The only difficulty is to know how to say nothing gracefully, which as I conceive is the great distinction between a simple ass and a complete man of the world. I go on the Thomsonian principle (G. W. T^2 I mean). Apologies on the first page—Reminiscences on the second, Exhortations to the correspondent to write on the Third—Love to all & the autograph on the last and a postscript asking a favor which it is ofttimes quite inconvenient to grant.

There are apostles of the newness here but nothing new except the mysterious Lady, who to make my bull[3] is rather old, and who is the main fashionable attraction at present. There was mesmerising at Mrs Bancrofts[4] last night, where Rolker[5] was, & came to the opinion "That it was for me, also, especially, very singular, more or less, and I, at once, came away unsatisfied at ha' p'st eleven." The concerts at the Academy still go on, & they played the Third Symphony of Beethoven the last time, played it pretty well which is more than I can say for their playing of the French overtures, which in the execution lack point finish & spirit, & therefore lack all that they possess of merit. Yes, there is one bit of news, which I would that you & Maria could have enjoyed with the Club,[6] we had a grand sleigh-ride, four horses in each sleigh—2 sleighs—27 people porters & a dance—& menagerie & games &c & home at 2 oclock—feeling as if the foul fiend had shampooed us when we got up the next morning.

How are the boys Page & Dougherty? Are they dead? Has Dr Elliot[t] cut all the blueness out of your eyes. Has Page painted you. Dont cut the moustache until I see you. "Shine forth, appear, be proud" in them when you return. Bill[7] is disconsolate, does not know who to take since Minns[8] has appropriated Anna Curtis,[9] but shows evident leanings toward Harriette Sturgis.[10] However this is none of my business, any man has a right to entertain his own intentions & views, without having all his friends at his key hole. I only wish Bill could be settled somehow, he would be so much happier.

I have now a proof to look over, and a Bankrupt waiting. Good bye. Get well soon & come home to the bosom of your anxious family

Yrs very truly
W.W.S.

We all remembered your birth-day Did you? and your mother & Father dined at Emelyns.

---

[1] Story contributed poetry, art criticism, and illustrations to the *Pioneer*, using his own name and the name of I. B. Wright. When difficulties arose during the preparation for the third issue while Lowell was in New York hardly able to use his eyes, Story generously came to the rescue by contributing almost a third of the issue. (Howard, *Victorian Knight-Errant*, pp. 128–9.) Edwin D. Mead, in an article entitled 'Lowell's *Pioneer*' (*New England Magazine*, N.S. V [October 1891], pp. 235–48) commented on the 'singular versatility' of I. B. Wright. Of particular significance is the pronounced interest in art that Story indicated in his prose articles for the *Pioneer*, for at this time he did not even dream of turning from law to art.

[2] Unidentified.

[3] Used in the sense of 'edict'.

⁴ Wife of George Bancroft (1800–91), historian and diplomat.

⁵ Bernard Rölker (d. 1888), LL.B. 1840, A.M. (Hon.) 1848, Harvard University. Instructor in German, 1838–56. (*Historical Register of Harvard University*, 1636–1936 [Cambridge, 1937].) Higginson said he was later 'well known as a lawyer in New York'. (*Cheerful Yesterdays*, p. 55.)

⁶ The Band.

⁷ Probably William Abijah White, prominent in temperance and anti-slavery movements. He was a fellow Harvardian of Lowell and Story and a member of the Band.

⁸ Probably George W. Minns, listed in the *Boston Directory* for 1848 as counsellor. Under the class of 1836 in *Harvard Graduates Magazine*, III (1894–5), 449, is the following: George Washington Minns LL.B. b. 6 Oct., 1813, at Boston; d. at Brookline, 14 Jan., 1895.

⁹ Probably Anna Wroe Curtis (d. 1860), daughter of Charles P. Curtis and wife of Benjamin R. Curtis, a distant relative.

¹⁰ Harriett Tilden Sturgis (1820–50), sister of Russell Sturgis. She married William Abijah White in 1846. (R. F. Sturgis, *Edward Sturgis*, p. 53.)

16 Court St. Boston
June 5ᵗʰ 1843.

Dear Jem

I received a letter from Page some two or three days since, accompanying the Cupid & Psyche which was rejected from the exhibition at N. Y.¹ None but a corrupted imagination could see anything indelicate in the picture & I shall put it in the Gallery, if it ever opens.

My object in writing is to convey to you a message relative to Dr Elliott, which I may have no opportunity of saying to you, before I forget it, & which may be of consequence to you. I quote "Tell Lowell, that I met Dr Elliott the other day, and he is anxious that James should write him all the particulars about his eyes, that he may send him the medicines that they require. E says, that it is not doing 'either of them justice to have gone home without having first seen him, and that now do the best they may, the cure has been greatly retarded in consequence.'

Therefore, the sooner he writes and tells all about it, the better. Don't forget" which injunction I have obeyed. Take Counsel, Cobus,[2] be a good boy & write and get well as soon as you can. These delicious days, which to-day prophecies, give me a yearning for green fields & trees—and sailing &c. After all, Court St is not so charming as Nature—but I am cooped up here, while you are luxuriating at your ease.

Are you preparing your book for the press—or writing anew the Present Life?[3] Success to you whatever you may be doing?

I send Emelyn's love for her. She unfortunately is not at my elbow to send it herself.

Yrs very truly
W. W. Story.

[1] Although the National Academy in New York accepted seven portraits by Page, his 'Cupid and Psyche' was rejected on the grounds of nudity. The painting was later exhibited in Boston. (Taylor, *William Page*, pp. 46–47, 62–63.)

[2] Shortened from Jacobus (James). Lowell sometimes signed himself 'Cobus'. (*New Letters of Lowell*, ed. Howe, pp. 137, 142.)

[3] Lowell's first volume of poems was entitled *A Year's Life*, published in 1841.

[Bussey Place, Boston
Late in 1843][1]

Our dear Mrs. Story,

We have been here in your little Eden half an hour & are obliged to depart into the world at large by (bad substitute for an angel with fiery sword, but as good as the age furnishes) the necessity of getting to *our* Eden in time for dinner. See Milton *in loc.*

And so in the best of highflying spirits
Goodbye & peace be with you

Maria &
Jemes.

[1] The underscoring of 'Mrs. Story', suggests that this letter was

written soon after Emelyn's marriage to William Story on October 31, 1843. On the fold of the letter is the following address: Mrs Emelyn Story / Bussey Place.

Elmwood Jany 1844.

My dear Will,

Expecting to see you in Boston, & having been condemned to an involuntary rustication which has hindered, I at last find myself compelled by all considerations of courtesy & friendship to take pen in (a very numb) hand & write you my sincere thanks for your notice of my book[1] in the daily Advertiser. It pleased all *my relations* & that gratifies me more than the individual pleasure which it gave myself. It shocked (I am told) some of the friends of the Psalmist,[2] but not that venerable harper himself who is a fine generoushearted fellow. I saw you & your wife at the concert last Saturday night, but was irremediably cut off from any contact with you by the musichunting multitude. Give my best love to Emelyn whom I hope to see before long. I have not got quite reconciled yet to your being independent householders[3] & having an oasis all to yourselves, but hope to live long enough to enjoy it thoroughly. I was very much grieved to hear on Thursday evening of our dear Mary's illness,[4] but found on calling at your Father's yesterday that she was better which relieved me much.

You will be glad to hear that a second edition of my volume has been demanded by an appreciating public & will be published in a few days. I am going to send Emelyn a copy of it on large paper as soon as I can get one from the binder.

Elliot Cabot[5] has a letter from Heath in which he sends remembrances to us & promises to write soon. I hear now & then from Harry Franco[6] who always desires to be remembered to you.

I shall most likely see you tomorrow, but write this in case of accidents. The thermometer's being but just above the freezing point in my room must apologize for my cacography.

Affectionately your friend
J.R.L.

¹ Lowell's second volume of poetry, *Poems*, appeared in December 1843 with the date of 1844 on the title page.

² Longfellow.

³ Story had recently married.

⁴ Mary Story.

⁵ James Elliot Cabot (1821–1903), who throughout his life was able to indulge his interest in flowers, drawing, and studying rather than confine himself to a profession. He had travelled and studied in Germany with John Francis Heath.

⁶ Charles Frederick Briggs. See JRL–WWS, August, 30, 1844, n. 3.

Dear Jem   July 29ᵗʰ 1844

I was very very sorry that you went before I knew your reason for so doing. The pleasure of having you there would have outweighed all pecuniary assistance in my power, & I should have insisted on your allowing me to persuade you to stay, at my expense. If I am really your friend, you would not scruple to let me do so, for this accident of money ought never to stand between those who are really in that relation. Let me entreat you to come back & spend the week more with us. You & Maria will be then together (a not unblessed thing for you) & I shall be also happier far.

I am here only for a moment & write in great haste. Believe me to be sincere & come.

Yours very truly
W. W. S.

My dear William,   Elmwood July 31, 1844.

I thank you as heartily for your hearty offer—which, however, it is not in my power to accept. I should have left Nantasket when I did at any rate, &, as it was, my "books" showed a balance in my favor of $2.50 when I left.

Have those imaginary guests of Worrick's¹ ("the Fessendens")² arrived yet? His Mrs. Harrises³ as Maria calls them?

Enter Worrick singing a verse of that highly popular ballad by David Mallett Esq[r], "I hear a voice you cannot hear,
I see a form you cannot see"—[4]
would have made a good scene in our drama[5] where the 1st . 2nd Sculteman & the Clown figured so pathetically. The scene might be "A wood" & the wood might be personated by Worrick's elm tree, an appropriate explanatory prologue having first been writ & spoken by the Neathead's servant in character. But why I am writing this nonsense when I am in a great hurry just starting for Boston. By the way you had better go over to Hingham tomorrow to the Emancipation Anniversary. There will be some fine speaking & some 3000 persons present.

Give my love to Emelyn & remember me kindly to the Parkers[6] & all the rest.

Affectionately your obliged
friend　J.R.L.

[1] 'In 1826 Mr. Worrick opened a public house near the south end of the beach, and called it "The Sportsman" . . . the resort of Daniel Webster, and other distinguished men. . . '. (M. F. Sweetser, *King's Handbook of Boston Harbor* [Cambridge, Massachusetts, 1882], p. 56.) The inn is still in use, known as Worrick Inn.

[2] Unidentified.

[3] Mrs. Harris was the mythical friend of Mrs. Gamp in Dickens's *Martin Chuzzlewit*.

[4] Probable reference to the well-known ballad 'William and Margaret' by David Mallet (1705?-65).

[5] A skit made up by Lowell and Story?

[6] Not Mr. and Mrs. Theodore Parker, who were in Europe from September 1843 to September 1844.

Elmwood. Aug 30. 1844.

My dear William,

I only write this note to shake hands with you & congratulate you on your yesterday's success. To congratulate you *&* *Emelyn,* I mean, for I know well whose heart was most anxious though absent in the flesh. A poem like that you delivered yes-

[222]

terday,[1] must necessarily shoot over the heads of all the "Fog-rums", who will go into ecstasies of applause over a bad pun if it be in rhyme, & I confess that I think you have reason to be proud of its reception.

Among other things let me particularly express my applause of the allusion to Slavery (coming in so of itself as it did) a point in your discourse at which I found myself on the point of ex-pogeing myself by a hurrah. But I need not speak of particulars, I went with you heartily throughout. Youth forever! against the world!

Your delivery struck me as eminently effective. I never heard any poem or speech so well spoken, as it seems to me. Though something of a Toilus I could find only one or two points to criticise. I have more to say when I see you. I am sorry that the *new* Miss Story[2] could not have been present.

I am in great haste, as I am to meet Maria shortly, & I have a letter to write to Briggs[3] who has just had a dead child born. It wrings my heart to think of it, & at the same time to say God bless you, on the birth of your fine child. Well, we only see in part & believe in part now. Give my best love to Emelyn.
Yr friend ever
   J.R.L.

[1] Story delivered his poem 'Nature and Art' before the Phi Beta Kappa Society of Harvard University on August 29, 1844. It was published in Boston as a pamphlet of forty-eight pages in this same year.

[2] Edith Story, born on August 23, 1844.

[3] Charles Frederick Briggs (1804–77), journalist and author, known to the public as Harry Franco. The letter Lowell wrote him is in Norton-Elmwood (I, 117–20).

Boston
September 2nd 1844.

Dear James

I thank you most truly for your very hearty words about my Phi Beta Poem. They were the most grateful that I have heard

[223]

coming as they did from one who could be so thoroughly depended upon both for sincerity and true judgment. You are the person who of all others I should prefer to like it.

I had many doubts concerning it & was at one time perfectly disgusted with the whole affair. I found myself writing under the eye of the public, & I was cramped & coffined. I was writing didactically & impersonally—& felt as if I dragged a lengthening chain behind me. This was when I was at Worricks. Then I intended to show it to you & ask your advice about it. But I thought it would be only a bore and if you did not like it, you might thereby be thrust into an unpleasant position. However, despite all this, I wanted sympathy and criticism, and I meant to ask it of you, as soon as I completed the poem—but your departure from Worricks before its completion prevented me from so doing.

I was well enough satisfied with my success, but not with my *poem*—neither am I now. The subject knocked me down as often as I strove to measure myself with it. I could not say anything that I wanted to say. I felt every thing slipping from my grasp, just as I thought I had it. I had hoped before pen went to paper that I should be able to condense in some measure my feelings, but the form & circumstances continually baffled that hope—and at the end, I found myself encumbered with the dead bones of my subject.

I have been repeatedly requested to publish the Poem, but I cannot make up my mind to do so. I really do not think it worth printing. I do hope, however, some of it will sink into the hearts & minds of those who heard it—for if it be stupid it is true.

But if that poem is worthless—one other poem, which I have, is not—my child (how strange that phrase seems to me) is a recompense for every thing. It is a fountain of joy, everincreasing, perennial. It is the best thing I have in life, except Emelyn. It winds itself round my heart, & teaches me a new life. It is a pure satisfaction. When you taste it for yourself which you will, you will know its value & also know how foolish all words are about it.

[224]

I have written nothing but about myself—but both Maria &
yourself have been so kind that I feel justified.

With love to Maria—believe me
Your sincere friend
W. W. Story.

Came Bridge Auct 11. 1844.[1]

Mi deer willyum,

Sense I see u i hev thort sum I shoed lik tu see thatair Brit-
isher[2] thet place uppon the staige! it aint reul repubblykin i no,
but considerin' he kils wun King & finely gits slortered himself i
think a tru democrat Might goe tu sea sech an exybishun With
prophit. i here a graydele About Brittish goald how thay ewes
it too korrupt hour Artillry hexions. ef u think thissar feller is
wun of um & is goin tu spilc ower fun nex Ma y i haint no idee
o goin butt as fur as i am kunsarned i kinder think I see mower
Brittish brass in one yere than evver I see goald in too howevcr
i giv in tu ewer opinyun coz u liv in the Sitty & no mower a bout
sech things then i do.

Ef u can git too Tick its so's Mariy cen goe if shee wunts too i
wil set L fer um. I wil let yu no a Mundy whither shee's agoin
or knott & ef u karnt fine no Boddy thet warnts the tick it y i ken
that's awl att enny Rate I will Bee sponceible fur it as is jest. i
shoed B.

i wornt tu C wun of these wild fellers amazin cuz thay tell mee
hee is a Sun off the mountin glen, hee & Mount the panther
(spelt painter out West but I gess i no) cuz the Song sez
"Mount & Macready then
Suns off the mountin glen[3] wich Menes hymn of
it menes ennybuddy. Sow wishin u awl helth & sperrits with luv
too ewer Wyfe & mi litel knees Edith I amm verry specfully ewers

yure O! begent servunt respectivly
JRL

[1] Lowell demonstrated his interest in dialect first in his imitation
of Burns (see Norton-Elmwood, I, 28–32) and later in his reproduction of the Yankee dialect (used in *The Biglow Papers*).

² William Charles Macready (1793–1873) made two tours in the United States, the second one beginning in New York on September 25, 1843, and ending in Boston on October 14, 1844. (William Archer, *William Charles Macready* [London, 1890], pp. 161–2.) Under the date of the last performance (October 14) Macready recorded in his *Diaries* that he received from Judge Story a note together with his miscellaneous writings. (*The Diaries of William Macready*, 1833–1851, ed. William Toynbee [London, 1912], II, 275.)

³ A play on two lines of Scott's song in *The Monastery* (Chapter XXV): Mount and make ready then,
Sons of the mountain glen.

Elmwood, Sept. 10. 1847.
My dear Emelyn,

You have by this time heard our good news, but in common with the rest of your sex (you know I have turned misogynist of late) arc probably dying for the particulars. At any rate, Maria is dying to communicate them to you. Items are naturally odious to me. I never read them in the newspapers (except on desolate islands) & then with a feeling of self contempt, as a child eats its supper after having proudly expressed its resolution to starve itself to death in order to reduce the too easily expugnable fortress of maternal discipline—a fortress which always has a traitor within. (I shall get to the Items presently—pardon a few preliminary wry faces.)

Consider this letter then as simply the "Elmwood Gazette," & read first under the title "Further particulars of the late happy event at Cambridge." On Thursday morning the 9th inst. the lady of James Russell Lowell Esq (late Captain of the Company of 'Cuirassiers' &c &c) was brought to bed of a fine girl. At one in the morning the first warning of the expected occurrence took place, & Thomas Scully (not a descendent of the traitor of that name who betrayed O'Sullivan More) the groom in waiting was despatched after Dr Hosmer¹ (Physician in ordinary at Elmwood) who arrived with the dowager Lady White at a few minutes before three A.M. Immediately after the more serious part of the ceremony began & a spunge [*sic*] dipped in

[226]

ether was held over the nose & mouth of the beautiful & happy sufferer. Before the hands of the clock indicated 1/2 past 3 the chamber resounded with the voice of Miss Lowell expressing a lively dissatisfaction at her extrusion into a cold & heartless world. Dr Hosmer was heard to remark that he had never witnessed so easy a labor. The happy intelligence spread like wildfire, & a general joy diffused itself in the bosoms of the tenantry. A feu de joie was kindled in every house at which (with that judicious thrift which characterises the management of this model estate) the several breakfasts were afterwards cooked. The fair mother is doing remarkably well. She was conscious of no pain, & is much stronger than was expected.

Now turn to the head "Further Items."

From 1 to 2 A.M. Mr Lowell makes himself generally useful.

From 2 to 3   ,,   ,,   ,,   ,,   ,,   ,,   ,,

At 3 Mr Lowell asks Dr Hosmer how he does.

At 1 minute past three Dr Hosmer observes that he is pretty well he thanks him.

At 3.5′ The ether is administered.

At 3.10′ Dr H. asks Mr L. whether his peaches have done well this season.

From 3.10′ to 3.15′ Mr L. gives a treatise on the culture of that delicious fruit.

At 3.20′ A general feeling of expectation.

At 3.27′ The child is announced as a daughter, to the satisfaction of both father & mother.

From 3 to 3.27′ Mr L. makes himself generally useful.

At 3.31′ The umbilical chord [sic] is cut & the "little treasure" wrapt in flannels, where it keeps itself from rusting by continual motion, while the solicitous attentions of all are devoted to the mother.

From 3.31′ till breakfast, Mr L. is puzzled what to do with his arms & legs & the other parts of his valuable person. During this period he gets in everybody's way & makes himself generally useful.

At 4 A.M. Miss Rebecca L. the aunt of the distinguished debutante is informed of the news.

At 5 A.M. The grandfather is let into the secret & forthwith embraces his distinguished son.

At 6 A.M. A handsome breakfast is served in a style doing credit to the Elmwood cuisine, over whose affairs Madame Ellen O'Something or other (née Scully) is understood to preside.

At 6.30′ Mr L. lights a little private bonfire of his own & his happy emotions so bewilder him that he does nothing but inhale the smoke & puff it forth again.

"Religious Summary."

A general feeling of thankfulness & a sense of the manifold goodness of the Father is diffused over the whole household at Elmwood.

"Further Particulars."

We have not learned what name has been selected for the young lady who arrived last night. Mabel is talked of—that having been the name of one of the wives of the first James Russell to whom the happy father is indebted for his own. Mr L. expresses his satisfaction with this arrangement on the ground that if the child should ever prove noisy, the name can be so easily & appropriately changed to Babel.

P.S. We are informed that Miss Robbins of Watertown has been selected to fill the responsible station of nurse.

Remarkable Child.

The weight of the child recently born in Cambridge has been ascertained to be exactly 10 pounds & a half.

Almost an accident.

As Mr L. was proceeding to weigh his daughter on Thursday morning, he adjusted the weight on the steelyards at the 9 lb notch, but on his proceeding to lift "the lovely burden," the child by a precocious exertion of weight, extraordinary in one so young, caused the beam of the balance to fly up so suddenly that, but for his great presence of mind, Mr L. who was leaning over it would have received a severe blow on the forehead. Gratifying intelligence.

Both Mr & Mrs L. are doing as well as could be expected.

Card. Miss Whatever-her-name-is-going-to-be Lowell takes

this opportunity of expressing her sincere thanks to Dr Hosmer
& the other friends who afforded her such ready & (on her part)
unsolicited assistance in her passage from Doubt to Certainty.

And so, dear Emelyn, with love to William, & hoping to see
you soon, I close my bulletin & remain

More affectionately than ever
Yours
J. R. Lowell, Father.

¹ Dr. Hiram Hosmer of Watertown, Massachusetts, father of the
Hatty Hosmer of these letters. In the Lowell papers there are records
of amounts paid to Dr. Hosmer at the end of various years. In 1847
the account for the family was $16.00 which included attendance
and medicine! (Houghton.)

Elmwood: March 10. 1848.

My dear William,

I begin with a cheerful confidence as near the top of the page
as I can, trusting that Providence will somehow lead me through
my three pages to a triumphant "yours truly" at the end.
Emelyn writes in good spirits, but I cannot help suspecting a
flaw somewhere. There must be not a little of the desolate island
where S.M.F.¹ is considered agreeable. It is hardly possible that
pure happiness should exist so far from Cambridge. One needs
not to go as far as Rome to find an attic, nor should I prefer an
Italian climb to an American one. As for ruins, you have there,
to be sure, plenty of them the work of Time & Goths & other
people with whom you have nothing whatever to do. But here
we have an excellent ruin on Mount Benedict² which we made
ourselves. And, if you mention political changes, Italy has been
getting itself born again ever since I can remember, & will have
to be delivered by a Caesarian operation after all. Beside, have
not we ours? It is not a week since Sidney Willard³ was elected
to our Cantabrigian mayor's nest in place of James D. Green.⁴
Mr Belcher has been dismissed from the office of field-driver. We
have two watchmen, who, I have no doubt, could put to flight

the Pope's whole civic guard. Deacon Brown has retired from business. Will not all these things be as important to the interests of mankind a hundred years hence as that Noodle VI sits on the throne of the two Sicilies, or Loafer XXI in the grand-ducal chair of Florence? If you have your Pio Nonos, we also can boast our Tommy Nonose, whom I meet every time I go to the Athenaeum.

Emelyn talks of roses in blossom. For my part, I think them no better out of season than green peas. I could never enter fully into these thermometrical and meteorological satisfactions. Have you had three weeks sleighing? Have you had the thermometer at 14° below zero? Have you stored twenty thousand tons of ice? I presume you have not even so much as an *ice-sickle* to reap such a crop with. But I will not triumph, seeing that these are things in which I had no hand, & it is not your fault that you have no winter. We are not without our roses either, & the growth of the open air, too. You should see them in Mabel's cheeks—roses without a thorn, as Saint Basil supposes them to have been in Eden. We are expecting a comet here every day as the newspapers inform me. I do not mention these things to make you discontented with your situation, but is [it] not rather wet in Rome of a winter? Make a clean breast of it now—if you should hear a party of English savages roaring their national anthem in a Casino, would not the "long to rain over us" seem to you touching & appropriate? Sometimes, as I have been walking briskly over our snow-crust, I have thought with a tender regret of Emelyn enjoying the interior of a hypaethral temple, with india-rubbers on her feet & an umbrella over her head. Never mind, you will come back to a civilized country and a decent climate one of these days. Men have different notions of things. You go all the way to Italy for the sake of stone-cutting, while we send all our rogues to Charlestown & set them at the same employment for a punishment. I suppose the occupation is thought to quicken the moral sense, & I shall accordingly expect great things of you when you return.

I confess I never had any very great opinion of the ancient Romans. They stole everything. They stole the land they built the Eternal City on, to begin with. Then they stole their wives, then their religion, then their art. They never invented more than one God of any consequence, as far as I know, & he was a twofaced one—an emblem of the treacherous disposition of the people. Niebuhr[5] has proved that they made up the only parts of their history that are creditable to them. Their descendants are said to be degenerate even from them, good for nothing but to loaf in the sun & do the world service by assassinating each other. God seems to have created them, or to have allowed them to continue as the natural food of fleas—a more valuable race than they. They are as useless as the coal-porters[6] (or whatever they are called) of the American Board of Missions. You may depend upon it that Americans will be objects of suspicion there if there be any outbreak of revolution. There are no warnings round the streets (as in decent Communities where a Christian tongue is spoken) to "Stick no Bills here", & you will doubtless be singled out as an early victim. My advice to you is to come directly home as soon as you receive this. I have it on good authority that the Austrian Government has its eye on Miss F[uller]. It would be a pity to have so much worth & genius shut up for life in Spielberg.[7] Her beauty[8] might perhaps save her. Is the Emperor unmarried? Pio Nono also regards her with a naturally jealous eye, fearing that the College of Cardinals may make her the successor of Pope Joan.

Mr Wetmore,[9] I suppose, will bring you all the news, & I do not know anything to tell you except what he will not be likely to mention. Mr Palfrey has been shot in a duel with Mr Winthrop,[10] & I have been elected to his seat in Congress. It is expected by my constituents that I should shoot Mr Winthrop & I am accordingly practising every day with blank cartridges. Longfellow has written a poem which Sumner & Felton do *not* think superior to Milton.[11] I have written one which has been popular. The American Eagle is anxiously awaiting the return of Miss F. whom he persists in regarding as the Genius of Columbia. A public dinner is to be given her in Boston at which the Bird of our Country will preside, supported by Abbott Lawrence & Peter C. Brooks as Vice-Presidents.[12] Page has captivated all the snobs by the urbanity of his manner, & is fast making his fortune. R. H. Dana has finished his life of Alston.[13] Somebody has written *"Four* years before the mast" and thereby become twice as famous as R. H. D. Jr.[14] But it won't last long, for I intend to write one hundred years before the mast which I think will finish the business, as the average life of a sailor is only seven years. Garrison[15] has at last found somebody to agree with him. (But I have discovered since that they only agree in thinking each other to be knaves). The new Review, the Massachusetts Quarterly has been united with the North American & the new journal is to be under the joint editorship of Parker & Bowen.[16] The Tale from the German in the Advertiser[17] is announced as to be finished in 1853. The Fourierites have built a successful phalanstery.[18] John Dwight, however, has left them & is a successful merchant on T. wharf.[19] Charles Sumner has written an oration without a single Latin quotation. G. T. C. has cut Mr Ticknor & made several new friends.[20]

I have been thinking all along that this was the fourth page of my letter & pluming myself accordingly. I should not have written the lines so closely if I had known where I was. However, so much the worse for you. I have told all my lies, & shall have [to] tell a few truths. Today J. Q. Adams's[21] body is received in Boston with great pomp. I am sorry that I cannot send you a programme of the procession that you might show the Romans that we can do a thing or two. The "Eastern magnificence" of the Theatres is nothing to it. The corpse will be followed by one consistent politician (if he can be found) as chief mourner. The procession will consist wholly of what the newspapers call "unmingled" patriots, & will, of course, be very large. I have sent in a bale of moral pockethandkerchiefs for the mourners & for wads to the cannon. The antislavery feeling of New England will bring up the rear of the cortege in a single carriage. There will be present on the occasion forty last survivers of the Boston tea party, & fifty thousand men who were in the Battle of Bunker's hill. But it just occurs to me that there may possibly be some kind of humbug in Rome also, so I will leave this part of my discourse, & ask you what you do for cigars? I know that the

Virginian nepenthe is so much esteemed there that one of the popular oaths is "per Bacco!", but it does not follow that the plant is any better for being deified. Weathersfield, I imagine produces as good onions as ever ancient Egypt did. But what *do* you do? I know that Vesuvius smokes, but do the people generally? And has the Pope shown himself to be a truly liberal prince by giving up the monopoly of tobacco? Tell him that it is expected of him.

By the way, I can tell you a good thing of Mrs Kirkland. You knew that she supports George Cabot[22] (who has turned Catholic I hear) & she informed some one the other day that "G. had never been in a situation to please his father so much as now. He has taken a nice house at the South End, keeps two domestics, & the young lady who consents to preside over his establishment, (Miss Livingston) is really a very respectable person for one of her class in life." But, if I expect to see the procession, I must stop here & I have written now more than you deserve. I expected to hear from you long ago.

Maria tells me that she has promised you a copy of my new volume.[23] But I shall think twice before burthening M^r W[et-more] with it. It has of course gone through ten or twelve editions but I shall send one (if I send at all) of the first, as being rarer. If you see my friend Dr Parsons,[24] give him my love & tell him that I have written him a letter in answer to his from Florence. I wish, if you can, that you would find out for me the address of the Brownings,[25] I mean to whose *care* &c. If the Pope should enquire, you can tell him that I am tolerably well I thank him & add any little complimentary speech which may chance to occur to you. It is as well to keep on good terms with these foreign potentates. You see I remain the same J.R.L. you left behind. I only add that I remain also the affectionate friend of both of you. *So goodbye.*

[1] Sarah Margaret Fuller (1810–50), a New England woman of remarkable intellectual powers, whose rebellious spirit and emotional frustrations characterized her unhappy and often misunderstood life in America. In outspoken recognition of her own intellectual superiority and unsparing criticism of contemporaries she

made an unfortunate impression on others as well as Lowell. She edited the *Dial*, the official magazine for the Transcendentalists, and wrote critical reviews for the *New York Tribune*. More important, however, were the influence of her dynamic personality and brilliant talk upon others and her book *Woman in the Nineteenth Century*, which shocked Boston and made her the leader of feminism in the United States. In 1846 she went to Europe, where life held promises of being congenial to her aspirations and intellect. She became an active supporter of Mazzini in Italy, married one of his followers, the Marquis Angelo Ossoli, and wrote a history of the Roman revolution. The ship in which she, her husband, and their child sailed for America was wrecked in a storm near New York; they were drowned and the manuscript of the history of the revolution was lost.

² Where an Ursuline convent was destroyed by a mob on August 11, 1834. Among the students who fled from the adjacent school was Maria White, later Lowell's wife.

³ Sidney Willard (1780–1856), professor in Harvard and writer, especially active in journalism and in public service. He was Mayor of Cambridge from 1848 to 1850.

⁴ James D. Green (b. 1798), elected first Mayor of Cambridge in 1846, re-elected 1847, 1853, 1860, and 1861.

⁵ Barthold Georg Niebuhr (1776–1831), author of *Römische Geschichte* (1811–32).

⁶ A pun on *colporteur*, a hawker, especially of religious tracts and books.

⁷ 'Moravian fortress-prison of the Spielberg, where the Emperor Francis played with his victims like a cat with maimed birds'. The Italian writer Silvio Pellico made its horrors the symbol of Austrian cruelty. (King, *A History of Italian Unity*, I, 38.)

⁸ In a description of Margaret Fuller by one of her contemporaries is the following statement: 'She certainly had not beauty; yet the high arched dome of the head, the changeful expressiveness of every feature, and her whole air of mingled dignity and impulse, gave her a commanding charm'. (Emerson, *Memoirs of Margaret Fuller*, II, 35.)

⁹ Thomas Wetmore (1794–1860), lawyer, the brother of WWS's mother. He was in Europe in the late 'forties. (*Diaries* in Story Col.) Phillips (p. 94) erroneously states that Mr. John Wetmore, an uncle of WWS, was in Europe at this time. There was no Uncle John. (James Carnahan Wetmore, *The Wetmore Family in America* [Albany, New York, 1861], pp. 455–78.)

¹⁰ Reference to a difference of attitude on slavery between two members of Congress from Massachusetts. When Robert Charles Winthrop (1809—94), who represented pro-slavery interests, was a successful candidate for Speaker of the House of Representatives in 1847, John Gorham Palfrey (1796–1881)—historian, editor, minister, and professor, who opposed slavery—voted against him. (See Robert C. Winthrop Jr., *A Memoir of Robert C. Winthrop* [Boston, 1897], pp. 67, 68–71, 76–77; also Elmwood, IX, 287–9 and X, 100, 106, 107.)

¹¹ The poem was *Evangeline*, published in October of 1847. Charles Sumner (1811–74), United States Senator and advocate of emancipation of the slave, who led New England opposition to the South; Cornelius Conway Felton (1807–62), professor of Greek in Harvard College and later president of the college; and Henry Wadsworth Longfellow (1807–82) were members of a club in Cambridge called 'The Five of Clubs', named by some 'The Mutual Admiration Society'. Both Sumner and Felton shared the general enthusiasm for *Evangeline*. (Edward L. Pierce, *Memoir and Letters of Charles Sumner* [Boston, 1893], III, 34; see Felton's review of *Evangeline* in the *North American Review* (January 1848].)

¹² Abbott Lawrence (1792–1855), prominent business man, politician, and philanthropist, who was minister to Great Britain from 1849 to 1852; and Peter C. Brooks (1767–1849), merchant, could hardly have been concerned about Margaret Fuller, idealist and promoter of feminism.

¹³ Washington Allston (1779–1843), artist and author. His second wife was the sister of R. H. Dana, Sr. (1787–1879), poet and journalist. Lowell's ironical remark referred to Dana's procrastination. Thirty years later, at the time of Dana's death, the biography was still not finished, the material being later used by J. B. Flagg for the most complete existing account of the artist. (See Lowell's description of Dana in *A Fable for Critics* [Elmwood, XII, 54.].)

¹⁴ Richard Henry Dana, Jr. (1815–82), lawyer and author, best known for *Two Years Before The Mast* (1840). He, Lowell, and Story were friends from their youth. (Norton-Elmwood, III, 96–97, 313–4.)

¹⁵ William Lloyd Garrison (1805–79), reformer, who devoted many years to the abolitionist movement. His violent uncompromising manner made it difficult for even his supporters to work with him. (See Higginson, *Contemporaries*, pp. 248–51; and Lowell's comment in Norton-Elmwood, I, 173–4.)

¹⁶ Lowell was not serious about the joint editorship. Theodore Parker, alive to the need for changes in religious, political, and social life and thinking, did not look with sympathy upon the *North*

American Review (1815–1939/40), a literary and historical journal. When Francis Bowen (1811–90), philosopher, author, and professor in Harvard College, edited it from 1843–53, he depended largely upon old subjects and old techniques and ignored the changes and vital problems of the time.

[17] *Boston Daily Advertiser* (1813–1929), the first successful daily newspaper published in New England.

[18] Lowell was thinking of the ill-fated Brook Farm phalanstery and the declining vogue of Fourierism. Brook Farm, a co-operative community with outstanding intellectual leaders, was set up near Boston, Massachusetts, in 1841. Two years later it came under the influence of the socialistic system of Fourierism, which was affecting reform groups in the United States at that time. In the summer of 1844 the building of a phalanstery, somewhat on the plan of a Fourierite community house, was begun; but in 1846, before its completion, it was destroyed by fire. Brook Farm did not recover from the loss and was dissolved in 1847. (See Lindsay Swift, *Brook Farm* [New York, 1900]; and Zoltán Haraszti, *The Idyll of Brook Farm* [Boston, 1937].)

[19] This is more irony. John Sullivan Dwight (1813–93), music critic and editor, was one of the most faithful members of Brook Farm, remaining until it came to an end. According to his biographer he had 'no financial skill' and 'no faculty for making money'. (George Willis Cooke, *John Sullivan Dwight* [Boston, 1898], pp. 83–84, 121, 266, 273.)

[20] This is written in the spirit of playful humour that pervades the letter. George Ticknor Curtis (1812–94), lawyer and writer, who married Mary Story, and his uncle George Ticknor (1791–1871), author and educator, were devoted kinsmen. It is not likely that Lowell was referring to William Davis Ticknor.

[21] John Quincy Adams (1767–1848), sixth President of the United States, had died on February 23 in Washington.

[22] The people in this paragraph are unidentified.

[23] With its failure to attract the readers that had made possible three editions of Lowell's 1844 *Poems*, his *Poems, Second Series*, published at the end of 1847, never reached a second edition; and Lowell himself seemingly had little interest in this book. (Howard, *Victorian Knight-Errant*, p. 230.)

[24] Thomas William Parsons (1819–92), dentist and writer, best known as translator of Dante. (See *Letters of C. E. Norton*, ed. Sara Norton, I, 119.)

[25] Lowell had just written a review of Browning, which was published in the *North American Review* in April 1848 (LXVI, 357–400).

Rome April 28—1848.

Dear James

To-night, when the Girandola[1] should be & is not on account of the rain, despite utter fatigue of various kinds, and a general stupidity I cannot help answering your letter which reached me some weeks ago by Mr Wetmore and gave me much pleasure. Write often, & let me know whether Sydney Willard really is mayor & whether he still "hangs his sign out" and keep me 'au fait' at the Cambridge news in the political & poetical line, and at the domestic news of the family at Elmwood. If I could sit down with you for an evening and talk freely there are many things which I could tell you of some interest—but on paper I can do nothing. There is here as much humbug as any where in the world, & if you were here you would enjoy laughing at your fellow creatures to your heart's content. All this week for instance has been a series of the most consummate humbugs that it has ever been my fortune to witness. Holy Week it has been, and all sorts of ceremonies have been going on, most of them senseless and superstitious, with a penny worth of religion to a ton of form. I have heroically done up the week, after crowding pushing & sweating and toiling day after day, and saving some one or two things the result has been 'bosh.' I have seen the Pope wash the feet of twelve fellows in white foolscaps, and at peril of my life have obtained over the heads of a garlic smelling & foetid crowd a sight of the same august person serving at the apostles table twelve fat fellows who eat away like mad & were the only people in the room who at all enjoyed the affair. It was with difficulty that the Pope himself could keep his countenance while he was performing this solemn farce and every now & then a grim smile would wrinkle up his features despite his best endeavors. Then again I have seen the washing of the pilgrims feet at the Trinita dei Pellegrini[2] the pilgrims being without exception the rummiest set of customers I ever saw, stupid dirty and bestial in their appearance—and indeed I have seen every thing that the week has. A crowd is always bad enough, but an Italian crowd is of all the very worst—such smells are not to be imagined—asafoetida would be Lubins choicest perfume compared with the breaths of some of the Italians—reeking as they do with snuff & garlic, & strong enough to strike a man of delicate nerves down. And in these crowds I have spent the better part of the last seven days.

Some things there have been which have been beautiful & affecting. To hear Allegri's Miserere[3] in the Sistine Chapel with the awful and mighty figures of Michel Angelo looking down on one from the ceiling—to hear Guglielmis Miserere[4] in St Peters while the gloom of evening was gathering in the lofty aisles and shrouding the frescoed domes was no humbug—but a deeply affecting and solemnly beautiful experience. Never can one forget the plaintive wailing of the voices which seemed to float in the air & to implore pity & pardon. Then again the illumination of St Peters, was as magical & fairy like as an Arabian night's enchantment the architecture seeming as if traced by a pencil of fire on the blue dark firmament. First it looked like a dream when it was covered with the lanterns, the whole body of the church being lost & only the lines of light gleaming along the outlines & ribs & cornices. Then when the second illumination came it was like a huge jewelled tiara, the gems of which flickered in the air. Bah! how can one give any idea of such a spectacle. Imagine a swarm of enormous cucullos gathering round the dome, & fluttering there—or fancy the stars falling like a snow of fire on to it and lodging in every nook & over every line—or recall every brilliant and magical & fantastic image that your dreams have given you & describe it for your self in your own imagination—or else come & see it. These things were worth seeing & cannot be forgotten.

I had hoped to get a glimpse of your book[5] nay rather to make a deep exploration into it and was very much disappointed when Mr Wetmore arrived without it. If you have a chance pray send it to me. What do you think of Tennysons new Poem?[6] I have not yet had time to find out Brownings address. He & his wife are however now in Florence—how long they are to stay there I do not know. Ida Hahn Hahn[7] is in Naples and we shall see her I hope. When I write again I will send you Brownings address particularly. Cigars are very good here & only cost a cent & a half. One can get Spanish cigars of any & every quality and price but not such ones as we have at home. I am now thinking of going to Naples, but as the time draws near, I hate the more to leave Rome—so utterly exhaustless is it & so strongly have I become attached to it. How I shall ever endure the restraint and bondage of Boston I know not. Still there are a great many things there which Italy has not & which are great & good. There is life & thought & progress of ideas & political liberty.

This is all now. If I am stupid set it down to fatigue & not to ill manners. Give my best love to Maria & give a kiss to Mabel for me & remember me as

Yr friend
W. W. S.

I hear nothing from Fr[ank] Heath although I have written to him. Emelyn's best love to you—and Maria & the whole family, in which I join also.

[1] In a narrow sense, a Catherine wheel; in an extended sense, a fireworks display.

[2] A hospital for poor convalescents was at Santa Trinità dei Pellegrini. (*Roba di Roma*, I, 55.)

[3] A work of the Italian composer Gregorio Allegri (1582c.–1652).

[4] Work of Pietro Guglielmi (1727–1804), Italian composer of operas and church music.

[5] *Poems, Second Series.*

[6] *The Princess*, published in December 1847. On April 24, 1849, Story recorded his opinion of the poem in his journal: 'I was on the whole disappointed with the Poem. It is pretty and in some parts beautiful—but it is not up to his mark. It has no serious aim & is often affected in manner'. A burlesque without humour in the beginning but ending well; the whole needing compression; beauty in some of

the lyrics—such were Story's criticisms of the poem. (Story Col.)
Lowell wrote a favourable review of *The Princess*, which was published in the *Massachusetts Quarterly Review* in March 1848 (I, 256–9).

[7] Countess Ida Hahn-Hahn (1805–80), German author of poetry,
novels, travel books, and—after her conversion to Catholicism in
1850—of religious works.

Rome March 21. 1849.

My dear Jem—
 Emelyn has just been reading me her long letter to Maria, in
which she has entirely exhausted all external topics of interest,
catalogued our movements & doing, and left me only a reaped
field to glean. But as the Crawfords[1] are just leaving for America,
& have offered to become the Harnden & Co of all scribblings,
without charge, I cannot forego the pleasure of heaping a large
basket of coals on your head in the way of a letter. You know
very well what twitchings of conscience you ought to have in
receiving this, for a gentleman of leisure like you, having nothing
to do but to rear hens and write verses, & patronize the landscape, & gather ideal crops of poetry ought fairly to be ashamed
of forgetting his friends as you have me. However assuming the
high pedestal, I forgive you. I stretch out my hand & pardon
you—as a true Christian like myself always does. Considering
this matter then settled let me tell you, that, (no thanks to you
however) I have known & seen you lately through your books[2]—
which at one instance were sent by Edward Eldredge & which
"cheered but not inebriated" many of our hours. I see that in a
moment I shall be telling you just what Emelyn has already,
how, one night as I was going out of the theatre, a stout fair
German with a moustache placed his hand on my shoulder, how
this figure resolved itself into Frank Heath—and how I caught
him brought him to No. 4272 Via della Scala 2nd piano back
room, gave him a glass of wine and stared at him & talked to
him until two oclock in the morning. Just then we had received
your books that very day—and as soon as we had got over our
surprise we took you into our company, & laughed heartily over
your jokes, true as good—& plunged into the deeper waters of

your poems—, feeling that we were all three together—once again. The Biglow Papers[3] I used to read to convulsed audiences at our weekly "at home" on Sunday eve[nin]gs, giving them as well as I could the true Yankee twang and one ev[enin]g I interpreted in the same tones one of them to the Brownings, who were quite as much amused & delighted as I. Always as I read— Frank as of old lifted his feet & burst forth bowing down under a storm of laughter. (You remember his way). The Fable for Critics[4] is admirable—and just what I think in almost all points. It is very witty and as the English say "amazingly clever." Once or twice you were biased by friendships (how can one help being, it is so graceful an error) and once by prejudice—but you know this really as well as I. There is but one thing I regretted, and that was, that you drove your arrow so sharply through Miranda.[5] The joke of "Tiring-woman to the Muses" is too happy—but because fate has really been unkind to her, & because she depends on her pen for her bread & water (& that is nearly all she has to eat) & because she is her own worst enemy, and because through her disappointment & disease, which embitter every one, she has struggled most womanfully & stoutly, I could have wished you had let her pass scot-free. But in all other respects I admired in the sense of wonder & delight at your great facility & felicity. You beat Butler at rhymes & everybody at puns, and men are all made to wait on true criticism. I know nobody in the world who could have written the Fable but you.

In your poems I find more poetry than in your previous volumes—true simple strength & a finer vein of thought & feeling—and as you know what I thought of the former volumes, you may judge how much I like this.

Frank H[eath] is as charming as ever—as Hamlet-like in every respect—his mind the same, but enriched and developed & Germanised. How much I enjoy his society & friendship here, you can easily imagine. It was a dream that I never expected to be realised to have him & Rome together—and now we are together every day riding on the Campagna, visiting the ruins, seeing the Vatican by torchlight & the Coliseum by Bengal lights, and sitting up to two & three oclock at night, talking over old days, philosophizing on art & criticising men & politics.

The Brownings & we became great friends in Florence[6]—and of course we could not become friends without liking each other. He, Emelyn says is like you—judge from this portrait. He is of my size but slighter—with straight black hair—small eyes, wide apart, which he twitches constantly together, a smooth face, slightly aquiline nose—and manners nervous & rapid. He has great vivacity, but not the least humor—some sarcasm, considerable critical faculty, and very great frankness—& friendliness of manner & mind. Mrs B is very petite, & resembles in manners & expression Augusta King[7] more than any one else I know. She used to sit buried up in a large easy chair, listening & talking very quietly & pleasantly with nothing of that peculiarity which one would expect from reading her poems. Her eyes are small, her mouth large, she wears a cap & long curls. Very unaffected & pleasant & simple hearted is she, and Browning says "Her poems are the least good part of her." I talked to them much about you & they seemed to feel a good deal of interest in American writers.

I have been hard at work—this winter, making a model statuette for the statue of Father & a statuette of Endymion which I wish I could show to you. Once in a while I write verses —& I think I have written better here than ever before—which is not perhaps saying much. I have hundreds of statues in my head to make but they are in the future tense.

Powers I knew very well in Florence. He is a man of great mechanical talent & natural strength of perception—but no poetry is in his composition & I think no creative power.[8] His busts are [by] far his finest works. I say this only to you—for it will not do for me to speak out my thought to the world in this respect. Besides Powers has been very kind to me & I would not for the world prevent the world from thinking him the greatest sculptor of the age. I can not however. When I compare him to Page, I feel his inferiority—and after all I have met very few if any persons who affect me so truly as men of *genius* as Page. Certainly there are very few *artists* like him.

This letter has been written during a visit from Mrs Cropsey[9] with whom I have been keeping up a constant conversation—& this may account for its fragmentariness. Give my love to Maria —kiss little Mabel for me write to me soon & with remembrances of kindness to your Father & sister believe me

Yours very truly

W. W. Story

[1] Thomas Crawford (1813–57), an American sculptor whose ability was often overrated by his contemporaries. Commissions for the bronze figure *Freedom* on the dome of the national Capitol, a group of figures for its north pediment, and the bronze doors for the Senate wing were acknowledgements of his countrymen's high regard for his work. In the 40s Rome became his permanent residence. (Gardner, *Yankee Stonecutters*, pp. 25–27, 62–63.) Harnden & Co. was a Boston passage and ticket office.

[2] Probably Lowell's *Poems, Second Series*, published at the end of 1847, though dated 1848, in addition to the books Lowell published in 1848: *A Fable for Critics; The Biglow Papers, First Series; The Vision of Sir Launfal.*

[3] The first series of *The Biglow Papers*, a political satire, was written in opposition to the Mexican War.

[4] A humourous verse satire directed at Lowell's American contemporaries.

[5] Miranda was Margaret Fuller. Irritation with Margaret Fuller for her criticism of him in an essay on American literature may have provoked Lowell to begin *A Fable for Critics* and caused her to stick in his mind as the poem advanced. (See Howard, *Victorian Knight-Errant*, pp. 261–4.) Although Lowell considered cutting Miss Fuller out of the poem, in the end he left her in, as unmistakably identified to the reader as the authors Lowell criticized by name. (Elmwood, XII, 62–64.) While M. Fuller was in Rome Story and his wife became intimate friends of hers. (Emerson, *Memoirs of Margaret Fuller*, II, 281–93; letters and journals in Story Col.)

[6] HJ says that the Storys and the Brownings met 'between the Storys' arrival at Genoa [1847] and their advance upon Rome early in 1848' (I, 96); and he leaves the impression that his information came from one of the notebooks that the Storys used for diaries, sketches, and other memoranda. I have not found this information in any of the notebooks in the Story Collection, and other references point to a later meeting. Lowell asked for Browning's address on

March 10, 1848, and Story, in his reply from Rome on April 28, 1848, implied that he had not yet met Browning, 'I have not yet had time to find out Brownings address. He & his wife are however now in Florence'. In the autumn of 1848 the Storys went to Florence and stayed there until February, when they returned to Rome. From Rome Story wrote Lowell in the present letter of March 21, 1849, 'The Brownings & we became great friends in Florence. . . '. Story's statement suggests that this was the first meeting, and a letter from Margaret Fuller (Ossoli) definitely shows that it was. In January 1849 she wrote from Rome to Emelyn Story, 'I have a letter from Mrs. Browning in which she expresses their pleasure in making your acquaintance'. (Story Col.) It seems, then, that the Brownings and the Storys met during the late months of 1848 or in January of 1849.

7 A friend of Story's sister Mary and a member of a group of young people that Lowell and Story had belonged to, 'the Band'.

8 Hiram Powers's outstanding reputation was ephemeral. Story's opinion of his work approximates the later and more considered criticism of the 'ingenious Yankee mechanic'. (Gardner, *Yankee Stonecutters*, p. 31; Taft, *The History of American Sculpture*, p. 70.)

9 Wife of Jasper Francis Cropsey (1823–1900), American land-scape painter.

Elmwood, September 23. 1849[1]

My dear William,

A conversation kept up (as between two deaf persons, with pen & ink) across three thousand miles of ocean, can hardly expect the merit of liveliness, however rich it may be in graver elements. It would be a good debating or controversial distance. The long space of time between the discharges of each gun would allow the smoke to clear away, in whose gathering fumes the disputants are apt to forget the original matter of argument. Or perhaps a loveletter—as that kind of composition is singularly retentive of life (witness those of Heloise—in Latin, too—witness those of many a defendant in suits for the least defensible of breaches) might carry its vital heat across those weary leagues of salt water, as easily as down through dry & cold centuries of time.

But I am not holding a disputation with you—be thankful for that & read on with cheerful hope. Neither am I writing a loveletter, yet I will satisfy here an emotion which enters into the composition of every solid & honest one, & discharge at least the debt of gratitude, however small the amount of assets may be that remains for the liquidation of my epistolary obligations.

How did you know anything about it? How did you guess that I had been wishing for one? that Maria had intended to surprise me with the New Year's gift of a Chinese one, & searched all Boston in vain? Yours came just in the nick of time to fill a gap of which I had precisely then become conscious in the furniture of my otherwise well fitted study. The very cigar I am now smoking came out of its kindly bosom—the hamadryad of that fortunate tree—smacking of Sorrento, & giving me a feeling of regard for the olive, a shabby tree in the main & no-wise comparable to our elm, & whose better part we get in flasks & jars. Not so neither—its fairest use is to be made into boxes with initials tastefully inlaid upon the cover, & sent as a *memento*. Had it been mulberry I might have added mori, & given a new turn to that tombstone morality. Think of this if you are sending one to any other friend, & give him a chance. I am talking all this time of your beautiful cigarbox. It has given me, moreover, a more favorable opinion of modern Italian art, & so enlarged my mind. Knowing that they had been so long in the habit of getting into bad boxes themselves, I had not supposed them capable of such an achievement. I was not so ignorant of the natural productions of our western world as not to know that all the nests of boxes came from Hingham, & had too rashly con-cluded that, as the nidification took place there, that was also the single locality for incubation. But possibly I was wrong in supposing this particular box to be the production of art. Perhaps it was brought into the world by mechanical contriv-ance, as chickens in Egypt? The egg may have been laid in Hingham & thence exported? I shall look upon it with all the more tenderness as never having known a mother's care, & put it in charge of a fullgrown Hingham box which I have in my closet. But, whatever solution of the problem we have recourse to, the box remains—like so many a poor devil's poems—an ornament to the centretable. I do not scruple to call it the handsomest piece of furniture I possess, except the table Maria made for me.

There is only one of your foreign experiences which I grudge you, only one which I envy, & that is the meeting with Frank Heath. If he be still within reach of voice or letter, give him my love, fresh as ever after so many years' silence, nay, seeming all the fresher, like a flower upon a grave. Yet for that buried friendship I live in the faith of a joyful resurrection—& in the body. Here I sit alone this chilly September morning, with the rain just beginning to rattle on the roof, & the writing of his name has sent my heart back to the happy, hopeful past when one was capable of everything because one had not yet tried anything. The years between have taught some sharp & some sweet lessons—none wiser than this—to keep the old friends. Every year adds its value to a friendship, as to a tree, with no effort & no merit of ours. The lichens upon the bark, which the dandyfiers of Nature would scrape away, even the dead limbs, here & there, are dear & sacred to us. Every year adds its compound interest of associations & enlarges the circle of shelter & of shade. It is good to plant them early, for we have not the faith to do it when we are old. I write it sadly & with tears in my eyes. Later friends drink our lees, but the old ones drank the clear wine at the brim of our cups. Who knew us when we were witty? who when we were wise? who when we were *green*?

You talk about my being a man of leisure. Why, beside what other writing I have done, I have for fourteen months contributed a column a week, & for four months a column a fortnight, to the Antislavery Standard,[2] which is of course advantageous to me, since columns, you know, do not allow poets to be mediocre. You are the man of leisure there in Italy, whose climate makes loafers of all. Now I will give you a commission. Leaving out Dante, Ovid & Boccaccio are the best part of Italian literature. Boccace was probably the best *man* of the three, & moreover, we who have the English tongue derive our poetical pedigree from him through Chaucer. Now you shall make a pilgrimage to Certaldo & make for me a sketch of Boccace's little tower—doubly interesting since Landor laid the scene of his Pentameron

[246]

there. Frank Heath shall go with you, & as you are both lazy dogs, & Frank no doubt fattish by this time, you shall perform your pilgrimage afoot. And you shall beside compose a *canzone* in alternate verses, your moiety being written in the most toothsome Tuskan, & Frank's in the very highest of High Dutch. This you shall engross fairly on a sheet of paper, & deposit with the parish priest directed to me, to await my coming whenever it shall take place.

I do not know what your movements are to be, nor when you will set your faces homeward. I have heard that you intend a journey to Egypt with Uncle Tom.[3] Do not go too far up the Nile. *Ex Nilo nihil fit,* nobody makes anything of it, & beside, there might be considerable risk to Mr Wetmore. There are savage tribes in the interior of Africa who devour white ants, &, if so, why not white uncles? Do think of this, for it is hardly probable that they are respecters of age or sex. Go rather to London, where there are quarters inhabited almost exclusively by uncles (with three golden balls over their hospitable doors).

It will seem a very old affair for me to speak of the "Fable for Critics." You know me well enough to know how it was written, the work (literally) of a few days & without any *malice* in it. I should have sent you a copy had I known that you were accessible by packages of that kind. Or, rather, I should not have sent one, it was so wretchedly misprinted. Set down the parts about Miss F[uller] as errors of the press. You speak of her as poor. I did not know that she was so, but that the departure of her uncle Abraham to his namesake's bosom had made her independent.[4] I only knew that she was malicious, & it was not what she had written of me, but what I had heard of her saying which seemed to demand the intervention of the satiric Nemesis. You may be sure I have felt more sorry about it than any one, only I always reflect *after* the thing is done. Nevertheless I imagine the general verdict was "served her right", though it was regretted that castigation was inflicted by my particular hand.

The only news I have to tell you about myself, apart from the blossoming of Rose, concerning which I suppose that Maria has written fully, is that I shall probably make an arrangement with

Ticknor[5] to publish a new edition of my poems in two volumes this fall.[6] By this means I shall profit by what I write more than hitherto, which is certainly a desideratum. With an unfortunate faith in my own future appreciation (I believe that is the phrase,) I have been in the habit of stereotyping my own books, so that, although the sale is tolerably large, I have barely more than paid expenses. Under the new system, if I enter upon it, you see that I have my plates already cast, &, the printing being the bookseller's share, whatever profit there is will be clear. Of the "Fable" three thousand copies were [sold] as fast as they could be printed, out of that I had given away the copyright.[7] Nevertheless it acted as an advertisement, for the authorship was at once guessed. The "Biglow Papers" also sold well, but cost me over two hundred dollars in stereotyping.

I know only a single item of news which you will be interested in hearing. That is the lamentable end of poor Edgar Poe. He was picked up in the streets of Baltimore staggering under *delirium tremens*, & taken to the Hospital, where he died. Sad enough, & a man of real genius, too.

I look forward with a great deal of pleasurable anticipation to your return home. I hope you will remain fixed in the plan which Emelyn mentioned of settling in Cambridge. Or perhaps we & some other decent people may choose some other spot & set up our rests *there*. At any rate, I see no reason why we should not renew a friendship to last as far as the grave, at least. I want somebody very much who will not only sympathize with me in literary & artistic matters, but whose early associations were the same as mine. You & I with our cigars in our mouths can talk & laugh over a thousand matters which would seem very poor stuff to most, indeed to all who had not been actors therein, or witnesses. By the way, there is another piece of news. *Our* Eustis[8] has been appointed professor of engineering in the Scientific School here with a salary of three thousand a year.

I have got to the end of my sheet & must for the present remain affectionately   *Your friend*
J.R.L.
Write me fully about Frank H[eath] his looks, &c. &c.

¹ HJ misread 23 as 25 for the September date. Norton read 23. (Norton-Elmwood, I, 222.)

² *National Anti-Slavery Standard* (1840–72), with which Lowell was actively associated for two years beginning March 1848—first as corresponding editor, then as associate corresponding editor. For a few years more he contributed occasionally to the magazine.

³ Uncle Thomas Wetmore.

⁴ Abraham Fuller, Margaret Fuller's uncle, died intestate; as one of a number of heirs she came in for a small share.

⁵ William Davis Ticknor (1810–64) founded the American publishing firm known after 1854 as Ticknor and Fields, at this time as Ticknor, Reed, and Fields.

⁶ The reissue of the two series of his poems (1844 and 1848) was published during the first part of December 1849.

⁷ Lowell sent Charles Frederick Briggs *A Fable for Critics* and gave him the copyright.

⁸ Henry Lawrence Eustis (1819–85), engineer, soldier, and professor. He resigned his assistant professorship of engineering at West Point in 1849 to become professor of engineering at Harvard College.

Berlin, Jan. 30th, 1850.

My dear Jim,—Your letter from Elmwood, dated some day in September last, had not the same disinclination to travel that possesses *you*. It spent nearly two months journeying backwards and forwards, between Vienna and Venice, to each of which places it made three or four visits before it could make up its mind to come to me in Berlin. At last, however, about a fortnight since, it abandoned the occupation of wandering Jew and, worn direfully by travel, much battered and over-scrawled, arrived at 9 Schadow's Strasse, "eine Treppe hoch," the present den in which we are domiciled.¹ Yet the prodigal, for all its wandering, had lost nothing of its welcome; it was warm and *geistvoll* as when it left your snug room at Elmwood, and a shout of gladness hailed its arrival. For a time we were with you as we used to be in staunch old New England; the wind was in the great elms,

[249]

and summer and youth in our hearts. I longed to stretch out my hand to you, with my heart in it, and unburden my soul, and claim your friendly sympathy, and sail down into the past with you along those shores so beflowered with happy memories. Yes, happy, though to me so sad. I must ever ferry across the dark river of death in order to enter into the elysium of youth beyond. We have now arrived at that point—I at least have—where I find myself looking backward oftener than forward, and I doubt if life ever will render an equivalent for what it has taken. . . . Sometimes I think—it is a dream, but a delightful one—that nothing could be so satisfactory and so easy as that we should make a little colony in Rome and there live in that old old home. Of all places in the world it is the true spot for us. I cannot tell you why it so haunts me and taunts me. But ever my heart goes back there in my dreams, and the thought of New England life cuts across me like a knife.

It was truly a joy to me to meet Frank Heath, and to meet him and be with him in Rome. He was to me all that a friend could be, so genial a presence, so unselfish, so noble, true and simple, that the old affection which always lay in my heart for him grew deeper and more vital with our renewed intercourse. His nature is so smooth and equable and deep that he was a constant consolation to me. I am irritable, quick, harsh, and am easily annoyed, but I could live for ever with him. Your commission to him and me to make a pilgrimage to Certaldo how gladly would I perform! But here I am shivering in Berlin, and Certaldo is away in the south, and I hear no toothsome Tuscan here, but only the rattling of the German cart-wheels. I am in [Frank] H[eath]'s old tracks, and his friend Dr Stadthagen[2] is my German master. As we drink our beer at Kneip's the Doctor recounts to me the vagaries of F. and we drink his *Gesundheit* with clinking glasses. I have for some weeks been a real student, and devoted myself to German, and attended the lectures, and sat on the student forms, and felt again as I did in old Harvard. The sensation with which I first entered the lecture-room was as if time had slid off my back and I was a boy again. I know not whether you will be interested to hear about any of the note-worthies here, but I venture to give you a sketch of some of them. And first for Neander,[3] their great man, in whom also your father will be interested.[4]

As you know, he is a Jew, and, as you don't know, is dirty and careless of externals. Small, with black clotted hair, very heavy, shaggy eyebrows and purblind eyes which seem never to have been used in seeing, he is completely absent-minded and abstracted from the world. He knows nothing of life or nature, cannot attend to his personal wants and necessities, can scarcely dress himself, and has been known to come into the lecture-room in his drawers alone. Some very good stories are told of him in this respect—of which take this as a specimen. One day he went home and complained of being lame, saying that he had hobbled all the way along the streets. On being asked if he suffered pain he said, "No, I feel no pain, no soreness anywhere, but I *am* lame, for I hobbled all the way home." His sister examined him carefully and found no injury, and a physician was called, who punched and twisted the poor old man all over, but to no purpose—he could find nothing wrong. Still, Neander insisted that he was lame and that he *had* hobbled. All were in perplexity till some one who had seen him returning solved the mystery by stating that he had walked home with one foot in the gutter and one on the sidewalk. His style of lecturing beggars description, and it at first struck me as so ludicrous that I confess to have not been able to be decorous. He has a high desk, reaching about to his neck, behind which, when he enters the room, he suddenly darts and disappears, so as to be visible from only one side. Leaning one elbow high up on the desk, he steps back, crosses his legs, droops his head down beside it lower far than the surface, seizes a quill which is always prepared and placed there, and twisting this round and round with both hands just about on a level with his chin, and tilting the desk so that one is in constant fear of its falling, commences his lecture—every sentence beginning with a spasm which convulses his whole body, stiffening it sometimes for a moment into a nearly erect position. His hands clench and his frame is in a paroxysm, but gradually, as the sentence proceeds, his body relapses and droops lower and lower, until at the middle of it he has regained his original position. His voice also accompanies this convulsion, loud at first and then lower and lower, until at last the conclusion of the sentence is utterly inaudible. There is a pause, he twirls his pen violently, spits five or six times, and then there is another convulsion and a second sentence. He literally punctuates his lecture by expectoration—once for a comma, twice for a longer stop. As he stands crouched down beside the desk and tilting it forward with one leg tied in a knot round the other and a long frock-coat coming down below his knees and swaying to and fro, he is certainly one of the strangest of spectacles. His lectures are good, though repetitive and technical. He likes, as all the Germans like, to use their magnificent metaphysical vocabulary, and very frequently they keep saying over the same thing in a different manner and without really adding to or developing the subject.

I have also been hearing Ranke,[b] whose style is the acme of flippancy, without dignity, grace or intelligibility. He is a little round-faced man, with a baldish forehead, a high voice and thin hair; his head just appears above his desk, and he rolls himself round, looking up at the ceiling and jerking out with the extremist rapidity and nonchalance, and in a most equivocal tone, which one knows not whether to take as jest or earnest, little fragments of sentences. If Neander always seems to be drawing his ideas out of a deep well, Ranke seems, on the other hand, like a garden fountain which keeps spurting up little futile jets and then stopping. Von Raumer[6] I likewise have heard—dull, dry, hard in manner, and his lecture consisting of the dry bones of history. Rudorf[7] on the Roman Law gave us a catalogue of acts and laws without the least development or explanation; I should have thought it impossible to be drier had I not heard Raumer and some others. Waagen[8] on Art was the stupidest old plodder I ever heard; nothing at all did he give us but a series of facts, and in the most mumbling, slovenly manner. Ritter,[9] the celebrated geographist, I found interesting; his lecture was devoid of all grace and delivery, but it was interesting and full of knowledge. Michelet,[10] in Political Economy, was really clever and also amusing. I do not believe at all in this system of instruction. The professors year after year repeat the same lectures. It seems to me the relic of a past age, when books were rare and what the professors gave orally was nowhere else to be found. The Germans are learned not in consequence, but in spite of, this system.

Now I am on these old worthies let me add to my catalogue a few others out of the University, whom I have met and whose acquaintance I have made. First there is Von Humboldt,[11] truly a noble old man, full of knowledge, of a calm clear mind, of great capacity and of very equally-balanced powers. His knowledge, is immense, even in respect to the most trifling subjects, and I was astonished, in the interview I had with him, to find that he knew everything in relation to our country, from the beginning to the end, in great and trivial things, as thoroughly as I did imperfectly. Common men I had never heard of, acts of our Government unknown to me, adventures of insignificant travellers, details of the gold mines, facts relating to the geology of every different portion, &c., all were to him "familiar as his garter." He is now eighty years of age and has a beautiful head and brow—full, expanded and open. He kept up a continual gush of talk from the moment I entered his room till I left it.

Von Savigny,[12] the celebrated jurist, I have seen repeatedly, and I can assure you that he is of all petrifactions the most remarkable I have seen. He is as dry as dust. Very courteous and affable and complimentary I found him, but living wholly in a book-world, and that book-world a law-book-world. He held up both his hands when he found out that I was an artist, and cried out, 'What, an artist and a lawyer? That is impossible!' But if he is dry, so is not Mme. von Savigny, who is lively, vivacious, chatty, elegant, and of great simplicity and kindness of heart. I always devote myself to her, and in return she introduces me to Gräfins with ugly faces and unpronounceable names, while the other men herd in one corner of the room, dressed in black and speaking monosyllables. It is odd that we are obliged to go to these parties in mourning for the Queen-Dowager of England.[13] We have serious thoughts of inviting Lord Westmoreland[14] to dinner with our landlady for cook. She is a creature only to be found here—with the dirt an inch deep all over her and the colour of her dress not to be distinguished below the incrustation of the same. We live here in the most simple and the least luxurious style—with two dinner-plates, at the most, alike, but not even two tea-cups. We help ourselves to soup with a tin dipper. We have our gravy in a cup. We have one tumbler that holds a pint and one that holds a quarter of a pint. When we came our landlady proposed to us to have our bedclothes and linen washed once a-month, and she offered us a towel a-week apiece. I have a big pudding-dish to wash in, with one bottle of water for my allotted quantity in connection with it. . . .

We have become acquainted with Bettina von Arnim,[15] who is just what you would suppose from the 'Conversations with a Child'—just so artless, plain, wayward, simple, frank and poetic. She received us in the most friendly manner and, taking Emelyn by the hand, said, 'You are beautiful. You are lovely.' At which we laughed, and then she said, 'Is not that English?' She kissed Emelyn and then shook hands with me and asked 'if I was for Liberty.' I cannot describe the conversation, but, generally, she talked about the King, and the horrors of the Hungarian war, and the suffering of many nobles who had been basely betrayed, imprisoned and robbed of all their fortune. She spoke of art, showed me her designs for her statue of Goethe, and said that the King had wished it to be made, but that she had declined because it would fetter her speech. She also told us the history of her book[16]—how she had refused to write it until permission should be granted to her to say all she chose, how this *was* granted, what a stir the book made, how it was condemned by all as improper to be written to a king (they are so servile here), and how the King said it should not be suppressed, it was laid at the footstool of royalty with so childlike a frankness. We talked about the aesthetics of art and agreed upon them, and she showed me her statue of Goethe, which she herself modelled and which is very clever, far better than Schwanthaler's[17] at Munich. . . .

[William Wetmore Story]

[254]

[1] The Storys left Rome in May 1849, and after visits to various places in Italy, Switzerland, and Germany they reached Berlin near the 1st of December and remained there until March 1850. (Story Col.)

[2] He also helped Story find his living quarters.

[3] Johann August Wilhelm Neander (1789–1850), German theologian and church historian.

[4] Because Lowell's father, Charles Lowell, was a minister.

[5] Leopold von Ranke (1795–1886), German historian.

[6] Friedrich Ludwig George von Raumer (1781–1873), German historian.

[7] Unidentified.

[8] Gustav Waagen (1794–1868), German art historian and director of art gallery in Berlin.

[9] Karl Ritter (1779–1859).

[10] Karl Ludwig Michelet (1801–93), German philosophical writer.

[11] Friedrich Heinrich Alexander von Humboldt (1769–1859), German scientist, author, and traveller.

[12] Friedrich Karl von Savigny (1779–1861), founder of the historical school of jurisprudence.

[13] Queen Adelaide, Consort of William IV of England, died December 2, 1849.

[14] John Fane, eleventh Earl of Westmorland (1784–1859)—distinguished soldier, diplomatist, and musician—was resident minister at Berlin from 1841–51.

[15] Elizabeth (Bettina) Arnim (1785–1859), German author as well as sculptor and musician of some accomplishment. She was the daughter of Maximiliane Laroche, whom Goethe had loved in his youth. Long after her mother's death, when Bettina was twenty-two and Goethe was fifty-eight, she became romantically obsessed with the idea of knowing her mother's lover and sought him out. Their association was made public after Goethe's death when Bettina, to suit her fancy, changed and added to their correspondence and published it under the title of *Goethes Briefwechsel mit einem Kinde*.

[255]

¹⁶ *Dies Buch gehört dem König* (1843), showing the miserable social and economic conditions in Berlin, was addressed to the Prussian king, Frederick William IV.

¹⁷ Ludwig von Schwanthaler (1802–48), German sculptor. In October 1849 Story had visited his studio in Munich, but he had not been favourably impressed. 'But I was not greatly pleased. I prefer to see a few finished works to a number of indifferent ones. There is certainly skill knowledge & cleverness in all these works—but no genius . . . . There was no one first-rate work'. (Diary, Story Col.)

Berlin March 1st 1850

My dear James

As I was reading some few days since a Boston newspaper I was startled & most deeply pained to see among the column of deaths the name of your little Rose. My heart instantly reached out across the waters to you—and I would fain have spoken to you at once my warmest saddest sympathy—and now, I cannot let this first packet, since that news reached me, go away without bearing a few words from me to you & Maria to tell you how deeply Emelyn & I feel for you in this bereavement. Consolation I shall not venture to give—that must you both find for yourselves—but sympathy will not I know be obtrusive.

If I were with you all that I could do would be to press your hand & be silent—and here I will do nothing more than say that the sting of your sorrow has also been mine—and I have been often with you in heart though away so far in body. I could not but lament too, that my last letter had gone to you. How must it have jarred on your sadness! When one thinks in how a different mood a letter may be received from that in which it is written— & how many things may occur to alter the life & condition of two correspondents while their letters are passing to & fro—it is a wonder that one ever dares to write gaily. I will only now copy for you some lines which I wrote after hearing that little Rose had breathed her last earthly breath—while I placed myself in your situation & felt for you. I never saw her and yet because she was your child I could not but be drawn towards her. If there be not much poetry in these lines you may yet be pleased to have them.

[256]

Borne in our loving arms her life was spent
Nor on the earth e'er trod her little feet,—
She made the chambers of our spirit sweet,
   And then the dear guest went.

Death like a sudden wind blew out the light
Of her unconscious life—& its pure flame
So that unfathomed thought from which it came
   Vanished from out our sight.

Our hearts all running oer with grief & love,
We laid beneath the sod the form she wore—
We look around & find her here no more,
   So must we look above.

We may not truly say, which most we own,
The joy that to our hearts from heaven she brought,
Or the deep pain of that abiding thought,
   That she is from us flown.

Joy holds us not so strongly to the earth
As once it held us—and the form of death
Grows younger fairer with each passing breath
   And Life of slighter worth.

The wind is in the trees this winters night
I hear it moan among the branches bare
I see the stars in the deep vast of air
   And long for morning's light.

We hope by the next steamer to get some words from you, which
will tell us more of the bereavement—and will show to us your
mental condition, at which we only can guess, now. With my
kindest remembrances to your Father & sisters—& my sincerest
love & sympathy for you & Maria believe me my dear James

                              Ever your most true friend,
                              W. W. Story

My dear James

I was very glad to hear a word from you the other day, giving good-news of your royal progress towards Venice.[1] Now you are in that old dream-city, floating in a gondola, & Page is with you —and you really see Titian. I think it seemed more like a dream to me when I was there than ever before or after my visit,—I never waked up till I left it—spite of Rölker & his confounded Marcus-Platz as he persisted in calling the grand old Piazza,—& his German associations of the Geisterseher,[2] of which he never failed to disburden his memory, when he nightly strolled there amid the crowd & the music & took ices under the lofty colonnades (I considered him as only one of the perverse visitants, which always intrude on a dream, to make it more really a dream.) The place had a fictitious & unreal air. Well from the Alban M[oun]t I hail you. We are perched just over the lake with the vast sweep of the Campagna stretching out from our feet & the old castello looking grimly down over the Popes gardens opposite.[3] We have taken the villa Cini & are here with Cass[4] or rather he is here with us. A villa more to my mind as far as the house goes I have not seen. Every bedroom fore—a magnificent salon of 63 feet in length & 25 in height—with a billiard table, at which I spend quite a third of my time playing with Cass—a grand dining room—beautiful loggia—balcony, looking over lake & mountain & Campagna—and three handsome girls with their mother in the mezzanino below, who are "so sociable." I would that you were here to saunter with us in the Grand Barberini Villa with its grove of pines—or to drive (for Cass's carriage is here stabled below & always at our command) through the galleries which lead off in all directions—or to make excursions to Gensano, L'Arriccia [*sic*], Itri or heaven knows where. Cass really walks, by the four & five hours together & abjures carriages while we are here. We find him very pleasant, not obtrusive, & though not genial (that's beyond his nature) agreeable. His wonderful sack of stories is never empty, and I have had an opportunity of verifying some which were exceed-

[258]

ingly mal trovati[5]—& been obliged to reverse the proverb. What we don't believe amuses us as much perhaps more than what we do. We have never found him untrue where we had an opportunity to know. Thank you for remembering the messages & enquiries in respect to a marble worker. It is of no use. Powers is in a fog as to all persons interests except his own—in respect to the latter it is always clear day with him. I am glad however to know that he has ceased to trouble himself about my marble—as I shall now look out for it myself. It is quite preposterous to tell me, that had he wished, he could not in *four* years, have obtained a block for me. He promised with such earnestness & so repeatedly to do this thing for me, that I believed him—more fool I.

As to your ring, which you have wondered about doubtless—the fact is, that Castellani[6] spent a week in finding a stone—it was as I thought too small. I set him again on the search—he found another,—it was too large. It required two days to cut it down, after he found it. The two succeeding days which should have been spent in this labor were grand festas & no one could work on them, & so the time has gone by. I urged hurry—& he answered Come si fa.[7] The ring at last however goes with this & I hope you will like it. I send it by post (taking insurance on it from the gov[ernmen]t in case of loss) directed to Freres Schielin.

In respect to the other affairs—I paid Dr Wahle's bill, which was L. 40. Freeborn's bill was as I considered exorbitant, but he pointed to a tariff & I could not much reduce it—it was, including every thing, the clergyman's fee &c. L.70.20. Civilotti's account was L.23—which is paid. The two first items covered all the money you left & Civilotti's I paid for you. I think, instead of troubling yourself in negotiating or drawing a bill in favor of Pakenham Hooker & Co or W. W. S. so as to reimburse us— that the shortest way will be to let me draw checks for all your debts here, in your name on P. H. & Co. & let them send the account to Boston to be paid there to their agents. I mentioned this to them, & they said it would be perfectly agreeable to them. Do however as you please, only let me know your decision. If you are to come back here to Rome, certainly you might postpone settling your acc[oun]t until your return. We found after your departure, quite accidentally the little acc[oun]t you gave Emelyn at Albano of money she lent you. It was L.3.90. Castellani's bill I have not paid as he has not sent it—but when I go to Rome (which will be in the course of a week) I will attend to it.

You who know the dilatoriness of Romans will not wonder, that the headstone for the Campo Santo is not advanced. I made three calls on Palombini, without finding him—and at last sent for him to come to me. He came in a couple of days & I gave him a rough sketch of a design which I asked him to draw out & give me an estimate. After waiting a week (during which time we left Rome) I wrote to ask about it. He answers sending me the drawing which he says all included will cost L.60—he undertaking to place it & to do every thing except the masonry. He says that it will be necessary or advisable that the marble slab instead of entering the ground, should be set in a shoulder of travertine. His design does not exactly carry out my ideas, & I have drawn another. Both of these I send you & shall wait for your answer, before allowing him to go on with his work as neither the design nor the cost may suit you. You can easily have the slab without the cross, which I suppose will somewhat diminish the expense, but not much. Shall the ℞⁸ go on the slab. Will you have it without the cornice—retaining the same general form. Is it high enough & broad enough. And most especially, what are your wishes about expense. And do you still wish an iron railing to be placed around the lot. Excuse me, my dear Fellow for troubling you about this & opening trains of sad thought, but I really know with so little exactness what are your & Maria's wishes, that I do not like to go on, without your sanction. Shall the cross be Latin or Maltese?

I am sorry to write you a letter of this kind—but you see I must. I most warmly hope that you will return to us in Rome next winter. Indeed I think you ought to do so. I cannot but think it of the utmost importance for Maria not to return for the present to New England[9]—and how greatly for selfish reasons we wish you here, I need not say. When I write home I shall whisper to Mr Eldredge, that the Parish should make a demonstration to your Father[10] & I feel sure that it would be a pleasure to them to do so, if they had wit enough to think of it. How is he now. We hear no word from home since you left. If I were to take heed of my premonitions I should fear all were not well there. During our last days in Rome we had the glorious illumination of St. Peters—and the Girandola on the Pincio, the latter of which we saw from Cass's windows. On St Peters Eve were vesperoni in the great church by both choirs which were very fine. The old bronze Jew-Peter was robed in a splendid costume with the triple crown on his head—flowers heaped the altars & were scattered on the floors—& the whole wall, where is Canova's kneeling Pope under the balustrade of chandeliers, was exquisitely mosaic'd in the richest flowers. This ceremony was not among the humbugs.

Your bust[11] is going rapidly on. I have done nothing since you left but a sketch of John the Baptist preaching "Repent Ye"—a wild enthusiastic figure, I meant to make him. Crawford has returned—having greatly enjoyed his journey & bringing home some admirable calotypes—(what is to be done with your Genius of the Vatican. You left no word with me, save to deliver it to H[ooker] P[ackenham] & Co when sent for) & being generally exceedingly 'popular.' He is now making a little model of the Washington Monument.[12] Greenough[13] painfully toils over the head of Pharaoh's daughter, which to me will squint. No hot weather here yet in Albano. A cracking & pealing thunderstorm after the Yankee fashion, wrested over us & crowded down along the Campagna this morning. It was a splendid sight—& the air is cool & delicious now. I never tire of leaning over the loggia rail & staring at the mountains and the magnificent view before us. Give my love to Page. What years since I saw him—how much we both must have changed. Tell him he must come here next winter. No place is like Rome. I have seen them all & I know it. Florence is nothing but a continental Boston—in its spirit.

Emelyn's love to Maria & you in which I join. Write soon a long letter & come back next winter.

Yrs affectionately
W.W.S.

send me back in your answer the two designs which I enclose. I have no copies. Mind & don't forget this or we shall be all at sea.

1 On the first part of a fifteen-month European visit the Lowells stayed in Florence in the autumn of 1851. Then they spent the winter and spring in Rome at Capo le Case, No. 68. Soon after they arrived in Rome, the Storys returned from America and settled on the floor beneath them for the winter. At the last of April 1852 the Lowells went to Naples for two weeks, returned to Rome, and from there went to Venice, one of the cities they visited in their European travels before returning to America.

2 The Storys were in Venice in November 1849. Story wrote in his diary on November 5: '. . . went to Piazza S. Marco . . . sipped our coffee . . . remembering Schiller's Geisterseher'. (Story Col.)

3 Castel Gandolfo, summer residence of the Pope.

4 Lewis Cass, Jr., American, was appointed chargé d'affaires to the Papal States in 1849 and promoted to the rank of Minister Resident in 1854; his resignation was accepted in 1858. (Leo Francis Stock, *United States Ministers to the Papal States* [Washington, D.C., 1933], pp. xxiv, 17, 100, 114, 115.) The Cass of this letter is incorrectly identified in HJ as General Lewis Cass, 1782–1866. (HJ, I, 243, n.1.) General Cass, the father of Lewis Cass referred to here, was not in Italy with the Storys at the time of this letter; he was in Washington at least during the first part of the summer of 1852, when he was a candidate for nomination to the presidency of the United States.

5 Story seems to have in mind this saying, '*Se non è vero, è ben trovato*', meaning, 'If it isn't true, it's well made up (or told)'. The reverse would be, '*Se è vero, è mal trovato*'—'If it is true, it is poorly told'. Story means that some of Cass's unconvincingly related stories turned out to be true.

6 In this and the following two paragraphs the proper names have to do with business that Story took care of for Lowell. There was a good deal of it because just as Maria and James Lowell were getting ready to leave Rome their son Walter became ill and died. Some of the references are clear from the context. Murray's *Rome and its Environs* (1853) includes Castellani under 'Jewellers'; Messrs. Freeborn and Co. and Messrs. Packenham and Hooker under 'Bankers'; Civilotto under 'Engravers of Cameos'; Civilotti under 'Roman Mosaics'. (Pp. viii–ix.)

7 A way of raising a question or objection, equivalent to 'how can' or 'how can one?'

[8] The most common form of Constantine's monogram, the first two letters of *Christ* in Greek, standing for Christ or Christianity.

[9] Maria Lowell, who was not a strong woman, never entirely recovered from her son Walter's death; she died within a year and a half.

[10] Lowell's father, who was pastor emeritus of the West Congregational Church of Boston, had suffered a stroke of paralysis in 1851.

[11] The bust Story made of Lowell.

[12] This was of the Washington monument in Richmond, Virginia. The commission was the result of a competition Thomas Crawford had entered during a visit to the United States.

[13] Richard Saltonstall Greenough (1819–1904), American sculptor, who lived in Rome for a time and died there.

Castel Gandolfo
Sept 20th 1852.

My dear James

I was sore afraid when you left us, that the Psora, prophecied by Dr Wahle, would break out ere you left the continent, it being those who are in-continent who are most subject to it. And by Maria's last letter, though she skillfully veils your illness with the pretence of too long swims, I see that this terrible disease has at last broken out. Does it itch like the old scratch. Is there no spot not already stracciato with nails. Does no imposition of hands cure the irritation. Is it worse than ten fleas under the waist-band, for that's where I believe they like a man the best. Have you found out where the *rub* is that makes calamity of so long life. Why do you not hire a rubber of whist, I mean a *silent* French scratcher, if such is to be found. You see how vain it was to pretend to deceive me, fortified with Wahle's opinion as I was, in any such pretence as that your illness was the result of your getting out of your depth any where in France unless indeed you went swimming in the French language, and hurt yourself in some hidden equivoque, of which there are plenty. But ere now I hope you are recovering—and I fancy you daily during your convalescence chanting the praises of "the Dieppe Dieppe sea"[1]

—though as far as I am concerned it has not been an 'oh pen' sea. Yet now that I think of it you are probably not there, but like Sophia[2] have 'crost the sea' & are on the shores of perfide Albion—or perhaps too, for I am rather in a mirmaze as to your whereabouts as you see, you are *fir* up on the All-Pine heights, [hearing] the herds—with a knapsack on your back & a snow mountain in your eye. Chi sa? If so tell me does the cheese smell as strong as ever. Have you found out the difference between an alpen-stock, and the mountain cows & goats. Have you learned to say in the Swiss dialect—Donkey (for so they say 'thank you') when a fair wooden-shoed short-petticoated Sweitzerinn offers you brod & milch. Have you seen the handsome girl on the top of the Grimsel. All that is very good but here is better. Such a summer as we have had I never passed—& never believed in before. Sea & mountain breezes all the time thunder showers varying with light & shade the Campagna. Donkey rides & rambles numberless—a long lazy-luxurious far niente of a summer, such as you would have thoroughly enjoyed. And how often have I wished to have you here. What excursions might we not have made together down in the Abruzzi where I long to go. What games of billiards at home. All that I wanted was to have some old friend with me. As for heat we have not felt it. There has always been a breeze & in the long shady galleries over-spread by ilexes one can walk even at noon for miles. Just now the Pope is here, & all is festa. Every day a new excursion he makes with all his cortege, & every town he visits, has a festa to receive him. You cannot imagine any thing more picturesque than are all these mingling costumes & bright colored-crowds— & fairs such as we saw at Gennezzano [*sic*], with sales of squash-seeds & pigs stuffed whole, and ciambelli,[3] and spring knives and false jewelry, and glaring bandanna handkerchiefs—& spouting fountains & almond eyed children & cleanly dressed girls with the white-peaked tovaglia on their heads. Up at the castle por-tone stand the striped Swiss guards with their long glittering lances, & the square is gay with soldiers and canonici and monsignori &c. When the pope walks or rides or drives in his great gilt coach with his four black giants of stallions what kneeling to his benediction as he enters the square, while tapestried hangings wave from the windows and boys cling to the gratings of the lower windows of the castello and the band bursts into a clash of music, & the organ inside the church, which is strewn with flowers & box & lighted with pyramids of lighted candles, groans & thunders softly. I never tire of these festas. Then the dancing to thumping tamborellas, & the laughter & gaiety & screaming, are really reviving. But why talk of this to you—you have seen enough of it to spur your imagination at Gennezzano [*sic*].

You have been imagining us at Frascati, as Maria writes but really we are at Castel Gandolfo. You never were here, were you? Poor fellow! been to Italy & never saw Castel Gandolfo. You might as well not have come. What will Lorry Austin[4] say. How will Gurowsky[5] growl, aiming that fatal eye over his nose at you when he hears this. You'd better swear that you've seen it when you return—have been at Castel Gandolfo, where the descendants of Aeneas's old white sow & thirty pigs,[6] now coal black, ramble round the streets & are tied out to posts, where with exquisite felicity, to the accompaniment of squeal and grunt, they snarl themselves up, with the legs of the donkeys that come to visit them, and are screamed & howled at by a score of ragged boys.

In a fortnight we intend to make a mountain excursion for a few days & then shall return to Rome where we have taken a beautiful appartimento in the Piazza di Spagna No 93 just opposite to Hookers bank. I am anxious to be at work in my studio, which is now completed uniformly with Crawfords. You see your grand schemes about the Palazzo Albano have fallen to the ground—but we like our new quarters better; they are more comfortable and better furnished & more fitted to our republican condition—although perhaps even they are a little too handsome. How we shall miss you & Maria in the winter evenings that we used to spend so cosily together. There is nobody to supply your place. We shall however probably see considerable Italian society this winter for we have made numerous friends here among the best of the Romans, and since we have been at Castel Gandolfo have only seen Italian friends. Some of them we find very pleasant and sympatica—& have become quite attached to some of them.

Boott[7] writes me from Florence that he is preparing an Inno to contend for a prize offered by some musical academy there. This however I suppose is a secret. He raves about Picchianti as ever and calls Rome by all the bad names he knows—& yet I'll venture that he longs to be back here. Greenough[8] & his wife have spent the summer in town & been neither of them very well. He is at work on an allegorical bas-relief—whether his allegory is taken from the banks of the Nile, deponent saith not. Crawford swears boldly to us, that it is ridiculous to go out of Rome into the country, that *he* & *his* family find *the Villa* good enough for them, to which the gentle Watson[9] sings a feeble echo —but at the same time sweet Mrs C[rawford] confides secretly in E[melyn]'s ear that Crawford has determined never to spend another summer in Rome, because he thinks that it wears upon the constitution. At the Correa[10] is a circus & during the summer I heard some admirable playing from a new company of actors. Of Black[11] I hear nothing since he left Switzerland but I suppose him to be in England & hope that he intends to return here in the winter. From the Lorings[12] we hear nothing. They have utterly forgotten us.

Your motions have been so erratic lately & we have been in such confusion as to your whereabouts & whatabouts that I have not sent you the letters of introduction that I promised. But herewith I send one or two & could send more, but that I doubt whether they will reach you in time to be of any service. How sorry I am that you can not be with us this winter. How sorry not only for the loss we sustain, but for the reason which prevents your return. When you write send us some good news of your Father, who I hope is doing well. But though you go now, I still hope to see you again here, when you can establish yourself for a year or two & we can go to the East together & make pilgrimages to the many nooks & spots of Italy, which both of us have left unseen. We must take some untravelled paths, which the English have not spoiled—& go into the wildest fastnesses of the

Abbruzzi [*sic*], perhaps to Sora. Though we say goodbye now you must come back. Every day, that I live here I love Italy better & life in America seems less & less satisfactory. All that I want here is a few old friends.

Maria in her last letters, left the final decision of the stone for the Campo Santo to you, stating that you would write. She says she inclines to something plainer than the sketch I sent, without cornice or shoulder—but that you would write & say the final word. I only wait for that. Forgive me for thus intruding this subject upon you—but with all good will to save you pain I want to carry out your wishes. Did your ring ever reach you & did you like it. Give to Maria the warmest love of E[melyn] & myself. E[melyn] also sends her love to you. Pray write soon & believe me

Ever truly yrs
W.W.S.

I have sealed these two notes to Forster & Leigh Hunt[13]— because I have availed myself of the occasion to write more than an introduction & also for fear that they may not arrive in time to serve you; in which case I wish you would transmit them to their address whether you use them or not. I have explained in the notes that they may arrive too late. Just write on the outside "Mr Lowell has left London" if so. If they arrive in time & you wish to avail yourself of the introduction—all that is to be done is to put them in another envelope with your card & address, put the proper postage stamp on the outside, & send them by the post. I should have sent you a letter to Browning[14] but I know not where he is.

[1] The Lowells went to Dieppe and from there to Switzerland.

[2] This is apparently an allusion to 'The Legend of St. Sophia of Kioff', a burlesque epic by Thackeray first published in *Fraser's Magazine*, XX (December 1839), 715–27, under the title 'The Great Cossack Epic of Demetrius Rigmarolovicz'. The title was changed when the poem was republished in *Miscellanies: Prose and Verse* (1855). The spoofing headnote accompanying the burlesque's first appearance claims that basis of the poem is a legend that St. Sophia's statue had walked up the River Dnieper to take its place in the church of

St. Sophia in Kiev. In the poem the statue boasts of having walked across the Sea of Marmora and other seas and on the Borysthenes (Dnieper). In a line near the beginning Sophia's statue 'Walks across the German Ocean' to Kiev, probably to satisfy the immediate needs of rhyme. This must have been the line that Story had in mind. '*Perfide Albion*' was Napoleon's phrase.

3 In *Roba di Roma* Story included the following in his description of the festival which took place on Twelfth Night: '. . . or, what is more Roman than all, long poles are carried about strung with rings of hundreds of *ciambelle* (a light cake, called jumble in English), which are screamed for sale at a *mezzo baiocco* each'. (I, 89–90.)

4 Loring Henry Austin (1819–92), a friend and classmate of Lowell's.

5 Adam Gurowski (1805–66), a European count, who, after a life of 'storm and stress amid the political intrigues of Europe', became in America a 'notable example of the vindictive radical type of the Civil War era'. (Le Roy Henry Fischer, 'Adam Gurowski and the American Civil War: A Radical's Record', *Bulletin of the Polish Institute of Arts and Sciences in America*, I [April 1943], 476–88.) He wrote several books on American life. For a time he was in Cambridge, Massachusetts, where his brilliance and eccentricities made a vivid impression. (See Underwood, *James Russell Lowell*, pp. 162–4.)

6 Aeneas was told by the river god Tiber that where he found a huge white sow suckling thirty new-born piglets his son (Ascanius) was to establish a city thirty years later. This city was to be called Alba Longa. (*Aeneid*, Bk. VIII.) Castel Gandolfo is on the site of ancient Alba Longa, twelve miles southeast of Rome.

7 Francis Boott (1813–1904), prominent in the artistic life of Cambridge, Massachusetts, was a pupil of Luigi Picchianti (guitar virtuoso, teacher, and composer) in Florence. Boott had been in Rome in the early part of 1852, when a stringed quartette of his had been played at Story's and had been much praised. (Scott, *Christopher Pearse Cranch*, pp. 188–9.)

8 Richard Greenough.

9 Unidentified.

10 'The theatre itself is built into the circular walls of the ancient mausoleum of Augustus, that fire, siege, and the efforts of barbarians have failed to demolish; and its popular name is founded on the fact that the entrance is through the *cortile* of the Palazzo Correa, on the ground floor of which the tickets of admission are sold'. (*Roba di Roma*, I, 233.)

[11] Charles C. Black was provisional assistant keeper of the Victoria and Albert Museum from 1863 until 1869 or 1870; before and after that period he carried out special commissions for the Museum. (Letter from P. R. Green of the Victoria and Albert Museum, March 31, 1954.) Mr. and Mrs. Black lived for many years in Italy, where they knew the Storys and the Lowells.

[12] Anna Loring (daughter of Ellis Gray Loring) married Otto Dresel, German pianist and composer, who moved to Boston in 1852.

[10] During his visit to England in 1850 Story recorded in his diary that he was with Forster. He probably met Leigh Hunt during the same visit. (Story Col.)

[14] The Brownings left Italy in late spring of 1851. They spent the summers of 1851 and 1852 in England and the winter of 1851–2 in Paris. Quite naturally Lowell, as he passed through London, wanted to see Browning, whose works he had reviewed and whose house he and Maria had stayed in when they were in Florence in 1851. The two poets did meet in 1852. In 1873 Mrs. Adams recorded a meeting of Browning and Lowell in London 'after twenty years'. (*The Letters of Mrs. Henry Adams*, ed. Thoron, p. 124.) The earlier meeting was obviously that of 1852.

Rome Feb[ry] 11th 1853.

My dear James

Admit that the date[1] gives a tug at your heart strings—that you as heartily wish you were here as we wish you were—that it would gladden your heart to see the Pantheon under water, & that you daily boast of the excellence of the Rorlonia cigars. Do you not lecture to the Club, there in your attic, on those bitter icy nights, when the very blood stiffens in the veins, & you hover round the grate, punching it to get more heat,—of the glories of the Eternal city. Does the enthusiasm for lobster keep you warm. Are politics any compensation for the Campagna. Have you become virtuous & foresworn all their potations. Are not the (w) ?rappers in great demand this winter, and have you a private spiritual table. Were I to consult a *tip*-top table I would desire especially to be put into communication with the spirit of John Knocks. Is it a fact that a Loring esquire is a medium gal.[2] If so why do we not hear from her. How is Maria?

Here the winter until the last week has been almost fabulously fine—clear—sunny & so warm, that as yet we have had no fires until the eve[nin]g. The grass is as green as in the spring—the birds sing constantly in the open air—and already the trees are putting forth their blossoms. But the Carnival has been a decided failure. It was so broken up with intervening festas, that one never got into the humor—and the weather was quite unpropitious; for the first time almost for a year we had some four or five days with rain—what mud—what soiling of pretty contadina dresses. I sought out our handsome contadina of last year but she was not to be found. Another very pretty one gave me one day a jumping jack, and a Roman smile, which were both highly satisfactory. We had a balcony under Clarisse's and had Perkins & wife Miss Willing Mrs Twisleton[3] & Mrs & Miss Rae (N Yorke.) were with us. I longed for you—and sulked all day at my studio because you were not here. If one could get rid of the ghosts of old times would it on the whole be an advantage?

What a world it is, America. There are you who used to [flower] so charmingly here in Rome, the moment you arrive in Yankee land with a novel—a 2[d] Edit[ion] of Poems—& a volume of Foreign Sketches on your shoulders.[4] Well I rejoice nevertheless—in all the misfortunes of our friends &c. A novel! That was a surprise. How what—when—where—who? Has Thackeray[5] put you up to that? I do not doubt you will write a good one and it will be fun to write it—and you have my best sympathy & warmest wishes. The Vol[ume] of Foreign Sketches I also shall take great interest in. Quorum pars magna (or parva rather) fui. And apropos of your Poems, you are creating at this time a furore in 28 Corso, Wood's Shakespere Woods[6] harem (scarem) as I call it—among the emancipated females who dwell there in heavenly unity—viz the Cushman, Grace Greenwood, Hosmer-Smith & Co—not forgetting the Bayne (who is here without his antidote)[7]—and for fear I should forget them let me tell you of them. They live all together under the superintendence of Wood—who calls them Charlotte, Hatty &c, & who dances attendance upon them every where, even to the great subscription ball the other ev[enin]g—& I could not help thinking what a pity it was that he could not dance polkas & waltzes as well as attendance, when he went stumbling round the room with his partner just as he stumbles through his speech. The Dr[8] was called by them all when he was here by the sobriquet "Elizabeth" & answered to it quite seriously. The Hosmer takes a high hand here with Rome—& would have the Romans know that a Yankee girl can do any thing she pleases, walk alone, ride on horseback alone & laugh at their rules. The Police interfered and countermanded the riding alone on acc[oun]t of the row it made in the streets—& I believe *that* is over—but I can not affirm. The Cushman sings savage ballads in a hoarse manny voice, & requests people recitatively to forget her not. I am sure I shall not. Page is painting her picture. He is well & happy & delights in Rome, & I am glad enough to have him here. After all one's old friends are the best. Those whom we make in later life are never so close to us as those who knew us when we were young. He has made some very fine copies from Titian which I suppose you have seen & is now painting Mrs Crodie[9] and Miss Cushman & is Titianising the Madonna della Seggiola.[10] Your old acquaintances the Duppas[11] are here, & we find them very pleasant. They give musical parties every Sat[urday] ev[enin]g. Frank Boott also is here. I told him when he returned to Florence, that he would repent—& so he has. Hemans[12] creeps round and "draws it mild." The Blacks are at Villeneuve on Lake Leman. Macpherson has betaken himself to photography & is eminently successful. (Poor Mac has lost his child. It died quite suddenly a couple of months ago.) He is to make a photograph tomorrow of my "Little Red Riding Hood." The Shaws[13] are here & Mrs S. seems to me to be well. She goes about every where & looks charmingly. There are a great number of Americans here but I have kept out [of] American society this winter—having exchanged it for Italian. We have now a large acquaintance among the best of the Italians, and have been to many balls & receptions & conversazioni this winter. I find it agreeable.

My life has been very uniform this winter. In November I began on my large Statue of Father[14]—and it is now about finished. Before this letter can reach you it will be in plaster. My marble for it is also purchased & my abbozzatore[15] engaged, so that there will not be a days delay in carrying forward the work. I hope in a year from now to have it entirely completed & on its way to Boston, but it may take longer to cut it. If I take the decision of my friends I have been successful & I am only too glad to think, that they are right. It was Page I think who said that the sketch I made last winter did not even give promise of the excellence of the large statue. Your bust[16] is nearly ready to send. I want to work three weeks on the marble & then it will be done. Where shall I send it & how. Do you wish it to be sent to you at once. I am also putting into marble my bas relief of "The Flight of Youth" for Fred. Sears.[17] My next work will be the Arcadian Shepherd Boy[18] in large—so much for me. I have been so consumed by my interest in my Statue that I have been nowhere & seen nothing by day. The Barbarini [*sic*] faun still spouts his fine column of water into the sunshine. I stop every day as I walk to my studio to admire it. In about three weeks I shall be at leisure & mean to go into the mountains that seem to woo me to them as I see them in the distance whenever I drive out on the Campagna—or over the Ponte Molle as I frequently do after the days work is over. The more I live in Rome the more I love it. All that I want is a few choice old friends—and especially do I long for you and Frank H[eath]. One cannot have both hands full. How you would have enjoyed this divine winter here. Do come back.

I confess to owing you a letter—for Dr Hosmer did bring me one from London—but I can not bear to give the fag end of time & mind to a friend—and every days close has found me weary & engaged. For him I did what I could—but he did not like to be done for. I got Miss H[osmer] a place in Gibson's studio but Wood took the credit of it. Miss H[osmer] is also, to say the word, very wilful & too independent by half—& is mixed up with a set whom I do not like & I can therefore do very little for her. The Dr is almost *fou* about her. She is doing very well & shows a capital spirit—& I have no doubt will succeed. But it is one thing to copy & another to create. She may or may not have inventive powers as an artist. If she have, will not she be the first woman who ever had?

I have had some capital Yankees to see my Statue—& one yesterday commenced his conversation with "Wal sir what is that intended to represent?" pointing to the Statue of Father & ended it on going out the door with "Stranger you dont happen to have one of your cards with you do you"—I have not I said "What is the name Sir then" said he—Story—Oh Ah wal good morning—we know that name well enough. But I must tell you a story of Pickering Dodge[19] of Salem. It comes from himself & is therefore a fact. He was travelling in Germany when a lady next him turned round and said "Sprechen sie Deutch Yes'm, Yes'm, said he—Pickering Dodge is my name, How did you know it" The lady somewhat aghast, repeated Sprechen sie Deutsch—Yes'm Yes'm Pickering Dodge is my name. But how did you know it. Fortunately an Englishman who was present explained. The story needs to be told aloud.

Pray in your next letter which must come soon tell us about Maria & how she is & your Father & how he is & give the united love of Emelyn & myself to both. Emelyn's love to you—& we both agree that every ev[enin]g that we quietly spend at home we wish you were here.

If you see the Eldredges please say to them that Charley has arrived & is well & enjoying himself. I shall write soon to them.

I have been very stupid but nine hours hard work at my studio leave me little spirits.

> Ever affectionately yr friend
> W.W.S.

Emelyn has [sent] the lamp which Maria wished. Is there anything we can do for you here. Everything that you left for me to do has been entirely completed.

[1] Story was born on February 12, and the Lowells and the Storys had been together in Rome on that date in 1852.

[2] Evidently this refers to Anna Loring. In an earlier letter Story mentions her failure to write and in a later one he mentions again her failure to write and also her interest in spiritualism. The playful

suggestion is that Anna is a spiritualistic medium and that she might communicate with her friends without writing. There seems to be a punning antithesis between 'lowering man' and 'woman of medium height', with 'Loring' pointing to Anna Loring and 'medium' to spiritualistic medium.

[3] In 1852 Ellen Dwight (1829–62) of Boston, Massachusetts, married Edward T. B. Twisleton (1810–74), politician and fellow of Balliol College and then of London University. In 1857 one of her kinsmen was impressed by the praise given her by the 'most exclusive society of London'. (*Life, Letters, and Journals of George Ticknor*, II, 366, 368.) In July of 1852 Mrs. Carlyle had taken Mrs. Twisleton to meet EBB in London, and there were other visits in Italy. (Huxley, pp. 288–9; Landis and Freeman, p. 184; *Letters of the Hon. Mrs. Edward Twisleton, 1852–1862* [Hallowell, Maine, 1925), pp. 71–72.) In a letter written during a visit to Rome early in 1853 (p. 75), Mrs. Twisleton identified other Massachusetts members of Story's party: 'Mary and Edward Perkins [a footnote explains that they were of Pine Bank, Jamaica Plain] and Miss Willing called and were just as usual, the ladies very, very pretty, and very well-dressed, the gentleman very well-mannered, and the sight of the home faces most agreeable'. I have not further identified Miss Rae.

[4] Lowell began a novel but never completed it. Before his trip to Europe he planned a group of poems called 'The Nooning', but the volume as planned was never published, though the poems were published at various times. The foreign sketches first appeared as 'Leaves from my Italian Journal' in *Graham's Magazine* (April, May, July 1854).

[5] In October 1852 Lowell returned to the United States on the ship that brought Thackeray, who was to give a series of lectures in America.

[6] Shakspere Wood (1827–86), English sculptor and journalist, who lived in Rome over thirty years.

[7] Smith and Bayne are unidentified.

[8] Dr. Hiram Hosmer, who, in the autumn of 1852, went with his daughter to Rome, where she was to study art.

[9] Unidentified.

[10] 'For many years [William] Page was the leading American portrait-painter in Rome, where his success in emulating the excellencies of the Venetian school was marked and memorable. One of his copies of Titian was stopped by the authorities at Florence as an original'. (Tuckerman, *Book of the Artists*, p. 297.)

[274]

[11] When the Storys were in Bagni di Lucca in the summer of 1853, WWS recorded in his journal: 'Miss Duppa and her brother [Frank Duppa] came to take the rooms below us'. They had picnics and excursions together. (Story Col.)

[12] Charles Isidore Hemans (1817–76), antiquary and author, was the son of the poetess Felicia Hemans. Lowell had been with Hemans, Black, and Macpherson in Rome. (Houghton, bMS Am 1239.2; Scudder, I, 331–4.)

[13] Francis George Shaw and his family.

[14] Story recorded in one of his diaries: 'Commenced Statue of My Father Oct. 20, 1852'. (Story Col.) The statue was completed in 1854 (according to an unsent letter from Story to Lowell dated July 10, 1854 [Story Col.]) and placed in the chapel in Mt. Auburn Cemetery, Cambridge, Massachusetts; it is now in the Law School of Harvard University.

[15] 'One who roughhews the statue for the artist'.

[16] That is, the bust Story made of Lowell.

[17] Possibly Fredcrick Richard Sears (1824–1907), who married Marian Shaw, sister of Francis George Shaw.

[18] The statue is now in the Boston Public Library.

[19] Pickering Dodge (1804–63), author of books on art, travelled in Europe from 1849 to 1853.

Bagni di Lucca
Aug 10th 53

My dear James

I was putting the last touches to the life sized model of my Arcadian Boy when your letter was brought to me, by a smiling penny postman in a tawdry chapeau. I was then alone in Rome, living with Crawford (both being temporary bachelors) and your handwriting looked so like you—so friendly & so redolent of old days & home & Cambridge, that when I read it, I felt half way between tears & smiles. How I longed to have you again on this side the water. How indeed I *always* long for you & Frank.[1] What is there that supplies the place of *old* friends. After reading your letter, I stripped off the covering from your bust & placed it in its best light—and stared at it a full quarter of an hour, after having lighted a baiocc' e mezz' cigar. I confess to having had a severe twinge of conscience, that the bust still stood in the studio. It ought to have been in Cambridge before now. But I only finished my Fathers statue in time to allow me to complete the Piper by strenuous working before the summer heat, and as I could command no workman sufficiently trustworthy, I was obliged to postpone the bust until I should return in the autumn. Then I will finish it at once and send it off to you. Indeed it is almost finished now. I thank you for your kindness in inserting the complimentary paragraph about my Statue of Father, in Putnam's Mag[azine],[2] and though I have not seen it, I have no doubt that it is "better than my deserts." I do believe you will like it despite its faults—and I really think, that it is not stupid. I am waiting to find an opportunity to send a photograph of it to my mother, & when *that* arrives, it will give you some idea of the mode in which I have treated it,—although a very imperfect and unflattering one. This by-the-way reminds me that Macpherson has just taken out a patent from the Papal Gov[ernmen]t for a new invention, by which he lithographs & engraves photographs —making the sun itself engrave on the stone & copper. The invention is not yet perfected but he has attained a considerable success—and his printed results have been so satisfactory that the Gov[ernmen]t has after examination granted him a patent. This makes Mac look up in the world—& he grows his beard & hair six inches longer in consequence.

We are all at the Baths of Lucca now—high up in the hills, amid the thick chestnut trees—retired from the bustle of the Ponte below, where gossip simmers round the café—and leading the most dolce far niente of lives. The place is beautiful. All about us tower the mountains, terraced with vines, and noble groups of chestnuts, and through the valley below sings a mountain brook & river as it sweeps under its over arched bridges, turns picturesque mills, and goes winding along through its rocky bed to the Mediterranean. Every eve[nin]g we drive along the picturesque richwooded banks of the wild roaring Lima—or drive beside the rushing Serchio where Shelley used to push his little boat, to the Devils Bridge. I have never lived an idler life. While the wind blows through the windows coolly, we sit and read & fall asleep over our books—and feel intensely virtuous when we achieve a letter. Of society there are none we care to meet but the Brownings who are living here.[3] With them we have constant & delightful intercourse interchanging long eve[nin]gs together two or three times a week & driving & walking together whenever we can meet. We like them very much, They are so simple unaffected & sympathetic. Both are busily engaged in writing. He on a new volume of lyrical poems —& she on a tale or novel in verse.[4] These they would like to make some arrangement to have printed or reprinted in America so as to secure some portion of the proceeds or at least so as to derive some pecuniary benefit from the republication. I suggested the publication of them in America so as to take out a copyright in the name of the publisher & a simultaneous publication in England with a copyright in their own names. They would prefer however to transmit proof-sheets to some house in America giving them the preference of printing. Would Field[s] make any proposition & what? By the way I was immensely amused to learn from Browning that the claims put forth by Fields to literary consideration in England were that he was the discoverer of Hawthorne.[5] And under that title he was presented to Browning. Was Hawthorne aware of his Columbus? Fields put forth, that Hawthorne being utterly unknown & unvalued, places in his hands the beginning of a manuscript of The Scarlet Letter. Fields reads & divines its excellence,—with prophetic prescience,—encourages H., pats him on the head—says 'macte vertute'—and in the most generous & self sacrificing manner proposes that he will print the Romance when written. Sad discouraged unrecognized Hawthorne, thus prompted & encouraged by the Maecenas of Washington so writes his book—& Maecenas Field[s] magnanimously prints it—& then appearing before the London audience & lays his hand on his heart & says —behold the Columbus of Hawthorne. Browning seemed somewhat to have suspected a rat,—but received Maecenas warmly, wondering at the oily curling whiskers. Suddenly a thought occurred. If this magnanimous Maecenas has thus sacrificed himself & purse for Hawthorne,—if he be so wondrously liberal & generous—perhaps, chi sa, there may be in his pocket one of those long red purses I have seen on the stage, brought over by him for me. So says B—By the way Mr Maecenas—I believe you republished Mrs Brownings poems & mine did you not. Magnanimous M. smiled & stroked his oily curling whiskers & said—somewhat embarrassed—The profits on the first editions you know (waving his hand)—risk of the publisher as you see (another wave). To which B responded Oh! Ah! I understand and B found himself none the better in purse although Maecenas had published his poems.[6] Will he or any one else do anything now? Both B & his wife seemed greatly have to taken to you & Maria & we all join in standing on the ramparts & waving our handkerchiefs for you to return. They go with us to Rome this winter. If you were only to be there also! B tells me that Clough[7] has a position in London as Superintendent of Public Schools or some such office to which he has just been appointed—you having some weeks before told me, that he was settled in Cambridge & dining every Thursday with you. How is it? He had to me a sort of shagbark nature—with a smooth hard shell, and a sweet kernel inside. It was hard work to get out the [kernel?].[8]

Putnam's Mag[azine][9] I have heard of—but not seen. I am delighted to hear that you are writing for it—& am quite disappointed not to have received any of "Our Own." I, of course, shall like it, & long to see it. What about the novel? You say nothing in your last letter. And the Nooning, when is that. The Mag[azine] ought to be good in the hands of such editors,[10] from the few extracts I have seen, I have great hopes of it. George Curtis's "[First] Society" I saw in part & thought it far the best thing I have yet seen from his pen.[11] He did not seem to have been as particularly pleased with the dancing girls of N[ew] Y[ork] as with those at Esne. This very morning I have been reading an article in the N. Y. Tribune on the sculpture in the N. Y. Exhibition[12]—which is very clever. Who writes those articles on art? I wish we had more criticism of the same kind, to prick those inflated reputations of the most mediocre men.

Nothing is more disgusting, nor more injurious to art, than the ignorant & wholesale adulation with which the most ordinary works of sculpture are lauded in our Public Prints. Every Smith is a Michel Angelo—& when a Tomkins makes a bust, Phidias is summoned to admire. Can anything be more utterly without artistic merit than that abomination—the Equestrian Jackson by Mills[13]—and yet see what parade of praise & solidity of cash it has brought. Was ever a farce enacted more ridiculous than its imagination. It makes one sigh to think how low the standard of excellence must be, which is more than reached by such a work. Crawford is going on with his [Perie][14] admirably. And Greenough[15] has left Rome with his wife & children en route for Paris. She will sail for Boston on August 29 and he intends to remain in Paris. They are both so whimsical that it is difficult to divine the real reason for their leaving Rome—but I suppose it is homesickness on her part, & a longing to see Anna Ticknor.[16] Both he and Crawford desire to be remembered to you. Page is just recovering from a fever he caught at Naples. He went with Sarah to make a visit to Sarah Shaw[17] at Sorrento, and could get no further than Naples on his return when he was taken ill—but he is now nearly well & has returned to Rome, which is to him home. He has become enamored of Rome & puts no other place in compare with it—and he has taken an admirable house on the Quirinal Hill, where the air is excellent, for which he pays some 35 or 40 scudi a month. The rooms are spacious and palatial & were formerly occupied by the Marchese Zappi[18] & wife. Of his pictures he has as yet shown me none save the portrait of Miss Cushman—which is wonderfully fine—the best portrait I think I ever saw. The picture of Mrs Crawford[19] is nearly done but he will not show it. And he is painting a head of Emelyn. He will find more to do in Rome than he can possibly attend to. I have a great impulse now to take a cigar but as dinner is almost ready I will postpone it. Browning does not smoke; it is his greatest defect—but he tells me that Tennyson does excessively—and that after he got to Florence on his way to Rome, he was so disgusted because he could not find a particular tobacco he liked that he turned back to England & never went to Rome. His brother Frederic[20] is living in Florence having married an Italian wife & B[rowning] says is full of poetry. Lytton[21] by the way is turning up a poet. I saw a couple of poems by him at B[rowning]'s, which were quite full of promise & richness. Boott is at Pratolino writing quartettes & experimenting with the "Spirits" but as yet he does not arrive at any satisfactory results in the latter department.

You were all too kind to pay that bill at the bookstore in Cambridge. I was sure that I either paid it—or left a special order with Edward Eldredge to do so—but my *strong* impression is that I went there the last day I was in America for the very purpose of paying the bill & that I did do so. I am quite distinct that I went out to C[ambridge] for the express purpose of paying that bill & giving some last directions about the Biography.[22] Edward E[ldredge] has the bill unless in my hurry I mislaid or overlooked it or tore it up. But I feel quite sure I paid it. Still I may be mistaken—I distrust my memory. None the less however do I thank you for your kindness—and whether or no I shall always consider the Chambers Cyclopedia as a present from you and value it a thousand times more on that acc[oun]t. The collection is an extremely good one and has been a source of great pleasure to me in these "furren" parts where books are so rare. There never was a day all last summer that I did not read in it. It is such pleasure to gossip with you now that I have begun that I regret the "mancanza"[23] of paper—but here I am at the end. Pray write me soon a good long closely packed letter and with the united love of Emelyn & myself to you & Maria & warmest regards to your household at Elmwood. Believe me dear James

Ever affectionately yrs
W.W.S.

P.S.
A word or two more dear James. Browning received your letter enclosing Centofanti's receipt for the rent of Casa Guidi[24]—& I believe it had the effect of utterly smashing C's credit with Browning. He was much obliged to you for it—and professed shame at not having answered it. In return for your batch of

engagement[s] I can tell you of only one. Camilla Bate has married a curiously ugly, dull, young Scotchman by the name of Watson[25] & gone with him to the land of cakes. It is supposed that Mamma Bête & Mac pushed her into this slough of matrimony—on acc[oun]t of a little money *W* had—& *they* coveted. Pray tell this fragment of news to Anna Loring. She will be interested to hear of the fate of her quondam friend Miss Bate. She was so pretty a Bait, that I thought she would catch a better fish. And while you are giving this bit of news to Anna ask her why she does not vouchsafe to us a single line. Has she forgotten us or has Titus ceased to be virtuous. When I remember those long weekly letters she used to write from Rome,—I sometimes think she might give us one. Every body here is interested about the moving & rapping tables & the spirit manifestations. What do you make of them. For myself I have as yet seen nothing to indicate spirits but my experience is small. Page however is a complete believer—& receives spirit communications daily—by writing. Sarah P[age] also says she is a medium. Boott is very warmly interested in investigation—and Mrs Browning is hungry for knowledge & information in respect to the manifestations.

We think of you often in your pleasant home at Elmwood amid the shade of those fine old trees and remember those pleasant days we spent there with you all[26]—with half a sigh. We both look forward to the day when you and Maria will be with us here again & hope that it is not long distant. We were so very sorry to hear of Maria's illness—which we feared might be laid to the charge of the climate. But your letter revived us in spirit, by telling us how much better she was. In the long summer days she must grow stronger; & ere the winter (dreadful thought) sets in, I hope she will be strong & well. But if you were only here where there is no winter! How is your Father's health? I hope improving.

Do you ever see Richard Dana. I received some time since a very pleasant letter from him which I wish he would repeat. Pray remember us kindly to him & his wife—and say to him that he must sometimes lay down the burden of the green satchel & send us a brief to Italy.

Do you have those Sunday reunions now at your room. What does the Dr[27] think of [Housalvania] stock. I saw "William A White. Wisconsin" signed to a call for a temperance convention the other day in the Tribune. Is that our Bill? Heavens how we are all scattered about. I was very glad to hear that Nat H.[28] was struggling to overcome his habits. It was really dreadful to see him so debased in mind, who was so brilliant in our College days.

I am sorry to have been so dull & stupid but you must take the will for the deed. Edie & Joe send kisses to Mabel & Aunt Maria & Uncle James. They are very well and devoting themselves to all sorts of pets. We have pet-snails pet-beetles pet-owls pet-cocks & pet-butterflies & spiders. Every living thing which can be found is brought in to clutter up the rooms. We are called upon to wonder at the extraordinary demonstrations of the beetles on their backs as they struggle again to get on their legs and at the one ragged dismal looking "Cockey" at every moment. Since I have been writing this little page I have thrice been called upon to admire Cockey's powers no less than three times. Edie says he has a remarkable ear for music.

> Well good bye again
> *Ever affectly yrs*
> *W.W.S.*

I suppose you know that our old friend Kestner[29] died last winter. Dr Wahle and Mr Kemble[30] the dentist are also gone— and poor Conte Giuseppe Canale.[31] You may recollect the latter. He was the brother of those two young ladies whom we saw take the veil in the church near S[an]ta Maria Maggiore one pleasant June morning. We afterward knew him very well.

I must tell you about the Correa or Mausoleo. Crawford Grenough & I used to go there almost every eve[nin]g during the month of June—to hear the [Santoni?] who was playing there better than ever & with a most admirable company. Among them was the curious fat Corsico with his little round mouth & eyes—but the [Preneo Grajico?] was far better than the one you saw. He was as powerful as [Santoni?].[32] But I never went there without thinking of you. I rejoiced most sincerely in Frank Heath's success. Will he never come out here again.

1 Frank Heath.

2 The *Putnam's Monthly* for April 1853 carried the following: 'Mr. Story has finished his model for the statue of his father, the late Justice Story. It is very highly spoken of by those who have seen it, and there is a rumor that a duplicate will be ordered for one of the Inns of Court in London'. (I, 472.)

3 This was the first of several summers that the Storys and the Brownings spent near each other in Italy. Story recorded details of the summer in his diary. (Story Col.)

4 RB's *Men and Women* (1855) and EBB's *Aurora Leigh* (1856).

5 For details of this account see James T. Fields, *Yesterdays with Authors* (Boston, 1889), pp. 48–52. Cf. interpretation of Field's behaviour in Louise Hall Tharp, *The Peabody Sisters of Salem* (Boston, 1950), p. 191; and Randall Stewart, *Nathaniel Hawthorne* (New Haven, Connecticut, 1948), p. 94.

6 Browning wanted to make arrangements with James T. Fields for his work, but the financial disregard by Fields in the unauthorized publication of the 1849 collection and Fields's treatment of EBB as well, which Browning refers to in this letter, taught him to be wary. (EBB to Arabel, November 18, 1851, in Berg; RB to Fields, October 16, 1863, in Houghton.) Soon after the date of this letter Browning wrote to Fields and arrangements were made to Browning's satisfaction. (Browning to Fields in *Century Magazine*, N.S., LXII, 130; DeVane and Knickerbocker, p. 87.) But Fields's behaviour provoked complaints in 1864, 1868, and 1880. (RB–WWS, May 3, 1864; Hood, pp. 114, 127; RB–JRL, September 6, 1880.)

7 Near the end of 1852 Arthur Hugh Clough (1819–61), as well as Thackeray, went to America on the same ship that took Lowell and his wife home from their European visit. Clough returned to England in July of 1853 on the spur of the moment, having planned to stay longer in America, and became Examiner in the Education Office.

8 Word torn away.

9 *Putnam's Monthly Magazine* (1853–7, 1868–70, 1906–10). In its early history Lowell contributed one poem, 'The Fountain of Youth'; three installments of 'Our Own', an unsuccessful poem which was discontinued after three numbers; and his more successful 'Moosehead Journal' and 'Fireside Travels'.

[10] C. F. Briggs was editor; G. W. Curtis and Parke Godwin were associate editors.

[11] George William Curtis (1824–92), lecturer and writer. The first word of the title is blotted; it looks like 'First', not 'Best', as it should be. Story must have seen 'Our Best Society' in manuscript, not in *Putnam's Monthly Magazine*, which he says he has not seen. It satirized social life of New York, appearing in *Putnam's* in February 1853 as one of a series of essays later published under the title of the *Potiphar Papers*. The essays had an immediate popularity.

[12] Later reprinted as a chapter in *Art and Industry as Represented in the Exhibition*, ed. Horace Greeley (New York, 1853).

[13] Clark Mills (1810–83), self-taught American sculptor, was given the commission with a contract of $12,000 (the bronze to be furnished) for an equestrian statue of General Andrew Jackson. He set up his own foundry and made the statue of a rearing horse with its hind legs under the centre of the body. It was dedicated in January 1853 with sensational success, and Congress voted Mills an additional $20,000 for his services. (Tuckerman, *Book of the Artists*, p. 585; Gardner, *Yankee Stonecutters*, p. 69.) The statue is in Washington D.C.

[14] HJ (I, 269) reads this as 'big thing', which could not possibly be right. I think it is a misspelling for 'Peri', a statue made by Crawford.

[15] Richard Greenough.

[16] The daughter of George Ticknor.

[17] Wife of Francis George Shaw.

[18] Unidentified.

[19] According to Page's biographer the portrait of the wife of Thomas Crawford 'caused almost as much stir as that of Charlotte Cushman'. (Taylor, *William Page*, p. 126.)

[20] (1807–98.) Browning persuaded him to print his poetry. His best volume, *Days and Hours*, was published in 1854. (Harold Nicolson *Tennyson's Two Brothers* [Cambridge, 1947], pp. 16–23; see also Kenyon, II, 113, 123, 126.)

[21] Robert Lytton, who visited the Brownings at Bagni di Lucca during this summer, joined in the excursions and visits of the Brownings and the Storys. Story and Robert Lytton had become acquainted in 1850. Lytton's urge to write became stronger after he went to Italy, where he was among writing friends. (See RB–WWS, June 11, 1854, n. 5.)

[284]

²² Story wrote a life of his father, which was published in 1851.

²³ 'Lack'.

²⁴ The Brownings rented Casa Guidi for twenty-five guineas a year. The Lowells subrented it for two months in the fall of 1851, and Centofanti took care of the rental. When the Brownings returned, there was some question of his honesty. (EBB–Arabel, November 13 and 15 and December 21, 1852, Berg.) RB dismissed him; seemingly, however, Centofanti's turning informer against rival lodging-housekeepers weighed more heavily against him than did the house business. (Houghton, bMs Am 1484.1.)

²⁵ Both unidentified.

²⁶ When the Storys returned to the United States in 1850.

²⁷ Possibly Dr. Estes Howe, who married Maria White Lowell's sister.

²⁸ Nathan Hale (1818–73), journalist and brother of Edward Everett Hale. In 1875 Lowell, in referring to the Harvard days, wrote of Nathan Hale as having been 'perhaps the cleverest man in the class'. (Norton-Elmwood, I I, 351.)

²⁹ Georg August Kestner (1777–1853)—Hannoverian minister, author of books on art, and amateur artist—was the son of Goethe's Charlotte (Buff) and Albert (Johann Christian Kestner) in *The Sorrows of Young Werther*. He published *Goethe and Werther*, which contained an explanation and history of the work and letters from Goethe to his father and mother. (See *Life, Letters and Journals of George Ticknor*, I I, 72–73.)

³⁰ Both attended Lowell in Rome. (Houghton, bMs Am 1239.2.)

³¹ Unidentified.

³² Both unidentified.

63 Avenue des Champs Elysées
Paris 9′ January 1855.

My dear James

I feel quite sure that you have not misinterpreted my long silence, and yet I cannot again speak to you without shame, that I should not long ago have responded to those few most kind & cordial words that Hamilton Wild brought to me from you months ago. But I have been daily intending and daily postponing until at last I find an hour with no visitors & no work & this I shall dedicate to you. Long ago while I was at Dieppe I wrote you a long letter, for there I could not but think of you daily, but it was thrown aside in my portfolio as too worthless & inadequate to send.[1] I shall say nothing to you of what has happened to us both since we parted. You will understand all that I feel & all that I would say. You will believe that my heart has bled for you & deeply sympathized in all your sorrows & I need no assurance that you equally have felt for me.[2] This must suffice.

I thank you for your hearty words—& I hope when my statue[3] gets to Boston that you will not be disappointed. When that will be, I do not know. It is at present at Leghorn awaiting a vessel for the modern Athens. Ere now, your bust should have arrived, for it is more than eight months since it was given into Hooker's hands to be sent to you It is not as good as the cast I am afraid for Nucci[4] turned out stupid and made me a great deal of extra work & expense on the marble. But such as it is I have sent it to you—and all that I can say is that I wish it were better than anything of mine ever will be—for your sake. It may recall to you our happy days in dear old [Rome] when we lived together in Capo le Case and saw the Sabine mountains out of the studio window of the Villa Negroni from which Shelley & Keats had looked before us when Severn painted in it.

I read months ago your genial and delightful paper on 'Fireside Travels' in the Putnam's Monthly.[5] Rarely does a number of that mag[azine] reach me across the water—but it happened that Cranch lent me this one copy before he had looked through it to while away an hour before going to bed. I had undressed me, stuck up my candle by my bed-post & was turning over the leaves, when the name of the "Edelmann Storg" caught my eye —& sent all the blood into my face. Before I slept I read the paper carefully through, & trod the old childish ways & nooks of Cambridge, & saw again the old worthies & characters we boys used to know, from Waterhouse[6] to the Fabulous Remie.[7] How well I saw the old places & faces that you so dearly & graphically painted! I shall never be more of a boy again than I was that night. This is the first word that ever was dedicated to me in print!

Let me thank you for making me acquainted with Hamilton Wild. I like him very much & we have got to be daily cronies. We agree in matters of art—& he puts up with my whims when I am bilious as a young man should. He is now painting two very pleasing pictures—one a charming group of the children in the wood—with night coming on and the two little creatures beginning to want to go home & to wonder where they shall go —the first twilight shadow of their forlorn condition beginning to darken over their minds, as the glooms gather in the woods. They are dressed in quaint dresses of the period & standing among the trees through the trunks of which the gleams of sunset show in the distance. The conception & treatment are highly poetical. The other is a silvery & delicate picture of a fiancée receiving a letter from her lover with flowers. The manner in which these pictures are painted give me a high impression of his talent & originality. They have a stamp of nature & beauty.

You have doubtless heard of poor Page's misfortune. Yet lest you have not let me tell you. Sarah has fled from him to become the mistress of Don Alfonso Cirella one of my friends at Rome a handsome spirited young fellow of about 21 years of age. I have long known that she had no love for Page & for more than a year she has been liée with Cirella in the most open manner. He was at her house morning noon & night, & in the constant habit of dining with the family. I do not understand how Page could be ignorant of their liaison, which formed the topic of gossip in American & Italian circles during all the last winter. In the summer he Cirella was at Albano, & Page hired a house there for Sarah & the girls, where they stayed, while Page remained at Rome—a most admirable arrangement for the two lovers & a most unfortunate one for the husband. At last, after they returned in the autumn to Rome, Cirella who is Neapolitan by birth returned to Naples, and about a month ago, Sarah procured a passport, had it viséed to Paris, said to Page, that she was going to Albano & disappeared. The visé to Paris prevented her from going beyond Civita Vécchia—& she was forced to return. She then went under a false name to a lodging in the Via del Gambano, & procured a visé to Naples. Page found her in this lodging, & implored her to return, but she was very decided in resisting every argument—and in a day or two disappeared as it is supposed to join Cirella who had come on to Albano. Nothing has been heard of her since. Cirella is the son of the Duke of Cirella a Neapolitan family of distinction, who were exiled in consequence of political troubles & who have been resident for some years in Rome. Alfonso being a boy when they were proscribed, was not under the penalties attaching to his three brothers & Father & Mother—so that on his coming of age he returned to Naples this last autumn & was there when Sarah fled. It is mere madness on her part—he is nine years younger than she—and will assuredly cast her off at some time. I do not in the least think that he was the seducing party. She fell in love with him—and led him on from step to step. He is a good-hearted spirited fellow & I am sure would never of his free will have become thus entangled with her. But so it is. Sarah had finally determined to leave Page with some one or other (as I know) and had made overtures to other persons, at least to one other person. This however is *in confidence to you*—and there are tales of her which are the worst that can be told of woman. I hope they are not true. I do not think Page will suffer from the separation other than in his pride,—they were not happy together. I hear that he is working again with spirit in his studio & is painting Crawford's portrait. But for Sarah the prospect is dreadful. She had many admirable qualities & was most kind & generous to us in our sorrow. I do most heartily pity her. I hear that she has left considerable debts behind her—but I hope not.

I see often Mr & Mrs Putnam[8] & in all long to see you again. Why will you not come abroad & live with us & let Mabel & Edie grow up together. We should be so glad if you would do this. Emelyn would take charge of Mabel & look after her in all respects & we could then be together. Pray consider this seriously. When I see you I shall urge it upon you. I do not know when or where we shall meet but I think it probable that I shall go to Boston in the summer & return in August making only a visit—& perhaps leaving Emelyn here.[9] At home, I cannot carry on my art & therefore could not live there. We think of returning to Florence to establish ourselves—but are not determined.

Pray let me hear what are your plans. Emelyn's best love to you & Mabel in which I join. Pray remember us most kindly to your Father & Rebecca—& believe me

Ever affectionately yrs
W.W.S.

Our little boy[10] is the sunshine of our house—but he is not like the other. I cannot but weep often & often when I look at him. He is a beautiful child very strong & healthy—and we take great joy in him. Emelyn already walks out & is quite well. Wild wished me to send you his kindest remembrances—& Edie if she knew I were writing would send love & a half-page of messages to Mabel.

[1] The letter that was never sent (dated July 10, 1854) is among Story's papers. There is a good deal of overlapping in content in it and this letter.

[2] Lowell's wife died in Cambridge in October 1853; and Story's son Joseph died in Rome in November 1853.

[3] Of his father.

[4] On February 5, 1852, Lowell recorded in his diary that he went to Nucci's studio—the marbleworker. (Houghton, bMs Am 1239.2.)

[5] 'Fireside Travels / Cambridge Thirty Years Ago / A Memoir Addressed to the Edelmann Storg in Rome.' The work was first published in 1854 in *Putnam's Magazine*, the first part in April and the second in May. 'Storg' was a Swiss innkeeper's misreading of Story's name. (Underwood, *James Russell Lowell*, p. 50.)

[6] Benjamin Waterhouse (1754–1846), physician and pioneer vaccinator in America. (See Elmwood, I, 61–62.)

[7] Marcus Reamie, the village barber, had a shop full of treasures, 'of wonder and delight' to the boys of Cambridge. (Elmwood, I, 24–26; see also C. E. Norton, 'Reminiscences of Old Cambridge', *The Cambridge Historical Society Publications*, I [June 19, 1905, to April 24, 1906], 13.)

⁸ Lowell's sister Mary (1810–98), author, married Samuel Raymond Putnam, merchant. Among her works are the following: *Tragedy of Errors* (1861); *Tragedy of Success* (1862); *Fifteen Days* (1866); magazine articles on Polish and Hungarian literature and on the history of Hungary.

⁹ In August both Mr. and Mrs. Story went to America, where they remained until the following summer.

¹⁰ Thomas Waldo.

Paris, 7ᵗʰ July, 1855.

My dear William,

I cannot easily tell you what a pang of disappointment I had when the *concierge* told me that you were gone, & that only the day before I got here. Unfortunately we had a ten days' calm, which made our passage (which at first promised to be short) an affair of twenty eight days.¹ I arrived here at 1/2 past 4 p.m. on the 4ᵗʰ & before six I was at your lodgings which I went to by a kind of instinct, only knowing that it was sixty something, but having forgotten the fraction. I confess I came hither chiefly to see you, & but for that hope should have probably gone right through to Dresden. I shall stay here about ten days longer. Now I want you to come over in time to go with me down to Cologne & Bruges & Brussells—or at any rate to come & spend a few days. I would come over to you without the least hesitation were I travelling for pleasure—but I am a kind of officer sent on a special mission & do not feel that I have a right to gad about. While here, I am at least perfectioning my French which (for a professor) to tell the truth, is rather in a lamentable condition. My professorship opens like the Exposition here before anything is ready. I need not say how much I should like to see Emelyn to whom I feel more closely drawn than ever now.² You say nothing of your plans. Shall you stay long at home? Of course you have heard about your statue,³ but you cannot hear too often or from too many. It has been an unqualified success. I have heard but one opinion.

When you write, give me your London address. Also is Cranch in Paris? or Heath? I saw that a Dʳ Heath⁴ had gone with our Minister[5] to some baths or other & it gave me a hope it might be Frank. My own address here is "Hôtel de France, rue Laffitte." Now do come over like a good boy. I will save a real cigar for you. I brought some with me on purpose.

 With best love to Emelyn

I am ever yours

J. R. Lowell.

Do you know Mrs Chapman's address.[6] Oddly enough I went to the Varietès last night & was put into the next seat to [J. A. L.][7] who has just come back from Spain. I did not know that he was to be in Paris again & should probably not have met him but for this accident.

 [1] In June Lowell had sailed from Boston for Le Havre. He had been appointed Smith Professor of the French and Spanish Languages and Literatures and Professor of Belles Lettres in Harvard College, and before taking up his duties was to study in Europe. After three weeks in Paris he went to London to see the Storys, who were on their way to America; and then he went to Dresden for six months.

 [2] Because of the close friendship that had existed between Emelyn Story and Lowell's wife, who had died in 1853.

 [3] Statue of Story's father, which had been sent to America.

 [4] See next letter.

 [5] John Young Mason (1799–1859), diplomat, served from 1853 until 1859 as envoy extraordinary and minister plenipotentiary to France.

 [6] Maria Weston Chapman. See RB–WWS, June 19, 1860, n. 4.

 [7] Lowell may be referring to his cousin John Amory Lowell (1798–1881), merchant.

London 9' July '55

My dear James
 I knew it would be so. I felt quite assured that as soon as the dust of Paris was off my feet, it would be on yours. I had already stayed nine days in hopes of seeing you—and should have stayed

much longer, but that our proprietaire was crooked & insolent and I could do nothing with him. My rent was up & I was forced to flee. Now the question is how we shall meet. It seems to me that you might at least appropriate a week or two to England without transgressing limits—and together I think we might enjoy ourselves here. You can have a room or rooms with us in the same house dine with us & be with us at all times. In this way we should be all together. If as you suggest, I should go to you, it must be *alone*. Emelyn could not go with me on account of the baby & Edie—& that would be hardly satisfactory. Let me therefore beg of you to come over here. It is only one day's journey. We will then either stay in London or go into the country or do whatever you like.

If you will not do this pray let me know exactly what your plans are and I will try to meet you. Shall you go down the Rhine? Where shall you stay & how long? But pray consider how much better it would be for us *all* to be together—here.

We are now at No 1 Bulstrode St. Manchester Sq. The Brownings are here. You will see them too & Leigh Hunt[1] & others. Cranch is to be found at No 51 Avenue de la Porte Maillott—Commune de Passy Paris. It is a little way beyond the Arc de Triomphe de L'Etoile. He has a little package for you which I left with him. Mrs Chapman is 21 Rue de Varennes-Faubourg St. Germain—Anna Greene (Shaw)[2] is I suppose still in Paris. She is at 144 Av[enue] des Champs Elysées. Herewith I send you a note of introduction to Mr [Lemousier][3] an admirer of you & a friend of Mrs Putnam—who wishes to see you—& who promised to prepare an article on your poems for his review. Pray see him. It was a brother of Frank Heath who was in Paris & accompanied Mr Mason to Nice. He has since married Miss Mason & gone home.

Emelyn sends her best love & urges you to come over & see her.

Have I congratulated Harvard Univ. yet on its discernment in appointing you Professor. I know of nothing which has given me so much pleasure for a very long time.

Just slip this note to [Lemousier] into an envelope & send it to him with your card & address. We are going home in the steamer of August 18' & how long we shall stay chi sa. It may be for years & it may be forever. Do come to us here.

Very affectionately yrs
W.W.S.

[1] Lowell did see the Brownings and Leigh Hunt. (Norton–Elmwood, I, 310–11, 313–4; Scott, *Christopher Pearse Cranch*, pp. 213–4)

[2] Anna Blake Shaw (sister of Francis George Shaw) married William Batchelder Greene.

[3] Unidentified.

Hôtel de France
Rue Laffitte
18th July, 1855

My dear William,

here I am still—chiefly because some clothes & shirts which I have ordered are not yet ready—& also because I have not been able to make up my mind whether I could go over to you or not. But I think I am decided now—&, if I hear nothing to the contrary from you, I may be looked for next Tuesday morning to stay a couple of days or so—not more if I can help it.

I have seen a great deal of Cranch[1] which of course has been a great pleasure to me. I like him very much. Today I meant to go to Chartres—but it rains & I fear I shall be cut off from it. My chief employment here has been the Louvre, where I know what I wish to see & so can go with profit.

I went with Cranch the other day to see a statuette of a musical man named Beetoven or Heatoven or something of the kind. It is the work of a *young* Italian named Ristori[2] (a relative, I believe, of the actress) & is in my judgment a most admirable performance. I never saw a portrait statue which I liked better, if so well. I felt a particular interest in it—for I knew Ristori in Italy—& as I am apt to criticize most severely the works of those in whom I am personally interested, I feel some confidence in my opinion. I was truly delighted with it & can hardly speak as warmly as I feel. I wish it could be made also of a life size. From what Norton writes me of Crawford's[3] (which had just got home) I cannot help regretting that this is not to go into the Music Hall instead of his. However, Ristori will have his turn.

If you stay at home "forever"—as you say—go to live in Cambridge, there is really good company there, & if you choose to build, I will give you the groundrent of the prettiest spot in the town for as long as you please, at sixpence a year rent with any arrangement you please to make about taking your "improvements" off your hands.

Give my love to Emelyn. I got a sweet little letter from Mabel last night & feel proportionably elated.

a rivederci

Ever yours

J.R.L.

[1] Christopher Pearse Cranch and Lowell met a short time before this letter was written, and they were to go to London together to visit their mutual friend Story. (Scott, *Christopher Pearse Cranch*, pp. 201, 212–13, 214; Miller, *Christopher Pearse Cranch*, p. 19.)

[2] Lowell is punning; he is referring to a statue Story made of Beethoven.

[3] Charles C. Perkins commissioned Thomas Crawford to make a statue of Beethoven for the Music Hall in Boston. When it was cast in Munich a musical festival was held, and there was another festival when it was placed in the Music Hall on March 1, 1856. (Winsor, *The Memorial History of Boston*, IV, 404, 436; Tuckerman, *Book of the Artists*, p. 307.) The Crawford statue is now in the Symphony Hall in Boston.

London July 20' '55

My dear James

We are delighted at your decision to come to us, but shall scarcely dare to believe in our luck—till we see you & touch you, —such unbelieving Thomases are we. Come straight to our house in Bulstrode St. (Manchester Sq) No 1—and you will find a room for you. We shall expect you to dinner on Tuesday unless you let us know that your coming is postponed. I suppose you will take the Folkstone-Boulogne route, as that is so much the pleasantest & if so you will be at our door at about 7 or 7 1/2 oclock. How glad we shall be to see you.

I heard from Cranch a day or two since, & he tells me that you & he have been doing all Paris together to his great satisfaction. Why cant you bring him over to our side. Don't leave Paris without seeing the Jardin Mabille & Chateau des Fleurs which is one of its special & remarkable 'institutions'—I know no better cicerone than Xtopher for those gardens of roses.

Will you be kind enough to call at Leroys (Horloger) in the Palais Royal 114—& ask him for my watch, which I left in his care to be put in order. There ought to be nothing to pay on it, as I have already paid him 60 francs for putting it in order, & his work broke down the second day, so that he *agreed* to re-do it for nothing. I say this lest he should claim pay[men]t.

Emelyn sends her best love & speed to your coming.

Yrs affectly
W.W.S.

What you say of the Beethoven is very kind, and I feel specially proud, for your good opinion is really worth having. I was afraid you did not see it under special advantages. I hope you do not think too well of it. As for your charming offer about Cambridge, I should not feel myself at home in America, were I distant from you & the old village—but we will be somehow together, will we not though I am not a Professor. How funny it sounds Professor Lowell,—I have a notion that Longfellow's house ought to be given up with the office—& that I ought to have the house & you the Professorship. But who has his deserts in this world.

au reservoir

I heard Palmerston & Dizzy last night at the House of Commons. P was like an old bull in fly-time as Hosea B[1] says—with a short tail, and a great gannenipper[2] called Dizzy stinging him. Tonight I am going to Leigh Hunts.

[1] Hosea Biglow, the New England farmer in Lowell's *Biglow Papers*.

² 'Gallinipper. Also galknipper, ganninipper, ganniper. A large mosquito or other insect capable of inflicting an exceptionally painful sting or bite'. (*A Dictionary of American English*, ed. Sir William A. Craigie and James R. Hulbert [Chicago, 1940].)

My dear William   Paris, July [23], 1855[1]

I ought to have written to you yesterday, and that is the only good reason I can give for not having done it. But the truth is that I went to Versailles to see the monster squirts which play there every other Sunday, and as I got up rather late, I had not time to write and see the *Granz-O*[2] also. I trust you give me credit for enough human nature not to expect me on the day I said I should come. There are so many last things to do that though not "loath to depart" I am "still taking leave."

I saw the Jardin Mabille and the Château des Fleurs when I was here before, and have been again—but found them rather stupid. The lights and all that are pretty, but the dancers seem to me like a French vaudeville made out of Dante's "Inferno." The flavour of hell is there, but every drop of poetry that would spoil the punch is left out. I have seen all I wish of Paris . . . If I wanted to be 'wicked' I wouldn't be so here as some of our compatriots, I believe, are, but at home where the thing would have a great deal more *tang* to it. Smoky London suits me better, and we will go and dine at the Cock—yes, and see the Tabard also, and old Gower's tomb close by at St Mary Overie's. We will have rational amusement, which means a beef steak and a pot of porter.

Don't expect *us* (for Cranch comes too) till Wednesday. If we should arrive Tuesday it will be something to thank God for, but I know my own habits too well to think it possible. I shall rescue the watch and shall ransom it if necessary. In these sad days one can't get together his retainers (I don't speak of lawyers) and go drub a tradesman into reason, nor am I facile enough (in French) to quarrel to any advantage. Cranch has just come in, and we debate the several routes. We want to see the cathedral at Amiens. But we are coming anyhow.

                                                      [James Russell Lowell]

¹ I have not the holograph for this letter. The text is from HJ (I, 291–2), where the day of the month is not given. The first paragraph of the letter indicates that it was written on Monday; the particular Monday was July 23, which fell between the Friday (July 20) of the preceding letter and the Wednesday (July 25) on which Lowell and Cranch arrived in London (Scott, *Christopher Pearse Cranch*, p. 212).

² A disguised spelling of *grandes eaux*, fountains in full play.

Dresden, den 10 Nov. 1855.

*hochwohlgeborner Edelmann!*¹

do you think, because you don't write to me, that I shall know nothing about you? Don't you know enough of human nature yet, (*you*, in the neighborhood of Forty—is *that* written plainly enough?) to conceive that I shall hear no good of you unless you write it yourself? Don't I know that you want to buy a great estate in Cambridge, & that you also want to buy it for nothing? Now let me reason with you a little. *What* do you want fifteen acres for? Do you expect to supply Europe with wheat? Do you mean to raise your own potatoes & pay three & ninepence apiece for 'em? Go rather & dig those of one of your neighbors & have the good of the exercise! Do you want to raise fruittrees? Farewell, then, your peace of mind forever! There are (ask Dʳ Harris)² if I remember, ninety six varieties of insects with a *penchant* for pears, forty three with an appetite for apples, thirty one that poison peaches, & twenty seven & three quarters that puncture plums. Your imagination will be as full of bugs as a drop of water under the solar mikroscope. You will go through every form of disease to which your pets are incident—(& all the beds in your garden will be beds in a hospital)—Edelmann Storg. You will have the blackwart with the plums, the yellows with the peaches, the cracks (or whatever they call it) with the pears, & worst of all, be bored with the apples—*Crede Experto!* Or do you want fifteen acres to walk over perhaps? Again I say walk over your neighbor's land & wear *that* out—there is some sense in that. Is it a sense of proprietorship you wish to buy? Then buy a dog with nomadic propensities, & you won't forget

[297]

for five minutes at a time that you own something. Archimedes was the only man who ever had right notions about landed property—δός ηον οζῶ³—enough to stand on for the time being was all he asked for,—and that a man can always borrow. Two feet square will hold a man with all his joys & sorrows, far-reaching hopes, & highpoising imaginations. *Cu jus est solum, ejus est usque ad coelum*,⁴ you know, & even on two feet square that is a very handsome piece of property, & one that takes most of us a good while to walk *to the other end of*. Perhaps you have eaten of the insane root Speculation? You mean to buy property that will rise? Invest in a basin of soapsuds & a tobacco-pipe, then; it is inexpensive, & will amuse the children. If you *buy* land, it *won't* go up any more than a balloon with carbonic acid gas in it. *Nothing* will start it. Everything and everybody conspires against you. They build railways in other directions on purpose—they put up offensive manufactories on the next lot—they swindle you with taxes—they run highways through you & make you pay for 'em—they carry off your rails for fuel & your stonewalls for the fun of it—& your land stays on your hands as a plain girl sits beside her mother in a ballroom—*eternumig: sedebit*⁵—& no one enquires after it.

The only gleam of reason in your plan is the desire to buy in Cambridge. *That* is sensible. There stick. 'Tis as good a climate to raise statues in as any in the world, not to speak of the resident gentry—some of the most agreeable of whom are now unhappily in Europe. But they will come back if they live. So, be a good boy & buy a house in Cambridge, but suppress all ambition. You can't expect to rival the *great hereditary proprietors*—that would be madness—but buy a modest house & you will not find even the Duke of Thompsonlot⁶ too proud to come & eat *maccaroni in tamburro*⁷ with you.

Maccaroni—that reminds me of what an Italian feast I have been having. La Ristori has been playing here—a head & shoulders greater than she was in Rome. The Germans call her eine der am grösten tragischen Erscheinungen,⁸ or something of the sort, but they don't go to see her because the prices are raised, & because—she is an Italienerinn. They would choose sourkrout rather than ambrosia because it is Dutch. They think no country beautiful, fertile, no people wise, brave, beautiful—out of their confounded Dutchland. However, there is one accomplished foreigner in Dresden & *he* goes every night & shouts *brava!* in the hope of giving a grammatical flavor to the *bravoes* of the audience, which of course the modest schauspieler[9] who leads in the heroine takes all to himself & blushes with pleasure through his paint. But she is splendid & I don't know whether it's association for I saw her in happier times[10]—but she makes me quite drunk with the sweetness of her Italian. I can't go to sleep after it.

But I am stealing the time to write this & I musn't go on about Ristori or I shall need another sheet. Would you know my condition—fancy yourself a savage without a squaw, who has to get all his food by the chase, to make his own moccasins, & to darn his own stockings—only they don't wear any—I forgot that. Well, who *would* have to if he did wear 'em. I read nothing but German & as I have considerable appetite for learning, you may fancy the excursions I had to make at first into the forest of the dictionary. *Now* I have a tolerable winter's store of this vocabulary venison salted & dried, so that I live more at my ease. But nothing have I got without my own hard work—for I found I knew intolerably little Dutch when I came here. I am in a state of nature, aesthetically considered, & shall continue more or less so for some time to come. And how is Emmeline? as I used to call her in the old, old times—times before the flood—God forgive me! Dear old times when the daughters of God loved the sons of men—the reverse of what it was before Noah—& horribly the reverse of what it is now, only in another sense. Goodbye. Be good & make a *Big* Beethoven. I heard from Cranch the other day. He is well—& poor as St Francis. Give my love to Emelyn. And has the boy[11] a name yet? The splendid great placidity! Tell him that Unkn James has not forgotten him. Dinner! zu Tisch! *Ever yours*

J.R.L.

Write me a good long circumstantial letter. You don't have to study Dutch!

My address is "beim Herrn Hofrath Dr Reichenbach N^r 4 kleine Schiessgasse, Dresden."

P.S. I never enjoyed any piece of property so much as a stack of hay which I saw carried off bodily by an inundation of the Charles. I was proud of the undecayed forces of my native stream and sacrificed the hay [with] exultation. I suppose he and his nereids stuffed their *beds* with it.

Tell Emelyn that I use those things she gave me for my bills & that there is not one on the "unpaid" side! Tell me about *Rachel*. I have not seen an American paper, nor even Galignani, for five weeks.

I tried to write this straight but my hands are too cold. I know 'tis offensive to a wellregulated mind to see such scrimble-scramble—but I can't help it. Fancy it talked & it will all be straight enough.

¹ 'High-well-born nobleman'.

² Unidentified.

³ 'Give [me] space to breathe in'.

⁴ A law maxim: 'He who owns the soil, owns everything above it'.

⁵ 'She will sit eternally'—a mixture of Latin and German.

⁶ Lowell is referring to himself as a landowner.

⁷ Obviously, food for the poor.

⁸ 'One of the greatest tragic appearances'.

⁹ 'Actor'.

¹⁰ Lowell and his wife, who died in 1853, had probably seen Ristori act when they were in Rome during the winter of 1851–2.

¹¹ Thomas Waldo Story.

Boston Decr 30' 1855.

My dear James

Your very kind & humorsome letter came a fortnight or so ago, with a round blood red post-mark of "Aachen"—most fitly coming from Aachen to aching—or from Aix to aches.[1] My dear James do you think I look like an "apostle" that you suggest that I make myself an "Eliot apostle"[2] of art here among these western savages. No, if I were in the apostle line I should stand a better chance as "Torquemada apostle" of slavery. It requires too much purse to apostolize art. Perhaps if I were worth a million of dollars, I might stay & have my labor for my pain—but no pay in—for my labor. Think of my spending $5000 annually on my studio, & being left to pay the bills—for my folly—or getting a pat on the head from the great autocrat of Park St.[3] on the credit account. It is true that as "*Eliot* apostle" Ticknorville[4] might rally to my support—the Advertiser[5] faintly bringing up the rear —but the support from them would be death to me. Suppose I should recommend you (being a poet and so specially gifted in English writing) to go to Kamchatka (or however the place is spelt) & publish your poems & clever writings of every kind for the benefit of those precious Kamchatkans—how would it seem to you. Suppose, I should further recommend you to publish at your own expense, import a printing press, types, &c out of your own pocket, & foreigners to use them—or else spend two years in teaching the sled-drivers to print. No! my dear friend. You & I want an audience which is intelligent & sympathetic, which can understand & stamp what is good—& what is bad—we do not write for idiots or boors. We gather strength from sympathy. We must have our sounding-board to give effect to the tune we play.

Allston starved spiritually in Cambridgeport—he fed upon himself. There was nothing congenial without & he introverted all his powers & drained his memory dry. His works grew thinner & vaguer every day & in his old age he ruined his great picture.[6] I know no more melancholy sight than he was—so rich and beautiful a nature, in whose veins the South ran warm, which was born to have grown to such height & to have spread abroad such fragrancy, stunted on the scant soil & withered by the cold winds of that fearful Cambridgeport. I look at his studio whenever I pass with a heart-pang. It is a terrible ghost. All is in fact ghostlike here. There is no such thing as flesh & blood; we hob-a-nob with spirits—freely. We *love* nothing—we criticise everything. Even the very atmosphere is critical. Every twig is intensely defined ag[ain]st the sky—the sky itself is hard & distant. Earth takes never the hue of the heaven. The heart is growing into stone. The devil-side of enthusiasm (irritability) possesses us. There is no hearty love of anything—for we are afraid of making a mistake. Smith is afraid that the great Thompson (not of Thompson lot) may sneer, if he Smith says he likes anything, & then the sky might fall—we do not connect together in Boston, there are large numbers of admirable people, but they are all isolated—their conversation is that of sand-links. Elements of an admirable society are here—but they never get consolidated into a real social mass. We are a people of personal repulsions. We love to criticise. We love unhappiness. "If theres anything we have a contempt for, its the moon." We are so wise, so practical, so commonsensical, so logical, that we give no play to the heart & the imagination. You think we are honest. I find Boston changed greatly in this respect. You say at least in the home-relations we are right—& tell a horrible exceptional story. Well! it is only some three weeks ago, that two husbands, under false pretences inveigled two handsome youths, one named Sumner, to their houses—at separate times —the husbands attacked each, drove Sumner down cellar, & beat him terribly, ending by kicking him over the wall in the back-yard. The poor youth is since dead of the wounds he received. The cause of this brutal cowardice is that the two wives behaved in a shameless manner, made Sumner's acquaintance in Vinton's confection-shop—led him astray—(he was only 19) & thus excited their husbands revengeful jealousy. They are now to be tried for manslaughter. Is this the "tang" of Boston which you allude to, is this the "character of its own" which you say it has? Vintons shop is little better than a whorehouse & the girls with naked arms & shoulders & bold painted faces behind the counter are no better than they should be. And Boston says, that the people who go there (legion in number) do what well-behaved people in Dresden do not do, at least openly. I disbelieve in the superior honesty of the Americans. They have little blood & few sensual temptations, but they do not resist what temptations they have. What do you say of Schuyler & Quincy & Brevoort. They are exceptional? Why then are they not caught & punished as Strahan and Paul[7] are in England? We are not shocked at these things,—they are a days wonder & that is all. Society is scabbed over with pretences, but it is not healthy for all that. Carter[8] & I have terrible growls together in the little back room at Little & Brown's[9] over America. He says we are the greatest & the best of people. I do not agree. But what a growl I have given you. I did not mean to when I began, but I have been going on until I should better stop & leave the other side for another time—but if there ever was a Little Peddlington[10] I know where it is.

One great charm that America had to me was that it held you within its limits and I feel the want very greatly. How I daily wish you were here. Yet it is a shame in me to complain. We are all well—and is that nothing? It is my brain that gets so overexcited here. What do you think I have been about these three months. Why, writing Law—in Little & B[rown]'s back room. I have actually written about 400 printed pages in that time to add to a new ed[ition] of my 'Contracts'[11] & I feel like a wet rag after it. Now it is nearly over, & I am thinking of making a basso-relievo of the Pied Piper with the children flocking after him. But what encouragement to do it? Nobody will buy it. Nobody cares for it. There would be real interest if I had imported a cargo of salt-petre.

Yesterday we had a great snowstorm and the snow is heaving like great surf waves over the walls in the country & the roofs of the houses. All along the eaves are *friezes* of icicles—jagged as a wolf's teeth—and now & then comes down a thundering avalanche. For the last few days we have had a crystal world, trees of pure glass, & electric wires of spun glass stretching for miles. The country looks like an enchanted land; the sombre green pines crusted with diamonds, & bending neath their weight, the slender birches bowing to the ground in arches of gleaming ice— all the weeds like crystalline fingers & the white smooth heaped snow shrouding every thing on the ground. The spectacle is magnificent.

Heaps of new books are out—but nothing American of any importance but Prescotts Philip II[12] which every body is reading. Stories & novels of wretched quality swarm—Augustine Duganne[13] appears in a splendidly got up volume of Poems—with no poetry in them. Longfellows Hiawatha[14] has raised a row a free fight into which all the editors have rushed—& in the meantime some 8 or 9 thousand copies have sold. It is in many respects excellent, graceful & simple, but diffuse & lacking in power. Thackeray[15] has been lecturing here to crowded houses—but people did not want to be pleased—& he was severely criticised. He was not heavy & instructive enough for Boston—& only a few dared thoroughly to like the light & genial sketches of manners & society he gave us in his inimitable way. Oddly enough our people objected to him, that he pitched into the Georges & called them names. The lectures were too *Republican* for our taste & too anti-Royalty. Powell Mason[16] objected to them on the score that he could find all the facts & anecdotes in books he had in his library. I told him I was astonished to hear him say so, for I thought Thack[eray] had invented them all—but this was too deep for Powell. Thack[eray] has been far from well here—& I am afraid, that he is in a bad way. Geo. Curtis begins on the 18' his course of lectures on the Novelists before the Lowell Institute.[17]

I was delighted to read what you wrote of Ristori. It was pleasant to see in Paris what a weight & value her character gave to her acting. Rachel seemed a sham after her. The Italians have the real elan of passion—the heart forces them into pathos & moves enthusiasm & sympathy in others. They are the most naturally powerful of all actors. The heat of their natures melts the casing of artificial rules. But I am no judge of Italy & Italians, the very names fire me. I love Italy. My taste is spoilt for everything else—foolishly enough. Shall I ever again be as happy as I was there? Ah heaven! we never can repeat. Ardently as I desire to return, I fear. Things are so changed I am so changed. Sometimes I dream I am there—& life is glad as it once was. I take great draughts of beauty & awake to find myself in Rowe St.—& to drudge the day after.

Do you hibernate with a great white ghost of a stove? Do you talk the horse language to unkempt Professors? Have you got through the swamp of the dictionary yet? Do you put & answer daily those admirable Ollendorfian Questions?[18] "I have been to Paris but I have not broken my sister's wooden table." You do not seem to overlike Deutschland. Yet there is good there—a homely picturesqueness of life & customs—which is good material for art. Our imitations here are very brummagem. Our Christmas tree is a ghastly sham. I wish you would send me the whole series of the "Jugend Kalender" published at Leipsic —by George Wigand with the illustrations of the Dresden artists. It is admirable & I keep the only one I have on my table & look at it daily. The drawings are so free & clever & full of Germanity. Reinick & Bürkner[19] are the editors. If you know Bürkner recall me to him. I saw him at Dusseldorf, I think, & was presented to him by Fraulein Sack. (Edie's governess)

Mabel[20] has been staying with us all Christmas week & we had a great time together—such romping at night with the wildest of shrieking was never known. We carried her out to Mrs Howe's[21] (Julia's) where was a Christmas tree & a dance, & tableaux from the Rose & the Ring[22] by us great people. Such fun! But Emelyn will have told you all about it. Rachel made a great sensation here. Everybody took a book & read to follow her. Nobody understood what she said—but every body thought her wonderful. Hurlbut wrote a tremendous article in Putnam[23]—& went wild for her. Nobody cared for her character. She was wretchedly supported by a set of dirty Jews—& they too were taken into the general admiration. She was Jewier than ever & tried to skin a flint in Boston, which created a little reaction. But you know we go by fashion & it was the fashion to consider her unequalled. It was as much as one's life was worth to intimate a question as to her. I have not yet bought any house or land—but if I do not I shall never return to America. Let us, if we can return all go to Newport & live there—or go somewhere & live together. Pray write me soon again & I will write to you now that I have got through with my Law Book. Up to this time I have not had a moment's time for anything but that. How I remember the day we waved our hats to each other when you embarked for Deutschland—& how I wish I had gone with you. Forgive my growling I will do better next time.

Ever affectionately yrs
W. W. S.

¹ Story is answering Lowell's letter from Dresden, November 10, 1855, which was postmarked as it came through Aachen (Aix-la-Chapelle). Passages in Story's letter raise the question of whether before replying he had received another letter from Lowell urging him to make his home in Cambridge.

² John Eliot (1604–90), writer and missionary who was born in England, went to Boston and became known as Apostle to the Indians.

³ George Ticknor.

⁴ Edwin Percy Whipple has the following sentence in his discussion of George Ticknor: 'His position was so assured [in 1838, after his second European sojourn] that one of his friends, Nathan Hale, pleasantly suggested that the name of Boston be changed into Ticknorville'. (*Recollections of Eminent Men* [Boston, 1886], p. 270.)

⁵ *Boston Daily Advertiser.*

⁶ At his death his great picture 'Belshazzar's Feast' was unfinished.

⁷ These men had committed fraud. For an account of Robert Schuyler and Josiah Quincy see 'The American Railway Defalcations', *The Bankers' Magazine*, XIV (September 1854), 494–9. For an account of William Strahan and Sir John Dean Paul see *The Times*, June 22, p. 5; June 23, p. 12; and June 28, p. 11, 1855.

⁸ Robert Carter (1819–79), literary adviser and miscellaneous writer, helped Lowell edit the *Pioneer.*

⁹ Publishers. According to the DAB article on James Brown, his 'store became the gathering place of those who made the Boston of that period a literary center'.

¹⁰ The term comes from John Poole's *Little Pedlington and the Pedlingtonians* (London, 1839), in which pettiness and hypocrisy of an English village are described.

[11] The fourth edition of his *Treatise on the Law of Contracts* was published in 1856.

[12] William Hickling Prescott (1796–1859), American historian, planned four volumes for the *History of the Reign of Philip II*. Three volumes were published—two in 1855 and another in 1858.

[13] Augustine Joseph Hickey Duganne (1823–84), American author of popular literature. His collected poems were published in 1855.

[14] Published on November 10, 1855. The historical representation and metre were attacked, but the poem also received much praise. The publicity helped the sale.

[15] On this, his second, American tour Thackeray gave a series of lectures on *The Four Georges*.

[16] William Powell Mason (1835–1901), lawyer and financier.

[17] The Lowell Institute, an educational institution in Boston, was founded by a member of the Lowell family to provide for lectures by prominent men.

[18] Heinrich Gottfried Ollendorff (d. 1865) had a 'new method' of learning foreign languages.

[19] Robert Reinick (1805–52), Georg Wigand (1808–58), and Hugo Bürkner (1818–97)—all did works for children.

[20] Lowell's daughter, Mabel, stayed in America during his year of study and travel in Europe.

[21] Julia Ward Howe (1819–1910), American author and social reformer, well known as author of 'The Battle Hymn of the Republic'.

[22] When Edith Story had not yet fully recovered from her illness after her brother's death in 1853, Thackeray read his *Rose and the Ring*, chapter by chapter, to the young girl from the manuscript. When Thackeray offered her the manuscript, she expressed a preference for the first copy of the book instead, a choice to be regretted in later years. ('Romance of Beautiful American Marchesa Peruzzi de [*sic*] Medici', *New York Sun*, April 27, 1913, Section 4, p. 4.) The manuscript and Edith's copy of the fairy tale are now in the Pierpont Morgan Library, having been acquired at different times. (*The Pierpont Morgan Library*: Review of the Activities and Major Acquisitions of the Library, 1941–1948 [New York, 1949], p. 13.)

[23] *Putnam's Monthly Magazine*, September 1855. The article was by William Henry Hurlbert, who changed his name from 'Hurlbut'.

Dresden 28ᵗʰ Janʸ. 1856.

My dear William,

Did I say anything about an Apostle *Eliot*? If I did, I forgot myself & take it apologetically back—I might as well have taken the opportunity to shake the moths out of a red blanket when an Urochs was going by in flytime.

As to what you say about Boston, I will drink up Essel & eat a crocodile[1] with you on that subject any day—you can't scold worse about it than I would. I know that the finest political institutions in the world don't make a country pleasant to live in, & that one may find unlimited freedom frightfully ofpressive.[2] I would gladly subscribe toward *offering* (a judicious phrase) a handsome reward to anybody who will find a cure for the (small:)—potato disease with which Boston is fearfully infected—but! For example, here you are asked to deliver an address or something at the inauguration of Crawford's Beethoven—which you can do very handsomely as you have made a better one yourself—well, give 'em a rousing orthodox discourse with a distant panoramic view of the Lake of Fire & Brimstone that is prepared for all nations who don't love Art, or who don't love it rightly. You have got plenty of fight in you —let it out so. You can do the people good—they are plenty of them who would be glad to think right if they only knew how. But to think of liking any country when your experience is such as you describe is preposterous. If Little & Brown had a shop in Elysium & I were shut up in a little backroom of it to write a lawbook, I would do something or other that would get me transported to hell—where, by the way, one would be much more likely to meet the booksellers.

But the truth was that when I wrote to you I was suffering under a horrible homesickness—& shall I confess it? longing for Italy.[3] I am going there! in a month! I got absolutely sick under it & have only begun to mend by agreeing with myself to let the real part of me go, if the professional part works hard enough in the meanwhile. When I wrote to you, I was trying to reason myself out of it. I couldn't sleep, I couldn't eat, I couldn't endure to be spoken to—in short I was very badly off—& my nerves are still not what I like.

I agree with you as to the wants one feels at home. When I look back & think how much in me might have earlier & kindlier developed if I had [been] reared here, I feel bitter. But on the other hand, I prize my country breeding, the recollections of my first eight years, my Hoz Biglow[4] experiences as something real & I mean to make a poem out of them some day that shall be really American. But we were born at an ill time—we must fight—we can't merely live, & unluckily we can't be born over again. But I like America better than Germany in many respects. They have too *many* ideas here—so many tools that they only handle them without doing anything. The beauty of Greece was that they had very few ideas & those simple & great. The Germans try to recreate Greece, by studying themselves into it & by acquiring a beehive of notions small & confused. The wise Göthe has talked as much twaddle as any man I know. When people jabber so much about Art as they do here & have all their terms so cut & dried they are only playing cards on Art's coffin—just as Aristotle's poetics was the funeral oration of Greek poetry. But I must quit that. "Take your hat & come out of that!" That reminds me how many good times we have had together. It was one of our old catchwords. But I must not think of old times either, it makes me sick. I will think of what is to come & namely of your Pied Piper. I am delighted with the subject (Charles Lamb ought to have put him with Herod in his famous toast)[5]—you will be able to have the nakedness & drapery too—that is the half & halfness which suits us. It is an admirable subject, & you must make something out of it fit to go up beside Luca della Robbia's singing children. There is a very good version of the story, by the way in Howell's Letters[6]—which may give you some hints—if you have it not already laid on a sketch of your proposed treatment. Why doesn't Charlie Perkins order a Mozart for the other niche?[7] Or it ought to be an Italian, Palestrina, perhaps. Do you remember our ride & the nightingales?[8] Well, we shall meet some day or other, I hope—if not here on some Italian planet. Addio. Love to Emelyn. Shall write her next post. Have only time to save the mail now.

[James Russell Lowell]

[1] 'Woo't drink up eisel? eat a crocodile?' (*Hamlet*, V, i.)

[2] A playful Lowellism.

[3] Lowell stayed in Italy about three months, and his spirits were considerably revived.

[4] The hero of the first series of *The Biglow Papers*, already published. The second series, which upheld the position of the North during the Civil War, was to appear periodically during the war and in book form in 1867.

[5] 'A story is told of him [Lamb], after he had been much plagued by a noisy family, rising to propose the health of the "m-m-much ca-calumniated good King Herod".' (E. V. Lucas, *The Life of Charles Lamb* [London, 1921], I, 491.)

[6] James Howell, *Epistolae Ho-Elianae* [London, 1713], p. 272.

[7] That is, in the Boston Music Hall, where Crawford's 'Beethoven' was to be placed.

[8] See Elmwood, I, 185–6.

[Boston]
Feb[ry] 18' 1856.
& in four days your 37
old boy. We shall fire
guns here on the occasion.

My dear James

I must add my mite to the contribution-box going to a friend cast away in Germany, if it be only to congratulate him on being there. I dare say you think yourself worse off in Dresden than you could possibly be in Boston—for it is the peculiarity of man to hate what he has, & cry for what he has not. But in this one instance you are wrong. The arctic zone has slipped down like a garter and got on to the temperate zone. Kane's account of his winter among the floes[1] is not an exaggeration of our Boston experience. The city has spent no less than $20,000 in ploughing up & carting away the streets. They are masks of hideous ice, with "ruffian billows" and pits—"thankee marms" as we used to call them in the "good old days"—that disturb the strongest stomach that goes over them, as much as a steamer in a head wind. The universal world growls & swears—& I foremost among them as you may suppose.

George Curtis's course of lectures on the Novelists was very successful. His manner was charming & his matter most genial & pleasant. Of course all did not agree to his criticism. Why should they? George would not probably agree with Jones & Jenkins on any other subject, why should he on novels. Ticknor[2] sat grimly beside me one ev[enin]g when the lecture was on Dickens & remarked after the lecture was over that he should probably have been more interested in it if he had ever read Dickens' books & knew the *pearsons* alluded to; but that he made three unsuccessful attempts at the Pickwick Papers & had failed to find any thing in them. All the girls fell in love with Geo. & said he was "perfectly splendid." I thought of you often & all your friends spoke of your lectures[3] constantly as being so very admirable. And by the way we drank your health in good warm-hearted Hungarian wine the other day at Longfellows & wished you were with us, or rather we were with you. I am in hopes that the Longfellows will go out with us in the summer, June probably, and the Henry Greenoughs seem disposed also to join us.[4] How I wish you were not a Professor & would go with us. However, we shall see each other somewhere in Europe —only let us know what your plans are, so as to be sure not to miss you.

I have got almost through with my book on Contracts which has now swelled to two volumes of 750 pages each—and am now preparing a volume of poems[5] for the press—which if I decide to publish I shall ask to dedicate to you if you are willing to take so poor a gift. I do not think they are bad. At all events they are so very far ahead of the old vol[ume] that I think it may be as well to print. I have given them to Carter to look over & if he & Underwood[6] think advisable to recommend Phillips & Sampson to publish them, I publish. If not—not.

Next week, I prologuize the Beethoven statue—which is to be inaugurated with considerable circumstance of music &c. I hate to do this, but for Crawford & Perkins sake I yielded, although I swore after the last poem in public, that I never would again publicly recite my verses.

Goodbye dear James—consider all that Emelyn says. Resign your Professorship & stay with those who love you.

Ever affectly
yrs
W. W. S.

---

¹ Elisha Kent Kane (1820–57), Arctic explorer, wrote of his first voyage to the Arctic in *The United States Grinnell Expedition in Search of Sir John Franklin* (1853). After a second expedition he wrote *Artic Explorations* (1856). (Jeanette Mirsky, *Elisha Kent Kane and the Seafaring Frontier* [Boston, 1954], p. 180.)

² George Ticknor.

³ At the beginning of 1855 Lowell had given a series of lectures at the Lowell Institute.

⁴ Passage was engaged for Longfellow and his family, but the poet injured his knee and the plans were cancelled. Seemingly Henry Greenough (1807–83)—painter and architect, brother of Richard Greenough—did not go. (See *Henry Wadsworth Longfellow*, ed. Samuel Longfellow, II, 315–16.)

⁵ Published by Little, Brown and Company, 1856. It is inscribed to JRL 'In testimony of a friendship / Which, beginning in childhood, has only deepened and / Strengthened with time; / And as a tribute of esteem, admiration, and love / For his high poetic genius; his exuberant / Humor and wit; his delightful social / Qualities; and his pure and / Noble character'.

⁶ Francis Henry Underwood (1825–94), literary editor and adviser for the Boston publishers Phillips, Sampson, & Co.

Catania, Sicily, 7ᵗʰ May 1856.¹

My dear William,

Your & Emelyn's letters followed me to Florence, & I have been running about so ever since that I have not had a quiet day

[312]

for answering them. I wrote you that I had resolved to go to Italy & that I meant to spend a month. Well, I came & found myself so much better for it that I am already in the first week of my third month. Having got to Rome, my sister[2] would have me go on with them to Naples, & being in Naples, she advised me very strongly to make the tour of Sicily which I have just been doing with Black, Norton,[3] & Field. We have come hither from Palermo on mules, I believe about two hundred & odd miles—tremendous work—but worth doing at any cost of discomfort. Enough discomfort there is—such inns it never entered into the heart of man to conceive—so nasty—so fleay, & all that. But one lives & likes it. I am staying at home today in the hope of accomplishing Etna tonight—but am afraid I shall funk as I do not find myself very well & unless I feel better this afternoon shall not try it. We are getting old, my dear boy. Black & Field will go at any rate, & Norton & I as far as Nicolosi. Thence we go to Messina & so back to Naples. In Italy proper I have done one or two places I skipped before—Ravenna, Parma, Mantova, Orvieto & the like. I cannot tell you how well it has been with me till now when I am getting a little downhearted again. Now I have given you a notion of my track & you know Italy too well not to be able to fill it out. The great days, of course, never come back, but Italy is still Italy. I dreamed night before last of being at Nantasket with Maria sixteen years ago & it has made me sad.

When I read about your book & your offer to dedicate it to me, my dear friend, the tears came into my eyes—it brought back so much. How could I be anything but pleased? I am sure the volume will do you honor, as the dedication will me. We are long friends & we shall be more to each other as we grow older. I am glad to have our names united in any way.

I hear in a roundabout way of your Beethoven-statue inauguration. It must have been a good time, but your own letter is the last I have received from home & I wait to hear directly from you. I can well understand that you were reluctant to undertake an "occasional" poem—but it was a graceful thing to do & I am glad that you did. I have seen the model of the statue since. My opinion of yours is raised, though I found C[rawford]'s better than I had looked for. But what things one sees in sculptor's studios, side by side with all that fulness of old art! The want of fancy in decorative parts quite perplexes me. I begin to believe that even Greek breath in frosty air took gracefuller forms than ours.

Now I am going to beg. We have got up a subscription to buy a Venus of Page's for the Boston Athenaeum.[4] We give a hundred dollars apiece up to three thousand, which is the price & I have counted upon you as one of the thirty. As for the picture, I need say nothing about that. Only it is very wonderful, & *everybody* thinks so which, you know, is not always the case with Page's pictures. Crawford, Norton, Field & I are among the subscribers. A brother of our Wales & Wales[5] himself have made themselves responsible for a thousand dollars. But think of sending such a stark-nakedness to proper Boston! We have some doubts the Athenaeum may decline it. But never mind, we wanted it to go to America, & if the worst comes to the worst we can make a raffle or Tontine of it. If you know anybody else who would subscribe get his name.

I shall do everything to meet you when you come. You must write to me at Dresden & tell me your plans & I will shape mine accordingly. I go back to Dresden & then home before long. I am quite homesick. But I would come to Paris on my way unless you come late enough to meet again in England, which I should prefer. I do not wonder at your coming back. I expected it, though I hoped you might stay in America. But you will be happier on this side.

I have been three weeks now without seeing a newspaper, & am wholly in the dark as to what is going on in the world. But I do not suppose the great clock has stopped because I am out of the way of seeing the dial. One event I must tell you to fill up my Italian experiences—a climb up Vesuvius which is sending out unheard of columns of smoke & groaning & sighing wierdly. We staid till after night & saw the smoke-wreaths lurid with the fires down below. Aetna is perfectly quiescent & covered with snow for almost a third of its height. The others are gone out to hear a famous organ at the Benedictine Convent. If they were here they would all send warm remembrances. Give my love to Emelyn, & tell her that Mrs Black is expecting to be confined. Only think of my being in Sicily & that three days ago I was at Syracuse! Goodbye I shall write again before long.

Alaways affectionately yours

J.R.L.

[1] Lowell held this letter for a month and then sent it with the one dated June 7, 1856.

[2] Mary, Mrs. Samuel Raymond Putnam.

[3] Charles Eliot Norton (1827–1908), author, editor, and professor of the history of art in Harvard University. He and Lowell were good friends; they co-edited the *North American Review* from 1863–8, and Norton edited two volumes of Lowell's letters, which he later included, with added letters, in the Elmwood edition of Lowell's works.

[4] The picture was 'refused on the ground of nudity' at the Paris Exhibition. (Kenyon, II, 316; see also EBB's remark on it in McAleer, p. 33.) It did get to the Boston Athenaeum, for a contemporary of Lowell's wrote of having seen it there. (*Letters and Journals of Thomas Wentworth Higginson*, ed. Mary Thacher Higginson [Boston, 1921], p. 78.) I learned from the director and librarian of the Boston Athenaeum that the picture became quite worthless and unexhibitable because of the deterioration of the pigments; consequently it disappeared from the scene early in the century. (Letter from Walter Muir Whitehill, November 30, 1953.)

[5] Dr. Henry Ware Wales (1818–56), a friend of Lowell's from boyhood, founded the Sanscrit professorship at Harvard. (Scudder, *James Russell Lowell*, II, 403.)

Dresden 7th June 1856.

My dear William,

You will see by my date that I have got back here to Germany again. The first sheet was written in Sicily, but I found the safety of the post thence very questionable & so kept the letter by me, & having travelled like a courier ever since by me it has remained.[1]

[315]

Pray write me here as soon as you arrive in London. I shall be here for a month longer, & then for home. Shall you make any stay in England? Or, if you go straight to Paris, couldn't we make some little excursion thence like that we made in England. I should like of all things to have you come here. Have you ever seen *our* Saxon Switzerland? It is worth a journey—but write & we will arrange some plan or other. I am sensibly better in body & mind than before my journey—only dreadfully bothered by having let all my correspondence fall into arrears.

I *must* be at home by the 1st Septr I have orders. But I hope to be there by the first of August. *Then* I shall have to work like —a professor on leave. I know no extremer comparison.

I trust everything is well with you & yours. Give my best love to Emelyn—& rest assured that Messina is duller than Boston. We had to wait a week there for a steamer. I shall work again when I am settled here. God bless you—Goodbye.

Ever *affectionately yours*
J.R.L.

---

[1] Lowell sent this letter with the one dated May 7, 1856.

Hôtel de France, Rue Laffitte,
Paris, 16th July, 1856.

My dear Emelyn,

Here I am back again just where I was a year ago at this time & as delighted to hear of your being in England as I was then disappointed to find that you had decamped thither—for in England I shall be in a few days. It is rumored in diplomatic circles that you are at the White Hart, Windsor which has a very comfortable sound, but are you to stay there? Shall we go & see another cathedral or so together?

What I wish you particularly to do now is to write & tell me where you got the *doll* which has so excited Mabel's cupidity.[1] If you can't remember the exact address, can you tell the street or the quarter? Also whether it is a gal of wax? Moves her eyes?

About how big? Cost *environ* how much? Has a wardrobe? I see ruin staring me in the face, & have just got a letter from Mabel ordering shoes, stockings & what not for the young foreigner. You see what a predicament I should be in were I to go home with the wrong baby. It is not a case for a warming pan, for the features of the child are already known to the expectant mother by vision—nay, by actual touch of the twin sister of elder birth. Not every supposititious child would answer. Were it not for this hitch I should leave Paris on Saturday, by which time, I shall have some books I have bought packed & some clothes ready.

I am already tired of Paris where ich langweile mich immer fürchterlich.[2] I am a great deal better in health than I was though not very well for me. You think I am suffering from the hypcomplaint? Very well, the result is the same. But I have really been ill [in] mind & body. Mind is better—body so so.

Cranch is not well. Took cold at Fontainebleau & is now bilious & all sorts of things, poor fellow—but more prosperous moneyly than last year. So the Longfellows are coming? Won't they have a nice time. Over here it is more of a reputation to *know* Longfellow than to have written various immortal works. Gather your laurels while ye may, old Time is still aflying! & old times, too, more's the pity. We will have one more, though, in England, I trust.

Since I wrote, I have seen William's Beethoven poem which I like extremely—both sentiment & style. It must have been very effective & is short enough to make one wish for more—a rare merit on such occasions when poets generally hang all their wardrobes fluttering on the lines. Is W. as savage as ever against that wretched town of Boston? Since George third nobody ever treated it so. Well, I give it over to him. I entrench myself in Cambridge, which is a good kind of place. For the country in general with Kansas & Brooks[3] & what not, I don't wonder you were in haste to get out of it.

Here is an extract from Mabel's letter—"Bobo[4] is just as pretty as he can be" which as the disinterested opinion of a young lady I attach some value to. *You* will think it too cautious &

measured, no doubt—for I was sharpsighted enough to notice your partiality for that young man. Perfectly proper, only don't let him take up all the room in your heart. Save a place for your old friends & especially

for your ever affectionate
J.R.L.

Of course it is understood that I send love to William.

---

[1] In the Lowell Collection in the Houghton Library are letters in a childish hand written by Mabel Lowell, aged nine, to her father while he was in Germany. In some of them she was insistent on the clothes for her French doll, specifying the need for 'stockings, and shoes, and dresses, petticoats, drawers, and chemises', because she didn't 'want to have her naked'. (bMS Am 1484.)

[2] 'Where I am continually fearfully bored'.

[3] The friction between the North and South had come to a head in trouble over Kansas. The feelings that ran high in Congress were matched by angry words on both sides. After Charles Sumner made a speech in May 1856, he was brutally attacked in the Senate by Preston Smith Brooks from South Carolina. The assault aroused tremendous feeling.

[4] Waldo Story.

Elmwood, 12th Septr 1864.

My dear William,

Dr Cogswell (whom everybody knows) wishes me to write an introduction to you & Emelyn in behalf of Mrs John Astor (whom he knows).[1] Of course I am happy to do it both on his account & hers. Mrs Astor, a South Carolinian by birth, is thoroughly loyal & refused a letter to you offered by a 'Copperhead' friend. So you see she deserves all kindness at your hands, whatever may be the case with *me* who have not written for so long.

I take this chance of sending you my *carte-de-visite* from Rowse's drawing[2] which is said to be like. With love to Emelyn,

Yours affectionately
as always
J.R.L.

P.S. I have just dedicated a book³ to you.

¹ Joseph Green Cogswell (1786–71), American teacher and librarian, who served as adviser to John Jacob Astor I in planning the Astor Library, now part of the New York Public Library. Astor's grandson, John Jacob III, who had been sent to Göttingen for two years with Cogswell as his mentor (Harvey O'Conner, *The Astors* [New York, 1941], pp. 74–75), married Charlotte Gibbes of a 'prominent but somewhat impoverished South Carolina family' (DAB).

² Samuel Worcester Rowse (1822–1901), American painter, illustrator, and lithographer, lived in Boston for many years. Of his crayon portraits, for which he gained national and international reputation, that of Lowell is one of the best. It was reproduced as frontispiece to Volume I of the Elmwood edition of Lowell's works.

³ *Fireside Travels*, including the 1854 essay that gave the book its title. (See WWS–JRL, January 9, 1855, n. 5.) The dedicatory poem of 1864 reads: 'Who carves his thought in marble will not scorn / These pictured bubbles, if so far they fly; / They will recall days ruddy but with morn, / Not red like these late past or drawing nigh!'

address me at
Palazzo Barberini
Rome. Decʳ 10. 1864

My dear James—

I was taken ill a month ago at Paris, & while I was lying on my bed Emelyn read to me your delightful book of "Fireside Travels" which I was fortunate enough to procure from London. As she read it all the old days revived; all the old passages of love & hope & joy which we had known together came before me, and my heart yearned towards you, as to one of the oldest & best-loved of all my old friends. For years our correspondence has ceased—why I know not—but my affection has never wavered for a moment & I have eagerly sought from all who had seen you news & information about you and yours. But as I read your book—so genial so rich in humor & fancy, I seemed as it were to be again talking with you, & I determined as soon as I should be well & have a half-hour of unoccupied time to write & break this long silence, & thank you—for the kindly mention of me which is scattered through your book—& for the dedication of it to me. I hear that there is a sonnet or some verses prefixed to the American edition—but this I have not seen as it is omitted in the English edition.

How I wish you were again here as in the olden times—& that we again could wander about the streets of the city & through the mountain towns, or sit long evenings before the fire late into the night and talk as we used to do. There is one great drawback to me in my Roman life, & that is the want of some friend, with whom I can thoroughly sympathise, & whom I can meet on the higher ranges of art and literature. For the most part, & with scarcely an exception among the American artists, art is but a money-making trade, & I can have no sympathy with those who are artists merely to make their living. As for general culture there are none of our countrymen resident here who pretend to it—and I hunger & thirst after some one who might be to me as you were. But nobody makes good the place of old friends. We are knitted together in our youth as we never can be in our older age—no new friends are like the old ones. But I suppose it is vain to hope that you will come again to Rome, at least for the present. You are tied down to Cambridge by strong ties, which it would be impracticable to break. Has the wild love of travel gone out of your blood as it has out of mine. Are you growing respectable, solemn, professional & dignified. I figure you to myself sometimes as sitting in the academic robes on the platform at Commencement, & cannot but smile as I see you there. Once in a while I hear your trumpet sound through the columns of the 'Atlantic'[1] or the 'N.A.R.'[2] & more rarely I read some new poem. But why are the poems so rare. Do not let the dust of the University drop too thickly upon you! Do not yoke Pegasus down into the Professors harness. You see I have not touched your hand & heard your voice for so long, that I cannot do more than grope after you in the dark—wondering about you, & fearing & hoping—& getting perhaps everything wrong.

This year I thought of going to America and seeing the old places again. But I hate to travel—& the expense added to my dislike of moving has prevented me. Besides, I was not quite well in England, & loved better to lounge on the lawn at Mt. Felix, than to be tossed on the restless & roaring ocean. But it is just possible that next year I may brace myself up to this terrible voyage, & then I shall see you. If I do come I hope to bring with me some statue of mine, to show as token of how I have spent my thoughts & my life here. At present there is nothing of mine in America of the best that I have done & I should like that something should be there containing my best which is nothing too good. I suppose as yet that nobody is convinced that there is much in me, & I fear that they are all right. They still pat me on the head & feebly encourage me now & then.

Edith has grown up to be a woman and so has Mabel. How I wish they could see each other & have the friendship their mothers had. But it has been ordered otherwise. Bobo you have seen—he is now ten years old—& yesterday was his birth-day. But Julian you have never seen. He is going to be an artist,[3] I think—but I let him work out his own way. If the love of art is real it will domineer, if not real it is useless to foster it. Emelyn knows not that I am writing—but she bears the same old love to you as ever & talks constantly of you—and constantly regrets your absence. We live in the Barberini Palace—& look down from our windows over all Rome—but there is not a person in any house so dear to us as you are.

This is a very stupid letter—but it will serve, perhaps. Set me a good example and write to me all about yourself and what you are doing. There is nothing that concerns you that does not interest us. *Even as of old your affectionate*

W. W. Story

[1] *Atlantic Monthly*, a political and literary magazine, was founded at Boston in 1857, with Lowell as its first editor. He edited it for four years.

[2] *North American Review*. Lowell was one of the editors at this time.

[3] He became a painter. In 1880 he painted a portrait head of Browning, which is now in the Lawrence Art Museum of Williams College in Williamstown, Massachusetts.

Elmwood, Thursday.
[July 27, 1865][1]

My dear William,

Remember that you are to dine with me at our Club (Union) on Saturday. I expect you & Emelyn to give us at least a week here before you go back. With old love to you & Emelyn.

Yours always

J.R.L.

[1] The envelope with this letter is postmarked July 27. Emelyn and W. W. Story visited America in 1865; July 27 fell on Thursday in that year.

Longwood
Monday morning.
[CA. September 1865][1]

My dear James

I was very sorry not to catch a glimpse of you the other day when you were in town, for my time grows short & I have really seen nothing of you.

If you like Emelyn and I propose to go to you at Cambridge & spend the night of Tuesday (tomorrow). If this be not convenient or if you would prefer any other night this week, please let us know & we will substitute it for tomorrow.

Address us to James T. Eldredge 23 Congress St. Boston.

Ever yours

W. W. Story

[1] In a hand other than Story's the date is written after Longwood as follows: [184–?]. The letter was not, however, written in the forties. James T. Eldredge was not at 23 Congress Street until 1858. (*Genealogical and Personal Memoirs Relating to the Families of the State of Massachusetts*, ed. William Richard Cutter [New York, 1910], IV, 2563.) The letter must have been written near the end of the Storys' 1865 visit, for Lowell was not in America during any other visit that they made to America after 1858. The Storys arrived in America towards the end of July (Norton-Elmwood, II, 103–4) and were back in London by October 15 (RB–WWS, October 15, 1865).

Elmwood, Tuesday
[ca. September 1865][1]

My dear William,

I fear you will not get this in time, but shall expect you all the same. I did not get your note till last night. Come early & come often. The cars pass my corner every quarter of an hour for Mt Auburn & Watertown. I shall be glad to get even a bit of you, though I should prefer the whole peach. If you get this in time, bring your photographs (of statuary) with you.[2] I should like to see them again & to have Fanny see them.

Yours always
J.R.L.

[1] The reference to Fanny, Lowell's second wife, dates this letter. Between Lowell's marriage in 1857 and Fanny's death in 1885, the Storys visited America only once when the Lowells were there—in 1865. The letter may have been the answer to the preceding letter in this collection.

[2] Lowell saw the photographs. (Scudder, II, 86.)

Oatlands Park Hotel[1]
Aug. 6' 1868.

My dear James

Mr Herman Merivale[2] is just leaving us here at Oatlands Park to sit under the trees while he takes flight to America—& I wish you to know each other. You will find him most agreeable full of fun & good stories, very clever, and the author of a very successful play "Time & the Hour" as well as of other things. I wish instead of his going over to you, you were coming here to us to make Time & the Hour delightful to us—& one of the things I most envy him in America is that he will see you.

Some day when you have nothing better to do why will you not give me one of your long letters as of old & tell me all about yourself & what you are doing. It is a long time since I have seen your handwriting, but a charming poem of yours from the Atlantic Mag[azine][3] came to us the other day which we read with great pleasure. So I know you are still alive.

[323]

If this were not a letter of introduction it would not be in my heart not to fill up these pages—but let us worship the God Proper whatever we do.

With our kindest remembrances to you & your wife and Mabel. Believe me ever as of old

Yours most affectionately
W. W. Story

[1] This was the hotel in Weybridge, Surrey, where the Storys sometimes stayed. (Story Col.)

[2] Herman Charles Merivale (1839–1906), English playwright and novelist. He, under the pseudonym of Felix Dale, together with John Palgrave Simpson published *Time and the Hour* in 1869.

[3] From January through August of 1868 Lowell published the following poems in the *Atlantic Monthly*: 'In the Twilight', 'After the Burial', 'A June Idyl', and 'The Footpath'.

Grosvenor Hotel.
Chester.[1]
28th July, 1872.

My dear William,

I am very glad to hear you are in London, & shall hope to see you there. I shall stay here till Friday, & should be glad to get your address before I leave—so that I need not travel down to Lombard Street.

Give my love to Emelyn & say that I should have answered her letter by Mabel if I had had any fixed plan. But my coming over at all was a contingency, & here I am at last the most astonished man in the three kingdoms. I went to bed in Cambridge & I wake up in Chester.

Send me your address that I may at least shake hands with you before you leave London.

We got here at 3 this morning & I am hardly yet awake.

Affectionately yours
J.R.L.

[1] Lowell and his second wife, Frances Dunlap Lowell, had just arrived in Europe, where they were to spend two years.

Thursday 1 Aug '72
Crosby Lodge[1]
Crosby on Eden
(5 miles from) Carlisle

Dear James—

We have just received your note from Chester & we have telegraphed back immediately to beg you to come & stay with us at our little house here. We all do so wish & hope that you & your wife will come to us. I know it is selfish—but I do not care. We want to see you. I don't see old friends every day—& you must come.

We are living very simply here—with a little box of a house— but with plenty of room for you & your wife & maid if she has one. Edith & the two boys are here & you will see them & they will be so glad to see you. You have never seen one of my boys & the other only when he was an infant.

You will see that it is not so very long from you to us—if you take the rail at Chester a very short time brings you here to Carlisle & our carriage shall meet you at the station & bring you to us. We have old castles to show you! Naworth for instance, the finest old border castle in the land. We have a charming country—shooting, if you like it—& I don't think you will be bored for a week at least—unless you have some special plan on foot which will carry you at once to London.

Kindest regards to your wife from us all—& to you all sorts of wild greetings from us all—& from

Yrs affectionately
W. W. Story

---

[1] In the early seventies the Storys spent their autumns partly in the North of England at Crosby Lodge, near Carlisle, and partly in Scotland. During their two-year stay in Europe the Lowells visited the Storys at Crosby Lodge and again in Rome in the early part of 1874.

[325]

11 Down Street,
Piccadilly
15th Aug. 1872.

My dear Emelyn,

I am siezed with a sudden panic that you may wish to know *precisely* when we are going to turn-up—because you may be expecting other guests & to have us suspended over your head all the while by the slenderest hair of chance must be dreadful. The truth is I came over hither with the express purpose of doing nothing & have thus far shown no small talent (I flatter myself) as well as industry in the business. Having got fitted to the chairs & things here I should probably spend the rest of my life here unless some such motive as Crosby Lodge intervened. You see it does not matter whether I start a day or two later or not.

My plan is to go down by way of York & Durham, taking Fanny over to Fountains Abbey on the way. From Durham there is a rail (& ergo a telegraph) to Carlisle, from Durham I shall *wire* you with exact dates. Meanwhile for probabilities. We shall start Monday or Tuesday, & I don't well see how we can use up more than a week on the road. Lincoln (I just remember) is also on the way & well worth seeing. Say a week, & that would bring us to Crosby Lodge on Saturday week—the 24th.

This strikes me as feasible & ingenious. It would be too absurd for an old fellow of fifty three to travel all that distance to see another old fellow & compare notes of hair & teeth & so on—but to make an instructive tour (don't you see?) puts another face on the matter. I drop in on you by accident, & we shall have no business with this profit & loss account of life. Then we can come back by the English Lakes.

As for J. H.[1] I could not persuade him & he is going over to the Continent intending to meet me again here or in Paris. I shall probably await the Nortons[2] here & then go over to the Low Countries & so South. Love to William

always affectionately yours
J.R.L.

[326]

[1] John Holmes (1812–99), brother of Oliver Wendell Holmes. In his quiet and simple life in Cambridge he had a few intimate but devoted friends, Lowell one of them, who left testimony of his humour and lovability. He and the Lowells went to Europe on the same ship in 1872. His correspondence during his travels is included in the volume of his letters, which reflect the charm of this thoroughbred New England Cantabrigian. (*Letters of John Holmes*, ed. William Roscoe Thayer [Boston, 1917]; see also Higginson, *Contemporaries*, pp. 168–91; W. D. Howells, *Literary Friends and Acquaintance* [New York, 1901], pp. 280–3.)

[2] Charles Eliot Norton was in Europe from 1868 to 1873. His wife died in Dresden in February of 1872, and he spent the following winter in London with his remaining family. On his way to London Norton stopped in Paris; and it was there, not in London, that he and Lowell were together. (Scudder, II, 154, 157, 158.)

Grosvenor Hotel,
Park Street
Tuesday. [July 31, 1877][1]

Dear William,

It sounds like old times, & I should like very much to be there[2] (so would Fanny) but I have made two appointments one just before & the other just after your hour. I tried to see you yesterday with Hughes,[3] but neither of us had the number, so after asking at five or six we gave it up. I shall try with this having got No 18 from James.[4] All success to you & your play.

Affectionately yours
J. R. Lowell.

[1] The date is established by date on the envelope and contents of letter. July 31, 1877—the date on the envelope—fell on Tuesday. Lowell, who had been appointed Minister from the United States to Spain, was spending a few days in London on his way to Madrid, where he was in diplomatic service for two and a half years. He came to England on the same ship that was to carry Story and his son Waldo to the United States.

[2] Lady Marian Alford and Story arranged for him to read his tragedy *Stephania* at her home on July 31. Lowell was invited. (Story Col., letters WWS–ES, July 30 and August 2, 1877.) *Stephania* was privately printed in *ca.* 1875.

[3] Thomas Hughes (1822–96), author of *Tom Brown's Schooldays*, had an enthusiastic admiration for Lowell's *Biglow Papers* and in 1859 prepared the first English edition of this work. In 1870, on his first visit to the United States, he and Lowell met and became lasting friends. (Edward C. Mack and W. H. G. Armytage, *Thomas Hughes* [London, 1952], pp. 131, 132, 185–6.) Story knew him and had been with him and Browning a few days before this letter was written. (Story Col., letter WWS–ES, July 30, 1877.)

[4] Henry James (1843–1916) had established himself in London in 1876. On July 30, 1877, Story wrote his wife from London, 'James [Lowell] asked me to dinner . . . & one other guest was Henry James'. (Story Col.)

Madrid, 18th Novr 1879.

Dear William,

Let me ask you to be kind to two dear friends of mine who have been very good to me, & who will be very agreeable to you. They will tell you the latest dreary news of me.[1]

With love to Emelyn,
Affectionately yours
J. R. Lowell

[1] Lowell's wife was seriously ill.

Il Lago
Vallombrosa
July 25, 1882

My dear James

You will be very sorry to hear that Mr Marsh[1] died at the Hotel at Vallombrosa on Sunday ev[enin]g at 9 oclock of paralysis of the heart. He had come here to pass the summer, and the air & the place seemed to agree with him, and we all thought him improving in health & spirits when suddenly all came to an end. He had been working all the morning, dictating a letter, & notes to one of his books, and after an early dinner went out and sat under the trees surrounded by his little nieces & there talked pleasantly to them about the clouds, & explained to them all sorts of little familiar facts of nature. After remaining there some time, he said he felt a little tired & thought he would go into the house. He did so & Mrs Marsh remained behind for a few minutes to speak with a friend—on her return she found that he was lying on the bed, but he complained of nothing save of feeling tired. She gave him at his request a couple of teaspoonsful of whiskey—& offered to read to him—but he said he thought he would go to sleep. From time to time she returned to his room & still found him awake & cheerful. Later he took a cup of tea—& still later asked for some lemonade. The servant prepared it & took it to him & he sipped a little of it. Mrs. Marsh was not then with him, and the servant came to her & said, that he seemed to be not as well as usual & found a difficulty in breathing. She went at once to him, & found him suffering from oppression, and gasping for breath—but there was nothing at first alarming—& she said to him Have courage it will all pass away, & you will be well again. To this he said No! No! Then asked that the window should be opened. But as he did not recover she became alarmed & summoned a physician in the house & gave him ether & some other restorative. Sinapisms were then applied to his feet & body—but it was of no avail. Within ten minutes of the time when she came in he sank back on the pillow and was gone—with no suffering, save a little distress for want of breath.

I have told you all this thinking you might desire to know all the circumstances—& in accordance with the wish of Mrs Marsh that you should be informed of them—& of his death.[2] She poor lady is utterly broken down—as you may well imagine. Peruzzi[3] & I went over to her immediately & passed the day there yesterday making all the necessary arrangements—and a melancholy day it was. We procured permission to place his body in a large room in the old convent, & this has been made into a Chapelle Ardente, until he can be removed to Rome where he will be buried in the Protestant Cemetery. Unfortunately at this moment there is no one to represent our country here. Mr. Wurtz[4] as perhaps you know has been turned out summarily by telegram from his place as Secretary of Legation —& though I hear that our government has with the utmost disregard of all propriety determined to unite the offices of Consul Gen[era]l & Secretary of Legation, & nominated Gen[era]l Richmond[5] our consul here to both positions, his nomination is not confirmed as yet I believe and he is absent on leave—so that all the duties of the occasion have devolved upon me & Peruzzi. In fact I know not what Mrs Marsh would have done had we not been near her. The telegraph to Wurtz [*sic*], but he apparently is not in Rome as he has not answered—and besides as he has no official position now he could do nothing more than we have done. This sudden & wholly unexpected act of the government in removing Wurtz & uniting the two offices of Consul & Diplomat was done without consultation with Mr Marsh and came upon him like a thunderclap.[6] He was very much affected & excited by it, & the agitation consequent on it undoubtedly determined his end. Not that he probably could have lasted long but this hastened his death. It certainly was not only a most unadvised act, but the suddenness & manner in which it was accomplished seems quite inexcusable. It remains to be seen whether this government & especially the King will accept this union of offices—and allow a commercial agent to be a diplomatic representative & it also remains to see how the diplomatic body will receive it. Will they receive a Consul as a Diplomat?

I am ashamed of the attacks which have been made upon you,[7] so low in character, so utterly unjustifiable. But I hope they do not wound you much. You may be sure that all the good sense of the country is with you & that every high minded man is on your side. But you are a shining mark at which the envious will throw mud and all decency goes out in our country when party spirit comes in. I hope that the government sustains you, & that it will not give way to all this mob-cry raised to court Irish votes—but will retain you in office. Be sure that my faith & affection for you will never die.

Who will succeed Mr Marsh here, God only knows—or perhaps the Devil. I am afraid we shall have some fearful appointment—some utterly incompetent & ignorant person, who can speak no language but his own, & that badly, & that we shall at the last be only glad that he will be able to make himself understood. Mr Marsh was an accomplished scholar & a gentleman to whom we could all look up with pride as well for his integrity & nobility of character as for his accomplishments in literature.[8] But who is to come after him? I am told that Schuyler Crosby has been pressing for this nomination—& that he has a chance.[9] God forbid! for he would be one of the worst possible appointments. His character or want of character is too well known here.

We are staying here at Vallombrosa with Edith—outside of the world in the peace & quiet of the woods. Were it not for the post—which is brought to us daily at our own cost from Pelago (there being no post here) the world might turn upside down without our knowing it. In fact I believe it is turning upside down & I don't much care.

It is possible & I am sorry to say probable that I may be obliged to go to America in August or early September on account of a statue which I am commissioned to make.[10] But I dread the journey—& hope to get off without it. If I do go I shall take Emelyn with me and we shall probably remain there for two or three months. Has John Field gone? or where is he? & when does he intend to go. I have heard nothing from him lately. If he has not gone we might possibly go together.

Emelyn & Edith send their most affectionate greetings. How is your wife now? Pray give her our kindest regards and believe me

Ever your affectionate
W. W. Story

Our address is *Pelago*—per Il Lago.

[1] George Perkins Marsh (1801–82), United States minister to Italy from 1861 to 1882.

[2] Lowell was United States minister to England from 1880 to 1885.

[3] Marchese Simone Peruzzi, who married Edith Story.

[4] George Washington Wurts, of Philadelphia, who arrived in Italy

in 1865 as unpaid attaché and later became secretary of legation, was 'invaluable' to Marsh. (David Lowenthal, *George Perkins Marsh* [New York, 1958], p. 300.)

5 Lewis Richmond (1824–94), soldier and diplomat, was secretary of legation and chargé d'affaires 1882–4.

6 For the effect upon Marsh of this act of the Government see Lowenthal's *Marsh*, pp. 328–9. From America, on December 7, 1882, Story wrote his son Waldo about the objection of the President and the Secretary of State to the combined offices. (Story Col.)

7 Lowell as minister was concerned with some of the agitators for home rule in Ireland. In a dispatch to his government he explained: 'Among the most violent are often the Irishmen who have been naturalized in America, and then gone back to Ireland with the hope, and sometimes, I am justified in saying, with the deliberate intention, of disturbing the friendly relations between the United States and England'. (Scudder, I I, 282.) These agitators were not willing to make a choice of countries, instead 'looking upon themselves as Irishmen who have acquired a right to American protection, rather than as Americans who have renounced a claim to Irish nationality'. (*Ibid.*, I I, 288–9.) Lowell acted on the principle that these troublemakers were subject to the laws of the British Government. His refusal to give them American protection (though he tried to remedy particular situations) resulted in attacks made upon him by some of his countrymen, but others defended his behaviour and his Government stood behind him.

8 Marsh, according to his biographer, was the 'broadest American scholar' of his time. 'He was at home in twenty languages, became the country's foremost authority on both Scandinavian and English linguistics, made important contributions to comparative philology, helped to found and foster the Smithsonian Institution, served as arbiter of public taste in art and architecture, established principles for railroad regulation, provided new insights into the nature of the history of man and of the earth. And from his pioneer work in geography developed the American conservation movement'. (Lowenthal, *George Perkins Marsh*, pp. vii–viii.)

9 John Schuyler Crosby (1839–1914) was American consul in Florence from 1876 to 1882. Not Crosby, but William Waldorf Astor (1848–1919), Anglo-American capitalist, became United States minister to Italy in 1882.

10 Of John Marshall (1755–1835), Chief Justice of the United States Supreme Court. Immediately after his death $3,000 was collected from members of the United States Bar toward a monument in his memory; the money was invested, and in 1880 the investment

yielded $20,000. Congress added another $20,000. The statue of Marshall, placed near the Capitol, was unveiled in May 1884. (*Exercises at the Ceremony of Unveiling the Statue of John Marshall* [Washington, 1884], pp. 11–14.)

Palazzo Barberini
Rome. Novr 1' 1884.

Dear James

Here we are "home again home again from a furren shore" & I wish you were here with us—that we two old fellows might have some more long talks together & make believe young, & wander through the old lanes of the past. We both did so much enjoy our visit to you that you and Fanny[1] (may I call her so) made so pleasant—and we hope that if the government at Washington don't know when they have got the right man in the right place, & foolishly remove you,[2] that you will come on here and make us a good long visit before you return to professorial duties at Cambridge. Yes! you both must come, and we will be as idle & silly as possible together, & shut out all serious fools—and have some more "Firooido Travolo" & real travels too into the Abruzzi among the mountains—and then we will go to Contrexeville & drink barrels of water, and get young again.

Our journey was prosperous after we left you. We passed a couple of days at Paris where we found Julian at work on a new picture, which promises to surpass the others—& then on to Florence where Edith Simone & Waldo were at the station, having come down from Vallombrosa to meet us. They were all well & gay, & after a day spent with them we came on here, & they returned to their mountain home. I was afraid that the weather would be too cold there for Emelyn, & persuaded her not to go. We had no drawbacks except that the train from Milan to Florence reeked with phenic acid that irritated our lungs & bronchial tubes, & gave us the privilege of cursing the stupidity of the Italians.

The weather here is magnificent—pure clear fresh & cloudless—three more splendid days than those we have passed since we arrived I never saw. The country is green, for there has been much rain in the early part of the month—and the whole country has an almost springlike look. We could scarcely find a hotel open and nobody seems yet to have arrived—and there is much wringing of hands among the hotel keepers at the prospect of a bad season for them. But there always is at this time & it don't trouble me.

Yesterday was the anniversary of our marriage—42 years ago! Good heavens! It seems impossible that this can be true but I am afraid it is. How swiftly they have gone.

With the kindest remembrances to your wife believe me

Ever affectionately yours
W. W. Story

1 The Storys visited the Lowells in London in October 1884. During the visit Browning and his sister had dinner at the Lowell's. (Whiting, *The Brownings*, p. 255.)

2 With the change of administration in 1885 Lowell's period of diplomatic life in England came to an end.

Rome. Feb 22^d '85

My Poor dear Friend,

My heart aches for you![1] how lonely is this your birthday! Her great festival & pride!! We had no word of her illness until a day or two ago & then it seemed, in the confusion of the reports, that *you* were ill!

I cannot tell you how glad I am that in the pleasant visit we made to you in Oct I had been so much with her. Her character was so direct & simple & her ways were so sincere that every day she made me love her more & more!

What devotion & unselfish love was hers! How proud & happy was she, no thought had she for herself it was all for you!! How fearful is your loss, what will you do what can you do without her? Somewhere perhaps you will find support but life will be very sad I am sure! We only wish that you were here that we might shield you from material troubles & worries which at this time must come to you! Why will you not come to us for the quiet peaceful life of a Roman Springtime.

Here, there is no call for interruptions or fatigues & we, your old friends, would seek in all ways to comfort you by peaceful surroundings! As yet we know nothing of her illness its nature, or duration. It is hard to be so far away from you at this time but you will know how deep is our sympathy. That we knew & appreciated her thoroughly gives us the right to share your grief & you may be sure that our thoughts are constantly with you as we know what you have lost.

Poor words these to express what I feel, but let me grasp your hand in deepest sympathy. God bless & keep you.

Yours as ever

Emelyn.

1 His wife, Frances Dunlap Lowell, died on February 19, 1885.

Palazzo Barberini

Romo Feb^v 29. 1885.

Dear James

We have just heard of your very sad loss[1] & I can not let a day go by without a word to assure you of our most deep & affectionate sympathy. I wish I could say anything to console you, but I know that to be impossible—all that we can do is to stretch out the hand & give a silent pressure and from my very heart I do this. Ever since the news came I have not been able to get you & Fanny from my thoughts, & have gone over the days of last autumn which you & she by your kindness made so pleasant to us. I then learned to know her better & more intimately than I ever had before & to appreciate her noble qualities of heart & mind & her sincerity her frankness her constant amiability & gentle efficiency, & the uncomplaining spirit with which she bore her bodily pains. It will always be to us a most pleasant memory.

We had been looking forward to greeting you & her this spring in Rome, & to renewing our long talks, & wandering about Rome & the Campagna. But now that she has gone, I fear that we cannot look forward even to seeing you here. Still, as one has to bear what is inevitable perhaps it would be the best thing for you to come away for a time at least, and if you will come to us, we will do all in our power to make the loss less grievous though help in such cases is of so little avail. At all events you may be assured that we feel for you most deeply. I know not what your plans are, & I suppose it is too soon for you to have made any, but I hope you will not go home at once but remain at all events for a time abroad—among your many friends in England. I could not bear to think of you alone in your house in Cambridge.

We scarcely had heard of Fanny's illness when the news arrived that she had gone—and the first reports were so hopeless that we did not dare to telegraph even—lest we should add to your trouble. Even now we know nothing of the circumstances of her illness and can get no information from any one. But I hope her illness was as painless as it was short. I know you will have many letters to write & much work to do, but if you can find time and inclination we should be most interested to hear something about her last days—and about your present plans—but do not do this if it troubles you.

Ever my dear James
Your most affectionate
W. W. Story

¹ His wife had just died.

31 Lowndes Square, S.W.
March 5th, 1885

My dear William,
I had had a letter to you on my conscience for a good while but never found a time when moods and leisure made it possible. I little dreamed that when I wrote it would be within these black boundaries. . . . I cannot yet say what my own plans will be. I suppose that there is little doubt that some one will be sent to take my place here. But I cannot now go back to live at Elm-

wood as I hoped. Probably I shall stay here for the present, as I took on my house till the end of the year. . . .[1] I cannot say enough of the kindness and sympathy I have received here. Lady Lyttelton[2] especially has been as a sister. It has done me all the good that can be done—and that *is* something. I thank you and Emelyn, dear old friend, as you know, but find it hard to say what I would *as* I would. God bless you both, and keep you together!

[James Russell Lowell]

[1] Lowell returned to the United States in June.

[2] Sybella Harriet Clive (1836–1900) married Humphrey Francis Mildmay and after his death married the fourth Baron Lyttelton.

[31, Lowndes Square
London]
March 31, 1885

[*Dear Emelyn:*]

I send you General Wallace's book[1] by to-day's post. It was touchingly characteristic that I should find it on her writing-desk done up and addressed to you. She never forgot or neglected a duty. But, not knowing the requirements of the Post Office, she had closed it at both ends, and sealed it. So I was obliged, much to my regret, to have it done up in the right way. But I ordered her original address to be left inside that it might show she had not forgotten.

I am on the whole glad to be rid of my official trammels and trappings. I do not know yet when my successor will arrive, but hardly look for him before July. I shall then go home, but whether to stay or not will be decided after I have looked about me there. If I decide to stay I shall certainly visit the Old World pretty regularly, and shall be sure to turn up in Rome.[2]

[James Russell Lowell]

[1] Probably *Ben-Hur*. Lew(is) Wallace (1825–1905), Major-General in the American Civil War, published it in 1880.

² Lowell made a yearly visit to England for the following four years. He never went to Rome again, though he was in Bologna in 1888. (See J R L–W W S, May 14, 1888, and n. 1.) After his visit to England in 1889 he was not able to travel to Europe.

2, Radnor Place,
Hyde Park. W.
2 June, 1887.

Dear William,

I am delighted to hear that Oxford is to do for you what she ought to have done sooner.[1] It will be no addition to you, but a very sensible one to me, since it will give me the chance to see you again. I won't say we are getting old, but we *are* getting on & every milestone is nearer to the inevitable twilight.

Now what I propose is this. I have very comfortable lodgings here & there is a bedroom over mine now vacant which I can engage if you are coming alone & will let me know in time when you are to arrive. You are to be my guest & I think we can contrive to be jolly together. Let me know also the date of Commemoration that I may go down with you to say *placet*. I will keep the day open.

London is unhappy just now with the eternal Irish indigestion, but I still find it pleasanter than any other place in the world. I who lived a hermit so long & thought my burrow delightful, find the sense of enormous human neighbourhood here comfortable in my old age. It shelters me from the wind somehow.

I was grieved to hear of your loss² & how great it was. There is nothing to be said, except that I am not without the experience that makes me capable of entire sympathy.

With love to Emelyn,
Affectionately yours
J. R. Lowell.

¹ On June 22, 1887, Oxford conferred upon Story the honorary degree of D.C.L.

[2] Margherita Umberto (b. 1881), the daughter of Edith Story (the Marchesa Peruzzi), died in May 1887. She was the godchild of the Queen of Italy. (Notes by W W S, Story Col.)

Paris June 6' 1887.
Place des Etats Unis.

My dear James—

Your most kind letter has reached me having been forwarded to me here (at Paris) from Rome. Nothing would give me greater pleasure than to accept your kind invitation & to be with you while I am in London. But Emelyn goes with me & so you see that it is not possible. But I shall see you very often I hope, & there will be no pleasure for me greater that London can offer. I should like to tell you that I am only 30 years of age —but the deuce of it is that you know better. Yes we are growing old—no! let us say older not old—though when I remember that my Father when he died was 2 years younger than I now am —it seems almost impossible to credit—that I am really as old as I am. We are neither of us dead yet for all that—& I thank God that there is still a good deal of foolish blood running in my veins.

I never was more surprised than when I heard that Oxford proposes to make me a D. C. L. But it was a most pleasant surprise & we can stand shoulder to shoulder there as we used to do at Cambridge—though you were so many heads taller then & now.

When I see you I mean to urge you to come to us at Rome next winter & then we can have long talks about everything & smoke indefinite pipes. The longer I live the closer I cling to the old friends.

This is Julian's pen & like every artist's pen an abominable one.

The Commemoration day is the 22'. I hope we can go down together & I also hope there will be no speeches (I mean on my part)—on your part I should like that there should be many.[1]

Love from Emelyn
Ever yours affectionately
W. W. Story

[339]

I say nothing about poor Edith & her terrible loss. In fact there is nothing to be said. Such losses we have to bear—& to suffer from—to suffer & be weak.

¹ For Story's account of the day given to his daughter see HJ, II, p. 291.

2, Radnor Place,
Hyde Park. W.
13th June, '87.

Dear William,

I can't say how sorry I am to have missed you. I had an errand to the Legation & I was out of baccy for my pipe. I get the humdungus they suppose here to be tobacco at the Army & Navy which is close by the perch of our Country's bird. It was mainly the baccy & here is a striking instance of our pleasant vices being made whips to scourge us. I shan't be able to lunch with you Sunday, for I spend that day in the country, but can't you breakfast with me on Wednesday at 10? Why not?

At any rate I mean to be at Oxford on the 22nd, D. V. that is to say Diabolo Volente, for I think it is he who puts a spoke in our wheel when we have a *good* intention. With love to Emelyn,
Affectionately yours
J.R.L.

2, Radnor Place,
Hyde Park.W.
14th May, 1888.

Dear William,

I am coming down to Italy in June, the University of Bologna having been bitten (by a centipede, I suppose) & celebrating its octocentenary some time in that month. I am the delegate from Harvard¹ & have not yet been informed of the exact date. I believe it falls about the tenth. By that time you will be in the Engadine if you are as wise as you ought to be at our time of life. (I hope you are not, by the way.) I am already engaged

[340]

here so far on as I think safe in my ignorance of dates. I should have been rejoiced could I have come to you for a few days.

I like to be back again in London, for there is a great deal that interests me here. But the whirl of society makes me giddy & 'tis after all a sad waste of life. One sees lots of interesting people & none of 'em well—lots of uninteresting ones & all of 'em too well.

I hope to see Italy (I mean at leisure) once more before I die. I have had a growing homesickness for it these two years now. But who knows? I am more or less necessary to Mabel & to my Sister Mary who is now seventy seven & expects me to spend next winter with her. So I shall probably go home in November instead of drifting southwards.

With much love to both of you,

Affectionately yours,

J. R. Lowell.

[1] Lowell received the Laureate of Honour in Jurisprudence from the University of Bologna. (Letter from Felice Battaglia, Rector, December 4, 1962.)

May 19, 1888.
Palazzo Barberini

My dear James

I am very sorry that you cannot come & make us a little visit here. But perhaps we may meet at Bologna. I shall make every effort to be there & then we may be able to persuade you to go to Vallombrosa & spend a few days with Edith—or to go on to Venice or somewhere together with us.

I have just received from Lady Galway[1] the letter which I now enclose. When she was in Florence some few months ago she wrote to me saying that she wished me to make a copy of my bust of Lord Houghton which she desired to present to Harvard —if they would be willing to accept it—otherwise to some other University or College or Public Institution in America. She wished to do this as a recognition of the kindness & appreciation which Houghton had received from our country & as a token of his interest & admiration in it. Now it would seem from her letter that you think Harvard would not accept it, because it does not represent an American. I cannot believe that you ever said that—and I suppose the old Lady must have misunderstood you. I for myself cannot see any reason why Harvard should refuse to accept this bust, if offered to it as a gift. You may be right, if you said so, for Harvard is peculiar—but I do not believe you ever said this.

If I am right in supposing that Lady Galway misunderstood what you said, will you be kind enough to put her right. I should like to make this copy, for other reasons besides this, that it would put money into my pocket. I have already made one for Cambridge (England).

But if Harvard would not wish to have it—is there no other college to which it could be given? Lady Galway had so much pleasure with the idea that Houghton's bust should have a place somewhere in some public College or Institution in America.

With love from Emelyn as well as myself

Ever affectly yrs
W. W. Story

---

[1] Harriette Eliza Milnes (1814–91), sister of first Baron Houghton, married George Edward Arundell, sixth Viscount Galway.

Villa Story—Campfer
Haute Engadine.
Sept 9. 1890

My dear James—

If it were not for the decencies of social etiquette and the distinction of the person addressed I should be tempted to say "My dearest old Jim" but I dont say so because I am afraid to—though I am greatly tempted—for the old days come back to me so vividly when I think of you that it seems a little improper that we are not boys again and playing on the old play-ground over the way—as we used to do in the good old days of youth & nonsense. I think of you constantly under the tall spreading elms & I wish I could ramble with you through the lane or smoke with you in the dear old study—where we have spent so many a pleasant hour. I suppose you do still smoke your pipe & I should like so much to light a cigar with you & talk and talk endlessly de omnibus rebus et quibusdam aliis. I was brave enough two years ago, at the instance of an old physician here to lay down my cigarettes—& with immense courage to deprive myself for all these two years of the satisfaction of tobacco —for he terrified me by a great long word—saying I was 'Narcotinised.' But at last after these years he said (of course a man has a right to change his views) I think on the whole you should smoke a few cigars every day. So I have again begun—& feel all the better for it—& ready to join you. I don't feel half as brave & good—but much happier for it.

What brings you so vividly before me today—& prompts me to stretch out my hand to you is a letter which I have just received from Holmes[1] in which he gives me news of you & a kind message—and makes an extract from a letter of yours to him— from which I learn to my great sorrow that you had been suffering very much. But it contained also the consolation that you were all right again—and able to be at work with your pen. I have been waiting to hear from *that* for a long time—& have wondered at your silence—& asking myself, where are the new poems & essays that I know are in his brain.

You are in very good hands with Dr Wyman[2]—but I also propose to prescribe for you. What it seems to me that you want —what I know that Emelyn & I & all of us want is that you should take a run over to us in Rome & occupy a room, ay all the rooms in Palazzo Barberini and put your legs under our table and over one of our arm chairs & let us have the satisfaction of seeing you again & renewing the dear old days & making excursions together into the Past and wandering about in the Present & scorning the Future. Do come—make up your mind —tear yourself away from Cambridge—& come immediately. It would make us, I mean E & I young again—& I hope it would do the same for you.

Those were pleasant days at Bologna & Milan[3] when I last

saw you. Let us have them over again. What do you think now of the Jews? or have you forgotten our talk about them? and do you still think that you & I are the only two persons you know who are *not* Jews? If you *are* a Jew—be a wandering Jew & come to us.

What are you doing? Are you writing & what. I shall look for the Introduction to the new edition of Milton's Areopagitica[4]—which I suppose will soon be published. But I want you to write a good long imaginative thing. You are old enough now to write a novel.[5] Why not do it. We can make excuses for your youth & inexperience. Write some nonsense—which is the best of sense. Where is Hosea Bigelow & Parson Wilbur? I hope nothing has happened to them. Nothing serious I mean.

Holmes wrote me a charming letter & I was immensely pleased to receive it. Dear man how his very name brings up the old days & the old recollections. I see him on the stage in the old meeting-house—all life & fire—flinging out his arms & enchanting us all with his coruscating lines. Those were splendid days. I shall never again hear such a poem delivered in public & so delivered as that—nothing at all events which will ever make such an impression on me. When you see him please tell him how glad I was to get that letter from him & tell him if he ever again calls me Mister I will peril my immortal soul with terrible words.

Here we are among the mountains that are covered with snow & flashing in the sunshine. I have built me a house here amid the pines out of the rocks of an old moraine & here we spend the summer months & see our friends who are many that come to drink the waters & fuse the iron into their blood but now we are soon very soon to take flight to the plains & to sail upon Como & to go to Milan where we last took leave of each other. Emelyn sends her love—& so do I

Ever affectionately yrs
W. W. Story.

or Edelman Storg—as you will—
& as you remember—

[1] John Holmes.

[2] Dr. Morrill Wyman (1812–1903) of Cambridge, Massachusetts.

[3] In 1888.

[4] See Elmwood, VIII, 115–33.

[5] Lowell had once started a novel, but it was never completed. (See WWS–JRL, February 11, 1853, and n. 4.) Hosea Biglow and Parson Wilbur were respectively the supposed author and editor of Lowell's *Biglow Papers*.

Elmwood,
Cambridge, Mass.
2nd Oct: 1890.

My dear William,

It was very pleasant to see your well remembered handwriting again & to see it without any hint of that quaver in it into which the hand as well as the voice is betrayed by the accumulating years. I say this not in malicious sympathy but as a respectful tribute to your seniority. It isn't great to be sure, but at our time of life even ten days have a value of which youth could not conceive.[1]

But why do I talk of old age, I, in whom autumn (of all seasons of the year) has renewed my youth? I was seriously ill last winter & spring, even dangerously so, I believe, for a day or two, & all summer have been helplessly languid & inert. Not that I didn't feel well enough in body, but my mind had no grip—"Couldn't seem to catch hold," as our vivid American phrase puts it. And my memory fumbled in vain when it tried to pick up anything smaller than a meetinghouse. But all of a sudden ten days ago I got up in the morning a new man. My memory still boggles a little about dates, but, as well as I can make out, I am about fifty. Pray Heaven it may last!

I am here in my birthplace & find it very gracious to me. I look upon the trees & fields I first saw & find them good as then. Your letter naturally recalled the old days. In my house & the ten acres in which it stands there is no change, but the Old

[345]

Road (now Brattle Street) as far as the corner of my lane is now crowded with houses, & the cross streets between it & the New Road thickly dotted with them. Mr Wells's grandchildren (*my* eldest, by the way, has just entered college) still live in the old house,[2] but a new one usurps the playground & two the garden. I still have elbowroom, but I am more & more persuaded that the new generation shouldn't be allowed to start till the old be off the stage. It would save much unseemly hustling & many heartburnings.

It is very good of you to tempt me with Rome & the Barberini, but, setting aside any scruples I might have as an American about living in a palace, I am anchored here for the winter. Even were Mabel not in question, Dr Wyman does not wish me to get beyond his reach as yet. (Indeed, I had a slight relapse towards the end of June.) And Mabel has been alarmingly ill of late so much so as to darken every outlook with foreboding. She is now slowly but steadily mending & my anxiety begins to lose its edge. She is living with me & I could not leave her. Then, too, if I am well enough, I am to read over again some old lectures in Philadelphia,[3] for it pleases me to earn a little money in this way & convince myself that my hand can still keep my head.

I shall send you one of these days a little book to which I have written a preface & which will have the value of being at once pretty & scarce—250 copies printed for a club.[4] It isn't much of a preface, but a good deal of a book, being Milton's "Areopagitica."

Though I cannot come now, I am not without hope of seeing you in Italy again before I vanish. A longing has been growing in me for several years now, chiefly, I confess, for Venice, but with subsidiary hankerings after Rome & Florence. Neither of them is the old one, of course, but they are better than anything else. But it grows harder & harder for me to get away. For reasons into which I need not enter, but which are imperative, I am not my own man so much as I should like to be & as I expected to be in my old age. For better or for worse one is married to duty & mustn't dally with the other baggages.

Give my love to Emelyn & thanks for her note. I suppose the Alpine air has driven you away by this time & so shall address this to Rome.

Goodbye.

Affectionately yours always
J. R. Lowell.

---

¹ Lowell is alluding to the fact that Story is ten days older than he is.

² Scudder, in taking his reader from one house to another on the Old Road (now Brattle Street) that led to Elmwood, Lowell's home, came to the 'Fayerweather house, occupied in Lowell's youth by William Wells, the schoolmaster'. He explained, 'Here the road turned to the south, and passed the last of the Row, known in later years as Elmwood'. (I, 3.) Lowell was prepared for college at Mr. Wells' boarding school.

³ Lowell was not able to lecture during the ten months left of his life.

⁴ It was written at the request of the Grolier Club of New York.

LETTERS EXCHANGED BY

ELIZABETH BARRETT AND JAMES RUSSELL LOWELL

My dear Miss Barrett,

It is rather late to acknowledge your kind reception of my little volume of poems,¹ but the pleasant memory of it, as a token of sympathy from a woman who has shown more true poetic genius than any poet of her sex, will be always green & fresh. The volume was published prematurely—(as a young author always feels after a year has passed) some of it was written when I was only nineteen, & all of it before I had finished my twenty first year. When I print another, I shall hope to send you something worthier for me to give & for you to receive.

I write this to ask a favor of you which, as I do it in right feeling, I trust you will not deem impertinent—a quality by which we Americans seem to be more known (or misknown) in England, than by any other.

Owing to the want of an international copyright law here, American authors are forced to compete with the cheap republications of English books, & the consequence is that all our literature is fast taking the periodical & cheap form of magazines. I am about to establish one² in Boston which I hope to make an instrument for the elevation of letters here, & for the creation of a right feeling in regard to many important matters.

Might I hope to print a poem of yours every now & then? I cannot afford to pay for it now, for I am poor. But if my enterprise is successful, I shall in time be able to render myself no longer your *pecuniary* debtor.

I suppose you know Mr Tennyson. Do you think that he would give me something?

Do not look upon this as if I came cap in hand begging for halfpence. If I thought less highly of you, I should not have asked this favor of you. Whether it argues a want of knowledge of propriety in me I cannot say: but I suppose the blood is of the same colour & hearts of the same warmth in England as here. With the truest wishes I remain *y^r friend J R Lowell*— Boston U.S.A. No 4 Court St.

¹ *A Year's Life*, published in 1841.

² *The Pioneer.*

London Wimpole Street 50.
Jany 4. 1843.

Dear Mʳ Lowell,

Whether the Americans are "known or unknown" for the tendencies you speak of, I cannot say. From the circumstances of a retired life & ill health it has happened that I never stood face to face with an American, except in my dreams. But I love the Americans & America for the sake of national brotherhood & a common literature. I honour them for the sake of liberty & noble aspiration—& I am grateful to them,—very grateful,—for their kindness to me personally as a poet. To all these feelings it is agreeable, when I comply with a request of Mʳ Lowell's . . and to another feeling beside, my respect for him individually: and I hasten into this expression of feeling from a desire to justify to himself *that part* of his good opinion of me which led him to trust me frankly,—the rest of it remaining I fear beyond the reach of my power of proving . . although *not*, believe me, of my gratitude.

I will write out a few poems below,¹—& they must stand for my *goodwill* in the matter & for my readiness to do a little more occasionally in the same way, should you continue to desire it. But I am unacquainted with Mʳ Tennyson,—I do not "side the gods" as you suppose . . & therefore I cannot forward your petition.

With every kind wish I remain

Your friend
Elizabeth B Barrett.

You must be good enough to transcribe these mss which are really ashamed of themselves in all ways (but I send hurriedly the verses nearest to my hand & am pressed for space) before you commit them to the printer. All his *diablerie* wᵈ not help him to put them into type from the present state—& I have fear lest you yourself "give them up" as riddles in Sanscrit.

[352]

[1] In answer to Lowell's request Elizabeth Barrett sent in this letter three poems—not four as Lowell said (Scudder I, 111), unless the small section of the letter torn away at the creases contained another poem. 'The Maiden's Death', part of which was written on one side of the missing section, was published in *The Pioneer* in March 1843; the magazine did not survive long enough for the other two to appear in it. Both were included in Elizabeth Barrett's *Poems* of 1844—'That Day' and 'Insufficiency', a sonnet which was entitled 'Imperfect Manifestations' in the letter to Lowell. 'The Maiden's Death' was first published in book form in 1914, in *New Poems*, by Robert Browning and Elizabeth Barrett Browning (ed. F. G. Kenyon).

50 Wimpole Street—July—
[1844][1]

Dear Mr Lowell,

As you have remembered me so long, & as so kind a word as "regards" accompanies the book you have sent me, you must try to forgive the freedom & *irreverence* of this address. It seems to come naturally, when the very next word on my part, must be an expression of cordial thanks for the honour you . . . in a welcome gift. Indeed I thank. . . . there seemed to be some signs of them in . . . poems, . . which appear to be the effect of select[ion] . . . of impulse, . . or of sympathy with the im[cut away] . . . writers, . . such as the Tennysons—rather than inward impulse: and these, . . it is certainly well to put away entirely. You will forgive me for speaking quite frankly. I have too much respect for the beauty attained on so many pages of the work before me, to speak otherwise. Your 'Legend of Brittany' is full of beautiful touches, . . to go no farther,—and the whole of the cathedral scene presents signs of no ordinary power. . . . that your object is (a noble one!) to teach not merely the holiness but hallowingness of love, I still shrink a little at the sudden escape from guilt & its results, which you confer on Mordred.

Then among the miscellaneous poems my pencil has marked various beauties & felicities. Chief of all I like the *Ode*, which struck a deep string in me, as it must in all, to whom Poetry has been as to me, the Life-light of existence.

If I ventured to make a remark in criticism on this new volume in a general point of view, it w^d be that there is a certain vagueness of effect, through a redundant copiousness of what may be called poetical diction (so that thoughts, images & descriptions rather swim dimly in a golden mist, than front the soul & eye with their individualities cutting upon the sense forcibly & arrestingly. . . .

[Elizabeth Barrett]

¹ The poems discussed were in Lowell's second volume, *Poems*, which had appeared in December 1843 (with the date 1844 on the title page). This letter has been mutilated. The portions cut away are indicated by the ellipsis marks.

LETTERS EXCHANGED BY

ROBERT BROWNING AND JAMES RUSSELL LOWELL

London, 19. Warwick Crescent, W
March 9. '73

Dear Mr Lowell,

On returning from France, last autumn, I found a parcel directed to me by Smith & Elder—containing some very striking & beautiful proofs of my poems having been fortunate enough to interest a true and original artist. I had no regular notice that they came from you, the kind conveyer, till my son, returning also from a distance, informed me to whom I was indebted. As it is,—I cannot guess how or why the honor was done me,—but in whatever shape it arose, I acknowledge it very gratefully, and trust that you will tell the painter as much. My friend Benzon has only just volunteered to communicate with you—I heard you probably might be in England this year: too pleasant news to come true, it seems.[1] But here, or wherever you are, I should like to say how much I have valued the marks of your remembrance which have reached me from time to time—that rare and delicate Cathedral,[2] which is immovably based on my table, being the last instance—except this very last.

I never was adroit—nor perhaps diligent at trying to express what I very really feel in these matters: those who have deserved the fullest expression, always must be able to anticipate and render it superfluous. I think you and I are good and familiar friends, in spite of distances and silences. I am sure I rejoice in your fame and desire your prosperity as heartily as any Bostonian of them all. So, all happiness to you from yours ever, admiringly and affectionately

Robert Browning.

[1] Lowell and his wife went to Europe in the summer of 1872 and stayed two years, part of the time in England and part on the Continent. In June of 1873 he was in England to receive the degree of D.C.L. from Oxford. If Browning did not see him then, he did see him in the summer of 1874. (See RB–WWS, June 9, 1874.)

[2] Published in book form at Christmas 1869 and in the *Atlantic Monthly* in January 1870. The inscription in the presentation copy reads as follows: 'To Robert Browning, with an appreciation heightening for thirty years, from the author, 30 Decr. 1869'. (Sotheby, p. 113, item, 881.)

Dear Mr Lowell,

The out-of-the way place from which I date this reply to your obliging communication of the 27th Ult must be my apology for the apparent delay in replying to the same.

It seems to me that no author, English or American, ought to —or could—pretend to a more favorable arrangement than that which you describe as contemplated: unluckily the difficulty which (judging by my particular experience) neutralizes any such transaction is a moral rather than a legal one: after all, a direct intervention of the law may put the old practice in a new light. Without reviving old grievances, I may simply say that I could have obtained, for many years past, a very decent remuneration for "early sheets" of my successive publications but that every Bookseller's Agent to whom application was made, declared his inability to print a new work of mine—seeing that its author "belonged" to another Firm: which Firm, till some years ago, was in the habit of offering that author a paltry sum on condition that publication in England should be delayed for a month after the receipt in America of the corrected sheets— (which might have been reprinted in a single day—) and this on the avowed ground that otherwise "copies would be possibly sent from England and sold (though at double the price) for the author's benefit"—and indeed one hundred so sent and sold would compensate the author for the loss of the American Bookseller's remuneration—to say nothing of his foregoing a month of the London "Season." For which,—and other reasons,—I have discontinued forwarding the proof-sheets—which are at once reprinted without any word—ever—of acknowledgement to me.

If there seem any touch of sourness in what I say, no one will better understand than yourself from what this arises. One writes to be read, and I value at its height the immense sympathy of which I have no end of instances—caused by the circulation of my books among the American people: if the case were put simply "we don't—or can't pay anything,—but will you be read *gratis* or left alone?" who can doubt what the answer would

[358]

be? But I am repeatedly told—"Every English author is in fault when he is not properly remunerated under even the present system"—and then—or rather, *now* for the first time, I have a word to say. Moreover I am the representative of my wife: and the last matter in which I was concerned respecting the publication of her works ended so dismally that I decline to associate her name with it. Nay,—why not tell the truth? Mr Fields[1] induced me, years ago, to write a letter, "on which he could act," desiring his House to print the Poems which "belonged" to another Firm: he did so, and, on the strength of it, made that Firm agree to "go shares" in a new Edition: which being done, I heard no more of the business. On Mr Osgood[2] calling on me some time after, I enquired into the reason,—and was told that Firm the First had proved that the author had been satisfactorily paid for all the poems—as witness her own declaration prefixed to the collection —which declaration—as I at once showed him—was that made (to another Bookseller) on the occasion of her publishing "Aurora Leigh"—and by him, or his successors, transferred to the complete edition as a receipt in full. Now, if ever you happen to hear that Mr Fields has written to me on the 7th of last month, respecting some honors proposed to be paid to her,—you will hardly wonder that I feel it impossible to reply with a corresponding "cordiality" to that of the writer.

Forgive this quite unwonted disburdening of what I wish out of sight and out of mind and believe me—Dear Mr Lowell,

Yours ever truly
Robert Browning.

[1] Browning's business difficulties with James T. Fields had started over thirty years before this letter was written, and from various references in Browning's letters it is clear that professional dealings between the poet and the publisher had not as a rule been satisfactory. (See WWS–JRL, August 10, 1853, and n. 6; and RB–WWS, May 3, 1864, and n. 12.)

[2] James R. Osgood. James R. Osgood and Company succeeded the publishing company of Fields, Osgood & Co.

19. Warwick Crescent, W.
Nov. 15. '80.

Dear Mr Lowell,

I should have at once acknowledged your very kind note but that I hoped to meet you last evening at our friend F. Lehmann's.[1] It will give me the greatest pleasure to dine with you in the way you propose, and I shall be happy indeed to become acquainted with Mrs Lowell.[2] Almost any day will suit me: shall I find you equally free next Friday? A word to mention your dinner hour—will oblige still further

Yours truly ever
Robert Browning.

[1] Frederic(k) Lehmann was the brother of the artists Henri Lehmann and Rudolf Lehmann, Browning's friend. Frederick was the business partner and brother-in-law of Browning's friend E. L. Benzon, mentioned in these letters. (See Moscheles, *Fragments of an Autobiography*, p. 320.)

[2] Lowell's second wife, Fanny. Browning's earlier association with Lowell had been during the life of Lowell's first wife, Maria.

[London] 5th November 1882.

[To Robert Browning]

. . . I enclose the letter of which I spoke to you the other evening. That anybody should suppose that the quadrupedans sonitus of your Courier's famous horse ever resounded on more solid fields than those of your imagination, or that a poem was less authentic because unsupported by any evidence in Haydon's Dictionary of Dates, is disheartening, but a line from you will make an honest admirer happy,[1] and I can only hope it may not result in his sending you the translation, which would probaby give you a shudder that I would gladly spare you. I hope the report is true that you are going to give us another book.[2] It will find no younger reader than I . . .   [James Russell Lowell]

[1] Inquiries about the historical basis of 'How They Brought the Good News', a popular poem, were not unusual. (For Browning's answers to questions on this poem see DeVane and Knickerbocker, pp. 203, 300; Hood, pp. 215–16; *Literary World*, XII [March 12, 1881], 104; Houghton, bMS Am 1408.)

² Browning's *Jocoseria* was published in March 1883.

31, Lowndes Square.
S.W.
21ˢᵗ Nov: 1884.

Dear Browning,

Will you dine with me on Tuesday, 25ᵗʰ, at 8 to meet a nice fellow who will be making me a visit & to whom I wish to show the Committés [*sic*]. Don't be engaged, please.

With kindest regards to your sister,

faithfully yours
J. R. Lowell.

31, Lowndes Square.
S. W.
21ˢᵗ May, 1885.

Dear Browning,

Will you & your Sister dine with us on the 26ᵗʰ at 8? I find that it is my only chance & fervently hope you are not engaged.¹

Faithfully yours
J. R. Lowell

¹ Lowell, who had been Minister to the Court of St. James, had just ended his period of diplomatic service. He was to leave for the United States in June. Browning accepted the invitation. (See R B–W W S, May 22, 1885.)

19. Warwick Crescent, W.
May 22. '85.

My dear Lowell,

I am not engaged on the 26ᵗʰ but if I were, I should consider your invitation of force to over-ride all others. My Sister and myself will be delighted to profit by what is also—I grieve to think—*our* 'only chance'—that is, for a long while. All thanks to you for the generous bestowal of it!

Ever truly yours
Robert Browning.

[361]

The following family groups include the names of the members that are referred to in the letters.

ELDREDGE–WETMORE–STORY[1]

Oliver Eldredge (1798–*ca.* 1857) married Hannah Smalley (1793–1867). They had ten children. Seven of them were
    Edward Henry (1816–65)
    Emelyn Bartlett (1820–94)
    Francis Oliver (1825–61)
    James Thomas (1828–89)
    Charles Warren (1830–95)
    George (1832–64)
    Mary Elizabeth (1835–94)

William Wetmore (1749–1830) married Sarah Waldo (1762–1805). They had six children. Two of them were
    Thomas, 'Uncle Tom' (1794–1860)
    Sarah Waldo (1784–1855)

Joseph Story (1779–1845) married Sarah Waldo Wetmore. They had seven children. Two of them were
    Mary Oliver (1817–48)
    William Wetmore (1819–95)

William Wetmore Story married Emelyn Eldredge. Their children were
    Edith Marion (1844–1917)
    Joseph (1847–53)
    Thomas Waldo, 'Dolo' (1854–1915)
    Julian Russell (1856–1919)[2]

Edith Marion Story married the Marchese Simone Peruzzi di Medici (1832–1900)

Thomas Waldo Story married Ada Maud Broadwood. Their children were
    Gwendolyn Marion Waldo (1884–1961)
    Vivien Waldo Story (1890–1944)

Gwendolyn Marion Waldo Story married Captain Arthur Courtenay Stewart.

Vivien Waldo Story married Colonel Alexander Baron Brant. Their son is
    Peter de Brant

BROWNING–BARRETT

Robert Browning (1782–1866) married Sarah Anna Wiedemann (d. 1849). Their children were
    Robert Browning (1812–89)
    Sarah Anna, or Sarianna (1814–1903)

Edward Moulton-Barrett (1785–1857) married Mary Graham-Clarke (1781–1828). They had eleven children. Five of them were
    Elizabeth Barrett (1806–61)
    Henrietta (1809–60)
    Arabella (1813–68)
    George Goodin (1816–95)
    Octavius Butler (1824–1910)

Elizabeth Barrett Barrett married Robert Browning. Their son was
    Robert Wiedemann, 'Pen' (1849–1912)

LOWELL-WHITE

Charles Lowell (1782–1861) married Harriet Traill Spence (1783–1850). Three of their six children were
    Rebecca Russell (1809–72)
    Mary Traill Spence (1810–98), who married Samuel Raymond Putnam
    James Russell (1819–91)

Abijah White (1779–1846) married Anna Maria Howard (1791–
1849). Two of their children were
    Maria White (1821–53)
    William Abijah White (1818–56)
James Russell Lowell married (1) Maria White
    Three of their four children were
        Mabel (1847–98)
        Rose (1849–50)
        Walter (1850–2)
James Russell Lowell married (2) Frances Dunlap (1825–85).

[1] The principal sources have been the following: *Genealogical and
Personal Memoirs Relating to the Families of the State of Massachusetts*,
W. R. Cutter, ed., New York, 1910, IV, 2563; James Carnahan
Wetmore, *The Wetmore Family in America*, Albany, 1861, pp. 446–78;
notes made by W. W. Story, in the Story Collection; Mr. Peter de
Brant of London.

[2] The DAB erroneously gives Julian's birth date as 1857. He was
born in England in 1856. (WWS's notes in Story Col.)

POEM TO JAMES RUSSELL LOWELL

(Published in *Blackwoods Magazine* (Edinburgh), Vol. CL, October 1891, pp. 589–90; reprinted in the *Critic*, Vol. XIX, October 10, 1891, p. 189, and *Littell's Living Age*, Vol. CXCI, December 19, 1891, p. 706.)

Friend of my childhood, boyhood, manhood, age,
　How can I fail thy bitter loss to mourn,
That from the book of life its glowing page
　So filled with golden memories has torn?

No! No! those memories still remain—more sad—
　That they are now but silent dreams that rise,
Faint phantoms, once so real, living, glad,
　Now only to be seen through tear-filled eyes.

Ah! of Truth's temples gone are nearly all
　Of its strong props, by cruel death o'erthrown;
And now, like some weak pillar near to fall,
　Amid the wreck I stand almost alone.

We roamed together through the fields of play,
　We strove through life as strenuous friends and warm;
No doubting shadows in our pathway lay,
　Nor o'er our friendship swept one passing storm.

Shoulder to shoulder, heart to heart, through life
　We went; ne'er asking which was best or first,
Unknowing envy, jealousy, or strife,
　Sure of each other—through the best and worst.

[366]

Fame, honor, fortune, crowned thee with its wreath;
  Justly the world to thee adjudged its prize;
But simple, heedless of its flattering breath,
  Thy path was onward with uplooking eyes,—

Onward through life, strong, earnest in the fight
  For freedom, duty, justice, all things good,
Sowing brave words, high thoughts, for truth, for right,
  And unseduced by all life's siren brood.

Nature to thee the poet's power bestowed,
  A genial humor and a trenchant wit,
That now like mild heat-lightning gleamed and glowed,
  Now with a sudden flash life's centre hit.

All the great gifts that lavish Nature gave
  By study, culture, art, were trained and formed.
As scholar, critic, poet—gay or grave—
  The world to thee with heart responsive warmed.

Thy loss, not I alone, a nation mourns,
  The double nation of our English speech,
Where'er the illuming light of letters burns,
  Where'er brave words and noble thoughts can reach.

Grateful I listen to the generous strain
  Of praise and grief, that through the whole world rings,—
But ah! what hand like thine will wake again
  The glad old music on my broken strings?

                              W. W. Story

When a book is referred to only once, full bibliographical information is given in the footnote. When a book is referred to two or three times, such information is given in the present list. When a book is referred to repeatedly, information about it is to be found in the table of abbreviations on p. xii.

Adams, *The Letters of Mrs. Henry Adams*, ed. Ward Thoron, Boston, 1936.

Adams, C. F., *Richard Henry Dana*, 2 vols., Boston, 1891.

Barclay, *The Diary of Miss Evelyn Barclay*, ed. A. J. Armstrong, 1932, Series V in *Baylor University's Browning Interests*.

Browning, *Robert Browning and Julia Wedgwood, A Broken Friendship as Revealed by Their Letters*, ed. R. Curle, New York, 1937.

DeVane, W. C., *A Browning Handbook*, 2nd ed., New York, 1955.

Emerson, R. W., *et al.*, *Memoirs of Margaret Fuller*, 2 vols., Boston, 1852.

Freeman, J. E., *Gatherings from an Artist's Portfolio*, 2 vols., New York, 1877–83.

Gardner, Albert Ten Eyck, *Yankee Stonecutters*, New York, 1945.

Greenwood, Grace, *Haps and Mishaps of a Tour in Europe*, Boston, 1854.

Harlan, A. B., *Owen Meredith*, New York, 1946.

Hawthorne, *The French and Italian Notebooks by Nathaniel Hawthorne*, ed. Norman H. Pearson, unpublished PH.D. dissertation, Yale University, 1941.

Hidy, R. W., *The House of Baring in American Trade and Finance*, Cambridge, Massachusetts, 1949.

Higginson, T. W., *Cheerful Yesterdays*, Boston, 1900.

Higginson, T. W., *Contemporaries*, Boston, 1899.

Hosmer, *Harriet Hosmer*, ed. Cornelia Carr, New York, 1912.

Howard, Leon, *Victorian Knight-Errant*, Berkeley, California, 1952.

King, Bolton, *A History of Italian Unity*, 2 vols., New York, 1899.

Locker-Lampson, F., *My Confidences*, 2nd ed., London, 1896.

Longfellow, *Life of Henry Wadsworth Longfellow*, ed. Samuel Longfellow, 3 vols., Boston, 1891.

Lowell, *New Letters of James Russell Lowell*, ed. M. A. DeWolfe Howe, New York, 1932.

Lytton, *Letters from Owen Meredith to Robert and Elizabeth Barrett Browning*, ed. A. B. Harlan and J. L. Harlan, 1936, Series X in *Baylor University's Browning Interests*.

McAleer, E. C., 'New Letters from Mrs. Browning to Isa Blagden', *PMLA*, LXVI (September 1951), pp. 594–612.

Miller, F. DeWolfe, *Christopher Pearse Cranch*, Cambridge, Massachusetts, 1951.

Milne, Gordon, *George William Curtis and the Genteel Tradition*, Bloomington, Indiana, 1956.

Minchin, H. C., *Walter Savage Landor*, London, 1934.

Moscheles, F., *Fragments of an Autobiography*, London, 1899.

Norton, *Letters of Charles Eliot Norton*, ed. Sara Norton and M. A. DeWolfe Howe, 2 vols., Boston, 1913.

Reese, Gertrude, 'Robert Browning and His Son', *PMLA*, LXI (September 1946), 784–803.

Scott, Leonora, *The Life and Letters of Christopher Pearse Cranch*, Boston, 1917.

Sturgis, Julian, *From Books and Papers of Russell Sturgis*, Oxford [1893].

Sturgis, R. F., *Edward Sturgis of Yarmouth, Massachusetts*, Boston, 1914.

Super, R. H., *Walter Savage Landor*, New York, 1954.

Taft, Lorado, *The History of American Sculpture*, New York, 1903.

Taylor, J. C., *William Page*, Chicago, 1957.

Ticknor, Anna, *Life, Letters, and Journals of George Ticknor*, 2 vols., Boston, 1877.

Tuckerman, H. T., *Book of the Artists*, New York, 1867.

Underwood, F. H., *James Russell Lowell*, Boston, 1882.

Vernon, Hope J., *The Poems of Maria Lowell*, Providence, Rhode Island, 1936.

Walburga, Lady Paget, *Embassies of Other Days*, 2 vols., New York, 1923.

Weiss, John, *Life and Correspondence of Theodore Parker*, 2 vols., New York, 1864.

Whiting, Lilian, *The Brownings*, Boston, 1911.

Winsor, Justin, *The Memorial History of Boston*, 4 vols., Boston, 1881.

INDEX

A., Lady, 123, 133
Abbé (Pen's teacher), 86, 87, 90, 94, 103, 117, 135
Adams, Charles Francis, 91 92–93, 106, 107
Adams, Mrs Henry, 269
Adams, John Quincy, 232, 236
Adelaide, Queen, Consort of William IV, 255
Advertiser, Boston Daily, 220, 232, 236, 301
Albert, Prince, 74, 92, 93
Albert Edward, Prince of Wales, 119
Alberti, 58, 59, 61, 64, 68, 70
Alessandri, 78, 80
Alexandra, Princess of Denmark, 118, 119
Alford, Marian Lady, 162, 171, 172, 190, 191, 207
Allston, Washington, 232, 235, 301; 'Belshazzar's Feast', 301, 306
Andrews, Joseph, 214, 215
'Angel', the, 202, 211
Annunziata (E B B's maid), 127, 128
Antonelli, 49, 51, 71
Apthorp, Robert, 63
Apthorp, Mrs Robert, 61, 63
Apthorp, William Foster, 63
Archimedes, 298
Aristotle: *Poetics*, 309
Arnim, Elizabeth (Bettina), 254, 255; *Goethes Briefwechsel mit einem Kinde*, 254, 255; *Dies Buch gehört dem König*, 254, 256
Ashburton, Louisa Lady, 108, 126, 128, 130, 137, 165, 168, 170, 171, 172, 175, 186–7, 188–9, 190, 191
Ashburton, Lord, 106, 108
Ashridge Park, 162
Astor, John Jacob I, 319
Astor, John Jacob III, 319
Astor, Mrs John Jacob III, 318, 319
Astor, William Waldorf, 332
Athenaeum (in Boston), 314, 315

Athenaeum (magazine), 67
Athenaeum Club, 99, 132, 136, 174, 175
Atlantic Monthly, 143, 145, 320, 321, 323, 324, 357
Austin, Lorry, 265, 268

Bancroft, Mrs George, 216, 218
'Band' (the 'Club', the 'Brothers and Sisters'), 204, 205–6, 217, 244
Barberini Palace, *see* Palazzo Barberini
Barrett, Arabel, 6, 75, 78, 84, 364
Barrett, Edward Moulton, 364
Barrett, Mrs Edward Moulton, 364
Barrett, Elizabeth, *see* Browning, Elizabeth Barrett
Barrett, George Goodin, 131, 133, 139, 140, 186, 364
Barrett, Henrietta, *see* Cook, Henrietta
Barrett, Octavius Butler, 64, 191, 364
Bate, Camilla, 281
Bate, Mr and Mrs Mac, 281
Bates, Joshua, 144
Bates, Mrs Joshua, 142, 144
Bayne, 270
Belcher, Mr, 229
Belper, Lady, 142, 144
Benson, Eugene, 176, 177
Benzon, Ernest Leopold, 165, 166, 172, 173, 174, 175, 357, 360
Benzon, Mrs Ernest Leopold, 165, 173, 174
Benzon, Lily, 174, 176
Biglow, Hosea, 344, 345
Black, Charles C., 266, 269, 271, 275, 313
Black, Mrs Charles C., 271, 275, 315
Blagden, Isa, 8, 22, 75, 76, 79, 85, 107, 136, 137, 141
Blickling Hall, 161, 162
Bloomfield-Moore, Mrs Clara Sophia, 180, 182, 183, 184, 185
Boncinelli, 96, 97
Boott, Francis, 74(?), 266, 268, 271, 280, 281

[371]

Bowen, Francis, 232, 236
Bracken, Mrs Mary E., 109, 110, 125, 128, 136, 155
Bracken, Willy, 109, 110, 125, 128, 136, 155
Brant, Colonel Alexander Baron, 364
Briggs, Charles Frederick (Harry Franco), 220, 221, 223, 249, 278, 284
Brevoort, 303
Broadwood, Ada Maud (Mrs Thomas Waldo Story), 180, 364
Broadwood, Gwendolyn Marion Waldo, 364
Broadwood, Vivien Waldo, 364
Bronson, Edith, 188, 190
Bronson, Mrs Katharine De Kay, 15, 188, 189, 194
Brook Farm, 236
Brooks, Peter C., 231, 235
Brooks, Preston Smith, 317, 318
Brown, Deacon, 230
Browning, Elizabeth Barrett: contributes to *Pioneer*, 213, 352, 353; marriage and settling in Italy, 1–2; feeling for America, 242, 352; with the Storys in Italy, 4, 21–22, 39, 41; Story's description of, 242; working on *Aurora Leigh*, 277; publication of her works in U.S., 278, 359; concern about Edith Story, 23, 25, 29–30; health, 4, 23, 42, 44, 45, 47, 48, 49, 57, 58, 59, 61, 67, 68, 69, 71, 72; defends Pantaleoni, 24, 26, 28–29; interest in Italian affairs, 2, 5–6, 42, 49, 53, 69, 72; interest in spiritualism, 8, 34, 53, 105, 186, 281; requirements for places to live in, 45, 50, 52; critics' attack on *Poems Before Congress*, 63; preparing new editions of her works, 61–62; reputation, 61–62, 75; effect of sister's death on, 66–67, 69; effect of Cavour's death on, 69; last illness and death, 6–7, 72–74; Story's bust of, 137–8, 139–40, 141, 151, 159; Hosmer's 'Clasped Hands', 35; Leighton's monument for grave, 138, 140; photographs of, 71, 72, 78, 79, 80, 96, 140
  ON: F. P. Cobbe, 81; Dall' Ongaro, 51; Lowell's poems, 353–4; Napoleon, 49; Rome, 31; Page's painting, 34; T. Parker, 57; Ricasoli, 72; Story's poems, 38; value of poetry, 353

MENTION: 21, 24, 25, 33, 36, 38, 45, 48, 52, 55, 62, 64, 65, 66, 73, 198, 274, 364
  WORKS: *Aurora Leigh*, 61, 277, 283; 'Curse for a Nation', 63; *Greek Christian Poets and the English Poets*, 118, 119; 'Insufficiency' ('Imperfect Manifestations'), 61–62; *Last Poems*, 95–96, 97, 99, 102, 104, 107, 108; 'Maiden's Death', 61–62; *Poems Before Congress*, 62, 63; *Selection from the Poetry of Elizabeth Barrett Browning*, 157; sonnet on Power's 'Greek Slave', 37; 'That Day', 61–62
Browning, Robert (father of poet), 76, 78, 101–102, 110, 112, 120, 143, 148, 364
Browning, Mrs Robert (mother of poet), 364
Browning, Robert: marriage and settling in Italy, 1–2; meets the Storys, 242, 243–4; Story's description of, 242; meets Lowell, 14, 269; with Storys in Baths of Lucca, 21, 277, 283; relations with Fields in American publication of works, 143–4, 145, 277, 283, 358–9; health, 23, 82, 116, 157, 166, 175; helps Storys during Edith's illness, 24–25, 26, 27; Lockhart's comment on, 27; reports on conditions of travel, 40, 58, 59; depends on Storys for assistance in finding places to stay, 23, 42, 45, 49, 50, 52, 55; and Landor, 42–43, 44, 45, 46–47, 48, 49, 50, 54, 55, 60, 61, 63, 64, 65, 80; interest in art, 6, 7, 58, 64, 135–6, 192; close association with Story, 6, 7–8; and E B B, preparing new editions of her works, 61–62; concern for E B B, 6, 26, 42, 44, 45, 58, 59, 61; tries to get apartment in Palazzo Barberini, 6, 68, 69–70; Miss Blagden's help after E B B's death, 75, 79; has picture made of rooms in Casa Guidi, 78; wants Storys to come to London, 76, 80, 82, 86, 98, 102; difficulties from Florence to England, 75, 76–77, 79, 80, 83; interest in Story's work, 77, 105–6, 110, 111, 112; sees Tennyson in France, 83–84; settles in London and concerns himself with Pen's education, 84–85, 94–95, 117, 120, 134; views on education, 76, 95; assists Story in

[372]

publication of writings, 8, 88, 113, 130, 132, 139; feeling for America and Americans, 90, 242, 358; love for Italy and dreams of returning, 95, 96, 100, 103, 107, 114, 117, 126, 130, 132, 138, 140, 143, 150, 156, 160; prepares his and E B B's works for publication, 8, 95–96, 118, 119, 157; made member of Athenaeum, 99; beginning of social life, 8, 99, 106, 116, 125, 135; considers and refuses offer of editorship of *Cornhill*, 100–101, 106–7; literary reputation, 101, 103, 135, 136, 144; objects to Thornton Hunt's publication of letters, 102; interest in Italian affairs, 86, 88–89, 111, 129; afraid for Story to make a bust of E B B, 138, 139–40, 141; rumours of a second marriage, 142; delays publication of *Dramatis Personae*, 143–4; sees Pass of Roland, 146; has working season, 154, 158; likes Story's bust of E B B, 155, 156–7; pleased with Pen's interest and work in art, 174, 179, 180; affected by Academy's rejection of 'Dryope', 182, 183; objects to Julian Hawthorne's misrepresentations, 185, 186; moves to De Vere Gardens, 192; last visit with Story in Asolo, 15, 193–4; last illness and death, 15, 197, 198; Hosmer's 'Clasped Hands', 35; Page's portrait of, 33; Julian Story's portrait of, 321; W. W. Story's bust of, 85, 87

ON: American Civil War, 77, 86, 87, 88–89, 111, 112; Mrs Bloomfield-Moore, 183–4, 185; Cavour's death, 68, 69; critics, 101, 102, 135; Mrs Eckley, 88, 120–1, 121–2, 122–3, 133; Gladstone, 188; his friendship with Lowell, 357; Italian affairs, 68, 70, 86, 88–89; Napoleon, 129, 166, 167; Page's portrait of him, 33; privacy, 102; Queen Victoria, 70–71, 74; spiritualism and Home, 103, 105, 132–3, 136, 185, 186; Story's poems, 37–38; works of Julian and Waldo Story, 191–2

MENTION: 25, 26, 29, 30, 32, 35, 38, 41, 53, 233, 238, 267, 364

PLACES LIVED IN AND VISITED: Asolo, 193–4; Bagni di Lucca, 21; Cambo, 145–8; Florence (Casa

Guidi), 22–74; Grantham, 169–72; London (39 Devonshire Place), 37–38; London (1 Chichester Road), 82–107; London (19 Warwick Crescent), 108–92, 357–61; London (29 De Vere Gardens), 192–4; Norfolk, 161–2; Paris, 81–82; Ste. Marie, 109–12, 128–30; Rome (43 Via Bocca di Leone), 23–32, 39; Rome (28 Via del Tritone), 57; St. Aubin, 172–3; St Enogat, 75–80

WORKS: *Balaustion's Adventure*, 163, 164, 165; *Bells and Pomegranates*, 44; *Dramatis Personae*, 118, 119, 121, 122, 130, 136, 143; *Fifine at the Fair*, 167, 169, 171, 172; 'A Forgiveness', 176; 'Gold Hair', 145; 'Hervé Riel', 165; 'How They Brought the Good News', 360; 'James Lee', Section VI, 145; *Men and Women*, 277; 'Mr Sludge, the Medium', 105; *Poetical Works of Robert Browning*, 118, 119, 121, 122, 136; *Prince Hohenstiel-Schwangau*, 166, 167; 'Prospice', 145; *Ring and the Book*, 148, 152, 153, 154; *Selections*, 101, 103, 112, 113, 115, 118, 119

Browning, Robert Wiedemann Barrett (Pen): health, 30, 76, 79, 83, 90, 95, 97, 103, 107, 111, 117, 121, 125, 128, 131, 134, 140, 142, 143, 162, 163, 166, 179, 185, 192, 194; early studies, 41, 87; pony, 56, 57, 75, 83, 114, 125; amuses himself, 76, 85, 109, 111, 114, 125, 142, 145, 151, 176; appearance, 85, 87, 151; character, 85, 95, 114, 117, 125, 134, 142; education, 76, 84–85, 90, 93, 94–95, 107, 114, 117, 120, 125, 134, 142, 162; fails examinations, 97; indifference to academic life, 119, 176; takes up art, 174, 176, 181; art teachers, 174, 176, 180; sells pictures, 179, 180; Wilde's picture of, 96, 98, 140

MENTION: 21, 26, 29, 31, 33, 36, 47, 60, 64, 66, 69, 75, 77, 79, 96, 101, 103, 112, 113, 118, 124, 126, 128, 136, 138, 139, 144, 152, 154, 155, 157, 162, 164, 165, 166, 171, 172, 173, 175, 179, 181, 183, 187, 190, 364

WORKS: 'Dinant-Market Woman', 179, 180; 'Delivery to the Secular Arm', 179, 180; 'Dryope', 182, 183

Browning, Mrs Robert Wiedemann Barrett, 197

Browning, Sarianna, 76, 78, 102, 110, 112, 120, 127, 143, 146, 147, 165, 173, 175, 178, 179, 180, 181, 182, 185, 187, 192, 194, 197, 364
Brownlow, third Earl, 162
Bruce, Lady Augusta, 102, 105
Bruen, Mrs, 67, 79, 87, 133
Bruen, Mary, 87
Bruen, Matthias, 87
Bruens, the, 86, 87, 96, 114, 140
Bull Run, battle of, 77, 78
Bulwer Lytton, Edward, 107, 108
Bürkner, Hugo, 305, 307
Burns, Robert, 225
Burridge, Dr, 82–83, 87
Butler, Samuel, 241
Byron, Lord, 96, 98, 178

Cabot, George, 233
Cabot, James Elliot, 220, 221
Canada, 151, 152–3
Canale, Conte Giuseppe, 282
Canova, Antonio, 261
Carlisle, Lord, 160
Carlyle, Jane W. (Mrs Thomas), 274
Carnarvon, Lord, 163
Carter, Miss Bonham, 142, 144
Carter, Robert, 213, 303, 306, 311
Cartwright, William Cornwallis, 50, 51, 52, 74, 86, 96, 98, 99
Cartwright, Mrs William Cornwallis, 51
Casa Guidi, 1, 6, 78–79, 80, 81, 280, 285
Casigliano, Duchess of, 53, 54, 60, 61, 73, 74
Cass, General Lewis, 262
Cass, Lewis, Jr, 258, 259, 261, 262
Castel Gandolfo, 265
Castellani, 259, 260, 262
Cavour, Camillo Benso, 68, 69, 72
Centofanti, Francesco, 280, 285
Chapman, Edward, 61, 63, 108, 109, 111, 113, 116, 122, 130, 132, 151–2, 153, 156
Chapman, Frederic, 61, 63, 108, 109
Chapman, Mrs Maria Weston, 63, 291, 292
Chapman and Hall (publishers), 63, 109, 111, 119, 130, 157
Charlemagne, 146
Child, Lydia Maria, 205, 206
Cholmeley, Mrs, 96, 97
Chorley, Henry F., 27, 28
Cirella, Don Alfonso, 35, 36, 287-8

Civil War, American, 77, 85, 86, 94, 111, 112, 317, 318
Civilotti, 259, 262
Cleveland, Duchess of, 143, 145
Clough, A. H., 60, 278, 283
Cobbe, Frances Power, 79, 81
Cogswell, Joseph Green, 318, 319
Coleridge, S. T., 214, 215
Colville, Lady, 143, 145
Cook, Henrietta (Mrs William Surtees), 66, 67, 69, 364
Cornhill Magazine, 100–101, 106–7, 165
Cowper, Lord, 163
Cowper, Lady, 163
Cranch, Christopher Pearse, 283, 290, 292, 293, 294, 295, 296, 297, 299, 317
Cranches, the, 26, 27, 32, 33
Crawford, Thomas, 240, 243, 261, 266, 275, 284, 314; 'Beethoven', 294, 308, 310, 314; 'Peri', 279, 284; Washington monument, 261, 263
Crawford, Mrs Thomas, 79, 80, 240, 266
Crodie, Mrs, 271
Cropsey, Mrs Jasper Francis, 243, 244
Crosby, John Schuyler, 331, 332
Crosby Lodge, 325, 326
Curtis, Anna Wroe, 217, 218
Curtis, Daniel, 181, 183, 188
Curtis, George Ticknor, 232, 236
Curtis, George William, 278, 284, 304, 311; 'Our Best Society', 278, 284
Curtis, Ralph, 183
Cushman, Charlotte Saunders, 28, 114, 115, 270, 271

Daily News, 90, 91, 92, 94
Dale, Felix, see Merivale, Herman Charles
Dall' Ongaro, Francesco, 49, 51
Dana, Richard Henry, Sr, 232, 235
Dana, Richard Henry, Jr, 232, 235, 281
Dante, 236
De Brant, Peter, 364
De Grey, Lady, 118, 119, 143
Dempster, Charlotte Louisa Hawkins, 80, 81, 100
De Vere, Aubrey, 100, 103
Dial, 234
Dicey, Mrs, 97, 98
Dicey, Edward James Stephen, 74, 75, 88, 91, 92, 93, 94, 97; 'Elizabeth Barrett Browning', 75; Cavour—a Memoir in 1861, 75; Rome in 1860, 75; Six Months in the Federal States, 75

Diceys, the, 86
Dickens, Charles, 100, 104, 126, 311;
  Bleak House, 104; *Martin Chuzzlewit*,
  221, 222; *Pickwick Papers*, 311
Disraeli, Benjamin ('Dizzy'), 295
Dodge, Pickering, 273, 275
Dougherty, Addison, 214, 215, 217
Downing, Andrew Jackson, 214, 215
Duff, Sir M. E. Grant, *see* Grant Duff,
  Sir M. E.
Duff-Gordon, Lady, 127, 128
Dulwich Picture Gallery, 192
Dugaine, Augustine Joseph Hickey,
  304, 307
Duppa, Miss, 271, 275
Duppa, Frank, 271, 275
Dupré, Giovanni: *Thoughts on Art and
  Autobiographical Memoirs*, 181, 182
Du Quaire, Frances Mary (Blackett),
  102, 104, 141
Dwight, John, 232, 236

Eckley, Miss, 122-3, 133
Eckley, David, 86, 88, 120-1, 121-2,
  122-3, 133, 140
Eckley, Sophia (Mrs David), 86, 88,
  102(?), 120-1, 121-2, 122-3, 130,
  133, 135, 140
Eldredge (several persons indistinguish-
  able), 60, 62, 159, 160, 161, 260, 273
Eldredge, Charles Warren, 273, 363
Eldredge, Edward, 240, 280, 363
Eldredge, Francis Oliver, 363
Eldredge, George, 363
Eldredge, James T., 322, 363
Eldredge, Mary Elizabeth (the 'Angel'),
  202, 203, 363
Eldredge, Oliver, 363
Eldredge, Mrs Oliver, 363
Eliot, John, 301, 306, 308
Elliott, Dr Samuel Mackenzie, 213,
  216, 217, 218
Elmwood, 11, 15, 345-6
Elphinstone, Lord, 71, 72
Emerson, Ralph Waldo, 214
Eustis, Henry Lawrence, 248, 249

Fane, Julian, 77, 78, 144; *Tannhäuser*,
  77, 78
Felton, Cornelius Conway, 231, 235
Fessendens, the, 221
Field, John W., 59, 60, 179, 184, 313,
  314, 331

Fields, James T., 143, 145, 277, 278,
  283, 359
Flagg, J. B., 235
Fletcher, Julia Constance (George
  Fleming), 176, 177, 178
Forbes, the, 61, 62
Forster, John, 44, 45, 46, 103, 112, 143,
  144, 267, 269
Fourierism, 236
Fourierites, 232
Franco, Harry, *see* Briggs, Charles
  Frederick
Frederick William IV, King of Prussia,
  254, 256
Freeborn and Co., 259, 262
Fuller, Abraham, 249
Fuller, Margaret, 229, 231, 233-4, 241,
  247, 249: *Woman in the Nineteenth
  Century*, 234

Gabriel, Mary Ann Virginia, 142, 144,
  168
Gajassi, Vincenzo, 96, 98
Galignani, Giovanni Antonio, 130
Galignani's Messenger, 66, 300
Galway, Lady, 341-2
Garibaldi, Giuseppe, 62
Garrison, William Lloyd, 232, 235
Gaskell, Miss, 100, 103
Gaskell, Elizabeth Cleghorn, 103
Gibson, John, 101, 103-4, 272
Gillespie, G. K., 94, 97, 134
Gladstone, William Ewart, 188
Godwin, Parke, 278, 284
Goethe, 254, 255, 309
Goldsmid, Julian, 109, 151, 152
Goldsmid, Lady, 108, 109
Goodban, Edward, 67
Grajico, Preneo, 282
Grant Duff, Sir M. E., 106, 107
Greeley, Horace, 284
Green, James D., 229, 234
Greene, Anna (Shaw), 292, 293
Greenough, Henry, 311, 312
Greenough, Richard Saltonstall, 261,
  263, 266, 268, 279, 282, 312
Greenwood, Grace, *see* Lippincott,
  Sarah Jane (Clarke)
Greville, Henry William, 168, 169
Grey, Mr, 114
Gurowski, Adam, 265, 268

Hahn-Hahn, Ida, 239, 240
Hale, Edward Everett, 285

[375]

Hale, Nathan, 282, 285, 306
Harris, Dr, 297
Harris, Mrs (in *Martin Chuzzlewit*), 221, 222
Harvard University, 341–2
Hawthorne, Julian, 185, 186
Hawthorne, Nathaniel, 9, 10, 47, 179, 185, 186, 213, 277, 278; *Marble Faun*, 9; *Scarlet Letter*, 277
Heath, Dr, 290–1
Heath, Frank, 203, 220, 221, 239, 240, 241, 247, 250, 272, 275, 283, 290, 292
Hemans, Charles Isidore, 271, 275
Heyermans, Jean-Arnould, 174, 176
Highclere Castle, 162, 163
Holmes, John, 326, 327, 343, 344
Holmes, Oliver Wendell, 188, 189, 327
Home, Daniel Dunglas, 103, 105, 132–3, 136
Hosmer, Harriet (Hatty), 33, 35, 55, 56, 79, 114, 135, 137, 140, 169, 170, 171, 172, 188, 190, 191, 270, 271, 272; 'Clasped Hands', 35; 'Zenobia', 137
Hosmer, Dr Hiram, 226, 227, 228, 229, 271, 272, 274
Houghton, *see* Milnes, R. M.
Howe, Dr Estes, 282, 285
Howe, Julia Ward, 305, 307
Howell, James: *Epistolae Ho-Elianae*, 309
Hughes, Thomas, 327, 328
Humboldt, Friedrich Heinrich Alexander von, 253, 255
Hume, Daniel Dunglas, *see* Home, Daniel Dunglas
Hunt, Leigh, 102, 104, 267, 269, 292, 293, 295
Hunt, Thornton, 102, 104
Hurlbert, William Henry, 185, 186, 305, 307
Hurlbut, William Henry, *see* Hurlbert, William Henry

Independent, 66, 160
Ingelow, Jean, 144
International Exhibition, 92, 93, 95, 104, 106
Ireland, 330, 332, 338
Ironside, Adelaide ('Aesi'), 101, 104
Italy, political situation, 2, 5, 68, 70, 86, 88–89, 111, 112, 129, 163; U.S. diplomatic situation in, 329–30, 332

James, Henry, 327, 328

Jarves, James Jackson, 52, 53
Jenner, Sir William, 193, 194
Jones, George, 50, 51, 52
Jowett, Benjamin, 117, 119, 120, 188

Kane, Elisha Kent, 310, 312
Keats, John, 54, 62, 63, 286
Kemble, Mr, 282
Kemble, Frances Anne ('Fanny'), 31, 32, 33
Kent, Duchess of, 74
Kenyon, John, 38
Kestner, George August, 282, 285
King, Augusta, 242, 244
Kinney, Mr and Mrs William Burnet, 33, 35
Kirkland, Mrs, 233
Kirkup, Seymour Stocker, 46, 47, 48, 52

Lamb, Charles, 309
Landor, Walter Savage, 53, 54, 62, 64, 66, 68, 118, 127; character, 42, 43, 46, 48, 55, 60, 61; family, 42, 44, 45, 46, 47; and RB, 42–43, 44, 45, 46–47, 48, 49, 50, 54, 55, 60, 61, 63, 64, 65, 80, 147; death, 148; 'Dialogue in Verse between Diana and her Nymphs', 53, 54; 'Lead for Casa Guidi Windows' ('Syracuse'), 61, 62
Lansdowne, Lord, 132
Lawrence, Abbott, 231, 235
Lee, S. Adams, 104
'Legend of St Sophia of Kioff', 264, 267–8
Lehmann, Frederic(k), 166, 360
Lehmann, Henri, 360
Lehmann, Rudolph, 360
Leighton, Frederic, 123, 124, 138, 140, 160, 161; monument for E B B's grave, 140
Lemousier, Mr, 292
Leopold, Prince, 193
Liberty Bell, 63
Lincoln, Abraham, 89
Lippincott, Sarah Jane (Clarke), 27, 28, 270
Liszt, Franz, 127
Little and Brown, 303, 308
Livingstone, Miss, 233
Locker, Lady Charlotte, 102, 114, 115
Locker (later Locker-Lampson), Frederick, 102, 114, 115
Lockhart, John Gibson, 27
Lodwick, Peter, 101, 103, 107

Longfellow, Henry Wadsworth, 220, 231, 235, 295, 311, 312, 317; *Hiawatha*, 304, 307
Longfellow, Mrs Henry Wordsworth, 80, 81
Loring, Anna, 269, 273–4, 281
Loring, Mrs Charles Greely(?), 204, 206
Lorings, the, 266
Lossius, Lucas, 110
Lothian, Lord, 162
Lowell, Charles, 217, 228, 243, 251, 255, 257, 260–1, 263, 273, 281, 289, 364
Lowell, Mrs Charles, 217, 364
Lowell, Frances (Dunlap), 175, 323, 324, 325, 326, 328, 333, 360, 365; character, 334, 335, 337; death, 334–6
Lowell, James Russell: early life and association with Story, 11–12; adopts writing profession, 12; sends copy of his poems to Miss Barrett, 351, 353; his aim for *Pioneer*, 351; asks E B B to contribute to *Pioneer*, 13, 351; is with the 'Band', 204; gives advice to Emelyn Eldredge, 205; goes to New York for treatment of eyes, 213, 214–5; works on *Pioneer*, 216; dedicated *Poems* of 1844 to Page, 206; finances, 221, 248; *Poems* (1844) have second edition, 220; interest in dialect, 225; marriage, 202; compliments R B and E B B in and out of print, 13–14, 351; writes about birth of Mabel, 226–9; R B's possible influence on, 14; contributes to *National Anti-Slavery Standard*, 246, 249; changes method of publishing his books, 248; reissues his poems, 248, 249; his daughter Rose dies, 256; stays in Browning's house (Casa Guidi), 14, 269, 285; his son Walter dies, 262; details for headstone for Walter's grave in Rome, 260, 267; meets R B, 14, 269; begins a novel, 270, 274, 278, 344, 345; is writing for *Putnam's*, 279; lectures at Lowell Institute, 311, 312; is appointed Professor at Harvard, 12, 291; goes to Europe to study, 12, 290; with the Brownings at Dulwich Picture Gallery, 192, edits the *North American Review*, 12; edits *Atlantic Monthly*, 12; expression of apprecia-

tion to R B, 13, 357; receives D C L from Oxford, 338; see R B, 13, 14, 174, 175, 188, 189; appointed U.S. minister to Spain, 13, 327; appointed U.S. minister to England, 13, 331, 332; his stand as U.S. Minister on the Irish question, 330–1, 332; death of second wife, 13, 334–6; end of diplomatic life in England, 13, 333, 334, 337, 361; attachment to England, 13, 338, 341; receives Laureate of Honour from University of Bologna, 340; longs to see Italy again, 15, 341, 346; last illness and death, 15, 343, 345; portrait of by Rowse, 318, 319; Story's bust of, 261, 272, 275–6, 286; Page's portrait of, 206
   ON: buying land, 297–8; E B's poetry, 351; Elmwood, 345; his first volume of poems, 351; Germany, 309; Italy, 11; London, 296; Margaret Fuller, 241, 247; Paris, 296; his professorship, 290; slavery, 223; Story's work, 223, 293
   MENTION: 1, 2, 36, 60, 201, 202, 282, 275, 328, 364
   PLACES LIVED IN AND VISITED: Boston, 201–11, 351; Cambridge (Elmwood), 220 347, Chester, 324; Dresden, 297–316; London, 326, 327, 336–8, 340–1, 360–1; Madrid, 328; New York, 215–6; Paris, 290–6, 316–8; Sicily, 312–5
   WORKS: 'Aeropagitica', introduction to, 344, 346, 347; 'After the Burial', 324; *Biglow Papers, First Series*, 12, 240, 241, 243, 248, 295, 328; *Biglow Papers, Second Series*, 310; Browning's works, article on, 13–14, 269; 'Cathedral', 357; *Conversations on Some of the Old Poets*, 13; *Fable for Critics*, 12, 240, 241, 243, 247, 248, 249; *Fireside Travels*, 11, 283, 286, 289, 319; 'Footpath', 324; 'Fountain of Youth', 283; 'The Gentle Una', 202; 'In the Twilight', 324; 'June Idyl', 324; 'Lady, There Grew a Flower', 201; 'Leaves from My Italian Journal', 270, 274; 'Moosehead Journal', 283; *National Anti-Slavery Standard*, contributions to, 246, 249; 'Nooning' (unpublished), 270, 274, 278; novel, beginning of, 270, 274, 278; 'Our Own', 278, 283;

Poems of 1844, 206, 220, 236; *Poems Second Series*, 12, 233, 236, 238, 240, 243; *Poems* (1849), 248, 249; *Princess*, review of, 240; 'Some Letters of Walter Savage Landor', introduction to, 203; Story, Judge Joseph, article on W W S's statue of, 276, 283; *Vision of Sir Launfal*, 12, 240, 243; *Year's Life, A*, 201, 202, 351, 352
Lowell, John Amory, 291
Lowell, Mabel, 226–9, 230, 239, 243, 282, 288, 289, 294, 305, 307, 316–7, 321, 324, 341, 342, 365
Lowell, Maria (White): marriage, 202; birth of first child, 226–9; death of children and effect on, 256, 262, 263; illness and death, 281, 286, 289; mention, 201, 202, 206, 208, 209, 210, 212, 213, 221, 223, 225, 233, 234, 239, 240, 243, 246, 247, 257, 260, 261, 263, 265, 267, 269, 273, 278, 280, 281, 282, 300, 313, 360, 365
Lowell, Mary Traill Spence, *see* Putnam, Mrs Samuel Raymond
Lowell, Rebecca, 227, 257, 289, 364
Lowell, Rose, 247, 256–7, 365
Lowell, Walter, 263, 365
Lowell Institute, 304, 307
Lyttelton, Lady, 337
Lytton, Robert Bulwer (Owen Meredith), 33, 34, 74, 77, 78, 80, 81, 107, 280, 284; *Tannhäuser*, 77, 78

Macmillan's Magazine, 75
Macpherson, Robert, 117, 119, 271, 275, 276
Macready, William Charles, 225, 226
Mallett, David, 222
Marsh, George Perkins, 328–31, 332
Marsh, Mrs George Perkins, 329, 330
Marshall, James Garth, 39, 40
Marshall, Mrs James Garth, 39, 40, 100
Marshall, John, 332
Mason, Miss, 292
Mason, John Young, 291, 292
Mason, William Powell, 304, 307
Massachusetts Quarterly Review, 232, 240
Matthew, Theobald, 143, 145
Maurice, Frederick Denison, 96, 97
Mazzini, Giuseppe, 234
Merivale, Herman Charles, 323, 324; *Time and the Hour*, 323
Michelet, Karl Ludwig, 252, 255

Mills, Clark, 284; statue of General Andrew Jackson, 279, 284
Milman, Mr and Mrs Henry Hart, 106, 108
Milnes, Richard Monckton (Lord Houghton), 53, 54, 99, 106, 142, 190, 191, 341–2
Milsand, Joseph Antoine, 152, 153, 173, 187
Milton, John, 231
Minns, George W., 217, 218
Mitchell, Mr, 132, 136
Monitore, 53, 54
Monteagle, Lord, 100, 103
Montecuccoli, the, 188
Morris, Captain, 21
Morton, Marcus, 214, 215
Mount Felix, 153, 154, 155, 321
Murray, John, 106
Mussy, Henri Guéneau de, 134, 137

Napoleon III, 5, 49, 51, 129, 166, 167
National Anti-Slavery Standard, 246, 249
Nazione, 67, 68, 70
Neander, Johann August Wilhelm, 251, 252, 255
Nencini, 58, 59, 63, 68, 70
New York Tribune, 234
Newton, Sir Charles Thomas, 147, 148
Niebuhr, Barthold Georg, 231, 234
Noel, Lady Anne Isabella, 177, 179
North American Review, 232, 235–6, 315, 320, 321
Norton, Charles Eliot, 313, 314, 315, 326, 327
Nucci, 286, 289

Ollendorf, Heinrich Gottfried, 305, 307
Orr, Alexandra (Leighton), 160, 161; *Handbook to the Works of Robert Browning*, 161; *Life and Letters of Robert Browning*, 161
Osgood, James R., 359

Packenham and Hooker, 78, 80, 259, 261, 262, 286
Page, Sarah (Mrs William), 35, 36, 215, 279, 281, 287–8
Page, William, 33, 34, 35, 36, 204, 205, 208, 213, 214, 217, 231, 242, 258, 261, 271, 272, 274, 281, 287–8; 'Cupid and Psyche', 218; 'Jephthah's Daughter', 205, 206; 'Venus', 314, 315; portraits of R B, 33; Mr Crawford, 288; Mrs Crawford, 279, 284;

Miss Cushman, 279, 284; Mrs Loring, 204; J. R. Lowell, 206; Emelyn Story, 279; 'The Italian Schools of Painting' (articles), 66
Paladin, 146
Palazzo Barberini, 6, 15, 106, 108, 143, 160, 321
Palazzo Manzoni, 187–8, 189
Palazzo Rezzonico, 15, 189
Palfrey, John Gorham, 231, 235
Palmerston, Lord, 295
Palombini, 260
Pantaleoni, Diomede, 22, 24, 25, 26, 28–29, 30
Parker, Theodore, 57, 87, 232, 235
Parkers, the, 222
Pass of Roland, 146
Paul, Sir John Dean, 303, 306
Parsons, Thomas William, 233, 236
Perkins, Charles Callahan, 86, 87, 96, 102, 114, 140, 270, 294, 309
Perkins, Mrs Charles Callahan, 79, 81, 86, 87, 96, 102, 114, 140, 270
Perkins, Mr and Mrs Edward, 270, 274
Peruzzi, Marchesa Edith, see Story, Edith
Peruzzi, Margherita Umberto, 339
Peruzzi, Marchese Simone, 329, 330, 331, 333, 364
Phillips, Sampson, & Co., 311, 312
Picchianti, Luigi, 266, 268
Pioneer, 212, 213, 214, 215, 217
Pippetta, 59
Pius IX, Pope, 2, 5, 49, 51, 230, 231, 233, 237, 264
Poe, Edgar Allan, 213, 248
Poole, John: Little Pedlington and the Pedlingtonians, 303, 306
Powers, Hiram, 36, 37, 242, 244, 259; 'Greek Slave', 37
Prescott, William Hickling, 304, 307
Procter, Bryan Waller (Barry Cornwall), 103, 105, 165, 166; 'On a Lady Slanderer', 166
Procter, Mrs Bryan Waller, 102–3, 105
Putnam, Samuel Raymond, 288, 290, 364
Putnam, Mrs Samuel Raymond (née Mary Traill Spence Lowell), 257, 288, 290, 292, 313, 315, 341, 364; Fifteen Days, 290; Tragedy of Errors, 290; Tragedy of Success, 290
Putnam's Magazine, 276, 278, 283, 284, 286, 289, 305

Quincy, Josiah, 303, 306

R., Mr, 121
R., V de, 175
Rachel, 300, 305
Rae, Miss, 270
Rae, Mrs, 270
Ranke, Leopold von, 252, 255
Raumer, Friedrich Ludwig George von, 252, 255
Reamie, Marcus, 286, 289
Reeves, Henry, 100, 103
Reid, Mayne, 41
Reinick, Robert, 305, 307
Ricasoli, Bettino, 72
Richardson, Col., 202
Richmond, Lewis, 330, 332
Ristori, Adelaide, 126, 127, 298–9, 300
Ritter, Karl, 252, 255
Robinson, Mrs W. C., 138
Rodin, Auguste, 180
Rölker, Bernard, 216, 218, 258
Rossetti, Dante Gabriel, 34, 100, 108, 128–9
Rowse, Samuel Worcester, 318, 319
Royal Academy, 143, 144, 182, 183
Rudorf, 252
Ruskin, John, 126
Russell, Arthur John Edward, 67, 121, 122, 132, 135, 137, 175
Russell, Odo, 65, 67, 78, 116, 130, 132, 135, 137, 162
Russell, Lady William, 64, 65, 67, 97, 99, 102, 107, 114, 116, 118–9, 121, 124, 125, 128, 130, 135, 140–1, 144, 147, 149, 152, 175

St Peter's, 238, 261
Salisbury, Lady, 132, 136
Santoni, 282
Sartoris, Adelaide Kemble, 29, 30, 31, 32, 33, 167–8, 169, 170
Sartoris, May, 168, 169
Savigny, Friedrich Karl von, 253, 255
Savigny, Madame Friedrich Karl von, 253
Schenk, Robert Cumming, 175, 176
Schiller: Geisterseher, 258, 262
Schuyler, Robert, 303, 306
Schwanthaler, Ludwig von, 254, 256
Sciamani, 29
Scott, Robert, 117, 119
Scott, Sir Walter: The Monastery, 226
Sears, Frederick Richard, 272, 275

[379]

Severn, Joseph, 286
Shaw, Mr, 159
Shaw, Francis George, 33, 34, 210, 271, 275, 284
Shaw, Mrs Francis George, 33, 34, 78, 80(?), 271, 275, 279
Shaw, Franklin, 206
Shaw, Jane, 203, 205, 214(?)
Shaw, Mrs Mary (Sturgis), 79, 81
Shaw, Mary Louisa, 79, 81
Shelley, Percy Bysshe, 276, 286
Shortall, John G., 190
Simpson, John Palgrave: *Time and the Hour*, 324
Spielberg, 231, 234
Stadhagen, Dr, 250
Stedman, Edmund Clarence, 35
Stewart, Arthur Courtenay, 364
Story, Edith (Marchesa Edith Peruzzi), 21, 23–30, 31, 32, 33, 36, 39, 47, 49, 50, 53, 55, 60, 61, 64, 69, 74, 75, 76, 77, 79, 81, 86, 90, 96, 97, 98, 100, 103, 107, 113, 114, 117, 118, 121, 124, 126, 127, 128, 129, 130, 134, 138, 139, 144, 147, 156, 175, 180, 223, 224, 225, 282, 288, 289, 307, 321, 325, 331, 333, 338, 339, 340, 341, 363, 364; translation of Giovanni Duprè's *Thoughts on Art and Autobiographical Memoirs*, 182
Story, Emelyn (Mrs W. W.), on Maria White (Lowell), 208, 213; comments on *Pioneer*, 212; engaged to W W S, 212, 213; first child is born, 223; with Brownings in Baths of Lucca, 3–4, 277; concern for Edith, 23–30; gives brooch to E B B, 39; death, 15; mention, 2, 21, 28, 30, 33, 43, 49, 55, 68, 70, 71, 76, 86, 90, 95, 98, 100, 107, 114, 116, 149, 165, 166, 172, 173, 178, 180, 187, 193, 194, 201, 202, 206, 217, 219, 220, 222, 223, 224, 225, 229, 230, 239, 240, 242, 248, 254, 256, 261, 267, 273, 288, 289, 291, 292, 294, 295, 299, 300, 312, 315, 321, 322, 324, 331, 333, 339, 340, 343, 347, 363
Story, Joe, *see* Story, Joseph
Story, Joseph (Judge), 2, 3, 35, 36, 226, 242, 271, 280, 285, 363
Story, Mrs Joseph (wife of Judge Story), 363
Story, Joseph (Joe, W W S's son), 4, 21, 24, 36, 282, 286, 289, 363

Story, Julian, 49, 69, 76, 92, 103, 112, 114, 117, 126, 135, 142, 149, 175, 179, 180, 182, 190, 191, 192, 321, 325, 333, 339, 363; 'Episode des Massacres de Septembre, 1792', 191; portrait of Browning, 321
Story, Mary Oliver, 220, 236, 363
Story, Waldo ('Bobo'), 35, 36, 49, 69, 76, 92, 103, 112, 114, 117, 126, 135, 142, 149, 175, 180, 182, 184, 289, 299, 300, 317, 321, 325, 327, 332, 333, 363, 364; Bassi Rilievi, 191, 192
Story, Mrs. Waldo, *see* Broadwood, Ada Maud
Story, William Wetmore: life before settling in Italy, 2–3; work for *Pioneer*, 215, 216, 217; legal work, 216, 217; with the 'Band', 217; writing and delivering 'Nature and Art' before Phi Beta Kappa Society, 222–3, 224; joy in first child, 224; meets the Brownings and describes them, 3, 242, 243–4; disapproves of Lowell's references to M. Fuller in *Fable for Critics*, 241; longs to be with Lowell, 250, 264, 275, 320, 323, 333, 339, 343; sends poem on Rose Lowell after her death, 257; takes care of business in Rome for Lowell, 260, 267; goes into Italian society, 265–6, 271; with the Brownings in Baths of Lucca, 3–4, 277; concern for Edith, 4, 23–30; death of Joe Story, 4, 24, 27, 36; effect of 'Fireside Travels' on, 286–7; comments on Lowell's professorship, 292, 295; dedicates poems to Lowell, 38, 311, 312, 313, 320; description of by Hawthorne, 10; assistance to Landor, 42–43, 44, 46–47, 63; is discouraged, 9, 82, 85; statues sent to London Exhibition, 9, 102, 104–5; placing of statues in Exhibition, 105–6, 107; sells statues, 9, 110, 111, 115, 141; reputation as sculptor, 9, 105, 115, 117, 119, 141; reputation as writer, 9, 116, 121, 122; health, 147, 149, 150–1, 174, 181; expression of affection for Lowell, 319; makes home in Palazzo Barberini, 321; made member of Athenaeum, 174, 175; private reading of his play *Stephania*, 327; gives account of death of G. P. Marsh and diplomatic

situation, 328–31; visits Lowell in London, 333, 334; receives D C L from Oxford, 338; in Asolo with R B, 197; writes to Pen on death of R B, 197

ON: art, 278–9, 320, 321; Boston and New England, 239, 250, 302, 317; Florence, 35, 36, 261; Mrs Bloomfield-Moore, 183–4, 185; Browning's letters, 161; Lowell's works, 241, 319–20; music in Boston, 216–7; Mrs Orr's *Life and Letters of Robert Browning*, 161; Page, 242; Paris, 35, 36; Hiram Powers, 242; Rome and Italy, 10–11, 36, 237–8, 250, 267, 272; slavery, 223; spirits, 281

MENTION: 21, 26, 28, 35, 36, 39, 44, 55, 57, 60, 64, 65, 67, 68, 81, 126, 128, 132, 136, 137, 138, 141, 148, 149, 155, 158, 165, 166, 172, 174, 178, 180, 201, 202, 212, 229, 318, 363

PLACES LIVED IN AND VISITED: Bagni di Lucca, 275–83; Berlin, 249–57; Boston, 214–25, 300–12, 322; Carlisle, 325; Castel Gandolfo, 258–67; Engadine, 342–4; London, 291–5, 323–4; Paris, 285–9, 339–40; Rome, 237–18, 269 791 Rome, Palazzo Barberini, 197–8, 319–44; Vallombrosa, 328–31

WORKS: poetry—Poem on Beethoven, 312, 313, 317; 'Borne in Our Loving Arms', 257; *Graffiti d'Italia*, 10; 'Nature and Art', 222–3, 224; *Poems* (1847), 37, 38; *Poems* (1856), 37, 38, 311, 312, 313; prose— *American Question*, 9, 88, 90, 91, 93–94; biography of his father, 280, 285; *Castle St Angelo and the Evil Eye*, 110; *Conversations in a Studio*, 10; 'Evil Eye', 110, 116; *Excursions in Art and Letters*, 10; *Fiammetta*, 10; contributions to *Pioneer*, 217; *Proportions of the Human Figure*, 10, 130, 132; *Roba di Roma*, 9–10, 109, 110, 111, 112, 113, 116, 118, 121, 122, 124, 130, 132, 139, 141; *Treatise on the Law of Contracts*, 303, 305, 307, 311; articles on *Macbeth*, 135, 137; on Lowell's *Poems*, 220; plays—*Nero*, 10; *Stephania*, 327; statues and busts of contemporaries—EBB, 87, 137–8, 139–40, 141, 151, 155, 156, 157, 158, 159; R B,

85, 87; Lord Houghton, 341–2; Lowell, 261, 272, 275–6, 286; John Marshall, 331, 332–3; T. Parker, 82, 85, 87; Josiah Quincy, 82, 85; Judge Story, 36, 37, 242, 271, 272, 273, 275, 276, 283, 286, 289, 290, 291; other statues and busts—'Arcadian Shepherd Boy', 272, 275; 'Beethoven', 36, 82, 293, 294; 'Cleopatra', 9, 85, 87, 102, 104, 106; 'Cleopatra Re-modelled', 135, 137; 'Endymion', 242; 'Flight of Youth', 272; 'John the Baptist', 261; 'Libyan Sibyl', 9, 85, 87, 95, 99, 102, 104, 106, 117; 'Medea', 126, 127, 151, 152; 'Pied Piper', 276, 303, 309; 'Little Red Riding Hood', 271; 'Saul', 114, 115, 116, 121, 122, 126, 140, 151; 'Sappho', 122, 124, 126, 127, 140, 141; 'Semiramis', 171, 172, 174, 175
Strahan, William, 303, 306
Sturgis, Harriett Tilden, 217, 218
Sturgis, Russell, 114, 115, 144, 147, 153, 154, 158, 218
Sturgis, Mrs Russell, 112, 114, 117, 118, 120, 125, 147, 153, 154, 155, 156, 158
Sumner, Charles, 2, 231, 232, 235, 318
Swiss Family Robinson, 41

Tappan, Mrs Caroline (Sturgis), 79, 81
Temple, Neville (pseudonym), see Fane, Julian
Tennent, Emerson, 100, 103, 106
Tennyson, Alfred Lord, 83–84, 125–6, 279–80, 351, 352; 'Enoch Arden', 126; *Princess*, 238, 239
Tennyson, Frederick, 280, 284
Thackeray, William Makepeace, 100, 101, 106, 140, 141, 270, 274, 283, 304, 306; *Rose and the Ring*, 305, 307
Thomson, G. W., 216
Thorwaldsen, Albert Bertel, 96, 98
Ticknor, Anna, 279
Ticknor, George, 232, 236, 301, 306, 311
Ticknor, William Davis, 236, 248, 249
Ticknor, Reed, and Fields, 249
Tilton, John Rollin, 159, 160
Tilton, Theodore, 160
Times on the American Civil War, 77, 86, 89, 94
Trent, affair of, 88, 89, 91, 94

Trevelyan, George Otto, 161
Trevor, Edward (pseudonym), see Lytton, Robert Bulwer
Trollope, Beatrice, 175, 176
Trollope, Theodosia, 152, 153
Trollope, Thomas Adolphus, 103, 105, 153, 176
Twisleton, Edward, 99, 274
Twiselton, Mrs Edward, 270, 274

Underwood, Francis Henry, 311, 312
Urquhart, 53

Vane, Lady Harry, 143, 145
Vatican Council, 162, 163
Vaughan, Miss, 33
Victor Emmanuel II, 5
Victoria Alexandrina, Queen of England, 70–71, 72, 74, 194
Villa Alberti (now Villa Marciano), 43, 48, 58, 59, 61, 63, 64, 68, 69, 127
Villa Bargagli, 41, 42, 43, 45
Villa Belvedere (also Villa Orr), 58, 59, 68, 69, 70, 72, 125, 127, 129
Villa Cini, 258
Villa Lustrina, 21, 22
Villa Marciano, see Villa Alberti
Villa Montauto, 185, 186
Villa Orr, see Villa Belvedere
Villafranca, treaty of, 5, 42, 43
Vinci, Leonardo da, 205

W., Mr, 22
Waagen, Gustav, 252, 255
Wahle, Dr, 259, 263, 282
Walburga, Lady, 51
Wales, Henry Ware, 314, 315
Wallace, Lew(is): Ben Hur, 337
Walmer Castle, 128, 130
Waterhouse, Benjamin, 286, 289
Watson, 266, 281
Webster, Daniel, 222

Wedgwood, Julia, 144
Wellington, Duke of, 130
Wells, Mr, 346, 347
Wentworth, Lord, 177, 178, 179
Westmorland, Lord, 144, 253, 255
Westmorland, Lady, 142, 144
Westminster Review, 57
Weston, Miss, 100, 142
Westons, Misses, 61, 62–63
Wetmore, Thomas, 231, 233, 234, 237, 238, 247, 363
Wetmore, William, 363
Wetmore, Mrs William, 363
White, Abijah, 365
White, Mrs Abijah, 365
White, William A., 214, 215, 217, 218, 282, 365
White, Mrs William A., see Sturgis, Harriett Tilden
Wigand, Georg, 305, 307
Wilbur, Parson, 344, 345
Wild(e), Hamilton G., 49, 51, 59, 60, 96, 98, 140, 184, 285, 287, 289
Wilkes, Charles, 91
Willard, Sidney, 229, 234, 237
Williams, Miss, 159
Williams-Wynn, Charlotte, 96, 97
Willing, Miss, 270, 274
Wilson, Elizabeth (Mme Ferdinand Romagnuoli), 127–8
Winthrop, Robert Charles, 231, 235
Wiseman, Cardinal, 116–7
Woods, Shakespere, 270, 272, 274
Worrick, 221, 222, 224
Wrest Park, 162, 163
Wright, I. B. (pseudonym), see Story, William Wetmore
Wurts, George Washington, 329, 330, 331–2
Wyman, Dr Morrill, 343, 345, 346

Zappi, Marchese, 279